¡Agítese bien!
A New Look at the
Hispanic Avant-Gardes

Juan de la Cuesta—Hispanic Monographs

EDITOR
Tom Lathrop

ASSOCIATE EDITOR
Alexander R. Selimov
University of Delaware

EDITORIAL BOARD
Samuel G. Armistead
University of California, Davis

Annette G. Cash
Georgia State University

Alan Deyermond
Queen Mary and Westfield College of the University of London

Daniel Eisenberg
Regents College

John E. Keller
University of Kentucky

Steven D. Kirby
Eastern Michigan University

Joel Rini
University of Virginia

Donna M. Rogers
Middlebury College

Noël Valis
Yale University

Ángel Valbuena Briones
University of Delaware

Amy Williamsen
University of Arizona

¡Agítese bien!
A New Look at the
Hispanic Avant-Gardes

Edited and introduction by
MARIA T. PAO
RAFAEL HERNÁNDEZ-RODRÍGUEZ

Juan de la Cuesta
Newark, Delaware

Copyright © 2002 by Juan de la Cuesta—Hispanic Monographs
270 Indian Road, Newark, DE 19711
www.juandelacuesta.com

MANUFACTURED IN THE UNITED STATES OF AMERICA
ISBN: 1-58871-022-X

Table of Contents

Introduction
    RAFAEL HERNÁNDEZ-RODRÍGUEZ and MARIA T. PAO vii

Herky, Jerky: Playing Fast and Loose
in Giménez Caballero's *Hercules jugando a los dados*
    ANDREW A. ANDERSON 1

Bodies in the City:
Sports and Beauty in São Paulo of the '20s
    MÔNICA RAISA SCHPUN 27

An Enormous Laugh:
The Comic Spirit in Brazilian Modernist Literature
    K. DAVID JACKSON 49

The Avant-Garde Oratory of Ramón Gómez de la Serna
    NIGEL DENNIS 77

Heading West with Rafael Alberti and Buster Keaton
    WILLARD BOHN 119

Alma: The First Complete Motion Picture in Print
    HENRY SCHWARZ 131

"The New Sweaty Beauty of the Century."
Avant-Garde, Sexuality, and Revolution in Mexico
    RAFAEL HERNÁNDEZ-RODRÍGUEZ 157

Transgressive Affinities (and One Difference)
in Buñuel's *La edad de oro* and Lorca's *El público*
    VÍCTOR FUENTES 177

In Hazardous Pursuit of Chance:
Mapping the Surrealists' Caribbean Sojourn (1941)
    GERARD ACHING 189

The View from the Wheel
    MARIA T. PAO 213

An Aesthetics of Transience:
Fashion in the Spanish Avant-Garde
    JULI HIGHFILL 243

The Commodification of the Image of Spain's "New Woman" by Mass Culture and the Avante Garde in José Díaz Fernández's *La Venus mecánica*
    SUSAN LARSON 275

Introduction

Shake well before using

ALONG WITH THE INNOVATIVE responses to the crisis of bourgeois culture that the early avant-garde movements represented—the baby talk of dadaism, futurism's frenzied rhetoric urging the destruction of museums, the return to the primitive of cubism, and surrealism's reliance on chance and the subconscious—the other aspect usually discussed when dealing with early twentieth-century art is the playful and creative force of these responses and the fact that since their origins they sought a connection with other cultural articulations. Most critics would agree that the art of the period aspired to reconnect with every aspect of life and society. Or as Peter Bürger famously put it: "The avant-garde intends the abolition of autonomous art by which it means that art is to be integrated into the praxis of life" (54). More recently, René Jara pointed out that the avant-garde feeds on "the very habit of living, dying, writing, and inscribing the world around" (285). He adds to the list of vanguard priorities the categories of the extraordinary and the prohibited, clearly following Matei Calinescu's idea that avant-garde artists wanted to overthrow tradition and explore the forbidden (95-97).

The idea of rebelliousness and novelty was common to all Western cultures at the dawn of the twentieth century, allowing avant-garde movements to develop in close collaboration with partners on both sides of the Atlantic. Even as American intellectuals traveled and lived in Europe, the power, energy, and beauty of the New World fascinated many Europeans. Artists from the Iberian Peninsula and Hispanic America replicated this pattern of cross-influence, and just as Spain received guests from Europe and Latin America, Spaniards found themselves abroad working with their Latin American counterparts. In 1926, for example, Basque writer Juan Larrea collaborated with Peruvian poet César Vallejo in France; the following year translator and literary critic Guillermo de Torre moved to Buenos Aires while remaining in contact with his Peninsular colleagues. Pablo Picasso and Diego Rivera met in Paris, while Jorge Luis Borges and Vicente Huidobro spent time in Madrid and actively promoted the avant-garde on both continents.

The 1920s were particularly important for the Latin American avant-garde, witnessing the creation of new groups and manifestos, as well as the occurrence of important historical and cultural events, such as the end of the Mexican Revolution in 1921 and the Semana de Arte Moderno of São Paulo in 1922. What distinctively marks American cultures of the period are the vitality and the sense of change present in their societies. According to Hugo Verani, it is in the twenties when we observe "una acelerada sucesión de manifiestos, polémicas, exposiciones y movimientos encaminados por propósitos distintos, pero contagiados de la 'furia de novedad'" (10-11). The fury of novelty, indeed, seems to have been one of the most attractive features of the avant-garde, and almost all the early manifestos are clear in their emphatic rejection of the "vieja literatura agonizante y apestada," as the first "Manifesto estridentista" puts it (Verani 88).

It is not surprising, then, that the association between a new society and a new culture, often understood only in terms of technology, appeared in the first manifestos of Mexico and Brazil, the two countries with a more developed economy. This dovetailing of culture and scientific advances, moreover, was articulated both as a celebration of progress and as a criticism of a capitalist system. In fact if we compare the editorial of the Brazilian magazine *Klaxon* (1922) and the flyer "Actual-Hoja de Vanguardia No. 1" (1921) by the *estridentistas* in Mexico, we can find in both documents the same principles, the same sensibility, and even the same vocabulary. For the latter, the criticism of capitalism was attained through an ironic and playful incorporation of the language of newspapers and publicity in their manifestos and poetry. For instance, the flyer "Actual"—an *affiche* glued to the walls of Jalapa just like an advertisement—had as one of its premises, "Se prohibe fijar anuncios." It promised to "cure" the old culture with a formula that "en veinte y cuatro horas extermina todos los gérmenes de la literatura putrefacta," but provided that you shake well before using it—"Agítese bien antes de usarse" (Verani 85), the verb "agitarse" meaning "to shake" but also, appropriately enough, "to disturb, excite, and stir up."

The use of other textual references besides publicity and newspapers is evident also in the case of Brazil. We can appreciate this particularly in Oswald de Andrade's manipulation of passages from both major European literary works and historical texts narrating the "discovery" of the country. The revision of European culture from the American perspective is especially relevant since it offers an opportunity to question the relationship between the continents through the appropriation, manipulation, and transformation of canonical literature. This cannibalization is ingeniously summarized in the famous "Tupy, or not tupy that is the question" of the "Manifesto antropófago."

A similar preoccupation with America, and particularly with the place Latin America occupied in Western culture, underpins one of the major avant-garde movements of Argentina—*martinfierrismo*. It is in the magazine *Martín Fierro* where Oliverio Girondo published his "Carta abierta a 'La púa'" in which he emphatically states that "fuimos nosotros, los americanos, quienes hemos oxigenado el castellano" (Verani 270). Later, the manifesto "Martín Fierro" would complement this idea with its declaration that "*Martín Fierro* tiene fe en nuestra fonética, en nuestra visión, en nuestros modales, en nuestro oído, en nuestra capacidad digestiva y de asimilación" (Verani 273). Once more, irony adds the sparkling note of subversion when the *martinfierro* artists acknowledge with humor that a big part of American identity is centered on the fact that "todas las mañanas nos servimos de un dentífrico sueco, de unas toallas de Francia y de un jabón inglés" (Verani 273). A statement that is apparently proof of cosmopolitism ("our capacity of assimilation") reveals itself as evidence of the cultural dependence of the region.

American identity is also fundamental in a more radical movement, this time with an indigenous focus and expressed in a somber if not pompous tone in the pages of the Peruvian magazine *Amauta*. Unfortunately, its writers lacked the humor and playfulness evident in other Americanist movements. *Amauta* established itself as a revolutionary vehicle that among other things supported the Indian cause and proclaimed the decadence of capitalism: "La decadencia de la civilización capitalista se refleja en la atomización, en la disolución de su arte" (Verani 182). For the artists and intellectuals gathered in its pages modernity and revolution were inseparable; the revolutionary essence of new art, however, was not in the exploration of innovative techniques, but "en el repudio, en el desahucio, en la befa del absoluto burgués" (Verani 183).

This idea of new art opposing the decadence of capitalist and bourgeois cultures echoes the view of the *estridentistas* in Mexico who imagined "el arte nuevo" as a vigorous, revolutionary, and virile expression at odds with the fragile, spoiled, weak poetics that produced verses representing nothing but "pseudo-líricos bombones melódicos" for *señoritas* and "niñas fox-troteantes" (Verani 84). It is clear that for *estridentistas* the ideal revolutionary artist (identified as brave and vigorous) was a virile adult male. New art, and new poetry in particular, were seen as important (read *masculine*) matters articulated against what they regarded as the girly ("bombones" for young ladies), infantile ("caramelos espirituales," Verani 90) attitude of old art. The *estridentistas*, though, kept their sense of humor.

The writers of *Amauta*, on the contrary, were overtly emphatic about their revolutionary intention and seriousness, to the point of correcting José Ortega y Gasset who, in their view, failed to differentiate the decadent from the revolutionary, leading him to the mistaken claim that "la nueva inspiración es siempre, indefectiblemente, cómica" (Verani 184). These writers and intellectuals agreed with their avant-garde counterparts that old art was obsolete and had to be replaced. However, they did not seem overeager to accept playfulness and humor as their weapons—for them, clearly, art was not a laughing matter.

As with Latin America, the 1920s also represented a significant period in Spain. Nineteen twenty-five, for example, saw the appearance of De Torre's *Literaturas europeas de vanguardia* and Ortega y Gasset's seminal essay "La deshumanización del arte." De Torre's book outlined general characteristics of the new sensibility, including a foregrounding of the autonomous image, formal innovations such as "neotypography" and the abandonment of rhyme, a "cosmopolitan spirit," and inspiration in photography and cinema. De Torre championed a novel role for poets: no longer prophets and conduits for divine inspiration, they have "abandonado sus antiguos sitiales deíficos y permuten su antigua solemnidad profética por una apetencia vital y una jovialidad desbordante" (20). Furthermore, he dismissed the concept of art as eternal expression. The literary work should no longer strive towards permanence, but towards ephemerality in order to make manifest its "now-ness" and recognize "el valor de lo pasajero, de lo relativo y del espíritu de nuestra época."

The other groundbreaking text published in 1925 was Ortega's "La deshumanización del arte," first appearing in *Revista de Occidente* one year earlier. Even though Ortega limits his remarks to the descriptive, rather than the prescriptive, it soon became "una especie de manifiesto" (Buckley and Crispin 8). If De Torre signaled the current irrelevance of the writer as high prophet, Ortega pointed to a parallel waning of art as the dead serious imparter of humanist values, realist representation, and personal expression. Instead, modern art increasingly focuses, not on the eternal and monumental, but on "los mínimos sucesos de la vida" (374). More important still, Ortega explains that traditional art, "cargado de 'humanidad'" (381), and new art differ fundamentally in that the former "[e]ra una cosa muy seria" whereas the latter is a "una broma, que es, esencialmente, la burla de sí mismo" (382). Today's art, no longer required to bear the cultural weight of its predecessor, "triunfa de todo, incluso de sí mismo" (383). Becoming "intrascendente," it allows its creators to accept the role ascribed to them by De Torre: that of modern artists and writers turning for the first time to the passing details of contemporary life. Modern art injects "puerilidad en un mundo viejo" (Ortega 384) and, eschewing connection con "los dramáticos movimientos sociales y políticos," aligns itself rather "al triunfo de los deportes y juegos." Finally off its pedestal, it engages in day-to-day "presentness"—sports and games, but also jazz, cinema, photography, fashion, spectacle culture, new technologies, cafés, and urban living.

Avant-garde art sought contact with everyday life through games and experimentation with such playfulness that made it difficult for some to accept. As we saw before, in Latin America many viewed the new attitude to be the result of an infantilization or childishness—precisely the "puerilidad" that Ortega encouraged—that represented the antithesis of maturity. And maturity, an attribute considered essentially masculine by tradition, was required to create serious art. As such, to play around, to laugh, and to create art as a joke was to allow oneself to get dangerously close to the infantile and perhaps even the feminine. In any case, it was to be weak, soft and to voluntarily renounce great and noble ideals like revolution and justice. If it is true that on both sides of the Atlantic avant-garde groups generally opposed traditional art, it is also true that in America many found it difficult to jettison entirely the notion of art as a symbol of humanist ideals and as a way of transcendence. Consequently, early on many criticized the "frivolity" of the European avant-garde, as we can see in a comment appearing in the Peruvian magazine *Variedades* in 1926, which clearly states that the reason why dadaism did not achieve greater transcendence as a more ambitious and coherent aesthetic position was because "[s]u clownismo, su humorismo fundamental se lo impedían" (Verani 185).

With time, this view became common to a great number of art and literary critics. Although most acknowledged the humor and playfulness of the avant-garde, they usually did so in a passing manner before immediately looking for some deep and transcendent idea to focus on. Very few books, therefore, have been published in Latin America or Spain addressing only the relationship between the literary avant-garde and other aspects of early twentieth-century culture. This volume attempts to begin to fill that void and to open a dialogue looking at fresh ways of experiencing the avant-garde. It is not meant, however, to survey all vanguard movements in all Hispanic countries. Instead of essays covering every region and every avant-garde manifestation in a comprehensive fashion, we have decided to include original articles that specifically explore the literary avant-garde's engagement with sports, fashion, games, gender identity, movies, urban life, and technology. This approach inevitably maps where these connections have been addressed and where they still require elucidation. In this respect, we hope that our book will be read as an indicator not so much of what has been accomplished, but of what is still left to be done.

¿Tiene usted forma?
The Hispanic authors represented here enjoyed double freedoms: a sense of play and irony resulting from the canceled obligation to weightier matters and the challenges of a changing environment. Suddenly, the strategies of dodges, feints, speed, and sheer audacity not only appeared in the sports pages. They also, as Andrew A. Anderson shows, made their way into Ernesto Giménez Caballero's *Hércules jugando a los dados* where the author's unique blend of social anthropology, arts commentary, and cultural studies *avant la lettre* took the form of free association and delirious wordplay, not to mention specious attributions boldly asserted. The vertiginous sleights of hand and spins and turns of logic leave the reader breathless and astonished at Giménez Caballero's unmitigated nerve—he fakes left, doubles back, rushes forward, and scores! One may never think of "literatura deportiva" in the same way again.

Sports played an important part in the emerging urban culture of many American nations. Urbanization became fundamental in the discourse of modernity in Latin America, as Mexico City, Buenos Aires, and São Paulo erected themselves as centers of culture that produced works dealing with the new city experience, such as Manuel Maples Arce's *Urbe*, Mário de Andrade's *Paulicéia desvairada*, and Oliverio Girondo's *Veinte poemas para ser leídos en el tranvía*. Many other works explored the masses and the new forms of leisure, including organized sports and sporting events where the city became the stage of a modern drama. In that context, Mônica Raisa Schpun, looking at the specific case of São Paulo, offers an excellent analysis of how literary and non-literary texts reflect an ideology that urban spaces helped to establish with their strict spatial divisions based on gender and race. The crowd, a phenomenon until then unknown in Latin America, becomes a perfect opportunity to reinforce the ideology of a patriarchal society where the masculine and the feminine correspond "logically" to the public and the private spaces, while sports aid to model the supposed characteristics of men and women.

São Paulo represented the Latin American city *par excellence*, which means that because of its fast industrialization and growth it also represented the internal conflict of a society divided between its traditional values and its modernizing pretensions. This conflict provided the soil for new ideas to emerge and be discussed. David Jackson argues in "An Enormous Laugh" that "humor was the chosen vehicle through which Brazilian society expressed its ideas." Professor Jackson focuses on the early or "heroic" avant-garde to rescue its playful and comic spirit, particularly that of the cannibalistic proposition of Oswald de Andrade's "Manifesto antropófago." He also contends that many of the literary and artistic manifestations of early Brazilian modernism were comic "tools for the clever dissection of a sharp social and psychological analysis" and that by reading them as solemn arguments, critics really miss the point.

Nigel Dennis points out that assessments of Ramón Gómez de la Serna's prose style — noted (though often criticized) for its jerkiness, chaotic development, and structural looseness — identify him, like Giménez Caballero, as another athlete or player of language. Best known for his invention of the *greguería*, Ramón sought to restore the original electricity of words. He did this through spontaneity and partial improvisation, not only in his written texts but also in his famously entertaining lectures. Aiming to delight his audience by deflating the pompous solemnity and tired rhetoric of politicians and academics, Ramón did not hesitate to don absurd costumes, climb atop an elephant, or munch on candles. In *El orador*, the only existing audiofilm in which he appears, Ramón demonstrates how props, caricature, and cock-crowing can transform a (mock-)serious aesthetic discussion complete with the requisite monocle (here glassless) into a giddy mix of art and entertainment.

Like Ramón, poet Rafael Alberti performed with aplomb, as he demonstrated in May 1929 before members of Madrid's Cineclub, where he accented his dramatic reading of poems dedicated to the comics of the silent screen with sound effects and pantomime. Willard Bohn reads Alberti's "Buster Keaton busca por el bosque a su novia, que es una verdadera vaca" against the film that inspired it, *Go West*, in a similar wry and playful spirit. In the poem the hapless protagonist searches high and low for his missing sweetheart, a bovine named Georgina. The pathos and poignancy is punctuated by whimsical imagery, animal utterances ("Pi, pi, pi, pi"), and sing-song repetitions expected more from children's stories than the verse of a poet who had won the National Prize for Literature just a few years earlier. The rhymes, near rhymes, phonetic effects, and recurring phrases create an imaginative performance poem, enchanting to ear and tongue.

Silent movies were as significant in Latin America as they were in Spain. In Brazil, Argentina, and Mexico moving pictures represented a phenomenon that arrived early and quickly established and developed native industries. However, the popularity and influence of movies from Hollywood, because they did not need to be translated, were so important that in at least one case they inspired a complete novel. Henry Schwarz argues in a very original essay that Oswald de Andrade created *Alma*, a novel read during the week of modern art in São Paulo, from the world of silent films. By identifying film elements in the book, he proves that *Alma* is a groundbreaking and highly experimental motion picture in print.

In the Mexican case, film was fundamental along with photography to the shaping and reshaping of the image of the revolution of 1910, the most important historical, social, and cultural event of that country's modern history. Along with literary texts, there is a considerable number of images that capture the turmoil of the nation at the beginning of the twentieth century—from monuments being inaugurated, parades, celebrations, beauty pageants, political rallies, and battles between the federal army and the rebel troops of Pancho Villa or Emiliano Zapata (who did not look like Marlon Brando) to portraits of the muralists at work as well as pictures depicting everyday life. And in the middle of all this noise and demand for a new culture irrupts the shrieking laugh of Salvador Novo, the homosexual poet who was equally eager and capable of writing a poem pondering aesthetic questions, composing a classical sonnet with a homoerotic theme, or chasing bus drivers through the streets of Mexico City. In his contribution, Rafael Hernández-Rodríguez revisits Novo's poetry and resistance to the self-proclaimed revolutionary artists that accepted only one way of being a Mexican avant-garde artist—not surprisingly, as a virile, aggressive, mature man. These artists fought for a unified, monolithic, manly new culture and excluded those who did not fit these parameters. Perhaps the perfect metaphor of Novo's rebelliousness and individuality is his studio decorated in the most theatrical Mexican style where he lived his sexuality, defying the macho demand for a national and revolutionary culture and art.

Individuality and freedom certainly represented some of the most important themes of the avant-garde, particularly when it came to sexual freedom and identity. Víctor Fuentes demonstrates that Luis Buñuel and Federico García Lorca turned to surrealism to produce provocative works that count among the avant-garde's most daring. That Buñuel's *L'Age d'or* instigated the audience at the film's debut to assault the screen and that Lorca's drama *El público* lay virtually unknown for some forty years testify to their unreserved flaunting of artistic and societal convention. Each extols the twin allures of Eros and Thanatos, death and desire that permeate surrealist texts in which normative restrictions of genre and gender yield to the imperative of personal freedom.

Surrealism's theory of contingency, the unexpected encounter, and "objective chance" are the basis for Gerard Aching's contribution, an essay where he analyses works of André Breton and Eugenio Fernández Granell and proposes an alternative historiographical model for surrealist activities during their voyage of exile through the Caribbean in 1941. According to Professor Aching, Breton's *Martinique, charmeuse de serpents* and Fernández Granell's *Isla cofre mítico* offer alternative ways of understanding the relationship between the European and American avant-gardes and the way this relationship has been studied and organized in literary history. He sees the surrealists' sojourn in the Caribbean as a speculative unfolding of certain kinds of knowledge about modern Western culture that goes beyond the simplistic interpretation of the avant-garde as a series of European movements mimicked in America.

Whereas Alberti turned to comic cinema to renew his writing, other members of his generation identified sources of inspiration in everyday life. The automobile had motored onto the scene, provoking celebrations of the car as an emblem of independence and *joie de vivre* in poems titled "Ford," "El último modelo," and "Conductora de auto." More significant, it provided new modes of visual apprehension as, through its windshield, drivers witnessed a landscape in motion. Maria T. Pao argues that texts by Guillermo de Torre, Pedro Salinas, and José María Hinojosa demonstrate not only that the speeding car alters both the manner and object of visual perception, but also that these transformations correspond to futurist, cubist, and surrealist modes of viewing external reality.

That the car soon became a key index of modernity was further underscored when Spanish writer Corpus Barga, in considering the fashions of artist and designer Sonia Delaunay, compared the architecture of her dresses to that of the automobile. As Juli Highfill observes in her reading of "París, abril, modelo" by Pedro Salinas, the avant-garde no longer located standards of beauty in classical models, but rather in the changing fashions now displayed on store-window mannequins. An "art of pure transience," fashion, represented by the modern woman on the move, epitomized an aesthetic sensibility predicated not on imitation of earlier patterns, but on the principle of self-invention and constantly renewed creativity. Just as the movement-generating engine of a car determined its external design, Delaunay conceived her fluid, multi-colored dresses to sheathe the mobile female form they covered. With the gendered body no longer static, but moving and changing with kinetic energy, Barga asks his male audience the disconcerting question: "¿Tiene usted forma?"

José Díaz Fernández, too, noted the intersection of fashion and mass culture in his 1929 novel *La Venus mecánica*. But rather than deploying these dimensions of modern life as signposts of a refreshing liberation from past models, this author uses them to critique the ultimately superficial and personally unsatisfying state of the Madrid avant-garde for working-class women. Drawing from cubist painting and consumer culture, Susan Larson traces the journey of the novel's protagonist from prostitute to fashion model to kept mistress. She demonstrates the avant-garde's collusion with market forces that finally annuls its emancipatory possibilities, nurturing Obdulia's resentment of a society that has used her. Larson's reading provides a thoughtful antidote to uniperspectival considerations of the vanguard and begs the question, "Avant-garde, but for whom?"

* * *

When we conceived of this volume, we had two principal criteria in mind. We wanted our contributors to focus on Hispanic avant-garde texts that engaged with extra-literary cultural manifestations, but we also wanted them to approach this writing on its own terms as high play, apparently ephemeral yet reflective of a supremely exciting moment in time. Our contributors responded admirably and we are very pleased to include them here. The texts that they read in the essays that follow, when considered alongside examples of more well-known vanguard writing, provide a much-needed shake-up, indeed.

RAFAEL HERNÁNDEZ-RODRÍGUEZ
MARIA T. PAO

Works Cited

Buckley, Ramón and John Crispin, eds. *Las vanguardias españolas (1925-1935)*. Madrid: Alianza, 1973.

Bürger, Peter. *Theory of the Avant-Garde*. Minneapolis: U of Minnesota P, 1984.

Calinescu, Matei. *Five Faces of Modernity*. Durham: Duke UP, 1987.

De Torre, Guillermo. *Literaturas europeas de vanguardia*. Madrid: Caro Raggio, 1925.

Jara, René. "A Design for Modernity in the Margins." *Modernism and its Margins*. Eds. Anthony L Geist and José Monleón. New York: Garland Publishing, 1999. 277-295.

Ortega y Gasset, José. "La deshumanización del arte." *Obras completas*. Tomo III. 5a ed. Madrid: Revista de Occidente, 1962. 353-86.

Verani, Hugo. *Las vanguardias literarias en Hispanoamérica. (Manifestos, proclamas y otros escritos)*. México: Fondo de Cultura Económica, 1990.

Herky, Jerky: Playing Fast and Loose in Giménez Caballero's *Hércules jugando a los dados*

ANDREW A. ANDERSON
University of Virginia

EVEN IF ERNESTO GIMÉNEZ CABALLERO (1899-1988) were only remembered today as the founder and editor of *La Gaceta Literaria* (1927-1932), in its day the best known and most influential of all the contemporary Madrid-based literary journals, as the founder and prime-mover of Spain's first cinema club, the Cine-Club de Madrid (1928-1931), and as the founder of La Galería (Madrid, f. 1929), a gallery showcase for modern architecture, furniture and crafts, he would still be considered as one of the outstanding figures from the second phase of the Spanish historical avant-garde, a period which spans the latter half of the 1920s. But during these same years Giménez Caballero was, in addition, the author of a series of books in diverse genres that also fit—more or less—into the category of the avant-garde: *Carteles* (1927), *Los toros, las castañuelas y la Virgen* (1927), *Yo, inspector de alcantarillas* (1928), *Hércules jugando a los dados* (1928), and *Julepe de menta* (1929). Of these, *Carteles*, which offers a radically new (and in part a mixed-media) approach to review writing and literary criticism, and *Yo, inspector de alcantarillas*, a heterogeneous work that contains a wild mix of creative prose fiction, have probably received most critical attention to date.[1] But this is not to say that the other three works—all essentially essayistic in nature—are any less interesting or in their own way radically innovative.

---

[1] See, for example, the articles by Dennis ("Ernesto") and Rodríguez Amaya.

In *Hércules jugando a los dados*² Giménez Caballero, faithful to that fascination with classical mythology evinced by so many members of the historical avant-garde, fixes his attention upon the most famous of all Greek heroes, Heracles.³ The opening pages propose athletics, cinema and the dice-shaker as the three defining attributes of the modern epoch (i.e. the 1920s) and locate Heracles within this triangle as the very embodiment of the spirit and sensibility of the new age. Giménez Caballero's avowed intention, then, is to analyze and characterize "la nueva juventud" (16), "la juventud de hoy" (21) and, in particular, modern literature and modern art. It soon becomes clear that for the purposes of this investigation athletics stands synecdochally for a wide range of sports, the principal connotations of cinema are adventure, speed and light (the flickering images), while the dice-shaker symbolizes both games (the ludic) and chance (the aleatory).

Of this motley triad it is the first component, namely sports, that, as it turns out, receives the lion's share of Giménez Caballero's attention. In this attempt to capture the spirit of the new age, and in the singling-out of an enthusiasm for sports as one of its fundamental, defining features, the influence of José Ortega y Gasset (1883-1955) (with whom Giménez Caballero had studied at the University of Madrid) is self-evident (Foard 26-29).⁴ One thinks immediately of *La deshumanización del arte* (1925), but in fact Ortega's preoccupation with sports can be traced at least as far back as 1920. In an article published that

---

² The publishers of the first edition of *Hércules* had a special fondness (one might easily say mania) for classification: thus the volume was described by them simultaneously as number 4 of Ediciones "La Nave," number 2 of Colección B: Autores [Españoles] Modernos y Contemporáneos (Siglos XIX y XX), and number 6 of the Serie Novena: Varia, of Publicaciones "Atenea!" The book was printed on the presses of Giménez Caballero's father, Imprenta E. Giménez (Huertas, 16 y 18, Madrid), with a print-run of 3200 copies. Although it is dated 1928, it seems very likely that the book was not printed—or at least not distributed—till well into 1929. The two reviews known to me (Salazar y Chapela, Ledesma Ramos) appeared in June and August 1929. All page references are to this first edition.

³ A few other examples of this fascination: Rafael Alberti's *Cal y canto*, José Díaz Fernández's *La Venus mecánica*, Juan José Domenchina's *La túnica de Neso* and *Dédalo*, or Antonio de Obregón's *Hermes en la vía pública*.

⁴ Concerning Ortega's influence on Giménez Caballero's *political* thinking, see Davidson 16-20, Foard *passim*, Selva Roca de Togores, "Plenitud" 45, and Selva Roca de Togores, "Giménez" 332-333.

year in *El Sol* and entitled "Biología y pedagogía, o el Quijote en la escuela," he wrote:

> La cultura no es hija del trabajo sino del deporte. Bien sé que a la hora presente me hallo solo entre mis contemporáneos para afirmar que la forma superior de la existencia humana es el deporte. [...L]a marcha de la sociedad, junto con los nuevos descubrimientos de las ciencias, obligan a una reforma radical de las ideas en este punto y anuncian un viraje de la historia hacia un sentido deportivo y festival de la vida. (qtd. in Polo del Barrio 92-93)

In *El tema de nuestro tiempo* (published as articles in *El Sol* and *La Nación* 1922-23; 1st ed. 1923), Ortega argued that:

> El arte, en el sentir de la gente nueva, se convierte en filisteísmo, en no-arte, tan pronto como se le toma en serio. [...] Si, por el contrario, desplazamos la ocupación estética y del centro de nuestra vida la transferimos a la periferia; si en vez de tomar en serio al arte lo tomamos como lo que es, como un entretenimiento, un juego, una diversión, la obra artística cobrará toda su encantadora reverberación.
>
> [...P]ara los jóvenes esa falta de seriedad es el valor sumo del arte, y, consecuentemente, procuran cometerla de la manera más decidida y premeditada.
>
> Este viraje en la actitud frente al arte anuncia uno de los rasgos más generales en el nuevo modo de sentir la existencia: lo que he llamado tiempo hace el sentido deportivo y festival de la vida. [...]
>
> Al trabajo se contrapone otro tipo de esfuerzo que no nace de una imposición, sino que es impulso libérrimo y generoso de la potencia vital: es el deporte.
>
> [...]
>
> Pues bien, una vida que encuentra más interesante y valioso su propio ejercicio que esas finalidades antaño ceñidas de sin par prestigio, dará a su esfuerzo el aire jovial, generoso y algo burlón que es propio al deporte. [...] Hará sus espléndidas creaciones como en broma y sin darles grande importancia. El poeta tratará su propio arte con la punta del pie, como buen futbolista. (140-142)[5]

---

[5] See Llera for a study of the centrality of *El tema de nuestro tiempo* to Ortega's thinking on sport.

Consistent with these previously expressed views, in an article published in 1924, "El origen deportivo del Estado," Ortega averred that he considered sporting activity "como la primaria, como la más elevada, seria e importante en la vida [...]. Es más, vida propiamente hablando es sólo la de cariz deportivo" (qtd. in Rota 37-38). Finally, in *La deshumanización del arte* (first chapters published as articles in *El Sol* early 1924; 1st ed. 1925), Ortega forcefully restated his opinions concerning the current historical moment:

> Todo el arte nuevo resulta comprensible y adquiere cierta dosis de grandeza cuando se le interpreta como un ensayo de crear puerilidad en un mundo viejo. [...] El nuevo estilo [...] solicita, desde luego, ser aproximado al triunfo de los deportes y juegos. Son dos hechos hermanos, de la misma oriundez.
> En pocos años hemos visto crecer la marea del deporte en las planas de los periódicos, haciendo naufragar casi todas las carabelas de la seriedad. [...] El culto al cuerpo es eternamente síntoma de inspiración pueril, porque sólo es bello y ágil en la mocedad, mientras el culto al espíritu indica voluntad de envejecimiento, porque sólo llega a plenitud cuando el cuerpo ha entrado en decadencia. El triunfo del deporte significa la victoria de los valores de juventud sobre los valores de senectud. Lo propio acontece con el cinematógrafo, que es, por excelencia, arte corporal.
> [...] No hay duda: entra Europa en una etapa de puerilidad.
> [...]
> El cariz que en todos los órdenes va tomando la existencia europea anuncia un tiempo de varonía y juventud. (63-65)[6]

If we turn now, for a moment, from the question of content to matters of style, two other writers can be identified as likely influences on Giménez Caballero. Trawling through *Hércules*, we find sentences such as these—

---

[6] Giménez Caballero was not as persuaded by other aspects of Ortega's argument in *La deshumanización*; his article "Eoántropo," published in Ortega's *Revista de Occidente*, is in large part a rebuttal of the ascendancy of the cool, rationalistic, objective, formalist qualities that Ortega sees in modern art. For commentary on this debate, see Soria Olmedo 187-189.

Ponerse a buscar algo en la pizarra, es ponerse a buscarle 3 pies al gato. O sea: 3—por lo menos—de las *n* dimensiones de las cosas. (34)

El radiador sorbe la cinta de la ruta y la devuelve, deglutida en humo. (72)

Una cabeza de héroe es hoy un conglomerado de cuero, duraluminio y mica. (76)

Suiza halló el fútbol en la manzana de Guillermo Tell. (107)

El mundo del primitivo era una sesión continua de cámara obscura. (137)

La sirena, erecta en su chimenea industrial—como sobre una roca oceánida—distendía su garganta gris con el aullido voraz de las apetencias humanas. (160)

Nada se parece tanto a una partida de ajedrez como un partido de fútbol. (196)

—and it is hard to imagine that Ramón—Ramón Gómez de la Serna (1888-1963), a friend of Giménez Caballero and contributor to *La Gaceta Literaria*—would not have been delighted to welcome each and every one of these observations or propositions among the thousands of his own *greguerías*.[7] Besides such witty or novel formulations, often involving a shift of perspective or an unexpected metaphor, we also find a goodly number of neologisms, such as "gimnosdérmica" (16), "agonotetas" (27), "ludigrama" (45), "plurigenismo" (95), "unigenista" (95), "teoplasma" (132), "sotolineando" (199), and many others. Mostly learned in nature, they recall the convoluted and dizzying vocabulary of Guillermo de Torre (1900-1971)—co-founder with Giménez Caballero of *La Gaceta Literaria*—that was so characteristic of his *ultraísta* phase in the first half of the 1920s.[8]

---

[7] This affinity has been noted by Hernando 302, and cf. Dennis, "Ernesto" 84.

[8] On neologisms in Giménez Caballero, see Hernando 280-282, Salazar y Chapela, and cf. Hernando 173.

Apparently of Giménez Caballero's own invention are several other stylistic tics that give *Hércules* a very particular and instantly recognizable flavor. Each chapter is divided into short sections, sometimes very short, separated by three asterisks; in places where this device proliferates, the pages seem to be covered with stars. The sections range in length from a single sentence, to a single paragraph made up of a few sentences, to several, normally short, paragraphs. Paragraphs, when they are more than a single sentence long, are frequently a sequence of short, staccato sentences that are often verbless.[9] Giménez Caballero makes much use of the parenthetical double dash within the sentence, and also deploys a non-normative mode of punctuation, with several successive colons used in a single sentence: e.g. "Y para vencerlo acudió a un medio genuinamente humano: reducirlo a álgebra: a signo: a dibujo" (143-144). Lastly, alongside the neologisms already noted, Giménez Caballero utilizes an array of rare but dictionary-listed words (Hernando 283), which often have the feel of neologisms, as well as a striking selection of foreign words, most of them drawn from English: ring, shop, match, stadium, knock-out, manager, driver, racer, performance, etc..[10]

As far as genre is concerned, if *Hércules* appears, broadly speaking, to be essayistic in nature, nevertheless it is rather more difficult to specify to which particular sub-category the contents of the book correspond. Is it aesthetic theory, art and literature criticism, editorializing on the contemporary scene, an excursus on mythology and the modern world, or what? The nine plates of reproductions of modern Spanish artworks[11] that are scattered through the text would seem to pull us in one direction, while the often present political concerns (which

---

[9] Salazar y Chapela: "Giménez Caballero se ha estacionado como para siempre (acaso amanerándose para tomar postura literaria, estilo) en el paso breve del párrafo corto."

[10] While this feature might be explained in part by Giménez Caballero's focus on sport and the fact that the Spanish language, in the 1920s, had not yet fully developed its own vocabulary for all the technical terms related to this topic, quite frequently he seems to be deliberately using the foreign word in preference to an existing Spanish equivalent.

[11] By, among others, Pablo Picasso (1881-1972), Benjamín Palencia (1894-1980), Pedro Flores (1897-1967), Ismael González de la Serna (1898-1968), Francisco Bores (1898-1972), Maruja Mallo (1902-1995), and Ramón Gaya (b. 1910). For further details, see Bonet *passim*.

crescendo towards the end) urge us in quite another.[12] A clue to Giménez Caballero's intentions may be found in the fact that among the group of articles in which form most of the chapters originally appeared, three offered the running title of "Folklor" and five more that of "Folklor de los juegos."[13] Furthermore, in the course of his observations and analyses in *Hércules*, Giménez Caballero twice portrays himself as a "folklorista":

> De todos los nuevos fenómenos que ofrece hoy el deporte al ojo del folklorista, pocos aparecen tan considerables como éste de *las mascotas*. (130)

> Yo veo en el *rey de bastos* algo más que un complejo social—como han venido sosteniendo los folkloristas hasta ahora—. Yo veo nada menos que el vago eco coloreado de un mito helénico. (195)

It is true that Giménez Caballero includes some material that could be considered as falling into the area of folklore, and, in addition, we find him several times quoting such authors as Lévy Bruhl and J.G. Frazer, talking of "etnógrafos," and dealing with topics derived from ethnography (e.g. 76, 135, 141, 146-147, 168, 206). But in part I believe that he has recourse to this kind of terminology because in the 1920s the words to describe exactly what he was doing, or attempting to do, simply did not exist. What he offers us here—as I hope will become more clear in an analysis of the range of topics treated—is a striking blend of social anthropology and commentary on the arts, one that seems very much to anticipate what today would be called cultural studies: he is, I would therefore suggest, a kind of pioneering practitioner of cultural studies *avant la lettre*.[14]

---

[12] Similar blends are to be found in Ortega's *La deshumanización del arte* and José Díaz Fernández's *El nuevo romanticismo* (1930), but in both cases the style of the essayistic prose is much more conventional.

[13] See the list of Works Cited and note 15 below. Giménez Caballero used the term "folklorista" at least as far back as 1924 in articles for *El Sol* that were later collected in *Los toros, las castañuelas y la Virgen* (Foard 46, 49, 76, 119; Hernando 209).

[14] Symptomatically, Hernando refers to Giménez Caballero as "situado ahora dentro de un plano de interpretación folklorista o cultural" (227).

Now, *Hércules* is arranged in twelve chapters. As mentioned above, chapter 1 establishes the principles of athletics, cinema and the dice-shaker. In chapter 2, Giménez Caballero laments the fact that almost all existing sports writing has been purely descriptive and asserts the pressing need for a more theoretical approach and a classificatory system; thereafter, he goes on to propose three axes on which different sports can be located: the horizontal (whether a sport is played naked or in protective clothing), the temporal (how old or new a sport is), and the vertical (what social class a sport corresponds to). At the very end of the chapter Giménez Caballero announces his intention of next offering three case studies: boxing on the vertical scale, car-racing on the horizontal, and mountain-climbing on the temporal, and a quick check of the index reveals that chapters 3, 4 and 5 do indeed offer precisely what has been promised.

At this stage, the first-time reader is likely to have formed a number of expectations based on the apparent rigor and symmetry of these opening chapters: 1 offers a general introduction and establishes the three defining principles; 2 considers one of those principles and defines three classificatory axes; each of 3, 4 and 5 focuses on a different one of those axes and an exemplifying sport. Based on these initial observations, it would be more than reasonable to anticipate that the latter two-thirds of the book would return to treat, in a more or less like manner, the remaining two defining principles, namely cinema and the dice-shaker. However, this is not the case at all. Instead, chapters 6, 7, 8 and 9 meander off in a number of directions: 6 reflects on another sport, this time soccer, 7 bemoans the woeful state of bullfighting, a judgment underpinned by Giménez Caballero's personal aversion for the *picador*, 8 investigates the vogue for mascots (yet another sporting theme), while 9 offers an extraordinary series of meditations on Russian factory sirens. Although a seemingly equal member of the opening triad, cinema receives scant attention: beyond a number of references in chapter 1, there is a brief section entitled "El cinema y el objeto" (135-137) included in chapter 8, "Las mascotas," but that is all. The third principle of the dice-shaker fares slightly, but not significantly, better. Dice games, games of chance, board games and all other leisure games and pastimes are (with one exception) not addressed; instead, asserting that the dice-shaker has already been more than adequately established on the contemporary cultural scene, Giménez Caballero decides to dedicate the last three chapters (10, 11, 12) to one game whose importance, he claims, has hitherto been overlooked: playing cards. Even then, he is not so much interested in the games that can be played with a pack of cards, as in the symbolism of the pack, with its four suits, sequence of thirteen card values (especially the face cards), and its association with the Tarot.[15]

Rather artfully, at the very end of chapter 1 Giménez Caballero creates a kind of analogy between the highest score possible from one throw of a pair of dice—double six—and the twelve chapters into which his book is divided, effectively suggesting that it too will be, as it were, a "winner":

> Permitidme que inaugure este breve devocionario heraclida con ese tercer ángulo del frontón de Hércules.
>
> Tomando a la divinidad alejada de la aventura y del músculo: en un momento de reposo y juego. Apoyada sobre una arista de su propio templo: echando sobre el ajedrezado del pavimento—negro-blanco—al aire, la prosa discontinua (6 doble) de unos dados: estos ensayos. (23-24)

---

[15] I would argue that the "prehistory" of *Hércules* is also relevant to this breakdown of an expected structure. The origin of the book seems to lie in a commission by the newspaper *El Sol* to review a series of four books on different sports published by Calpe. The review appeared in five installments with the title "Bajo el signo heraclida" (see list of Works Cited): "I" was a general introduction, "II" considered two books on "Concursos atléticos" and "Deportes atléticos" by Federico Reparaz, while "III", "IV" and "V" became part of *Hércules*, as chapter 5 and the first and second halves of chapter 6, respectively. This sequence was followed by eight individually titled articles, all headed "Folklor" or "Folklor de los juegos" (see list of Works Cited), which became chapter 4, chapter 2, chapter 3, chapter 10, chapter 11, two-thirds of chapter 12, and the first and second halves of chapter 8, respectively. Thus, almost exactly 75% of the book was originally published between August and November 1927, and only three chapters, 1, 7 and 9, plus the last part of chapter 12, seem to have been written later and specifically for *Hércules*.

This chronology also has implications for those interested in the political content of Giménez Caballero's book, as by the turn of the decade he would have explicitly espoused Italian fascism (cf. Davidson, Foard and Labanyi). Most of his thinking as reflected in *Hércules* can be dated to the summer and autumn of 1927, though it should also be noted that the most explicitly protofascist section, the last third of chapter 12 (208-215), was one of the later additions. For an overall view of Giménez Caballero's contributions to *El Sol*, see Dennis's edition of *Visitas literarias* 67-76.

But besides the witty conceit, in these paragraphs we also encounter an example of sleight of hand, of crafty, dextrous, now-you-see-it-now-you-don't substitution: the third side of the pediment, i.e. *the dice-shaker*, with which Giménez Caballero says he is planning to open his devotions, connects seamlessly enough with the *games* found in the title of chapter 2, "Tablero de los juegos,"[16] but as we read on we discover that the kind of games that Giménez Caballero proceeds to talk about are actually *sports*, which in turn strictly correspond to the first side of the pediment, i.e. *athletics*.[17]

Furthermore, as the second paragraph of this same quotation unfolds, the syntax becomes ambiguous or confused: Giménez Caballero pictures Heracles ("la divinidad") sitting on the ground, propped ("apoyada") against the wall of his temple. The following Spanish gerund, "echando," *appears* to refer to Heracles playing a game of dice. But as the sentence develops, another colon serves to equate the dice with Giménez Caballero's essays ("unos dados: estos ensayos"), and it then seems as if "echando" is to be taken in a different way, in parallel with "tomando" (both governed by "inaugure"), in which case it would refer back to Giménez Caballero rather than to Heracles. Once this is perceived, the phrase "al aire" can be connected with the verb "echando"—"echando al aire" (throwing into the air), rather than functioning as a descriptor of the Greek temple (with its geometrically paved floor and the dice game that would of course be "in the open air"). The whole passage has an unstable, elusive feel, with Heracles and Giménez Caballero floating in and out of focus, the one partially superimposed upon the other.[18]

A little way into chapter 2, Giménez Caballero outlines the limitations of sport-related literature written to date, and proposes that the present vein of inspiration has in all likelihood run its course:

---

[16] For a discussion of punning and the polysemy of the word "tablero," see note 27 below.

[17] Later on Giménez Caballero would offer this already quoted *bon mot*: "Nada se parece tanto a una partida de ajedrez como un partido de fútbol" (196). Notice too that the word he uses here for the temple pediment "frontón"—also refers to the court or playing-space of the game of *pelota* (this court is also sometimes referred to as a "jai-alai").

[18] Underpinning the initial analogy—double six: twelve essays—there is evidently an implicit allusion to the twelve Labors of Heracles (Davidson 82). No false modesty here on Giménez Caballero's part!

> Tal vez la etapa lírica del deporte ha tramontado ya.
> (Quizás, la novelística también.)
> Y recaer hoy día en la oda muscular o en el relato lúdico, es posible que constituya un acto zaguero: Una esquivada; un *sidestepping*—en la literatura deportiva. (27-28)

This kind of composition, he says, is already "over the hill," and to go back and write more of the same would be to lapse ("recaer") into senseless repetition. But Giménez Caballero changes his metaphor in midstream: such a doubling-back would indeed be an "acto zaguero," in the sense of being in/bringing up the rear (from "a la zaga"), but the root of this word also reminds us—acoustically—of another spatial motion, namely "zigzag," "zigzaguear." Using his ubiquitous appositional technique, Giménez Caballero goes on to gloss "acto zaguero" as "Una esquivada; un *sidestepping*," perhaps relying on the intermediate, but only implied, notion of zigzagging to get us from "going to the rear" to the perpendicularly different action of "sidestepping."

It will be my contention in the rest of this study that the blurring of details, mixed metaphors, argument by analogy, and misdirection that we have detected in these two illustrative examples are integral to a particular mode of writing that permeates *Hércules* at all levels of the construction of the text, a mode which constitutes its most novel and arresting feature. In fact, throughout the book Giménez Caballero is constantly ducking and dodging, skirting the issue, elusively slipping and sliding away, meeting matters more usually aslant than head-on. By analyzing several passages drawn from Chapter 1 as well as others from elsewhere in the book, I hope to isolate the variety of mechanisms at work in producing the disconcerting impression that the author is deliberately sidestepping traditional logic and indeed "playing fast and loose" with his writing—and with the reader.

As mentioned above, Giménez Caballero's starting point (or opening gambit?) for his cultural inquiries is the identification of the three defining principles of his times. Beginning with a series of references to the durable appeal of the triad in Europe through the ages, he then observes that:

> Es raro que no se haya evangelizado antes por la joven literatura la nueva divinidad que venía preformada en el siguiente triángulo:

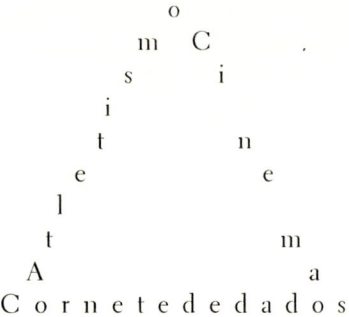

Que no se haya inscrito en ese polígono—definidor absoluto de nuestro tiempo—al dios a que todos estábamos rindiendo fervor y entusiasmo. (13)

Several items are of interest here. First of all, Giménez Caballero merely states that this miscellaneous threesome *is* the very essence of the modern age, and to bolster this bald—and decidedly arguable—assertion, he adopts the rhetorical pose of mock surprise, finding it inexplicable that others before him have not already seen and affirmed the patently obvious. His diagram is vaguely reminiscent of a *calligramme*—the words form a triangle which in turn represents the pediment on a Greek temple wherein the "nueva divinidad" is to be inscribed (cf. *Hércules* 11). Notice also the slippage from "la joven literatura" in the sentence before the typographical illustration, to "nuestro tiempo" in that which follows: from "youthful [i.e. modern] literature" to the whole of "our age" is quite a leap.

Of course, the new divinity is none other than Heracles, and Giménez Caballero goes on to tell us that:

Tras Hércules marchó toda la nueva juventud. Quitó el cielo azul de los hombros del Atlas y se lo colocó sobre los suyos, heredando así el sublime mito de ese monte negro de sabor picassiano: Atlas.

Hijos del Atlas (monte hercúleo): los atletas. (16)

In this passage "la nueva juventud" now seems to synthesize the two terms previously employed ("la joven literatura," "nuestro tiempo"), but of primary importance here is the considerable compression and sleight of hand that these at-first-sight simple sentences contain. Giménez Caballero alludes to the Eleventh Labor, in which Heracles proved strong enough to assume Atlas's burden while Atlas went to fetch the golden apples from the Garden of the Hesperides; he was also wily enough to trick Atlas into taking back his burden afterwards.[19] Here, Heracles's *temporary assumption* of Atlas's role/burden is perceived as somehow allowing him to *inherit* the myth of Mount Atlas, though we know that Heracles and Atlas are also linked by other mythological stories and beliefs beyond their encounter in the famous scene from the Eleventh Labor. Using this connection as a springboard, then, Giménez Caballero presses on, striving for further insights, and if we turn our attention to the last sentence of the quotation and bear in mind all the mythological material adduced so far, his pithy conclusion can be expanded discursively and rendered approximatively as a sequence of ideas: Atlas is Mount Atlas, Mount Atlas is a "monte hercúleo" (the southern Pillar of Heracles), Heracles was a paragon of physical prowess (and was held to have founded the Olympic Games),[20] the sons of Atlas are "at*letas*," the Heraclids are the sons, descendents (and followers) of Heracles,[21] and so the Heraclids are likewise consummate athletes, not only because they take after their

---

[19] A review of the mythology surrounding this episode yields the following data: Atlas was a Titan who originally was "the guardian of the pillars of heaven (which hold up the sky)" (Howatson 76); Graves describes his original task as the Titan "who separated the waters of the firmament from the waters of the earth" (1: 146). In the war between the Titans and the Olympian Gods (i.e. Zeus and his brothers and sisters), Atlas was asked to be their leader, and when the Titans were eventually defeated, "Atlas, as their war-leader, was awarded an exemplary punishment, being ordered to carry the sky on his shoulders" (Graves 1: 40-41). The Garden of the Hesperides, that is, Hera's garden with the golden apple-tree, "lay on the slopes of Mount Atlas" (Graves 2: 145), and as Graves explains: "later mythographers understood Atlas as a simple personification of Mount Atlas, in North-western Africa, whose peak seemed to hold up the Heavens" (1: 145). Furthermore, by extension and by geographical proximity, "[Atlas] became identified [...] sometimes with the southern Pillar of Hercules" (Howatson 76), one of the two Pillars near the Straits of Gibraltar that figure in the Tenth Labor. Heracles was, of course, one of the many offspring of Zeus by a mortal woman, in this case Alcmene, and while his name means "glory of Hera," his conception and birth aroused Hera's indignation and jealousy (Graves 2: 85-86).

[20] Howatson 392; Graves 2: 90, 178.

[21] Throughout *Hércules* Giménez Caballero uses "heraclida" as an adjective meaning related to, associated with, or derived from Heracles; as a noun the Heraclids or Heracleidae are the children and further descendents of Heracles (Howatson 269).

father/ancestor Heracles but also because Heracles is identified with Atlas and "atletas" are the "hijos de Atlas." If we recall Giménez Caballero's opening statement that "tras Hércules marchó toda la nueva juventud" (16), then it follows that, in his view, present-day Heraclids are to be identified precisely as:

> [E]sta nueva juventud ginnosdérmica, [que] no sólo quiso restaurar en sí el culto de "los anchos hombros sustinentes del mundo"—y coger las manzanas de oro que ocultaba el gigante—, sino también equipararse en "velocidad" y "sentido de la aventura" a este supremo Heracles. (16)

When all the intermediate steps are teased out, it can readily be appreciated that Giménez Caballero's conclusion is arrived at much more by a process of free association than by anything approaching true argumentative logic. However, the most revealing discovery of all is that the linchpin of the whole passage, located in that appositional phrase "Hijos de Atlas [...]: los atletas," is actually based on an implied etymology that turns out to be false. Given the acoustic similarity, it certainly seems as if the one is derived from the other, or both from a common root, but that proves not to be the case.[22] Instead, Giménez Caballero has created the fleeting illusion of a real and substantive underpinning founded on solid erudition, and readers are prevented from questioning or scrutinizing too deeply as they are carried along by a combination of rhyme, a fast, lapidary style, and a relentless succession of bald (and bold) assertions. Thus Giménez Caballero's sometimes abstruse, often sophistical, but always imaginative association of ideas is all the more persuasive for its headlong forward rush, for the speed, terseness and aplomb with which it is consistently dispatched.

---

[22] Howatson suggests that Atlas's "name probably means 'he who carries' or 'he who endures'" (76), while Graves gives "he who dares, *or* suffers" (1: 383). Corominas traces the origin of "atleta" back through Latin to the Greek *athletes / athleo / âthlon* (he who competes for a prize, to compete for a prize, a prize [in a physical competition]) (71).

For another instance of decidedly creative etymologizing in *Hércules*, this time regarding the word "hacha," see 190-191. Salazar y Chapela approvingly notes Giménez Caballero's "engaños—literarios—de profundidad," while Hernando writes of his "estilo de alusiones poco determinadas" (257) and observes Giménez Caballero's fondness for "etimologismos," but finds that "muchos de estos 'paladeos etimológicos' son utilizaciones estilísticas, poco ortodoxas en filología" (284-285).

Still in Chapter 1, Giménez Caballero proceeds to offer an unlikely disquisition on "el Cinema: invento heraclida," wherein he is able to find "esta línea hereditaria: *Hércules—Caballero medieval— Douglas Fairbanks*" (19); he also provides an equally provocative excursus on "Hércules: el primer don Juan" (20).[23] At the end of this latter section, he closes with a brief recapitulation of the three preceding ("anchos hombros"—Atlas, "sexo genial"—Don Juan, "alegría veloz"—cinema) followed immediately by a new transition: "La juventud torna a este Hércules de los anchos hombros, del sexo genial, inventor de la alegría veloz del cinema cosmopolita de paisajes, viajero innumerable. Y jugador de dados" (21-22). While Heracles's travels during and after the Twelve Labors would certainly qualify him as a "viajero innumerable," Giménez Caballero makes no attempt to prepare us for the sharp turn (sidestepping?) that occurs in the last verbless sentence of the paragraph. The reader might well be forgiven for wondering where in the world this came from; in fact, Giménez Caballero has simply decided that this is the next subject for discussion, and so he veers off towards it merely by tacking on one more fresh attribute ("Y...") to the list of topics treated so far.

The next paragraph elaborates a little more—"Dicen que Hércules tuvo muchas debilidades. Que fué amigo de Dionisos, y que su libro dilecto era 'El manual del perfecto cocinero'" (22)—but these rumored reputations are summarily rejected, despite the fact that Heracles was indeed "also known for his appetites, gluttony and lust" (Howatson 269). Instead, Giménez Caballero concludes: "Hércules tuvo sólo un juego pacífico: jugar a los dados" (22). While the reference to *El manual del perfecto cocinero* is patently and transparently humorous, a passing joke based on anachronism and playful allusion (to Fray Luis's *La perfecta casada*, among others), the short, blunt and unequivocal statement regarding dice as Heracles's only leisure pastime appears to bear all the hallmarks of authority and authenticity. Now, as we have seen, Giménez Caballero's bald assertions are actually often articulations of unsubstantiated interpretation or quirky, subjective opinion, but this latest one allows us to add yet another category to this list: that of pure invention. An exhaustive search of Greek and Latin databases, including the Internet Classics Archive and the Perseus Project (Tufts University) as well as the *Lexicon Icono-*

---

[23] Note how in all these cases the strikingly new perspective that Giménez Caballero proposes is first established by a pithy appositional phrase articulated around a colon.

graphicum Mythologiae Classicae (4, pt. 1: 728-838, pt. 2: 444-559; 5, pt. 1: 1-262), reveals not only that no classical text supports this exclusive linkage of Heracles and dice, but indeed that Heracles and dice are never even mentioned together![24] Elsewhere Giménez Caballero demonstrates considerable familiarity with Greek mythology as well as a panoply of other more or less arcane subjects, and this overall impression of wide-ranging erudition enables him to smuggle in, undetected, the occasional fabrication that nevertheless has the ring and the feel of the truth.[25] It also permits him to change direction on the spot: what could be wrenching transitions, from Atlas to the cinema to Don Juan to dice, are made succinctly and effortlessly, and Heracles's supposed fondness for dice allows Giménez Caballero to introduce what he really wants to talk about next, namely Cubism.

Once again the colon serves as the visible mark of equivalence, the fulcrum point of equilibrium, though here—unlike previous occasions, where the syntax is very simple and straightforward—the sentence continues with a further phrase that serves as a gloss and that in turn creates a second equivalence or identification: "Hércules: descubridor del cubismo, de verter sobre tableros un cubilete con dos cubos de marfil" (22). The steps of the "argument" run something like this: Heracles's only non-violent game was dice; the two dice are thrown on a board from a shaker with no prior knowledge or control of how they will fall; the cubic shape and the unpredictability—"Azar y matemática" (mentioned twice [22-23, 23])—of the dice are also the defining characteristics of Cubism (artistic and literary).[26] The whole

---

[24] The closest we come is a dice-oracle in a shrine sacred to Heracles at Bura, mentioned by Pausanias in his *Description of Greece* (cf. Graves 2: 176), some of the Heracleidae playing dice (Herodotus, *History*, book I), and the keeper of a temple dedicated to Heracles proposing to his deity a game at dice (Plutarch, *Romulus*).

[25] This apparently factual but actually unsubstantiated claim is both echoed and recalled much later in the book, where Giménez Caballero writes, "La taba: testigo adámico. Adán no jugó a otra cosa en el Paraíso. De ahí esa cosa paradisíaca, de mundo balbuceante, que trajo el cubismo con su restauración del 'hueso tallado' de los dados" (168-169).

[26] Despite Giménez Caballero's breezy highhandedness with matters of logic, there is nevertheless something of a problem here: if we accept for the moment that dice and Cubism share certain essential qualities, if Cubism can be glossed as "verter sobre tableros un cubilete con dos cubos de marfil," then Heracles becomes not only the discoverer of Cubism very much *avant la lettre* but also, strictly speaking, the discoverer (inventor) of the game of dice, which

set of ideas seems to come full circle and can be neatly wrapped together:

> La juventud ama hoy los dados y el cubilete. Los arroja sobre las telas de los nuevos pintores, en los poemas de los nuevos líricos, en los bocetos de los nuevos ensayistas. Azar y matemática. Cornete de dados: tercer ángulo del frontón de Heracles. (23)

Giménez Caballero establishes a kind of physical analogy between dice and Cubism to reinforce his outlandish theory: just as the two dice are turned out ("verter") of the shaker by the player onto the board, so the young painters and literati of the day throw ("arrojar") — figuratively — the dice over their canvases, poems and essay drafts. Given the rich semantic range of the word "tablero" — as bulletin board, playing board, gaming board (for chess or checkers), blackboard, or quite simply the top of a table, the dice board is, again in terms of the analogy, equated to the stretched canvases — or indeed wooden planks — of painters, and to the sheets of paper of writers (and the desk tops on which they work).[27] Furthermore, an element of self-

---

is not what Giménez Caballero had asserted (however fallaciously) moments earlier. I suspect that his elliptical tendencies almost get the better of him here, while we also need to take a second look at that word "descubridor." Any explicit inconsistency or contradiction is eliminated if a more metaphorical reading is adopted. The gist of Giménez Caballero's argument then becomes that just as the Heracles of antiquity personifies the spirit of the modern age, so his fondness for dice prefigures the artistic movement which corresponds to that age, namely Cubism: he is the "discoverer" of Cubism inasmuch as he also discovered — that is, he discerned and appreciated — certain fundamental or "transcendent" features inherent in the game of dice.

[27] A further exploitation of the numerous meanings of "tablero" can be found in Chapter 2. That chapter's title — "Tablero de los juegos" — appears at first sight to mean "board for games," but as we read on we rapidly discover that "tablero" is now being used to refer to a chart or grid, and that the chapter is concerned with establishing a classificatory system (27, 32). Further on, via a kind of pun or semantic slippage, "tablero" also comes to be associated with the blackboard (another of its meanings, though Giménez Caballero most often refers to the blackboard with the word "pizarra" [27, 34, 40]) on which the classificatory chart/grid is drawn and worked out (40). There are further connotations of the stereotypical maths or physics professor in the classroom, and possibly also of a coach and a sports team (Davidson 39).

In addition, there may be a further punning reference to *Tableros* (remember that Giménez Caballero uses the plural in "verter sobre tableros" consciousness or a gesture of self-referentiality can likely be detected in the phrase "los bocetos de los nuevos ensayistas."

One other aspect of Giménez Caballero's treatment of dice and Cubism merits comment. In the opening pages of Chapter 1, where he is concerned with configuring the triangle that defines the age, it is noteworthy that Giménez Caballero substitutes in it the acoustically similar word "cornete" for the more likely or expected "cubilete." "Cornete" only figures in María Moliner as a highly technical term for bony plates inside the nose, but its derivation—from "cuerno" and the diminutive suffix "-ete"—is obvious. Corominas reminds us that traditionally the cone-shaped dice-shaker was made out of a horn (182), so nothing really seems amiss.[28] But by establishing the "cubilete" = "cornete" equivalence early on, I believe that Giménez Caballero is strategically preparing for a wider-ranging series of observations that occur in the dice/Cubism discussion.

Immediately after the sentence that introduces the initial proposition—"Hércules: descubridor del cubismo, de verter sobre tableros un cubilete con dos cubos de marfil" (22), he goes on to pose the rhetorical question that, given the way in which it is phrased, leaves little room for doubt or alternative perspectives: "¿Qué otra explicación se puede dar a su famoso *cornete* de Amaltea? Azar y matemática. Sacar el 6 doble en un golpe de taba. ¡Bello juego, único y posible juego heraclida!" (22-23). Clearly, this is another example of Giménez Caballero's specious argumentation: he first substitutes "cornete" for "cubilete," then makes an extravagant (and mainly metaphorical) connection of Cubism with dice, then goes on to "justify" or "support" it with an obscure, erudite reference to two mythological stories about a horn, stories that bear little relevance to the matter at hand and which he is only able to adduce thanks to that substitution of "cornete" for

---

[22]), as this was the name of one of the literary magazines of *ultraísmo*, directed by Isaac del Vando Villar, with four numbers appearing between 1921-1922 and with contributions from many of the best known *ultraístas*.

[28] Another factor here may well be Max Jacob's *Le Cornet à dés* (Paris, 1917), which was translated by Guillermo de Torre as *El cubilete de dados* (Madrid: Editorial América, 1924), with a prologue also by de Torre. An exhaustive treatment of Giménez Caballero's possible indebtedness to Jacob would go far beyond the scope of the present article, but suffice it to note that Jacob's collection of prose poems is typically characterized as containing humor, playfulness, puns, word play, verbal acrobatics, jumps, illogic and false causation.

"cubilete."[29] In this way, then, Giménez Caballero uses the reference to Amaltheia in order to trigger an implicit allusion to one of Heracles's feats of strength (the fight with Achelous) and to remind us of Amaltheia's horn as the magical cornucopia; from there, he implicitly equates both Achelous's horn and the cornucopia with the dice-shaker made out of a horn, and concludes—with totally unfounded and truly spurious logic—that Heracles's receipt or winning of the cornucopia must be the explanation of his predilection for dice and, hence, his "discovery" of Cubism.[30]

Although this kind of discursive zigzagging and syllogistic legerdemain is perhaps densest in Chapter 1, nonetheless it permeates the whole of *Hércules*. For instance, Giménez Caballero can present as a foregone conclusion some newly introduced point that is in fact far from proven or established: thus, after stating the need for a more critical, thoughtful kind of writing about sport, he continues, "Desde luego, el primer hueco a rellenar en esta alta literatura deportiva se ve que es el destinado al encasillamiento de los juegos" (32). Sometimes he will present a choice as if it were random, whereas in fact, on closer examination, it turns out to be a perfectly deliberate and premeditated one that enables him to further his "argument": "La mejor verificación de que el éxito hodierno del boxeo tiene un sentido vertical es tomar un país cualquiera y someterlo a prueba. [...] Un país—por azar—como el nuestro" (53). In this example, Giménez Caballero's "experimentalism" is entirely sham: it is self-evident that he really wants to

---

[29] Amaltheia was a Goat-nymph who suckled Zeus as an infant (Howatson 10). In gratitude, Zeus "set Amaltheia's image among the stars, as Capricorn. He also borrowed one of her horns, which resembled a cow's [...]; it became the famous Cornucopia, or horn of plenty, which is always filled with whatever food or drink its owner may desire" (Graves 1: 39 and cf. 42). In a related story, Heracles fought the River-god Achelous, and in the course of their struggle Achelous turned into a bull and charged Heracles; "Heracles nimbly stepped aside and, catching hold of both his horns, hurled him to the ground with such force that the right horn snapped clean off. [...] Some say that Heracles returned the broken horn to Achelous in exchange for the horn of Goat Amaltheia; and some, that it was changed into Amaltheia's by the Naiads [...]; Others say that in the course of his Twelfth Labor, he took the horn down to Tartarus, filled by the Hesperides with golden fruit and now called the Cornucopia, as a gift for Plutus, Tyche's assistant" (Graves 2: 191-192).

[30] Giménez Caballero returns very briefly to the subject in Chapter 12, where he observes, again somewhat capriciously, that: "Su fecundidad divina radica en el cuerno de una cabra" (205).

steer the discussion around to Spain. A somewhat similar strategy involves conceding one point and then introducing a second, different one as if it genuinely "followed" from the first, whereas the connection is actually tenuous:

> El arte nuevo ha cumplido un encargo delicioso cerca de los juegos milenarios del hombre: restaurar el cornete de dados. Salpicar, telas y poemas, de cubiletes y poliedros arrojados al azar.
> Pero le falta una nueva rehabilitación: la baraja. (167)

Finally, a comparison or simile, however stretched or far-fetched, can also serve as a launching pad for leaping from one topic to another, as in the following, where Giménez Caballero describes the racing-car driver in his leather helmet: "En el casco, desafiador de los elementos, como las caretas de los chamanes frente a los espíritus malignos" (68). These are all essentially techniques for guilefully making a radical change of direction, for, as it were, turning on a dime and heading off immediately to whatever new idea Giménez Caballero wants to treat next (cf. Hernando 256).

Furthermore, a number of the choices he makes in the course of his disquisition seem to be totally arbitrary as well as perhaps ludic in nature. Thus the main reason for deciding on *three* axes for his classificatory grid in chapter 2 would appear to be that he had just been reminded of the proverbial phrase "buscarle 3 pies al gato" (34)! Elsewhere, we encounter an inventive, quirky, and almost jokey delineation of cause and effect: "El alpinismo comenzó por originarse de una elucubración sentimental y pedagógica. (¡Oh Rousseau!)" (83).[31] In this false, tendentious yet at the same time humorous attribution of origins, it is sometimes difficult to know where whimsy ends and a kind of allegory begins:

> En Italia el fútbol fué inventado por Marinetti.
> Se cogió la cabeza pelona de d'Annunzio. Se la afeitó la perilla. Y se la echó a rodar por la cuneta de la velocidad. Todo el equipo futurista dió sus coces a esta pelota. (106)

---

[31] The joke depends in part, of course, on ellipsis, and on the ability of the (knowledgeable) reader to catch the allusion to works such as *Les Rêveries du promeneur solitaire*.

Is Giménez Caballero alluding obliquely to the brutal Aztec game that gives the impression of being an early, atavistic forebear of modern soccer, is he suggesting that a new generation needs, so to speak, to decapitate a preceding one in order to differentiate and establish itself (and thereby work out any "anxiety of influence" or Oedipal rancor), or is he genuinely associating this modern sport with a modern artistic movement that he admires? I find that it is almost impossible to say.

A final and notable example of Giménez Caballero's fervid imagination occurs in his treatment of Lindbergh's transatlantic flight of 1927. Here the reader will in all likelihood be initially baffled by a reference to the aviator's mascot:

> Solamente el instinto popular explicó la feliz travesía de Lindbergh de acuerdo con Lindbergh mismo. O sea: gracias al gato o pingüino que Lindbergh portó, en su genial escala, *como mascota*. (131)
>
> *El pingüino de Lindbergh.*
> [...]
> (Lindbergh puso de moda en París "el pingüino de Lindbergh," bajo el más variado aspecto utensiliario.) (145-146)

Research reveals, however, that Lindbergh carried with him on his record-breaking flight a picture of Felix the Cat, a popular cartoon character created in 1919, and so this is an authentic detail from the zone of popular culture that Giménez Caballero has evidently seized upon and pressed into service. The black and white appearance of Felix apparently stimulates the free play of Giménez Caballero's associative processes, prompting him to write of the "gato o pingüino," where the insidious conjunction "or" demonstrates perfectly the surreptitious introduction of what is in fact a wholly unjustified alternative; a few pages later, the animated feline has been completely forgotten or rather transformed definitively into "el pingüino de Lindbergh." No wonder, then, that in a later chapter Giménez Caballero could himself introduce another of his visions with the phrase "Imagino muy bien—delirantemente—..." (162): delirious is a fine and entirely apt characterization of much of his play with words and ideas.[32]

---

[32] Guillermo de Torre writes of Giménez Caballero's "expresiones desgarradas" [ripped expressions] and finds that "sus aciertos y sus desvaríos, son buenos ejemplos de un tiempo de invención y subversión desatadas" (248).

In his now classic study of "La Métaphore filée dans la poésie surréaliste" Michael Riffaterre demonstrated how Surrealist extended metaphors differ fundamentally from non-Surrealist extended metaphors. In the latter case, sequences or chains of derived metaphors are spun out from a primary metaphor by means of an associative process based on synonyms, metonyms, synecdoches, and other connections that in some way express one or other modality of the primary term (48-49). However, in the case of the Surrealist extended metaphor, the creation of those sequences or chains is very different, in that semantic links are abandoned, indeed avoided, and in their place the controlling factor is now, rather, one or other of the *formal* features of words; that is to say, the associative process is based on rhyme, assonance, puns, homonyms, syllepsis, spoonerisms, set phrases, clichés, quotations, and so on (49-50). What remains unchanged, of course, are the linguistic structures, but where in traditional extended metaphors the grammatical construction and the meaning go hand in hand, in Surrealist writing much of the effect is derived from the tension generated by encountering semantically incompatible metaphorical elements (present because of some *formal* connection) within familiar and "correct" grammatical environments.

Turning back to *Hércules jugando a los dados*, in the preceding analyses of passages from the book we have found examples of the use of rhyme, assonance, acoustic similarity, free association, associative leaps, semantic slippage, false etymology, neologism, smoke-screen humor, the ludic, the arbitrary, tangential transitions, unfulfilled expectations, loose ends, unsupported assertions, specious argumentation, the seamless mixture of genuine and spurious erudition, and a racy, telegrammatic style, all wrapped up in a sleek, self-confident and often fast-moving package that discourages careful and pondered critical scrutiny.[33]

---

[33] Compare *Yo, inspector de alcantarillas* (1928), a completely "creative" prose work, wherein Dennis pays particular attention to Giménez Caballero's "exercises in word association" and "free association" ("Ernesto" 84, 91-92), describing one of the processes thus:

> Giménez Caballero [...] begins by allowing sound to dictate sense: phonic similarities combine or collide with semantic ambiguities [...] each word builds on the final syllable of the preceding one [...] enabling the text to pirouette—somewhat haltingly—and return to its point of departure, having demonstrated that sound and sense can be harmoniously

Although these features do not provide a perfect match with the characteristics identified by Riffaterre, there is some measure of overlap and a good deal of similarity between them. While I should stress that it is very far from my intention to portray *Hércules* as any kind of Surrealist or even quasi-Surrealist work, the comparison does allow us to get a better sense of the book, and it does reveal to what extent the prose is radically different from what one would normally expect in an work of essayistic non-fiction.[34] Approaching an extended essay or a set of essays for the first time inevitably arouses a certain set of conventional expectations in the reader, but as we have seen *Hércules* does not deliver on or actively undermines many of these, both in its overall structure and development and in its discursive manner and style.

My conclusion, then, is that the book is actually a kind of rare hybrid, a mix of non-fiction and avant-garde creative prose, a blend, as it were, of essay and prose poem, a heady and uniquely-flavored cocktail (an oddball rather than a highball, a screwball rather than a screwdriver—after all, his next book would be entitled *Julepe de menta!*), for which there are few analogues in modern literature.[35] The blend of authentic and falsified erudition, the sophistry, the uncertainly about

---

fused if the writer works hard enough at creating the illusion of the mind hopping unfettered from one thought to another. (92-93)

Writing of *Genio de España* (1932), a later "essayistic work," Labanyi notes Giménez Caballero's practice of acoustic word association and makes repeated mention of the "huge imaginative leaps" (380-381). It is clear, therefore, that Giménez Caballero effectively made little or no distinction between "creative writing" and "non-fiction."

[34] Nonetheless, Giménez Caballero's views on Surrealism, expressed just about the time that the first edition of *Hércules* appeared in bookshops, are interesting and quite revealing: for him "superrealismo es retorno a la inspiración, a la libertad. Es revuelta contra el clasicismo" ("Libros y márgenes," 1 May 1929), and "Superrealismo quiere decir: *mística del heraclida*. Músculo y libertad: vitalidad" ("Libros y márgenes," 15 May 1929"). Together with his muscular and dynamic view of Surrealism, the mention of the "heraclida" is of course suggestive.

[35] Selva Roca de Togores describes *Hércules* as "un conjunto de brillantes ensayos, cercanos al poema en prosa" ("Plenitud" 45), and Hernando talks of "el aspecto poemático de *Hércules*" (256). Referring to *Genio de España*, Labanyi notes Giménez Caballero's "crossing of generic boundaries" and asserts that it "is as much a text of the literary avant-garde as it is a political tract; its hybrid nature can be understood only in the context of its author's multifaceted activities" (377).

the principal thematic focus, the humor and the general quirkiness might put us in mind of the writings of Jorge Luis Borges, while the unlikely mixing of genres perhaps finds an echo in the original version of Virginia Woolf's *The Pargiters*, where five chapters of fiction were to be combined with six essays. Closer to home, and beyond the already noted connections with Ramón Gómez de la Serna and Guillermo de Torre, comparison with the contemporaneous work of José Bergamín (1895-1983) may also prove illuminating. Nevertheless, despite our best efforts to locate him, Giménez Caballero retains a considerable originality, and the author of *Hércules jugando a los dados* may already have provided us with the best description of his own work, first as "prosa discontinua" (24) and then as "literatura deportiva" (28), though clearly it is less a question of Giménez Caballero writing literature about sport and much more one of him having sport with literature.

Works Cited

Bonet, Juan Manuel. *Diccionario de las vanguardias en España (1907-1936)*. Madrid: Alianza, 1995.

Corominas, Joan. *Breve diccionario etimológico de la lengua castellana*. 3rd ed. Madrid: Gredos, 1973.

Davidson, R.A. "*Hércules jugando a los dados*: obra prefascista de Ernesto Giménez Caballero." M.A. Thesis. Queen's University, Kingston, Ontario, 1998.

Dennis, Nigel. "Ernesto Giménez Caballero and Surrealism: a Reading of *Yo, inspector de alcantarillas*." *The Surrealist Adventure in Spain*. Ed. C. Brian Morris. Ottawa: Dovehouse Editions, 1991. 80-100.

———. "De la palabra a la imagen: La crítica literaria de Ernesto Giménez Caballero, cartelista." *El universo creador del 27. Literatura, pintura, música y cine*. Ed. Cristóbal Cuevas García and Enrique Baena. Málaga: Publicaciones del Congreso de Literatura Española Contemporánea, 1997. 363-377.

Foard, Douglas W. *The Revolt of the Aesthetes. Ernesto Giménez Caballero and the Origins of Spanish Fascism*. New York: Peter Lang, 1989.

Giménez Caballero, Ernesto. "Revista de Libros. Bajo el signo heraclida. I. Una Biblioteca de Deportes." *El Sol* 28 July 1927: 2.

———. "Revista de Libros. Bajo el signo heraclida. II. Atletas, índice." *El Sol* 31 July 1927: 2.

———. "Revista de Libros. Bajo el signo heraclida. III. La crisis del alpinismo." *El Sol* 7 Aug. 1927: 2.

———. "Revista de Libros. Bajo el signo heraclida. IV. Explicación del fútbol." *El Sol* 11 Aug. 1927: 2.
———. "Revista de Libros. Bajo el signo heraclida. V. Explicación del fútbol." *El Sol* 12 Aug. 1927: 2.
———. "Folklor. Los cascos mágicos." *El Sol* 19 Aug. 1927: 1.
———. "Folklor. Vertical del boxeo. I. Tablero de los juegos." *El Sol* 29 Sep. 1927: 1.
———. "Folklor. Vertical del boxeo. II." *El Sol* 5 Oct. 1927: 1.
———. "Folklor de los juegos. Rehabilitación de la baraja." *El Sol* 19 Oct. 1927: 1.
———. "Folklor de los juegos. Los ases." *El Sol* 25 Oct. 1927: 1.
———. "Folklor de los juegos. El rey de bastos." *El Sol* 3 Nov. 1927: 1.
———. "Folklor de los juegos. Las mascotas. I." *El Sol* 13 Nov. 1927: 1.
———. "Folklor de los juegos. Las mascotas. II." *El Sol* 27 Nov. 1927: 4.
———. "Eoántropo. El hombre auroral del arte nuevo." *Revista de Occidente* 57 (March 1928): 309-342.
———. *Hércules jugando a los dados*. Madrid: La Nave, 1928.
———. "Libros y márgenes. Salvador Dalí. Superrealismo." *La Gaceta Literaria* 57 (1 May 1929): 3.
———. "Libros y márgenes. Por ejemplo: el superrealismo." *La Gaceta Literaria* 58 (15 May 1929): 3.
———. *Visitas literarias de España (1925-1928)*. Ed. Nigel Dennis. Valencia: Pre-Textos, 1995.
Graves, Robert. *The Greek Myths*. 2 vols. Harmondsworth: Penguin, 1990.
Hernando, Miguel Ángel. *Prosa vanguardista en la generación del 27. (Gecé y "La Gaceta Literaria")*. Madrid: Prensa Española, 1975.
Howatson, M.C., ed. *The Oxford Companion to Classical Literature*. 2nd ed. Oxford: Oxford University Press, 1989.
Labanyi, Jo. "Women, Asian Hordes and the Threat to the Self in Giménez Caballero's *Genio de España.*" *Bulletin of Hispanic Studies* (Liverpool) 73 (1996): 377-387.
Ledesma Ramos, R. "3 libros: 3 perfiles. I. Giménez Caballero y su Hércules." *La Gaceta Literaria* 63 (1 Aug. 1929): 1-2.
Lexicon Iconographicum Mythologiae Classicae. Zurich/Munich: Artemis, 1988.
Llera, Luis de. "Ortega y Gasset, filósofo *mondain* o metafísico de lúdico?" Morelli 13-32.
Morelli, Gabriele, ed. *Ludus. Gioco, sport, cinema nell'avanguardia spagnola*. Milan: Jaca Book, 1994.
Ortega y Gasset, José. *El tema de nuestro tiempo* [1923]. Madrid: Revista de Occidente/Alianza, 1981.
———. *La deshumanización del arte* [1925]. 10th ed. Madrid: Revista de Occidente, 1970.
Polo del Barrio, Jesús. "El fútbol español hasta la guerra civil." *Revista de Occidente* 2nd epoch. 62-63 (1986): 85-101.

Riffaterre, Michael. "La Métaphore filée dans la poésie surréaliste." *Langue Française* 3 (September 1969): 46-60. [English version: "The Extended Metaphor in Surrealist Poetry." *Text Production*. New York: Columbia University Press, 1983. 202-220.].

Rodríguez Amaya, Fabio. "I *Carteles literarios* di Giménez Caballero (Gecé): invenzione e critica tra ludus, poesia e pittura." Morelli 351-367.

Rota, Ivana. "Il dibattito tra sport e cultura nel primo novecento spagnolo." Morelli 33-55.

Salazar y Chapela, E. "Revista de libros. Literatura. Giménez Caballero (E.): 'Hércules jugando a los dados.' Edición La Nave. 215 páginas. Madrid, 1929." *El Sol* 15 June 1929: 2.

Selva Roca de Togores, Enrique. "Plenitud vanguardista de Gecé." *Anthropos* 84 (1988): 44-46.

———. "Giménez Caballero en el vórtice de la vanguardia hispana." *Revista Canadiense de Estudios Hispánicos* 18 (1994): 328-337.

Soria Olmedo, Andrés. *Vanguardismo y crítica literaria en España (1910-1930)*. Madrid: Istmo, 1988.

Torre, Guillermo de. *Historia de las literaturas de vanguardia*. 3rd ed. Madrid: Guadarrama, 1974.

Bodies in the City: Sports and Beauty in São Paulo of the 20s[*]

MÔNICA RAISA SCHPUN
Università degli Studi di Milano

AS THE RESULT OF an immigration policy that brought in a glut of workers serving the booming coffee plantations, the city of São Paulo experienced an extremely rapid and dramatic increase in its population at the turn of the century, as we can see in the following chart.[1]

Year	Population	Increase (%)	Annual Growth (%)
1872	31, 385	—	—
1890	64, 934	107	4. 1
1900	239, 820	269	14. 0
1920	579, 033	141	4. 5
1940	1, 326, 261	129	4. 2

---

[*] This text is part of a larger research project about gender relations in São Paulo during the 1920s. An extended version of the same topic was published in Les Années folles à São Paulo: hommes et femmes au temps de l'explosion urbaine (1920-1929), with a preface by Michel Perrot.
[1] Source: Instituto Brasileiro de Geografia e Estatística, Anuário estatístico 42.

The decade of the twenties was a special moment in the history of São Paulo, particularly from an urban perspective. It was a time of great transformations in the physical and symbolic landscape that touched multiple dimensions—political and social, as well as economical. These changes were related, moreover, to the forms in which the space was organized, inhabited, perceived, and even read. The interrelationship of the factors above makes the *paulistano*[2] twenties a laboratory of history, since many of the changes observed during that period confirm a pattern of transformations that speaks to the way in which modernity places itself in the emerging urban life.

The urban life taking shape in São Paulo was highly marked by the emerging of new forms of socialization and leisure. In fact, among the disquieting aspects of the period, according to witnesses, were the new rhythms of life that introduced velocity, simultaneity, and fragmentation—a result of the until-then-unknown crowds, product of the sudden increase of the city's population. Not only did people live faster, but they also lived collectively; more occurred at one time and organized public events took advantage of the new spaces and emotions.

Multiplicity and fragmentation in an urban space do not exist without a simultaneous—and seemingly paradoxical—unification and convergence. The situations that called people to public spaces also affected the physical body of the individual whether isolated or in the crowd. If we look closely at the codes of conduct, which are extremely gendered, we will see a reality taking shape that was anything but homogeneous.

In this context I will examine below the new practices and discourses that define, institute, discipline, and separate masculine and feminine corporal experiences during the twenties. At the same time I will look at the social imaginary that binds these experiences to the city of São Paulo where new forms of defining citizenship were being exercised. Focusing my reflections on the urban elites, I will first review some of the practices documented in the press of the time—most notably, competitive sports. That sports occupied so much space in the printed media is not surprising since the masses of spectators, the passion for the game, as well as the variety of sports practiced constituted a privileged expression of masculinity. Women, on the contrary, occu-

---

[2]*Paulistano* and *paulistana* refer to a person, thing, or situation related to the *city* of São Paulo, while *paulista* refers to a person, thing, or situation related to the *state* of São Paulo.

pied a marginal space—athletics was definitely not her "natural" terrain. Her absence in the stadiums, tracks, fields, and swimming pools was precisely the consequence of those gendered urban codes of conduct that we will examine in this article.

Second, when dealing with the specific feminine practices of the new urban culture, I will address issues related to physical representation and beauty. Of all the social groups mingling in the city, women of the dominant classes formed the newest group on the urban scene, which demanded a learning process as well as the development of a pedagogy of public exhibition.[3] This gave origin to a series of gendered codes that aimed to regulate contact between the sexes in integrated spaces, at the same time creating ways of distinguishing and reaffirming social identities. For example, a woman from an elite class was always required to keep her distance, her essential difference, from the masses with whom now she shared spaces and situations.

Gendered forms of urban sociability reveal the relationship between corporal practices and different ways of occupying the city. These social practices are responsible for regulating the interaction between men and women of the dominant classes while intensifying the divisions between the masculine and the feminine. We are dealing, then, with the establishment of identities that are urban, collective, and above all gendered. I base my observations on printed sources taken from sports and women's magazines, literary and medical journals, as well as documents and photographs kept in archives of athletic and social clubs in São Paulo.

The Sex of Sports

Sports were introduced in São Paulo at the turn of the century by immigrants and members of the oligarchy familiar with the development of sports in Europe. Essentially elitist in structure, its practice was restricted to upper- and some middle-class groups.[4] The concept of pro-

---

[3] We know now that women from the lower classes had already figured in the space of the city. In the case of the dominant classes, the process seems to be the opposite—urban expansion occurs together with a series of administrative norms and policies of exclusion or at least of limiting this presence in the public space. See Maria Odila Leite da Silva.

[4] Particularly in the cases of immigrants from urban societies that wanted to continue their sportive habits, like the English or the Germans who organized teams and matches to practice sports since the end of the nineteenth century.

fessional sports—including soccer, a sport that would later give poor children the possibility of social mobility and prestige—did not exist at a time when teams, leagues, and clubs still insisted that people play only for the "love of the game." Sports emphasized enjoyable interaction among equals through activities that functioned as important elements of social distinction while providing cohesion and identity among the members of the group. By the thirties, when the professionalization of sports became common, the teams composed exclusively of members of the elite withdrew from public life to continue practicing in select private settings.

The prestige offered by coffee's success in the international market, together with the crisis of Europe after World War I, allowed the upper classes of São Paulo to determine economic and political policies for the rest of the country, apparently confirming their impression that "O future é aqui." This new elite, flush with capital, optimism, and pride, became a symbol of the promising future of the nation. In this context, the preoccupation with the physical formation of boys and girls grew increasingly important, not only to guarantee healthy and attractive children, but also to help promote and prolong the much-valued youth of the citizenry as a whole. An editorial published in the magazine A *Cigarra* illustrates such an ideal:

> São Paulo é, talvez em todo o mundo, o meio mais propício para a adoção de boas iniciativas, por mais adiantadas que sejam. As idéias novas circulam aqui livremente, e se há pessoas que lhes opõem obstáculos, é porque têm fortes capitais empenhados em explorações ameaçadas de ruína, caso as novas idéias saiam vencedoras. Mas por que São Paulo é tão progressista? Pela simples razão de que aqui não há velhos. É uma cidade de moços e de adolescentes [. . . .] O predomínio dos anciãos em França explica a razão porque esse país oferece uma tão teimosa resistência a todo progresso. (1st fortnight of August, 1923)[5]

The association between youth and social success triggered a proliferation of discourses that demanded more attention to the physique of young people and established a marked distinction between the prac-

---

[5] A *Cigarra* was a magazine that appeared without pagination every fortnight or "quinzena," therefore whenever a quote from this magazine appears, the bibliographic information will follow the quote in parenthesis in the text indicating the fortnight, the month, and the year.

tices recommended for men and women, predicated on their different "natures."

Guidelines for men's physical training reveal a concern with the formation of "virile" citizens. Most strikingly, they separate gymnastics from the general field of *sports*. For men, gymnastics are recommended only during childhood to assure muscular endurance and discipline. Later they are advised to turn to competitive sports, such as soccer or other athletics more appropriate for the development of masculine qualities. This is exactly what Ariel suggests:

> Entra então o esporte em cena. Está completa a educação física primária do homem e passa ele para a secundária e superior [. . . .] Nela aprende o adulto a lutar, a vencer e a ser vencido, despertando-lhe a vida esportiva emoções tanto mais valiosas quanto são livres de toda a dosagem rigorosa e precisa e também porque são voluntárias [. . . .] Fica esclarecida a questão. Justamente o que à ginástica dá maior valor—a sua dosagem rigorosa e a monótona singeleza dos seus métodos—tornam-na imprópria para a mocidade que quer e vai se virilizar. E o esporte, condenável para os meninos e adolescentes [. . . .] faz-se então absoluta, imperiosamente necessário, pelas suas duas grandes qualidades—a espontaneidade da ação e a emotividade que por ela se desperta. (24)

For women, even though other activities were accepted, gymnastics remained the most recommended physical activity. Repetitive and monotonous, lacking spontaneity and suitable for controlling "tendências corporais e psíquicas,"[6] gymnastics offered great "advantages." For example, it required no special equipment, no large spaces, and no other participants. Further, it could be practiced at home, thereby combining the demand for physical activity with domestic responsibilities.

Based on a strictly gendered perception of the physical needs of young people, such discourses and practices defined the physical fitness of girls and boys in terms of force or strength, which was deemed "natural" and different in men and women. Since strength and stamina were considered to be of lesser duration in females, women were offered less demanding activities with fewer options. Walks, for example, were not just recommended, but often considered sufficient for

---

[6] An expression used by the gymnastics instructor from Club Athlético Paulistano in articles published in the bulletin of the club.

women's exercise needs, while men were expected to participate in the more elaborate and regulated world of organized sports.

Even though the physical education of women was the object of countless references in the specialized press of the time, such references were intended, more than anything, to circumscribe a particular field of specialization around women and to promote a specific conduct. The primary topic with regard to physical activity, however, remained, all through the twentieth century, the athletic practices of men. The discipline intended for masculine bodies was structured and imposed according to their "natural" tendency: young men are "spontaneously" attracted to competition and to the cultivation of physical strength and muscle development because these activities reinforce virility and emphasize their "masculine nature."

That young men discover their "nature" through the practice of sports is an idea that begins to take shape during this time. A young *paulistano* was expected to follow sports, participate in organized stadium events, root for a soccer team, be concerned with his physical shape, and, of course, practice competitive sports. These behaviors implied the acceptance both of his own masculinity as well as of the discourses that demanded that he keep his body active to build a race worthy of the promising future of the country. Above all, a young man belonging to the elite and adhering to the modernizing values of his group must discipline himself in order to adapt to the new social demands. He participated in the sophisticated new forms of urban socialization centered on sports as practiced in private clubs, with modern equipment, and according to international regulations.

Women's bodies, on the contrary, were defined not only in opposition to male characteristics, but also given more thorough attention since it was assumed that the goal of physical education for women was to create aesthetic effect. In fact, feminine bodies had to conform to specific norms of beauty. As women became more visible, they required greater "civilizing" physical discipline to assure that their public display followed precise social codes. The literature of the period, for instance, frequently alluded to the graceful movement of the female body:

> Os exercícios, pois, que mais convêm à mulher são aqueles que aumentam a flexibilidade e a destreza da coluna vertebral, isto é, os movimentos que, sujeitos às leis da cadência e do ritmo, se tornam, por assim dizer, a poesia da locomoção.

É que da flexibilidade do tronco e da harmonia dos movimentos depende um dos maiores encantos da mulher: a GRAÇA. A educação física para moças deve ser, pois, higiênica e estética, e nunca "atlética," visar sobretudo o desenvolvimento da parte inferior do corpo, dar a graça e a destreza dos movimentos, procurando antes a ligeireza do que a força. (Azevedo 46)

At a time when the female body was more and more visible on the street and in places of leisure, it was important to transform the way it looked and moved since, proportionally, it also became a target of surveillance. The practice of gymnastics, producing a delicately trim upper body and arms combined with conditioned legs and hips, seemed ideal for this suddenly increased attention to feminine bodies. If the presence of women on the street grew, revealing an irreversible trend tied to the process of urbanization, the interaction of women in the street in turn was filtered through a series of rules that sought to control and organize, rather than simply "limit" her. In order to counteract the female "invasion" of the public space interfering with the masculine experience and the relationship between *men* and the city, women were often reminded that *their* space was that of the private sphere. In any case, women still represented a minority at civic gatherings as well as sporting events, and the urban masses continued to be predominantly masculine.

But although access to public spaces was not easy for women, we cannot ignore the fact that reality was changing dramatically. Even upper-class women, traditionally guarded with more zeal and confined to the private space, started to have more excuses to be in the street. Indeed, many texts from the period depict men fascinated and seduced by the feminine presence. The very existence of these texts and the observations that they contain reveals the novelty of women in public, as the poet Mário de Andrade demonstrates:

SAMBINHA
Vêm duas costureirinhas pela rua das Palmeiras.
Afobadas braços dados depressinha
Bonitas, Senhor! que até dão vontade pros homens da rua.
As costureirinhas vão explorando perigos...
Vestido é de seda.
Roupa-branca é de morim.
....

> Parece que a rua parou pra escutá-las.
> Nem trilhos sapecas
> Jogam mais bondes um pro outro. (175)

Being on the street without a male companion or an older woman is an adventure for a girl who exposes herself to "dangers," the poem says. It also reveals the reasons behind the preoccupation with female movement, harmony and presence: the eyes following the women on the street pay attention even to the clothes that they are wearing under their dresses. For women, the masculine surveillance implied a constant self-consciousness; corporal movement became a means of guarding against a closely trailing and scrutinizing gaze. And although such preoccupation affected upper-class women more directly, Mário's poem shows that it was an aspect of modern life that women of all classes had to take into consideration.

An extremely moralist attitude underscoring the "natural" innocence of girls permeates this discourse. However, in the transition from private space to public, in the encounter of people in the street, "innocence" becomes embarrassment as seen in a passage from Laura Villares's *Vertigem* that depicts two women strolling. Whereas Liliane, a prostitute, exercises her role of "public woman" to perfection, Luz expresses the discomfort of a woman who was not brought up to be in the public eye and therefore is not prepared for it:

> Na rua, vendo o desembaraço com que a companheira caminhava, a pequenos passos, com a cabeça alta, os olhos dominadores, pensou com tristeza que *mademoiselle* Louise tinha razão quando dizia que uma mulher mal vestida sente-se desarmada e fraca, como Sansão sem a cabeleira. (29)

Beyond any simplistic opposition between the two women, what Luz lacks is street culture: "E andava no meio da gente entontecida, procurando não mostrar os pés, envergonhando-se do vestido" (Villares 30).

Yet when we review the press of the time, particularly women's journals, facts are constructed differently. Above all the magazines show the transformation in the behavior of women now free of old constraints; they underscore the modernity, the cosmopolitan mentality of the *paulistanos*: "Sozinha: para as mãos já não faz falta o embrulhinho cúmplice e dissimulador [. . . .] Já sabe o que fazer com as mãos, que são igualmente adestradas para empunhar a direção de um auto ou para mover-se sobre o teclado de uma máquina de escrever" (*Revista Feminina*, March 1928).⁷ This view is obviously an attempt to construct the image of a modern city and modern citizenship. However, it is important to point out that it is the sharing of the intense life of the city by both men and women that constitutes the most significant marker of modernity. Besides showing the novelty of the feminine presence in public space, what these texts confirm, not always overtly, is the embarrassment that still permeated the visibility of women on the street.

Physical fitness and activities in this context aim to prepare the public for the appearance of women in the city. As observed earlier, grace was the "natural" characteristic to develop in girls in order to preserve harmony in her social, corporal, and mental comportment. Let us see, for example, how the girls' gymnastics classes at the Club Athlético Paulistano were conducted. Intended to be a complete experience, the course offered not only an instructor, but also a pianist who would play next to the swimming pool and provide rhythm for the feminine movements.⁸ As taught at the Paulistano, gymnastics deemphasized competition, aggression, and the desire for victory, downplaying development of personal ambition. What was fundamental in the practices designed for boys, was disdained in those specified for girls. In fact, in its zeal for beauty and rhythm, gymnastics resembled "classical dance." This term was used frequently, especially in the sports press, which also linked gymnastics to the success of Isadora Duncan's style of dance inspired by ancient Greece.⁹ While we do not know exactly how classical dance was taught in São Paulo, media images show girls in tunics and bare feet. Several texts also mention an applied methodology. An instructor of classical dance, Ms. Rego Cavalcanti, for example, describes her technique in the pages of *Sports*:¹⁰

---

⁷*Revista Feminina* was a monthly magazine published without pagination; whenever a reference to this magazine is made, the information, month and year will be given in parenthesis in the text.

⁸The club's magazine published photographs of the gymnastics course in its December 1928 and March 1929 issues.

⁹ Brazilians embraced and emulated Duncan's art particularly after her triumphant visit in 1916.

¹⁰Dance classes following introductory sessions of rhythmical gymnastics were offered by the Instituto Jaguaribe. Founded in 1901, this institute became a center for the dissemination of gymnastics in Brazil and was frequented by the elites of São Paulo.

> Ao ar livre, pés descalços, leves túnicas que lhes não dificultem os movimentos, ao ritmo simples de músicas sonoras, a mulher desde menina até moça deve expandir-se em movimentos espontâneos, gestos graciosos, atitudes harmoniosas, poses estéticas, revivendo assim essa esplêndida arte que foi a DANÇA CLÁSSICA.
> A mulher não necessita músculos de Hércules. Os exercícios de estética, a harmonia das formas, a graça dos movimentos são próprios e característicos da fisiologia feminina. A Dança Clássica é o atletismo da mulher. (11)

And another writer in the same magazine affirms that

> Tudo é natural; muito embora essa naturalidade exija um cuidadoso treino a fim de que, sendo simples, os gestos não sejam por isso menos graciosos e significativos [. . . .] Inspirada pela melodia de um ritmo primitivo e cantante, a alma domina os músculos e os nervos, exteriorizando suas mais íntimas sensações [. . . .] Em graciosas atitudes o corpo molda-se ao som da música e essa expressão natural dos nossos sentimentos cadenciados pelo ritmo musical é característica da dança grega. (Maya, "Uma renascença," 113)
>
> ....
>
> [A dança clássica] é ritmada, sem ser mecânica e automática, e [é] sobretudo verdadeira e vivida e pessoal, porque cada um dos seus intérpretes tem a livre escolha de expressão, traduzindo as suas emoções individuais inspiradas pela mesma melodia. (Maya, "Eurítmica," 190)

A clear contradiction is evident in discussions of classical dance, since those "spontaneous" and "natural" movements are actually the result of methodical training, a training that responded in part to an already existing code regarding female "nature" which deemed certain movements beautiful, harmonious, and graceful. The "spontaneous" corporal expression of the students, then, confirms their feminine sexual identity.

Sports discourses and practices created a situation in which "natural" differences between men and women were reaffirmed and promoted. For instance, texts on classical dance are very explicit about this differentiation; they deem dance an athletic terrain exclusive to women since "masculine" sports do not cultivate the characteristic considered the epitome of femininity—grace. Dance, particularly practiced outdoors, is connected also with health benefits. Many texts stress the advantages of outdoor activities particularly dance, over indoor activities including salon dancing, a mundane activity always practiced at night in enclosed places and with little air. Classical dance also offers little or no contact with men and thus neutralizes possibly seductive postures in favor of discrete harmony and grace.

Soccer and Masculinity
Charles Miller, born in São Paulo in 1874 of English parents, became member of a British soccer team, the Hampshire, while studying in England. In 1894 he returned to his hometown and four years later, along with other members of the English colony, founded the São Paulo Athletic Club. In 1897, Hans Nobiling, a German ex-soccer player from Hamburg, came to São Paulo with the idea of creating a soccer club in the New World associated with the organization to which he had belonged. He arrived in Brazil with a ball, the jersey, socks, and rules of his club, and two years later formed a team that trained at night and on holidays. In 1899 the team played its first match against Mackenzie College.

Two soccer clubs, offshoots of Nobiling's team, began in 1899: the Sport Club International (formed by Germans and Brazilians who had studied in Europe and therefore already were familiar with soccer) and the Germania (comprised of members of Brazil's German colony). Among the Brazilians who contributed to the introduction of soccer in São Paulo was Antonio Casimiro Costa who created the Liga Paulista de Futebol in 1901 based on models and rules that he brought from Switzerland; he was also the club's first president. The Liga Paulista was responsible for the establishment of regular championships. By 1903 São Paulo had five major soccer teams—Athletic Club, International, Germania, Mackenzie, and Paulista. Other teams would increase the list and spread the popularity of this sport during the twenties.[11]

Alongside organized soccer teams formed by upper- and middle-class players, teams from the popular substrate emerged, such as the Palestra Itália representing the Italian community. Soon the entire city of São Paulo became caught up in the passion for soccer. In working-class neighborhoods local "teams" practiced in vacant lots where chil-

---

[11] Among others we can mention the Americano, the Ypiranga, the Corinthians, the São Bento, and the Floresta.

dren enlisted any available space to improvise and improve their skills, using balls made from stockings and wearing wooden shoes. Workers even took advantage of their breaks for impromptu matches.[12] Regardless of neighborhood—inner city or suburb, wealthy enclave or poor—soccer represented the dominant form of pleasure.

In a city strongly marked by immigration with an accelerated growth in population since the nineteenth century, soccer became one of the most effective elements of collective identity. The emotions provoked by the sport united people from diverse origins, particularly those suffering feelings of uprootedness as we can see in the following anecdote. In 1925, Antônio Prado Júnior, whose name appeared in practically all the organizations related to the direction and promotion of sports, chose a team from his club, the Paulistano—a four-time winner of the local championship—to represent Brazil in Europe. He organized the trip and arranged the European matches. Of a total of ten games (eight in France, one in Switzerland, and one in Portugal), the Paulistano won nine (losing only in Sète, France one to zero).

The return of the team to its homeland was celebrated everywhere in Brazil. Their first stop was Recife, where people were already awaiting the players of the "Glorioso" (as people started calling the Paulistano). Many official celebrations were organized in Rio to welcome the boys and included military honors and personal congratulations from the president of the republic. In São Paulo, the team's last stop, the city was practically paralyzed at their arrival. Some two thousand cars were arranged to bring the players to the club where an official reception was waiting, but instead a multitude spontaneously carried them through the city. The newspaper O Estado de São Paulo even started a campaign to erect a public monument to honor the Paulistano.[13]

The victories of the team were seen as victories of the country as a whole; they were interpreted as evidence of the potential of the young nation. It was the spirit of renewal and progress that was believed to have defeated an old Europe under her very nose. Nothing could have been more glorious and more effective to reaffirm the project of national identity. And in the context of São Paulo, a prosperous urban society with a large investment in discipline and sports, it made perfect sense that the winner team was *paulistano—the* Paulistano.

[12]See Nicolau Sevcenko 60-61.
[13]This monument still exists near the headquarters of the clube paulistano.

It is not surprising, however, that the connection with sports—whether in the soccer fields themselves or in those moments of collective explosion in the streets—was not experienced in the same way by men and women. Already excluded from public life and competitive sports, as we saw, women were excluded also from the practice of soccer and, subsequently, from the rituals surrounding it. As photographs from the period confirm, women appeared only occasionally and in very few numbers at events related to soccer games. The euphoric demonstrations in the streets of the city, perhaps even more than the matches themselves, were experienced almost exclusively by men. The matches as well as the post-game celebrations included noise, bodily contact, displays of emotion, and yelling, with women kept to the margins in both cases.

In contrast to men's more "natural" presence in public urban spaces, women's social sphere—strongly limited, filtered, and ritualized—was established mainly in private settings. Cícero Marques in *Tempos passados* offers a revealing picture of this when he evokes young law students and their bohemian habit. He describes the public places that the different groups would frequent for pleasure, as well as the times and the specific situations each group would prefer for socializing. In such descriptions, it is interesting to note that the only feminine names that appear are those of cabaret artists or high-priced prostitutes.

Some of the same cafes and teahouses where the students met were also frequented by families, although always under very specific conditions. But apart from these occasional informal encounters in which women of "decent" families circulated in public places, the interaction, exchange of information, meetings, and bonding rituals took place almost exclusively among men. The masculine population occupied the city, experiencing and exploring everything in their own company. Marques insists on the forms of masculine leisure that enact ties of friendship and sociability between men. Achille Tartari confirms that as we can see in this quote that explains how a man could stay out late, see the last show at the movies, walk home, or meet friends:

> Moça, a senhora não era nascida naquele tempo, por isso não sabe [. . . .] Não pode imaginar como era gostoso sair do cinema, depois da última sessão, e ir pra casa a pé, batendo papo, ou ficar andando à toa por aí, quando não se estava com sono; a gente

sempre acabava encontrando algum amigo, que sempre tinha alguma coisa pra contar, ou a gente contava alguma coisa. (qtd. in Galvão 70)

Descriptions like these appeared frequently in textual references to the São Paulo of the time. In what Tartari presents as a fact of urban life there is no reference to the feminine sector of the population. His natural and matter-of-fact tone reveals his inability to imagine a mixed social sphere, much less the existence of an urban feminine sociability parallel to the masculine. One more example illustrates this point. In his memoirs, Geraldo Sesso Júnior compares the São Paulo at the turn of the century with the São Paulo of the 1920s: "Nas esquinas, onde antes se agrupavam rapazes, preparando-se para as futuras festas e serenatas, em seu lugar, a canto de esquina, encontram-se meninas-mulheres que, quando não assaltam os transeuntes, convidam-nos para fazer amor" (161).

The writer above describes the transition from a traditional urban life perceived as tranquil and comfortable to a more violent one characterized by the presence of women. He describes encounters between friends on their way to parties, and the reader cannot help wondering, where were the girls with whom these young men would dance at those parties? Most likely they had gone by quickly on their way to the socials, rather than stopping on the corners or lingering in the streets — those masculine points of encounter. The tone of the description, nostalgic of a time when men occupied the city freely without being subject to aggressive advances by women, masks the gendered nature of that freedom. The image that expresses the author's negative feelings toward the disappearance of an old male intimacy within the city is presented as an inversion, as a world turned upside down where certain women replace the young men on the corners. It is interesting to note, however, that these women were, in reality, the same women that had always been there—those who did not observe the imposed rules regulating their presence in the urban space. The others, the "decent" ones, were deemed chaste precisely because they obeyed the rules of appearing—or rather, *not* appearing—in public. In stadiums or in the streets, ties of urban community, almost without exception, were constructed among men.

Beauty: A Ritual Apart

And yet, the abundance of commerce and leisure, along with the frequency of urban gatherings, invited more and more women from the elite and the middle classes to cross the threshold and leave their house. More visible in the city now, women faced another concern — preparing their physical appearance to appear in public. The appearance of women in the visual culture of the city, then, was accompanied necessarily by a constant reworking of the culture of beauty.

Just as physical beauty seemed to constitute an element of progress in the sense that modern urban life demanded that women invest in their appearance as a condition to participate in it, it is also clear that women derived pleasure from such engagement. Discipline became paramount in order to limit and channel the culture of beauty so that it would not result in disorder with respect to the assigned roles of men and women. This culture of beauty implied strict regulation — exposed to the male gaze and men's opinions, feminine bodies must conform to rigid "civilizing" norms. The attentions that a woman dedicated to her body must always account for a social gaze that is not her own and yet regarded as the carrier of order. The female body, then, had to repudiate the excesses of overt seduction as well as avoid diverging from the prescribed models of feminine beauty.

Becoming increasingly prevalent was an ethos that we may describe as "beauty-as-work;" in other words, a beauty that required an increasingly systematic and methodical learning process. The unacceptable appearance of "ugliness" compelled women toward an endless investment of time and energy in the hope of improving every detail of their appearance. Meanwhile, a proliferation of mirrors and the popularity of photography permitted improved control of the way women presented themselves, banishing every gesture that had not been rehearsed and mastered.

In the case of women from the elite classes, the pedagogy of public appearance contained an additional onus. In presenting themselves in public, these women inevitably represented their social position as well. By their mere appearance, they underscored the insurmountable distance separating them from women of other classes. The intricate social complex gave way to new strategies that emphasized differences and avoided integration since, although the arrangement of urban space allowed for some private enclaves for the elite, urban life per se implies the collective use of spaces and structures. Counterweighing physical proximity, social distances had to be protected by rearranging physical activities and by providing each individual with an appearance that assures the immediate identification of his or her social status.

What can be observed in women's public appearances is a series of regulations intended to limit female freedom on the street, often supported by an ideology of the "natural" in opposition to anything "artificial," including the use of make-up. Renato Kehl, one of the spokespersons of the "pensamento higienista,"[14] recommends cosmetics only as a last resort:

> Só se deve, pois, empregar os cosméticos na impossibilidade de recorrer à terapêutica naturalista, que consiste na vida ao ar livre, no regime alimentar adequado, ou quando com isto não se consegue reparar as injúrias do tempo, das doenças, ou das desordens acidentais supervenientes. ("Introduction")

Clearly, the problem to correct mentioned here is ugliness. At the same time, other printed sources yield techniques, advertisement, and numerous resources that each woman can use to improve her looks, bring out her physical attributes, and preserve a youthful appearance. These media reinforced the message that women had to invest in their faces and bodies to attain beauty, either naturally or with the help of artificial products.

Even Kehl in a more moderate tone tried to conciliate natural and cosmetic methods for obtaining the desired result. In the second half of his *Formulário de beleza*, for example, he provides a long list of beauty recipes to be made at home or requested in a pharmacy. The list includes make-up, but also all kinds of body lotions, perfumes, hair products, white powders, as well as black, red, and white facial masques. Beauty tips—not too different from those of Kehl— published in women's magazines justified the investment in beautifying oneself, stressing the element of seduction. Moreover, they openly recognized the importance of flirtation and of a certain affectedness in order to increase women's aesthetic value. And yet a woman could be regarded as "decent" or taken for a prostitute depending on the amount of make-up she wore. A woman with just the right amount of tastefully applied make-up stands out for her polished sophistication

---

[14] Translators' note: The term "pensamento higienista" does not have a precise English translation, but refers to the promotion of physical health, fitness, nutrition, and beauty.

and for the fact that she has the time and money for such luxuries. Used with precision and restraint, make-up became a sign of distinction and refinement as well as wealth.

Physical movement, however, remained the most important code defining the feminine presence and walking the privileged element of this code—knowing how to walk, controlling every movement, and keeping an upright posture, epitomized feminine elegance. The obsession with the comportment of the female body figured constantly in the press, and not only in beauty magazines: all promoted the development of hips and legs or advocated a disciplined gait. These texts attempted to regulate the presence of women in the public space, which was, as we have noted, a phenomenon tied strongly to the new urban order. The polemic that occurred at this time with regard to skirts and dresses represents an eloquent example.

Comparing the styles shown in photographs from the beginning and the end of the twenties, we observe a clear shortening of skirts. The debate takes place in the pages of sports magazines, but also and particularly in Catholic publications such as *Revista Feminina*. The element that immediately captures our attention is the fact that some magazine articles defend the use of shorter skirts, considering them appropriate for the education of the girls. According to some fashion writers, by wearing short skirts, girls automatically are forced to pay closer attention to the way they walk, their posture, their gestures and movements, as well as the way that they sit. Furthermore, some authors believed that the use of long skirts since childhood resulted in a woman walking carelessly, inelegantly, or even indecently.[15] This last was particularly serious since long skirts concealed young girls' bodies from the corrective eye of their mothers. In this regard, then, although short skirts represented an affront to morality, such practice could be defended if it improved vigilance of one's body. In the end, those who won the polemic represented the new logic—the urban logic of physical perception and feminine beauty in *public*.

Similar to the case of sports in relation to men, the culture of beauty reached beyond elite circles. The new urban order united and mobilized women, producing a general acceptance of the work needed to improve personal appearance; it is not coincidental that beauty pageants also surged at the beginning of the decade. Along with

---

[15]See the regular column of Annette Guitry "Crônica de elegâncias" in *A Cigarra*, particularly in the issues of the first fortnight of October 1921 and October 1923.

movies, beauty pageants disseminated the patterns of what was considered beautiful. Kehl himself defends the pedagogical importance of these "Olympiads" of beauty: "Os concursos de beleza, com a exibição honesta de corpos bem modelados, constituem, pois, fatores indispensáveis de educação estética masculina e feminina. É necessário ver e comparar afim de poder fazer juízo do que seja um corpo verdadeiramente perfeito" (Kehl 57).

In this way, face, smiles, hairdo, and make-up should adhere as closely as possible to those of the pageant participants. Meanwhile, the way of walking in public and the movement of the body, as well as the use of flirtatious devices in moderation, can be learned from movie stars. Indeed, these elements coincide in one aspect—the photographs of the competing women and the movie stars from the Brazilian silent film industry show the mimetic force of the models of beauty previously propagated by American movies.

However, some elements included in the new aesthetic movement go beyond those proposed by movie stars. The praise of youth, for example, was fundamental, with efforts concerted toward maintaining a beautiful—read, *youthful*—appearance. Youth is strongly identified with a svelte figure, physical activity, and a healthy diet. In many illustrations and articles of the time, obesity has an aura of ridicule, identified with ugliness and the grotesque, but also with advanced age. In slim bodies, youth and beauty go hand in hand.

Furthermore, in a country with a history of slavery whose abolitionist movement occurred as late as 1888, it is easy to imagine how models of beauty distanced themselves from any sign of blackness, an avoidance manifested in dyed hair, the use of creams and whiteners, and an ambiguous relationship with the sun. Even though medical advice promoted sunbathing as a healthy activity that prevented people from excessive paleness—which was not recommended—there was great reluctance to engage in it. Long exposure to the sun could be misinterpreted as a sign of manual labor, something until very recently associated with slavery and therefore exceedingly negative. Women of the elite did not work, and any association with labor construed as anathema. The association of women's chasteness with whiteness, in addition, contributed to the class bias.

Maids represented the majority of black characters in the press of the twenties, embodying ugliness, ignorance, and even obesity. In contrast, their female employers are portrayed as delicate, refined, slim, young and, of course, white. A passage from *A Cigarra* illustrates this well arguing that even though there is in "França a voga da tez morena, podemos de antemão garantir que ela nunca será adotada em São Paulo. Aqui, as morenas continuarão a dissimular a sua morenez natural, com o uso das pastas e cremes brancos e a oxigenar os cabelos" (Guitry, "Crônica das elegâncias," issue of the 1st fortnight of February 1922).

Literary works also offer a portrait of this seamless union of fitness, whiteness, elegance, and refined taste, considered essential to feminine beauty. For example, the novels of Albertina Bertha express this ideal of beauty correlating class distinction with skin color. Voleta of the novel of the same title is a woman of principle and deep soul who does not care for worldly possessions. The wife of a leftist political leader, her beauty provokes admiration everywhere she goes, in spite or perhaps because of the sensuality and eroticism of her presence. All the men she knows fall in love with her or at least recognize the power of seduction that she holds over them. Senhorinha Sieg, the secretary and disciple of Voleta's husband is presented as the opposite of Voleta in both personality and social origins—while Voleta descends from aristocratic lineage, Senhorinha Sieg comes from working-class stock. Their physical appearance also reinforces their apparent differences: "Paulo [. . . .] comparava mentalmente os gestos aristocráticos, a beleza patrícia de Voleta com a sobriedade máscula e a pele amarelada da Senhorinha Sieg" (Bertha, *Voleta* 56).

The social and racial origins of Voleta provide her with the features of both her physical and moral beauty, something that is understood to come with birth. By the same token, Senhorinha Sieg's stigmas—yellowish skin foremost among them—are also understood as a product of her class (which in Brazil is also related to race) and therefore prevent her from having access to the category of classical (meaning pure European) beauty. Clearly, the beauty of Voleta resides in her whiteness, the maximum sign of class difference, of her distance from the masses.

> A sua silhueta esguia, flexuosa, o seu tipo clássico, de euritmias estonteantes e a vivacidade álacre de seus gestos atraíam a atenção, a curiosidade dos passageiros.
> —Não é brasileira, é por demais branca—ouvia Voleta de passagem, em vários idiomas. (320)

On the same level, Ladice, the protagonist of *Exaltação*, another novel by Bertha, is the incarnation of classical Greek beauty. At a charity ball intended to save an orphanage, a woman is needed for the flower stand. The organizers want the most beautiful and elegant lady, the one who most corresponds to their ideal of beauty. Ladice, of course, embodies the group's expectations. The effect of her presence is so impressive that the text can only provide fragmented physical descriptions to tell us in the end that "A Senhora de Assis com sua palidez de magnólia e seu corpo abietino de ânfora grega e a graça de suas atitudes orientais, atraía irresistivelmente os olhares dos homens" (*Exaltação* 124). Other details, like "a mão de Ladice, fina e branca" (125) or "a boca pequena, fechada" (126) confirm this model. Ladice's hands are surely more beautiful if they are kept away from manual labor, and the fact that her mouth is small—and closed—signals her as a delicate and feminine lady of European origin. The characterization of Ladice stands in sharp contrast to the images published in *A Cigarra*, where coarse-lipped black women only emphasize the delicate features of their white counterparts. Women's hair comprises an equally important sign of class and race and that of characters like Voleta and Ladice is invariably fine and gracefully wavy. Not surprisingly, a black woman often is presented next to a white woman to point up the physical difference between the races.

Elitist at their root, these normative examples of feminine beauty gained acceptance, but only up to a point. If it is true that cinema, advertisement, and beauty pageants disseminated models of the ideal woman that met with positive reception, it is also true that the imposition of these standards on society clashed with a less visible, but still palpable resistance. In the case of slim bodies, for instance, the press reveals an inconsistency in popular sentiment. Whereas *Revista Feminina* reproduced images that had appeared in foreign magazines in which the female figure was usually tall and erect, *A Cigarra* employed Brazilian talent such as the well-known illustrator Belmonte. A comparison of the styles reveals that the European figure does not correspond completely to that of the national imaginary. National illustrators had a tendency to bring out the rounded forms of the feminine bodies clothed in tight dresses to emphasize the full-figured hips, buttocks, and legs, in contrast to the often-small bosoms.

Significantly, in the foreign illustrations none of these characteristics exists, resulting in a considerably different representation of the female body. But the rigidly upright European model also had detractors. Articles published in the issue of June 1923 of *Revista Feminina*, for example, explicitly observe that men appreciate women with rounded forms and urge slim women to gain weight. Other articles from the March of 1926 issue of the same journal criticize French women for their flat, even, and erect body. Renato Kehl joins in praising a model that is half Scandinavian and half Greek, although he is forced to recognize that this example does not entirely reflect the taste of Brazilian men.

> Para a maioria dos homens, pouco importa a conformação do corpo e sua modelagem desde que o volume e a rotundidade sejam notórias.
> ....
> Quantos homens continuam a apreciar erroneamente as proeminências dos seios e nágedas, as coxas e pernas grossas! Querem "carnes," mesmo [. . . .] de má qualidade, desprezando o tipo esguio e leve das Evas helênicas. É, em geral, no volume dos seios, assim como na amplidão dos quadris, que residem, para eles, os elementos primordiais de atração feminina. A muitos o excesso de gordura dessas partes não constitui defeito, ao contrário, e dizem [. . . .] que "belas ancas tem aquela mulher," como elogiam as pernas grossas [. . . .]. Pendem, pois, mais pelas gordas que pelas magras; preferem as mulheres rochunchudas, *potelées*, desdenhando as de carnadura seca e firme, cuja solidez plástica garante uma mocidade mais duradoura e sadia, ao contrário daquelas cuja tendência é para o acúmulo de gordura e subsequente deformação do corpo. (Kehl 17; 56-7)

In this discourse, which values slim young girls, obesity is a sign of feminine ugliness. This, however, does not mean that such an ideal offered by the health and fitness set (the "higienistas") was representative of the people's feelings at large. In Brazil, the sensuality of feminine curves, particularly of the hips and buttocks, seemed to resist the foreign model proposed by Kehl.

As we have seen, the demand to invest in physical beauty for women is as taken for granted and representative of the times as the expected masculine passion for sports. Both attitudes are privileged vectors for the construction of collective identities, while remaining strongly gendered and essentially urban. Nonetheless, these two forms of urban life were essentially unequal, the feminine presence more greatly ritualized and mediated than that of men.

[Translated from Portuguese by Rafael Hernández-Rodríguez and Maria T. Pao]

Works Cited

Andrade, Mário de. *Clã do jabuti. Poesias completas*. Belo Horizonte/São Paulo: Itatiaia/EDUSP, 1987.
Ariel. "Ginástica e esporte." *Sports* 2 (January 1920): 24.
Azevedo, Fernando de. "Para as mulheres." *Sports* 2 (January 1920): 46.
Bertha, Albertina. *Exaltação*. Rio de Janeiro: J. R. dos Santos, 1931.
———. *Voleta*. Rio de Janeiro: J. R. dos Santos, 1926.
Cavalcanti, Rego. "Dança clássica." *Sports* 2 (January 1920): 11.
Galvão, Maria Rita Eliezer. *Crônica do Cinema Pulistano*. São Paulo: Ed. Ática, 1975.
Instituto Brasileiro de Geografia e Estatística. *Anuário estatístico*. Rio de Janeiro: IBGE, 1971.
Júnior, Geraldo Sesso. *Retalhos da velha São Paulo*. São Paulo: OESP/Maltese, 1986.
Kehl, Renato. *Formulário de beleza (fórmulas escolhidas)*. Rio de Janeiro/São Paulo: Livraria Francisco Alves, 1927.
Leite da Silva Dias, Maria Odila. *Quotidiano e poder em São Paulo no século XIX*. São Paulo: Ed. Brasiliense, 1984,
Marques, Cícero. *Tempos passados*. São Paulo: Moema Editora Ltda., 1942.
Maya. "Dança clássica—uma renascença magnífica." *Sports* 4 (March/April 1920): 113.
———. "Dança clásicca—eurítmica." *Sports* 7 (July 1920): 190.
Sevcenko, Nicolau. *Orfeo extático na metrópole: São Paulo, sociedade e cultura nos frementes anos 20*. São Paulo: Companhia das Letras, 1992.
Schpun, Mônica Raisa. *Les Années folles à São Paulo: hommes et femmes au temps de l'explosion urbaine (1920-1929)*. Paris: L'Harmattan/IHEAL, 1997.
Villares, Laura. *Vertigem*. São Paulo: Casa Editora Antonio Tisi, 1926.

An Enormous Laugh: The Comic Spirit in Brazilian Modernist Literature

K. DAVID JACKSON
Yale University

> Amor
> Humor
> *Primeiro caderno do aluno de poesia Oswald de Andrade*

Laugh slowly!

SCRIBBLING IN RED INK across a page of the large diary-scrapbook kept in Oswald de Andrade's São Paulo *garçonnière* in 1918, the witty young muse Deise jotted the words "Ri devagar!"[1] With this phrase, she cleverly satirized the aesthetic pretenses of the gentlemen's club that had adopted her, inhabited by young artists and bohemians in cloistered retreat from the city, while at the same time prefiguring the comic spirit that would pervade modernist literature and the arts throughout the 1920s. The scrapbook's playful title, *O perfeito cozinheiro das almas deste mundo* communicates the humor in their equation of art and life. Deisi's laughing imperative has the air of a manifesto, a mocking challenge to perform a harlequin's trick or to unmask a social façade, acts highly valued by pre-modernism. Viewed as a pure marking in red ink, her inscription draws upon the primordial wisdom

---

[1] Oswald de Andrade (1890-1954), one of the most important modernist writers and intellectuals, was at this time a recent law school graduate linked to bohemian or decadentist literary circles. The diary of this moment of pre-modernist ferment surfaced in a sumptuous facsimile edition (*O perfeito cozinheiro das almas deste mundo*) in 1987. All translations are by the author unless otherwise noted.

of laughter as remedy, touching the grandeur and misery of the human and social comedy. At age 18, Deisi reached the pinnacle of universal comic play. Her large red laugh occurred at the culmination of her role as muse of early modernism, the height of the effervescence of a life that ended tragically at age 19.[2]

For expressing their intelligence through humor and irreverence, the literary bohemians were allies and precursors of the modernists. Perhaps to compensate for the lack of a national philosophical tradition, humor was the chosen vehicle through which Brazilian society expressed its ideas.[3] Jorge de Sena explains how humor was employed both to undermine pretense and to exploit the extremes in the social structure between modernist and traditional values in the early years of urbanization and industrialization of São Paulo:

> E como a expressão literária e artística estava sendo ridicularizada pelo modernismo europeu, que tinha de lutar contra a falsa seriedade, era evidente que o uso de graças, de transformação de algumas criações estéticas e coisas cómicas, o humor, a ironia, a demolição de tudo que era considerado sagrado e respeitável iria ser dirigido, no Brasil, não só contra o estabelecido intelectual, mas também contra o abismo que nele existia entre a vida real e a contemporânea que tinha apenas a externa aparência de progresso. (100)

During the decade before the main event of a generation, the Modern Art Week of 1922, São Paulo's magazines were filled with caricatures and pastiches of a city swelling with immigrants and incipient modernization.[4] Oswald de Andrade's magazine *O Pirralho* (1912-18) introduced the *Cartas d'abaixo piques* in Italo-Paulista maccaronic dialect by Alexandre Ribeiro Marcondes Machado (1892-1933), who used the pseudonym Juó Bananere. The magazines *Papel e Tinta* and *Fon-Fon*, more art nouveau than esprit nouveau, carried caricatures of

---

[2] For the clever and tempestuous story of "Daisy" or "Miss Cyclone" (Maria de Lourdes D'Olzani de Andrade), consult Tereza Virgínia de Almeida, *A ausência lilás da semana de arte*.

[3] Lustosa 72. In addition to Brazilian history, José Madeira de Freitas also published a comic Portuguese grammar by the "confused method."

[4] For a portrait and history of the city, see Richard Morse, *From Community to Metropolis*, also published as *Formação histórica de São Paulo (de comunidade a metropole)* [São Paulo: Difusão Européia do Livro, 1970].

Oswald and other denizens of the elite circles, while the yellow press shouted scandal. *O Parafuso's* photo of Oswald in a white suit over the caption, "Seducer of Minors," alluded to the writer's insistent but frustrated pursuit of a young dancer met on board a first voyage to Europe.⁵ The social world of Brazil's *fin-de-siècle* tropical *belle-époque*, fashioned in the styles of *commedia dell'arte* and "sorriso da sociedade" made popular by the writings of Afrânio Peixoto, intentionally blurred distinctions between play and reality, art and life. It spawned character-narrators of the 1920s, Oswald's alter-egos "João Miramar" and "Serafim Ponte Grande" and Mário de Andrade's Amazonian hero without any character, "Macunaíma."⁶

The voyage, the carnival fantasy, the artistic persona, the regional stereotype, and the ethnic immigrant are main ingredients of a humorous self-portrait of Brazil's early twentieth-century modernity. The first number of the avant-garde journal *Klaxon* in 1922 proclaims a just revolt against the past, which is to be accomplished by constructing happiness, as if exuberance were a material component of the building of a new national society. *Klaxon's* manifesto states: "Farce and burlesque do not repulse us, as they did not repulse Dante, Shakespeare or Cervantes."⁷ The crossing of laughter with revolt provides the theo-

---

⁵ For the story of these and other adventures in the life of Oswald de Andrade, consult Maria Augusta Fonseca, *Oswald de Andrade: biografia*. An overview of Brazilian urban culture at the time can be found in Jeffrey Needell, *A Tropical Belle-Époque: Elite Culture and Society in Turn-of-the-Century Rio de Janeiro*.

⁶ These constitute three major avant-garde novels of modernism: Oswald de Andrade's *Memórias sentimentais de João Miramar* (1924) and *Serafim Ponte Grande* (1933), and Mário de Andrade's *Macunaíma*. The English translations are *Sentimental Memoirs of John Seaborn* (1972), *Seraphim Grosse Point* (1979), and *Macunaíma* (1984).

⁷ In 1919 modernist Ronald de Carvalho, who had ties to Portuguese futurism, published a book in French on Rabelais (*Rabelais et le rire de la Renaissance*), while Oswald de Andrade used an illustrated citation from *Don Quijote* in an early fragment published in *O Pirralho* in 1916, announced as part of his novel in preparation, *Memórias sentimentais de João Miramar*. *Dom Quixote* was also the title of a magazine in which Mendes Fradique serialized his comic essay, *Brasil pelo método confuso*. In the "Manifesto antropófago" (1928), Oswald appropriated famous quotations from Shakespeare, deformed to fit a Brazilian context ("Tupy or not Tupy, that is the question"). Such examples show that Brazilian modernist writers were aware of their relationship with the comic tradition in European literature, which had been so well ex-

retical focus necessary to understand modernism's overriding comic spirit, both in its historical moment and in its recapitulation of universal comic themes.

Comic Theory: From the Ridiculous to the Sublime
English and French essayists who have analyzed the nature of the comic, from Meredith to Baudelaire and Bergson, posit differences both in kind and in degree concerning comedy in literature. As described by these essayists, the comic could be said to operate on two strands, the first kind representing distance, separation, and criticism of reality, characterized by wit, satire, or mockery; and a second representing empathy, wholeness, and identification with reality, marked by unawareness of self, intoxication, and the sublime. The former is composed of conflicts, differences, reactions, and contradictions, while the latter is made of harmony, acceptance, play, synthesis, and participation. Another way of conceiving this dynamic lies in the difference between rational criticism of life, the incompatibilities of mind and matter, on the one hand, and the incorporation of the narrative voice into a superior yet ultimately ephemeral reality beyond reason and the self, on the other.

In seeking to define the nature of the comic along the first strand, the essayists address perceived differences in degree, which a narrator or subject observes in the usual workings of external reality. Baudelaire writes that humor is "essentially contradictory" and arises from a "double feeling." Bergson, more abstractly, states that it is a "crossways" resulting from "rigidity applied to the motion of life." Humor would thus be an inherent feature of any single individual observation of the change and multiplicity of reality, which is often said to be stranger than fiction. The contradictions between an observer's expectations and observed reality, the essence of what Baudelaire calls the "misery" of comedy, motivate a sequence of reactions and forms of behavior in the observer which are considered to be characteristic of the comic in its widest sense. While the essayists do not arrange their insights into such reactions in any particular order, their observations nevertheless suggest a structure to the reader. Ever deeper and more expressionistic levels of involvement with the human and social world result in a roller-coaster effect, based on a narrator's level and intensity of criticism. On the first level would be a narrator's feelings of mental superi-

---

plored in the major novels of Machado de Assis, upon which they also drew in their works.

ority, followed next by pastiche, mockery and satire, and finally by moral or physical debasement, involving the grotesque, violence, and bodily disfigurement.

Along the first strand, the superiority and distance of observation place the narrator above the misfortunes, ailments, failures, and madnesses—the categories are Baudelaire's—of what the French poet terms, prefiguring Bakhtin, a carnivalesque world. The level of pastiche involves, on the other hand, Baudelaire's concept of "significative" humor, which is humor derived from cultural content originating within society, although innocent in intent. The third level, that of moral debasement associated with Rabelaisian expressions of "spleen" or "comic savagery," comes from the body, while physical debasement and disfigurement are also manifestations of Baudelaire's idea of the "diabolic origin" of the lower comic mode. When at the service of morals, laughter is a means to express rage and violent attack; when physical, the comic embodies rage, suffering, or disfigurement. Both cases were considered by Baudelaire to be kinds of hyperbole, whereas the contemporary reader may think of them as ritualistic. Bergson likewise distinguishes between moral and physical sides of comedy, defining them as *de facto* and *de jure* comic; for him, the contrast of the lower aspects of comedy with reality is the origin of farce. In the social sphere, laughter is often aimed at the customs and complicity of a social group. While its social significance is understood as a corrective, Bergson goes further to find an implied unconscious intent to humiliate or reprimand. Such a prime, veiled intention is described using psychological terminology in place of Baudelaire's earlier recourse to "comic spleen."

The essayists further suggest a difference in nature between humor, as a way of treating and conceiving reality, and that of common descriptive logic. The comic in its most distilled form is described as pure idea, genius, or wit, directed at a subject without any obligatory measure of mercy, understanding, or sympathy. For Meredith, the comic is a form of genius, which exists to vindicate reason, and its ideal form of expression is wit. Meredith conceives it as working from inside society to gain a subtle understanding of the current moment, which in his age would best be expressed subtly, as through a knowing smile. Satire in this scheme would be taken for a violent blow, and ridicule considered altogether out of bounds, beyond the comic. Bergson similarly describes humor as disinterested and indifferent, appealing only to the intelligence. Pure wit, while admired for its brilliance and genius, is both powerful and insensitive in intent and should be handled with reserve or restraint by gentlemen.

The notion that humor is different by its nature, forming a second hermeneutics, underlies the definition of a second strand. Baudelaire posits a primary aesthetic and philosophical role for comedy, affirming that humor constitutes a form both of beauty and of knowledge. Comedy is "one of the eternal elements of beauty," held as one of the prime categories and goals of philosophy. The sage may be comic as well as the fool, in that wisdom is also expressed through what Baudelaire calls "the primordial nature of laughter," which forms part of the grandeur of the comic genre. Bergson evokes the sublime as one of two sides of the comic; from its perspective, art and life are seen together as a whole. Rather than spring from differences in perspective, the sublime comic remains closely identified with real life and thus, in Bergson's opinion, leads to a more profound analysis of it than that which results from the clash of different perspectives or modes of being. Baudelaire speaks of the "dizzying intoxication" of an absolute comic state, which is unaware of itself and of its oneness with the beautiful, wise, and sublime comedy of life.

Frank Muir's introduction to the *Oxford Book of Humorous Prose* suggests a working hierarchy for the nature of the comic, whose categories can be adapted usefully for a comprehensive analysis. Muir discusses different types of comedy based on perspectives of satire or the corrective criticism of life, as well as mocking reactions to life's contradictions that cut against the grain. What Muir terms "comedy" refers to the curative process of moral correction, in which laughter expresses the caricature or pastiche of the innocent comic. His second category, "humor," especially associated with the English, is closer to a comedy of human types or persona closely identified with social customs, manners, or place, especially those acting in the disguises of a theatrical, masked, or carnivalized society. The psychological and erotic impulses inherent in such humor may produce instances of deviance and madness, in the first instance, or of spleen, debasement, the physically grotesque and diabolical in the second. His third category of "buffoonery" suggests a state of atavism or primitivism beyond the social play of humor. The buffoon embodies an intuitive undercurrent that defies rational wit by transmuting its critical perceptions and attitudes into a primal or ritual state of ridicule and foolishness.

Although Muir does not mention the universal comic of Baudelaire and Bergson, found in knowledge, beauty, or the sublime, this second strand is still, in our opinion, a crucial category of analysis of the comic. It represents the superior reality of humor defined as philosophy and play, whose awareness is "out of self" and beyond agency. An insight into the foolishness of everything and one's inevitable participation in it is one of the revelations of laughter and a prime path for reaching Bergson's idea of the sublime. Significantly, this second strand of the comic effectively completes a circle by providing a meaningful conclusion or resolution to the dialectic of comic difference and criticism. Wit, Meredith's pure idea and genius, stands between the two strands of the comic, linking them and completing the circle. Wit's "disinterested and indifferent" intelligence can be inclined either to the withering criticism of social life and customs or to a superior awareness of its own comic nature, its role in the universal comedy and laughter of the world. Ruled by the linchpin of wit, the categories of the first strand (comedy, humor, buffoonery) and the second (the universal comic) provide a comprehensive structure for the presentation and analysis of humor. The two strands, with their negative and positive poles, build up a current that will explode in the enormous laugh of Brazilian modernist literature.

The First Strand of the Comic: "Very Interesting" Manifestos
The wit of Brazilian modernist authors after 1922, the expression of their "pure genius," is the result of a startling synthesis of widely disparate elements. It is a synchronic cut that unites diverse sources of aesthetic information to epitomize a concept or bring an idea to a single point of sharpness or resolution. In Raul Bopp's poem of Amazonian lore, *Cobra Norato* (1931), for example, trees in the forest telegraph each other. The unsettling symbiosis of organic and electric creates a modern architectural frame and futuristic language for Brazil's vast interior landscape. In the wake of the Week of Modern Art in São Paulo in 1922, Mário de Andrade published the poems of *Paulicéia desvairada* with a vanguard preface titled "Prefácio interessantíssimo." In the style of a letter or note, it is addressed "To Mário de Andrade, Beloved Master" and signed "Mário de Andrade," who in the guise of a disciple praises the "other" Mário as his master and his lord. Using the language of a manifesto, Mário dramatically proclaims his martyrdom at the service of the master's ideal. The preface exploits the question of author and persona, an overture to the world of virtual authorship perfected in the heteronyms of the celebrated Portuguese poet Fernando Pessoa. In a comparable rhetorical inversion and play on identity in

the novel, Mário de Andrade's Amazonian hero, Macunaíma, who has traveled to São Paulo to recover a magic amulet, writes his famous "Carta às Icamiabas" to his female subjects the Amazons left behind in the jungle. His epistle imitates the ornate Latin style of a Roman emperor who is visiting the capital city of a outpost of civilization, where the women are uncouth in their dress, speech, and body painting when compared to the classical goddesses of the jungle.[8] In another pre-classical city invoked by modernists, the Persian Pasargadae, poet Manuel Bandeira indulges in the Utopia of patronage and sensuality that, he wittily suggests, was lost with the end of Empire in Brazil:

> Vou-me embora pra Pasárgada
> Lá sou amigo do rei
> Lá tenho a mulher que eu quero
> Na cama que escolherei.
> Vou-me embora pra Pasárgada. (117)

The Brazilian past is recovered in a displaced Orientalist vision, which suggests yet another voyage that carries a native away from Brazil's heartland and returns him to classical origins.[9]

Oswald de Andrade had the reputation of being willing to sacrifice a friendship for the sake of a witticism. He was "the man who knew how to laugh."[10] The recently published collection of his thumbnail sketches and clever observations about colleagues and society in *Dicionário de bolso* (1990) is a case in point, although some of his most biting or scathing remarks were not included. Oswald refers in manuscript notes to his counterpart in the modernist movement, the musicologist, ethnographer, and poet Mário de Andrade, as a "Macunaíma

---

[8] In terms of the satirical essay, the city-country opposition is the theme of *Cartas de um matuto*, published between 1908-14 in the *Careta* of Rio de Janeiro. A rancher from Minas Gerais, Tibúrcio da Anunciação, writes to his wife about his experiences in the city where he has come to visit the National Exposition of 1908. The art of satirical letters is continued by Mário Brant (1875-1968) and Arístides Rabelo, who ridicule the snobbishness of bourgeois society, following João do Rio. In Lima Barreto's *Os bruzundangas*, a stranger describes the land of Bruzundanga, that is, Brazil of 1920.

[9] The paradigm had been fixated in the celebrated romantic poem "Canção do exílio" ("Song of Exile") written by Antônio Gonçalves Dias in Portugal and recapitulated in José de Alencar's legendary novel, *Iracema* (1865).

[10] See Marília Pacheco Fiorillo, "Oswald, o homem que sabia rir," 39; and Maria Augusta Fonseca, *Oswald de Andrade: o homem que come*.

in the Conservatory who, seen from behind, resembles Oscar Wilde." The discoverer of Brazil, Pedro Álvares Cabral, becomes "o culpado de tudo;" Freud is the "Diretor espiritual da burguesia" and Krishnamurti, whose ecumenical Hinduism was popular in Europe and Brazil at the time, is a "Deus arrependido."[11] The column "Brasiliana" carried in the *Revista de Antropofagia* reproduced quotes from the press that unwittingly revealed comic foibles of the national character:

MÃE
De um artigo de Manoel Victor na *Folha da Noite* de S. Paulo, n. de 28-9-28:
"A qualidade de ser mãe não exige distinção de raça, de classe ou de côr."

The outer limits of civic discourse were later craftily tested by architect and poet Flávio de Carvalho's "Experiências," in a form of experimental social anthropology that introduced anomalies and antithetical components into social and religious rituals. In *Experiência Nº. 2*, Carvalho participated in an Easter procession without removing his hat, and in the second he introduced a new men's fashion garment in "summer style," in actuality a short skirt in which he paraded along São Paulo's downtown avenues.

Some of the cleverest and most infamous aphorisms of Brazilian modernism can be found in Oswald de Andrade's "Manifesto antropófago" of 1928, which is widely considered a central document of modern Latin American cultural theory. Under this manifesto, Brazilian intellectuals became cannibals who devoured and neutralized foreign influences. The manifesto's slogan, "Tupy or not Tupy, that is the question," has been deconstructed and interpreted by critics as a cannibalization of Shakespeare.[12] Its fields of reference are indeed far ranging, crossing Hamlet with an allusion to the Indianism dear to romantic nationalism that inspired many Brazilian intellectuals to propose Tupy as Brazil's official language in place of Portuguese, with the purpose of ridding the country of linguistic vestiges of colonial domina-

---

[11] The clever, biting aphorism is a genre continued by humorist Barão de Itararé (pseudonym of Apparício Torelly, 1895-1971) in *A Manhã*, the weekly whose first phase was 1926-35. He described Brazil as "uma república 'generalizada.'"

[12] See Maria Eugênia Boaventura, *A vanguarda antropofágica*.

tion.[13] The slogan at the same time alludes to the first published account of life with Brazilian cannibals by the German traveler in sixteenth-century Brazil, Hans Staden. His account of life among the Tupinambás (Warpurg, 1557) was published with red and black woodcuts that were selectively reproduced by Oswald de Andrade to illustrate the *Revista de Antropofagia*.[14] The slogan's cross-reference in the plastic arts is to Brazilian artist Tarsila do Amaral's celebrated painting of a cannibal in a stylized tropical landscape, the "Abaporu," created for Oswald on his birthday in January 1928 and a prime conceptual source of the manifesto.[15] The pure wit of the slogan resides, however, in the crossed images: a cannibal delivering a soliloquy on ontological doubt, confusing the Shakespearean "to be" with a local homophone; or an urban, elite intellectual practicing ritual cannibalism on the European colonizers of Brazil, who are in all likelihood family relations.

Satire: A Top Hat in Senegambia
Comedy in Brazilian modernist literature is mainly expressed through social satire based on caricature or parody as commonly practiced since the advent of journalism in the mid-nineteenth century. Oswald de Andrade's 1924 "Manifesto da poesia pau-brasil" highlights the contrast between exaggerated, legalistic rhetoric imitating classical and European oratory and the popular speech of a syncretic Brazilian culture. The contrast shapes his caricature of senior statesman Rui Barbosa: "uma cartola na Senegâmbia." In the manifesto, convoluted rhetoric is elevated to the status of a national ill, the pain of excessive erudition: "País de dores anônimas, de doutores anônimos." Critic Roberto Schwarz theorizes that cultural imitation of Europe has always been inevitable in Brazil, whereby truly national characteristics

---

[13] Oswald had access to the Tupy grammar published in the sixteenth century by Ruiz de Montoya. He incorporated a poem in Tupy into the "Manifesto da poesia pau-brasil" ("Brazilwood Poetry Manifesto") of 1924, taken from *O selvagem* by Couto de Magalhães.

[14] Staden's book was of great interest to modernist primitivism and was republished by the Frankfurter Gesellschaft für Anthropologie, Ethnologie und Urgeschichte (1925 and 1927) and in English translation (London, 1928). The first English translation of 1874 by Albert Tootal, with annotations by Sir Richard Burton, had been published by the Hakluyt Society.

[15] The "Abaporu" has become one of the most important paintings in twentieth-century Latin America, perhaps enhanced by its exposition in New York in 1993.

can only be derived by subtracting imitation.[16] The high degree of originality found in the local encounter with European models would suggest, to the contrary, that comedy and national identity form a strong and positive bond that feeds on imitation, through symbiotic and isomorphic relationships. Bandeira's famous verse, "fala errada do povo, fala certa do povo," reinforces the strength of culturally hybrid, imitative forms, as does the classic line from Oswald's "Brazilwood Poetry Manifesto:" "a contribuição milionária de todos os erros."

The satire of overly embellished rhetoric in the voice of social conservatism or obscurantism is a target of Oswald de Andrade's 1924 novel, *Memórias sentimentais de João Miramar*. Penned by an anachronistic character named Machado Penumbra ("Nathaniel Webster Darkling," in the translation), the preface represents legal rhetoric and privileging of traditional literary expression. The comedy resides in Penumbra's uncertain attempt to encourage the young writer ("I cannot help but recognize the sacred rights of innovation" in spite of "a few lamentable abuses" that threaten "the golden treasures wrought by the Parnassian era"). While endorsing the young writer, Penumbra draws the line at "violation of common rules of punctuation," an influence of the Cubist Salon d'Automne on this "satirical essay, as witty as it is biting." The bite goes deeper in the parody of a patriotic speech pronounced by the moral guide Pôncio Pilatos da Gloria at the Ping Pong Recreation Club. Pilate praises the abstinence and chastity of the youth of both sexes during the "extinguishment of the lights" by a "perfidious current" that interrupts a waltz with sudden darkness. Invoking the high literary and moral behavior of the youth ("Here no one reads novels of low literary ilk or futurist verses. One only reads Rui Barbosa"), Pilate notes that when the lights went out young men "upheld themselves at such a dangerous hour in the posture which will later carry them as husbands to the fulgurant firmaments of married bliss!" The unwitting similarity between the moral and erotic metaphors enhances the satire through double entendre.

In poetry, the succinct satiric poem "sets off a grenade of desacralizing humor," as Haroldo de Campos comments (1991). Oswald de Andrade invents the "poema-piada" or joke poem, which produced what is undoubtedly the shortest poem in Portuguese language. The *Primeiro caderno do aluno de poesia Oswald de Andrade* (1927), composed in a deliberately ingenuous style of playful innocence, begins

---

[16] See Roberto Schwarz, "Brazilian Culture: Nationalism by Elimination."

with a minute poem that should be read as a manifesto. It consists of the title "Amor" printed in red and the single-word response "Humor" printed in black. The play with rhyme, form, and meaning catches "a satiric note in the ossified national customs," affirms Campos, and signals as well a trend in Brazilian poetry whose influence can be noted in contemporary experimental poets such as José Paulo Paes, Augusto de Campos, and Paulo Leminski.[17] The modernist style of playful yet critical innocence is also practiced by Bandeira, as in the humorous satire of first love in "Porquinho-da-Índia":

> Quando eu tinha seis anos
> Ganhei um porquinho-da-Índia
> Que dor de coração me dava
> Porque o bichinho só queria estar debaixo do fogão!
> Levava ele pra sala
> Pra os lugares mais bonitos mais limpinhos
> Ele não gostava:
> Queria era estar debaixo do fogão.
> Não fazia caso nenhum das minhas ternurinhas...
>
> —O meu porquinho-da-Índia foi a minha primeira namorada.
> (100)

The history of Brazil became a prime target for cultural irreverence and provocation, resulting in poetry that Schwarz classifies as both humorous and sharply nationalistic: "Ingenuous and jingoistic. Libertarian, enlightening, and provincial" (7). In his "história do Brasil" in the 1925 *Pau-brasil* poems published in Paris, Oswald produces ironic versions of the colonial encounter by reproducing passages from historical documents and chronicles of discovery selected for double entendre:

> *festa da raça*
>   Hu certo animal se acha também nestas partes
>   A que chamam Preguiça...
>   Que ainda que ande quinze dias aturado
>   Não vencerá a distância de hu tiro de pedra. (OC VII, 83)

---

[17] Augusto de Campos's isomorphic "Viva Vaia" (1972) is the equivalent in Concrete poetry of Oswald's "Amor."

Poet Murilo Mendes writes a more comprehensive parody of signal events in national history in *História do Brasil (1932)*, a collection in which Jorge Amado identified a master of the "poesia-piada:"

> Itararé: a maior batalha da América do Sul / Não houve.
> Homo Brasiliensis: O homem / É o único animal que joga no bicho. (*História* 89)

Under the pen name Mendes Fradique, an inversion of the pseudonym of Portuguese author J.M. Eça de Queiroz (Fradique Mendes), José Madeira de Freitas begins to publish chapters of his *História do Brasil pelo método confuso*. The first chapters appeared in the humor magazine *Dom Quixote* in Rio de Janeiro in 1919. Employing the format of didactic textbooks of national history used in the public schools, the "confused method" presents mixed information:

> A Terra – Sob o ponto de vista geográfico era o Brasil um dos países mais originais do globo...
> Limites—Ao sul, o Borges de Medeiros, a leste, o cabo submarino, a oeste, o Acre. Não tem norte.
> Superfície—Foi sempre um país muito superficial, em tudo. (*História* 49).

According to Isabel Lustosa's reading, Freitas presents a vision of a joyful Brazil that brings to life the modernist vision of Macunaíma, in which the new "elite" is represented by the miscegenated *caboclo* and Indian in a picaresque atmosphere of play and carnivalization (149).

Satirical poetry also targeted well-known and often-recited verses. Oswald de Andrade and Murilo Mendes each penned parodies of the romantic war horse, "Canção do exílio" by Antônio Gonçalves Dias. Oswald's "Canto de regresso à pátria" reduces the poem's argument of abundance ("Minha terra tem mais flores") to tautology, "Minha terra tem mais terra." Murilo Mendes humorously notes the new internationalism of the Brazilian landscape in his own "Canção do exílio":

> Minha terra tem macieiras da California
> onde cantam gaturanos de Veneza.
> Os poetas da minha terra
> São pretos que vivem em torres de ametista,
> Os sargentos do exército são monistas, cubistas,

Os filósofos são polacos vendendo a prestações...(*Poesia* 87)

La divina increnca (1924) is a collection of verses in the city's Italian dialect which parodies the recitation of classic poems of Brazilian literature. Juó Bananere includes a "translation" of the "Canção do exílio" that deforms the phonetics and morphology of the Portuguese language, comparable to contemporary "Spanglish" or "Portuñol":

>Migna Terra
>
>Migna terra tê parmeras,
>Che ganta inzima o sabiá
>As aves che stó aqui
>Tambê tuttos sabi gorgeá.
>
>A abobora celestia tambê
>Che tê lá na mia terra,
>Tê moltos millió de strella
>Che non tê na Ingraterra.
>
>Os rios lá sô maise grandi
>Dus rio di tuttas naçó;
>I os matto si perdi di vista,
>Nu meio da imensidó.
>
>Na migna terra tê parmeras
>Dove ganta a galligna dangola;
>Na mingna terra tê o Vap'relli,
>Chi só anda de gartolla. (Bananere 14)

In the final stanza, the *sabiá* bird (a Brazilian thrush), whose song is identified with romantic nationalism, is substituted by the Guinea hen ("galligna dangola"), an allusion to Brazil's miscegenated populace. The final verses parody elite fashion associated with anglophiles and conservatives: "Na mingna terra tê o Vap'relli, Chi só anda de gartolla." Vap'relli refers to a professor in the Law School, whose top hat reinforces the caricature that Oswald applied to Rui Barbosa.

The Social Body: "Artificial Sugarloaf"
Humor in modernist literature springs from a more intimate connection with the social body, its customs, language, and civilization. The farce and burlesque endorsed by *Klaxon* are employed to dramatize the charm and madness at the core of social organization, portrayed by Oswald de Andrade in "capital da república:"

> O orgulho de ser branco
> Na terra morena e conquistada...
> A Avenida se abana com as folhas miúdas
> Do Pau Brasil
> Políticos dormem ao calor do Norte...
> O Pão de Açúcar artificial. (OC VII, 108-109)

The fantasy of a young country of pure appetite spawns parodies of its legal and rational traditions that fit within the cannibal metaphor of 1928: "Perguntei a um homem o que era o Direito. Ele me respondeu que era a garantia do exercício da possibilidade. Esse homem chamava-se Galli Mathias. Comi-o." Attempting to discredit the European façade of Brazilian society, the modernists repeat Hans Staden's quote from the Tupinambás as a slogan for the *Revista de Antropofagia*: "Lá vem a nossa comida pulando."

The discrete, poetic charm of modernist social organization is often captured in depictions of carnival and fantasy. In *Pau-brasil*, a "dispute between the warring hosts of Laughter and Madness" describes a carnival procession, in which fantasy is a transparent social allegory:

> 20 crianças representando de vespas
> Constituem a guarda de honra
> Da Porta-Estandarte
> Que é precedida de 20 damas
> Fantasiadas de pavão
> Quando 40 homens do coro
> Conduzindo palmas
> E artisticamente fantasiados de papoulas
> Abrem a Alegoria... (OC VII, 113)

In her 1933 novel, *Parque industrial*, the militant muse Patrícia Galvão (1910-1962) portrays a darker side of the celebration, the mad carnival of the sensual and exploited women in São Paulo's Italian district:

> —Quer fazer uma vaca pra comprar uma lança-perfume?
> —Eu não. O meu bigodinho me dá.
> Cadeiras na rua... Italianas gordas... Meninos grandes chupam as mamas de quilos... Todas as meninas bonitas estão sendo bolinadas... A burguesia procura no Braz carne fresca e nova.
> —Que pedaço de italianinha!...
> As filas de automoveis se misturam, engrossam, levando a promessa das meninas pobres, cheias de ventarolas e rolos catados. Pierrots vermelhos. Arlequins. Dominós. (42-43)

The attractive mulatto woman Corina becomes the victim of the quasi-ritual exploitation of race, sex, and class; her story is a comic undercurrent and critique of an elitist and Europeanized society.

Madness becomes a useful motif of social insight, as illustrated by an episode of Oswald de Andrade's second "novel-invention," *Serafim Ponte Grande*:

> Senhores e possuidores de fundos e de largos latifúndios... fizeram construir num arrabalde de Juqueri um Asilo para tratamento da loucura sob suas formas lógicas. E encomendaram a um pintor vindo da Europa uma fotografia a óleo do falecido...
> O pintor, louco como um silogismo, inaugurou as celas de luxo do Asilo Serafim. (OC VII, 257)

In Mário de Andrade's masterful short story, "Peru de natal," a young male narrator who is navigating his way through a family drama of death and redefinition finds madness to be a very useful guise for protecting his unorthodox points of view from criticism and prohibition:

> Foi decerto por isto que me nasceu, esta sim, espontaneamente, a idéia de fazer uma das minhas chamadas "loucuras." Essa fora aliás, e desde muito cedo, a minha esplêndida conquista contra o ambiente familiar. Desde cedinho...eu conseguí no reformatório do lar e na vasta parentagem, a fama conciliatória de "louco." "É doido, coitado!" falavam... Pois foi o que me salvou, essa fama. Fiz tudo o que a vida me apresentou e o meu ser exigia para se

realizar com integridade. E me deixaram fazer tudo, porque eu era doido, coitado. Resultou disso uma existência sem complexos, de que não posso me queixar um nada. (*Contos* 96)

Bodily humor, in which physically erotic and grotesque images and themes are conveyed through farce, is a strong current in modernist literature. In the *Sentimental Memoirs*, fragment 19, "Bicicleta de Onã," threatens the practice of vices if there is no bicycle to assuage the boredom of the interior town of Águas Enxutas: "Passo os dias que nem na fazenda que não tinha nada para fazer senão vícios. Vou fazer como lá se mamãe não quiser mandar a bicicleta que já estou pedindo" (20). The physically grotesque is exploited for comic value, as in satire of advertisements in *Pau-brasil* poems:

> *reclame*
> Fala a graciosa atriz
> Margarida Perna Grossa
> Linda cor – que admirável loção.... (OC VII, 127-128)

Vulgarity in the picaresque *Ponte Grande* leads to the first expulsion of a character from a novel in literature:

> Movietone
> Mas Serafim insiste; dirige-se atrás dele até o reservado dos homens e grita-lhe:
> —Diga-me uma coisa. Quem é neste livro o personagem principal? Eu ou você?
> Pinto Calçudo como única resposta solta com toda a força um traque, pelo que é imediatamente posto para fora do romance. (OC VII, 193)

Erotic themes run throughout modernist humor. An image of popular classes concludes the novel *Parque industrial*, when the destitute Corina, suffering from hunger and the exploitation of prostitution, meets the worker Pepe in a café: "Os dois, agarrados, vítimas da mesma inconsciência, atirados á mesma margem das combinações capitalistas, levam pipocas salgadas para a mesma cama" (Galvão 145). In the parody of a Portuguese romantic novel in *Serafim*, the hero's praise of Paris is cast as a rhetorical and sexual farce: "Fornalha e pêssego! Domingo de semi-deusas! Egito dos faraós! Roma de Garibaldi! Dás dobrado o que as outras capitais oferecem! Ao menos, dentro de tuas muralhas, se pode trepar sossegado!" (OC VII, 197).

Many of Macunaíma's adventures reproduce the coarse humor of the folktale. In an initial encounter with the Curupira, Lord of the Forest, Macunaíma accepts a grilled slice of flesh from its leg, which was a trick intended to allow the monster to follow and eat Macunaíma:

> O Curupira...amontou no viado, que é o cavalo dele ...e lá se foi gritando:
> —Carne de minha perna! carne de minha perna!
> Lá de dentro da barriga do herói a carne respondeu"
> —Quê foi? (15)

In another tale, Macunaíma encounters a monkey in a city park cracking babassu palm nuts between his legs with a stone. The monkey convinces Macunaíma that he is cracking his own "nuts" for a painless, tasty treat and convinces the hero to try it. When Macunaíma smashes himself, he drops dead and the monkey jeers, "Pois, meus cuidados, não falei que tu morrias! Falei! Não me escutas! Estás vendo o que sucede pros desobedientes?" (106).

Buffoonery: 400 Years of Beef, Horrors!
Buffoonery carries modernist literature further into the hyperbole of farce and carnivalesque, erotic humor. In the *Revista de Antropofagia*, the cannibal faction aggressively formulated a social and political agenda in the aftermath of the manifesto, describing in comic hyperbole the utopian, matriarchal alterations to be made in Brazilian civilization, without any pretense of being taken seriously. In the column "A 'Descida' Antropophaga" in the first number, Oswaldo Costa explained the philosophy of a new cannibal paradise:

> Nós queremos o homem sem a dúvida, sem siquer a presumpção da existencia da duvida: nú, natural, antropophago.
> Quatro séculos de carne de vaca! Que horror!

Costa's farce pretends that Brazilians have been eating the wrong kind of flesh and as a consequence have lost contact with the natural world.

Oswald de Andrade's play *O rei da vela* (1937) introduces surrealistic hyperbole and buffoonery into the Brazilian theater. Parodying the French medieval romance of Heloise and Abelard; the play exploits and inverts social roles and passions. Act I presents a usury office in the newly industrialized city of São Paulo, administered by Aberlardo I and Aberlardo II. The Abelards are examining the records of small debtors who cannot pay the hundreds of percent interest charged on the most insignificant loans. Rejecting humane excuses, the usurers imprison their "clients" in large animal cages, while defending all political measures necessary to support a corporate, fascist state:

> Os clientes aparecem atropeladamente nas grades... Homens e mulheres mantêm-se quietos ante o enorme chicote de Abelardo II.
> Abelardo II dá um tiro para o ar. Os clientes recuam gritando. Ele corre a porta de ferro ruidosamente. (OC VIII, 72)

The decadence of the old colonial system is portrayed in financial and sexual hyperbole, ripe for the exploitation of the amoral Abelard, a lackey of foreign capital. Abelardo I plans to marry the lesbian Heloisa to gain access to her family's plantation wealth. The "lesbian" American financier chases a chauffeur, to the relief of the young couple Totó Fruta-do-Conde and João dos Divãs, the jealous gay offspring of the patriarch, Colonel Belarmino. Plantation patronesses are ex-prostitutes from Poland. The intellectuals are judged to be too weak and ineffectual to confront the new system of calculated exploitation:

> Abelardo I—Não pratica a literatura de ficção?
> Pinote—No Brasil isso não dá nada!
> Abelardo I—Sim, a de fricção é que rende. (OC VIII, 79)

Farce and erotic humor are woven into the caricature of scientific and social issues of the day. In Brazil, writers Monteiro Lobato and Menotti del Picchia create the regionalist stereotype caricatures Jeca Tatu and Juca Mulato, respectively, representing the *caipira* from the interior of São Paulo and the mulatto. The modernists laugh at Sérge Voronoff, a Russian physician renowned internationally for his experiments with a youth tonic made from monkey testicles, who is the subject of a novel by José Madeira de Freitas in 1926 and makes an appearance in the final Utopian voyage of Seraphim:

> Foi ordeando que se jogasse ao mar uma senhora que estrilara por ver as filhas nuas no tombadilho que passava a se chamar tom-

bandalho. Mas ela replicou que chorava de saudade do célebre curandeiro Dr. Voronoff. (OC VII, 263)

Language is also subject to buffoonery, in São Paulo's "babel of improper vocabulary from all races."[18] *La divina increnca*'s satire of a poem of longing for São Paulo telescopes its virtues into the memory of the Italian daughters of Bom Retiro district:

> "Sodades de Zan Paolo"
>
> Tegno sodades dista Paulicéa
> Dista cidade chi tanto dimiro!
> Tegno sodades distu céu azur,
> Das bellas figlia la du Bó Ritiro.
>
> Tegno sodades dus tempo perdido
> Xupano xoppi uguali d'un vampiro;
> Tegno sodades dus begigno ardenti
> Das bellas figlia lá du Bó Ritiro.
>
> Tegno sodades lá da Pontigrandi,
> Dove di notte si vá dá un giro
> I dove vó spiá come n'un speglio
> As bellas figlia lá du Bó Ritiro.
>
> Andove tê tantas piquena xique,
> Chi a genti sê querê dá un sospiro,
> Auano perto per caso a genti passa,
> Das bellas figlia lá du Bó Ritiro.
>
> Tegno sodades, ai de ti – Zan Baolo!
> Terra chi eu vivo sempre n'un martiro,
> Vagabundeano come un begiaflore,
> Atraiz das figlia lá du Bó Ritiro.
>
> Tegno sodades da garôa fria,
> Agitada co sopro du Zefiro,
> Quano io durmia ingopa o collo ardenti
> Das bellas figlia lá du Bó Ritiro. (Bananere 48-49)

---

[18] See Maria Eugênia Boaventura, *A utopia antropofágica*, 176.

The villainous Italian Mafioso, Venceslau Pietro Pietra, who possesses the magical amulet, meets his farcical end in *Macunaíma* by falling into a pot of boiling spaghetti, yet with time to make a final culinary observation, "falta queijo!" Buffoonery and hyperbole in modernist literature are tools for the clever dissection of a sharp social and psychological analysis.

Universal Comic: The Enormous Laugh
The dimension of the universal humor that began with Deisi's red laugh resounds throughout Brazilian modernist literature as its highest expression of the comic spirit. Jorge de Lima's great universal circus privileges play as the comic principle of the world:

> Senhores, hoje há espetáculo no mundo...
> ("Poema de qualquer virgem")
> [...]Marie e Helene se apresentam nuas,
> Dançam no arame e deslocam de tal forma os membros
> Que parece que os membros não são delas.
> A platéia bisa coxas, bisa seios, bisa sovacos.
> Marie e Helene se repartem tôdas
> Se distribuem pelos homens cínicos,
> Mas ninguém vê as almas que elas conservam puras.
> E quando atiram os membros para a visão dos homens,
> Atiram as almas para a visão de Deus.
> Com a verdadeira história do grande circo Knieps
> Muito pouco se tem ocupado a imprensa. (448)

Lima has changed the grotesque of bodily humor into a transcendental communion through play. The comedy of the great spectacle of the world exposes, separates, and shares the universal body, beyond which are the unseen souls of a spiritual paradise.[19] Murilo Mendes shares Lima's universal sense of comedy and carnival in poems parodying scenes from the history of Brazil. The poet imagines a tropical birth of Venus in the discovery in 1500:

> O Pão de Açúcar sonhou
> Que um carro saiu da Urca
> Transportando com amor
> Meninas muito dengosas,

---

[19] See Luciana Stegagno Picchio, "Jorge de Lima: Universal Poet."

> Umas, nuinhas da silva,
> Outras, vestidas de tanga,
> E mais outras, de maillot.
> (*História do Brasil* 10-11)

In the "Manifesto antropófago," Oswald de Andrade posits happiness as an endemic quality of Brazilian life before the discovery: "Antes dos portugueses descobrirem o Brasil, o Brasil tinha descoberto a felicidade" (OC VI, 18). Happiness exuded from indigenous mythologies in contact with the soil, capable of transforming taboos into totems, thus creates valid equivalents of Western religion, justice, and science. The manifesto's slogan "A alegria é a prova dos nove" is raised as the measure by which to judge the progress of civilizations. A reader of Freud and Lévi-Bruhl, Oswald excoriated Western dress as the first indication of repression of natural society in the tropics:

> O que atropelava a verdade era a roupa, o impermeável entre o mundo interior e o mundo exterior. A reação contra o homem vestido. O cinema americano informará. (OC VI, 14)

The manifesto proposes a new Brazilian matriarchy to remedy the patriarchal ills registered by Freud: "Contra a realidade social, vestida e opressora, cadastrada por Freud—a realidade sem complexos, sem loucura, sem prostituições e sem penitenciárias do matriarcado de Pindorama."

The finale of Oswald de Andrade's novel, *Serafim Ponte Grande*, coins a metaphor for permanent Utopia in the travels of the picaresque anti-hero, which culminate in a never-ending voyage on the ocean liner *El Durazno* that elevates play to a universal sustaining principle of comic freedom. Following precepts announced in the "Cannibal Manifesto," Seraphim's hijacked ship sails the oceans in order to escape the "peste dos chamados povos cultos e cristianizados." In a reversal of definitions, the ship's antennas proclaim plague on board in order to assure their isolation from society. Shipboard ethics constitute an inverse society based on natural order, sexual license, nudity, recitation of poetry, and the imagination of dreams. Although without money, the passengers refuse to disembark and take on cargo on credit, voyaging throughout the tropical world. This final voyage in the section, "Os antropófagos" carries an epigraph from the seventeenth-century *Spiritual Conquest* of Ruiz de Montoya which describes the actions of a dishonest priest who "seduced some girls and several young ladies in his service, and with them he fled." The utopian voyage eliminates the possibility of sin and deception by voiding the "coercion" of moral catechism and replacing it with the natural ethics of a marooned society.[20] In his essay, "*Serafim*: A Great Non-book," Haroldo de Campos explains the utopian perspective fully developed by Oswald de Andrade in the series of articles "March of Utopias" in 1953:

> Oswald foresaw a new golden age, an anthropophagic-technological culture, in which the national technicized man under the shield of matriarchy (that is, without the ties of family, property, and the class state natural to patriarchal culture, messianic) will rediscover social happiness and playful leisure, propitious to the arts. (131)

Seraphim's ocean liner avoids all but essential contacts with civilized ports: "*El Durazno só pára para comprar abacates nos cais tropicais.*"

The incomprehension of the world may also form part of a universal comic sphere, through a lower human comedy consisting solely of Rabelaisian appetite and the physically grotesque. Mário de Andrade's *Paulicéia desvairada* ends with a grand finale in the form of a profane oratorio, "As enfibraturas do Ipiranga," performed in a park near the Municipal Theater. The soloist is a soprano, "Minha loucura," whose arias are interspersed with choruses sung by groups representing different ideological orientations: "As juvenilidades auriverdes," "Os sandapilários indiferentes," "Os orientalismos convencionais." After building to a tremendous crescendo, the soprano intones a lullaby that casts the principals into an eternal deaf sleep. Outside, along the city streets and in the buildings of downtown São Paulo, the maddened crowd rises to an apotheosis of the world carnival in a frenzy of denunciation:

> ([…]enquanto das janelas de palácios, teatros, tipografias, hotéis—escancaradas, mas cegas—cresce uma enorme vaia de assovios, zurros, patadas.) (Mário, OC II, 82)

The last laugh punctuating the modernists' philosophy of humor belongs to Macunaíma. The Amazonian hero has gone to Rio for an

---

[20] To this extent, Brazilian utopianism is undoubtedly influenced and shaped by its slave society. Oswald foreshadows Gilberto Freyre's *Grande casa e senzala* (*The Masters and the Slaves*), published in the same year as *Serafim Ponte Grande* (1933).

Afro-Brazilian religious rite, a condomblé ceremony through which he seeks magical recourse to take revenge on the terrible giant Piamã, eater of people, who in actuality is the villainous industrialist Pietro Pietra, possessor of the *muiraquitã* amulet. The ritual drumming and dancing of condomblé that precede the trance states that propitiate receiving the spirits of the gods is accompanied by cigar smoke and *cachaça* liquor, a sugarcane distillate first produced by plantations in Northeastern Brazil. The condomblé ceremony is Mário de Andrade's equivalent of the great mystical circus of Jorge de Lima. Macunaíma prepares for it by removing his shoes and socks and hanging a charm around his neck made of wax and herbs. The litany of the processional singing evokes the god-devil Exu, a malignant demon who brings about wickedness. The candles, drinking, and chanting in the closed atmosphere lead to a frenzy and crazed ecstasy of naked revelry: "Já quase todos tinham tirado algumas roupas e o respiro ficara chiado por causa do cheiro de mistura budum coty pitium e o suor de todos" (*Macunaíma* 59).

Macunaíma is about to face the swinging, loose breasts of an overpainted whore, dancing into a trance with foaming lips and a piercing cry in front of the devil-saint Exu. For the first time Macunaíma tastes the distilled drink, unknown in the Amazon jungle, and he immediately shows physical signs of incantation or epiphany that symbolize his grotesque, comic communion with the universal body:

> E foi lá que Macunaíma provou pela primeira vez o chachiri temível cujo nome é cachaça. Provou estalando com a língua feliz e deu uma grande gargalhada. (*Macunaíma* 59)

Macunaíma's enormous laugh enounces his initiation and entry into the magical rituals of a carnivalized world, his new awareness of the universal comic spirit of Brazilian modernism.

Works Cited

Almeida, Tereza Virgínia de. *A ausência lilás da semana de arte moderna*. Florianópolis: Livraria e Editora Obra Jurídica Ltda., 1998.

Amado, Jorge. "Introdução." *Máximas e mínimas do Barão de Itararé*. Sel. and org. Afonso Félix de Sousa. Rio de Janeiro: Record, 1985.

Andrade, Mário de. "The Christmas Turkey." Trans. Richard Breneman. *Latin American Literary Review* 7. 4 (1979): 96-102.

———. *Contos Novos*. 7th ed. São Paulo: Martins, 1976.
———. *Hallucinated City*. Trans. Jack E. Tomlins. Nashville: Vanderbilt UP, 1968.
———. *Macunaíma*. São Paulo: Cupolo, 1928; republished in Rio de Janeiro and São Paulo: Livros Técnicos Científicos; Secretaria da Cultura Ciênica e Tecnologia, 1978; English translation, *Macunaíma*. Trans. E. A. Goodland. New York: Random House, 1984.
———. *Obras completas de Mário de Andrade*. Vol. II. *Poesias completas*. São Paulo: Martins, 1955.
Andrade, Oswald de. "Cannibal Manifesto." Trans. Leslie Bary. *Latin American Literary Review* 19. 38 (1991): 35-47.
———. *Dicionário de bolso*. São Paulo: Globo, 1990.
———. "Manifesto of Pau Brasil Poetry." Trans. Stella de Sá Rego. *Latin American Literary Review* 14. 27 (1986): 184-87.
———. *Obras completas*. Vol. VI. *Do Pau-brasil à Antropofagia e às Utopias*. Rio de Janeiro: Civilização Brasileira, 1970.
———. *Obras completas*. Vol. VII. *Poesias reunidas*. Rio de Janeiro: Civilização Brasileira, 1971.
———. *Obras completas*. Vol. VIII. *Teatro*. Rio de Janeiro: Civilização Brasileira, 1976.
———. *O perfeito cozinheiro das almas deste mundo*. São Paulo: Ex Libris, 1987.
———. *O primeiro caderno do aluno de poesia Oswald de Andrade*. São Paulo: Globo, 1991. [1st ed. 1927].
———. *Sentimental Memoirs of John Seaborne*. Trans. Ralph Niebuhr and Albert G. Bork. *Texas Quarterly* (Winter 1972): 112-160.
———. *Seraphim Grosse Pointe*. Trans. Kenneth D. Jackson and Albert G. Bork. Austin: New Latin Quarter, 1979.
Bandeira, Manuel. *Estrela da vida inteira*. 7th ed. Rio de Janeiro: José Olympio, 1979.
Baudelaire, Charles. "On the Essence of Laughter." Ed. Corrigan. 448-465.
Bananere, Juó. [pseud. Alexandre Ribeiro Marcondes Machado]. *La divina increnca*. São Paulo: 1966. [1st ed. 1924].
Bergson, Henri. "Laughter: An Essay on the Meaning of the Comic." Trans. Cloudesley Brereton and Fred Rothwell. [London: Macmillan, 1911]. Ed. Corrigan. 471-477. [Also pub. as *O riso: ensaio sobre a significação do cômico*. Rio de Janeiro: Zahar, 1983].
Boaventura, Maria Eugênia. *A vanguarda antropofágica*. São Paulo: Ática, 1985.
———. *A utopia antropofágica*. São Paulo: Ática, 1985.
Bopp, Raul. *Cobra Norato*. São Paulo: Irmãos Ferraz, 1931.
Campos, Augusto. *Poesia, 1949-79*. São Paulo: Duas Cidades, 1979; 2nd. ed. São Paulo: Brasiliense, 1986.
Campos, Haroldo. "Seraphim: A Great Non-Book." *Seraphim Grosso Pointe*. By Oswald de Andrade. 113-131.

———. "The Rule of Anthropophagy: Europe Under the Sign of Devoration." Trans. María Tai Wolff. *Latin American Literary Review* 14. 27 (1986): 42-60.
Carvalho, Flávio de. *Experiência No. 2 realizada sobre uma procissão do Corpus Christi*. 2nd ed. São Paulo: Irmãos Ferraz, 1931.
Carvalho, Ronald de. *Rabelais et le rire de la Renaissance*. Pref. Luc Durtain. Paris: E. Hazan, 1932.
Corrigan, Robert W., ed. *Comedy, Meaning and Form*. San Francisco: Chandler, 1968.
Fonseca, Maria Augusta. *Oswald de Andrade: biografia*. São Paulo: Art Editora; Secretaria de Estado da Cultura, 1990.
———. *Oswald de Andrade: O homem que come*. São Paulo: Brasiliense, 1982.
Freyre, Gilberto. *The Masters and the Slaves*. Trans. Samuel Putnam. New York: Knopf, 1944.
Galvão, Patrícia. *Industrial Park*. Trans. Elizabeth and K. David Jackson. Lincoln: U Nebraska P, 1993.
———. *Parque industrial*. 2nd. ed. São Paulo: Alternativa, 1981.
Itararé, Barão de. *Máximas e mínimas do Barão de Itararé*. Sel. and org. Afonso Félix de Sousa. Intro. Jorge Amado. Rio de Janeiro: Record, 1985.
Lima, Jorge de. *Obra completa. Vol. 1. Poesia e ensaios*. Org. Afrânio Coutinho. Rio de Janeiro: Aguilar, 1958.
Lustosa, Isabel. *Brasil pelo método confuso: Humor e boemia em Mendes Fradique*. Rio de Janeiro: Bertrand, 1993.
Madeira de Freitas, José [Pseud. Mendes Fradique]. *Doutor Voronoff*. São Paulo, 1926.
———. *História do Brasil pelo método confuso*. Rio de Janeiro: Leite Ribeiro, 1922.
———. *Gramática portuguesa pelo método confuso*. Edição fac-similar. Vitória: UFES/Rio de Janeiro: Rocco, 1984.
Mendes, Murilo. *Poesia completa e prosa*. Ed. Luciana Stegagno Picchio. Rio de Janeiro: Nova Aguilar, 1994.
———. *História do Brasil (1932)*. Org., intro. e notas Luciana Stegagno Picchio. Rio de Janeiro: Nova Fronteira, 1991.
Meredith, George. "The Essay on Comedy." Ed. Corrigan. 466-470.
Morse, Richard. *From Community to Metropolis*. Gainesville: U Florida P, 1958.
Muir, Frank, ed. and intro. *Oxford Book of Humorous Prose*. Oxford: Oxford UP, 1992.
Needell, Jeffrey. *A Tropical Belle-Époque: Elite Culture and Society in Turn-of-the-Century Rio de Janeiro*. Cambridge: Cambridge UP, 1987.
Pacheco Fiorillo, Marília. "Oswald, o homem que sabia rir." *Folha de S. Paulo-Caderno Ilustrada* (20 Oct. 1984): 39.
Revista de Antropofagia. Facsimile edition. São Paulo: Metal Leve, 1979.
Schwarz, Roberto. "Brazilian Culture: Nationalism by Elimination." *Misplaced Ideas*. Trans. and intro. John Gledson. London: Verso, 1992. 1-18.

Sena, Jorge de. "Modernismo Brasileiro: 1922 e Hoje." *A vanguarda literária no Brasil*. By K. David Jackson. Frankfurt: Vervuert, 1998. 97-110.

Stegagno Picchio, Luciana. "Jorge de Lima: Universal Poet." *Portuguese Studies* 1 (1985): 151-67.

Süssekind, Flora. *Tal Brasil, qual romance*. Rio de Janeiro: Edições Achaimé, 1984.

Szafran, A. Willy and Adolhe Nysenholc, orgs. *Freud et le rire*. Paris: Editions Métaili e Diffusion Seuil, 1994.

The Avant-Garde Oratory of Ramón Gómez de la Serna

NIGEL DENNIS
University of St Andrews

"¡Lo necesitada que está la vida de nuevas experiencias
e intentos, de tocar nuevos cielos, de abrir nuevas cajas
de sorpresas!
Hay que predisponerse a los contrastes más bravos
y que la vida literaria tenga un valor espectacular, haciendo
que alcance la metáfora combinaciones siderales."
— Ramón Gómez de la Serna

WHEN ERNESTO GIMÉNEZ CABALLERO, himself a major figure of the Spanish avant-garde, called Ramón Gómez de la Serna in 1934 "padre de todos los 'ultras' españoles" (50), he rightly signalled the pioneering role that Ramón had played in the opening decades of the twentieth century in shaping and defining a new creative sensibility in Spain. During those years Ramón was the embodiment of modernity, championing everything that was stridently new and innovative in literature and the arts. As Valéry Larbaud famously wrote in 1923, "Modern Spain is Ramón's Spain" (qtd. in Gómez de la Serna, *Echantillons* xiv).[1] He was such a compelling and inventive writer that Guillermo de Torre, another alert observer of the times and chronicler of the most radical changes taking place in Spanish literature before the Civil War, considered that Ramón's work between the years 1919 and

---

[1] My translation.

1925 constituted on its own an entire avant-garde.[2] From this kind of acknowledgement of his colossal presence on the literary scene sprang the notion of "la generación unipersonal de Gómez de la Serna," an affectionate hyperbole that Ramón himself, always eager to promote his exceptional status, actively encouraged.[3] But if, in a sense, his uncontainable energy did seem to overshadow those around him, his example was also a generous and fertile one, providing many other writers of the pre-war period, as critics like Luis Cernuda later noted, with the expressive strategies they would make use of in their own work.[4]

Ramón's approach to literature amounted to what has been called "cultural terrorism."[5] It involved the systematic demolition of everything that tradition and convention had to offer and the implementation of a militant program of ongoing reconstruction. Reacting vio-

---

[2] See his response to the survey on the avant-garde undertaken by Miguel Pérez Ferrero in *La Gaceta Literaria* in June 1930, reproduced in Buckley and Crispin 406-13, 408.

[3] The hyperbole was, in fact, set in motion by Ramón himself in the remarks he made in 1923 at a banquet offered to him by Azorín: "Soy el único de una generación que se anuló, que no existió. Parece que en mi año no nació nadie al mismo tiempo que yo, que fui el único aparecido en una laguna de las generaciones" (*Automoribundia* 373). Future references to *Automoribundia* will be indicated directly in the text with the abbreviation "AM." The idea was picked up by other critics such as Melchor Fernández Almagro and became something of a topical perspective on Ramón.

[4] In "Gómez de la Serna y la generación poética de 1925," Cernuda wrote: "[E]n Gómez de la Serna encuentra nuestra lírica el antecedente histórico más importante para ciertas formas de 'lo nuevo', captadas por la visión y la expresión [...]. En la visión y lenguaje poético que caracterizan, si no todos, algunos de los poetas entonces jóvenes, al menos en la etapa primera de su labor, se observa una influencia evidente de aquella visión de la realidad introducida en nuestra literatura por Gómez de la Serna bastante años antes, hacia 1910" (173). Ignacio Soldevila significantly calls Ramón "sol fecundante, padre Nilo prolífico en descendencias" (62).

[5] Rafael Flórez describes the young Ramón as an "activista impertérrito de un terrorismo cultural y lúdico repleto de víctimas y de procesos, como corresponde a un anarquista de la época" (407). According to Flórez, this practice gave rise to "libros-bomba, artículos-petardo, teatro-explosivo, conferencia-atentado" (407). Other critics have made similar remarks. In "Escorzo de Ramón," for example, Salinas calls the writer "una especie de demoledor Hércules de las letras" (140).

lently against the "estado comatoso, rígido" ("Proclama," *T* 97)[6] of Spanish literary society, complaining that "todos los moldes han resultado estrechos después de fecundados" ("Concepto," *T* 65) he embarked singlehanded on a mission to liberate literature from its constraints and to engineer the forms of expression that a new age demanded: "La entrada en nuevos tiempos exige nuevas formas, nuevas invenciones" (*Greguerías*, *T* 138). For him, innovation was the determining principle of art and his commitment to it was unconditional: "No hay otra forma ni concepto de la distancia en Arte que el innovar [...]. El deber de lo nuevo es el principal deber de todo artista creador" (*Ismos*, *T* 115).

While such attitudes as these may be viewed as typical of the restless, adolescent iconoclasm that reconfigured a good deal of European art and literature at the beginning of the twentieth century, they corresponded in Ramón's case to a kind of permanent dissidence, what he himself called "mi interminable posición de rebeldía" (*Ismos*, *T* 110).[7] To avoid the stultifying effects of complacency and repetition, which he believed led to creative paralysis, Ramón needed to reactivate constantly his pursuit of originality. Novelty in any form, with its attendant notions of revelation and revitalization, was for him an antidote—both festive and lyrical—to the prosaic tedium of life: "Alcánzame el delirio poético de cada día, y no me dejes morir de monotonía, que es de lo que se muere realmente" (qtd. in Ynduráin 74).[8] Ramón's entire creative endeavor can be viewed as an attempt to sustain and enact this daily "delirio poético," redeeming a drab and empty existence with the

---

[6] This text, "Primera proclama de Pombo," is reproduced in the useful anthology of Ramón's essays edited by Ana Martínez-Collado and published under the title *Una teoría personal del arte. Antología de textos de estética y teoría del arte*. Future references to texts included in this anthology will be given parenthetically with the initial "*T*." A list of the essays quoted, with their original dates of publication, is given in "Works Cited" following the *Teoría* entry.

[7] Soldevila stresses how Ramón applies in his work the principle of "la revolución permanente" (39-40). See also Ramón's declaration in *Muestrario* [1918]: "Preparémonos a una terrible movilización constante, permanente, indisculpable" (*T* 22).

[8] Ynduráin is quoting from Ramón's "La diosa de muchos brazos." Monotony, for Ramón, was bound up with the idea of repetition. To avoid repetition the writer had no choice but to pursue relentlessly originality (of form and expression). See his comment in his prologue to *Ismos*: "lo antiguo, por bueno que sea, es monstruoso en la repetición" (*T* 115).

torrential products of his imagination. In this sense, art was a reassuring consolation, a way of calming anxieties by assigning sense where none was apparent: "[P]ara conseguir la paz hay que llenar la vida de sentido y sólo lo logrará de nuevo la grandeza del arte, la pasión por la literatura, el don elocuente del monólogo" ("Torre," *T* 34).

In order to achieve these ends, Ramón pursued with extraordinary tenacity the absolute value of what he called "la libertad superior." Such freedom would enable him, he believed, to enrich and elevate life in such a way that it could enjoy the imaginative expansiveness of art. In a highly revealing section of his autobiography he defined the sense of these fundamental convictions and identified the creative imperatives that consequently informed his own writing:

> Creo en la libertad superior para poder hacer proposiciones nuevas, para tener suposiciones originales.
> Hay que ampliar la conciencia por el arte, por el teatro, por el cine, por la poesía, por la nueva manera de hablar.
> Hay que sensibilizar a las gentes y crear el sentido lírico de la exaltación. Hay que conseguir mayor imaginación y más posibilidad de vida extraordinaria, no de vida ordinaria. (*AM* 422)

What Ramón advocated essentially was the fusion of art and life. By exercising this "higher freedom," he believed he could invigorate both, engineering a reciprocal relationship whereby, on the one hand, the virtues of the extraordinary—the products of an unfettered imagination—would be incorporated into the humdrum routine of the everyday and, on the other, the modest realities of the everyday would fuel his creative drive. Art would not just be the protagonist of his own life but would also, through him, scatter its light and heighten awareness, illuminating the sense of "la poesía de lo que se levanta sobre lo cotidiano" (qtd. in Ynduráin 75).

In pursuit of these goals, Ramón developed, among others, two inter-related strategies, implicit in some of what has been said above. The first involved deconstructing existing genres and adding new ones. Only by doing this could he devise effective outlets for the expression of his unusual sensibility and imagination. As Pedro Salinas accurately observed: "Temperamento en libertad, Ramón rechaza módulos, normas, se acerca a un género literario, entra en él y sale corriendo por el otro extremo en una especie de juego que a veces se ofrece con fulgores dramáticos" (139). His approach to standard genres, such as the novel and theater, was emphatically subversive and produced results that were so disconcertingly original and personal as to be incomparable. He pushed other established genres—the biography and the prologue, for example—to new extremes, radically altering their status. And, quite naturally, he devised new genres—the *diálogo trivial*, the *disparate*, the *capricho*, and, above all, the *greguería*—in order to be able to express his own distinctive way of perceiving the world around him.[9]

His second strategy, as Salinas suggests, involved privileging the playful aspect of creativity, tying art to amusement and packaging it as entertainment. Ramón has often been labelled a "humorous" writer and it is perfectly legitimate to draw attention to the comic qualities of the incongruities and surprising insights present throughout his writing; but humor was a serious business for him as he made clear in his famous essay of 1930 "Gravedad e importancia del humorismo." His treatment of the subject links up with what has been said above about his view of the redemptive power of art. Humor for Ramón was, in Salinas's words, "una terrible forma evasiva del dolor" (140), a way of offering relief from the mournful dreariness of life lived in the shadow of death. The provision of amusement, of joyful distraction, was a life-affirming impulse in Ramón. It enabled him, he believed, to lighten our burden, give direction, recreate the world in a new, more palatable form. In his prologue to the 1917 edition of *Greguerías*, he made this point explicitly:

Dediquémonos a la diversión pura y diáfana, que defiende la vida y la aúpa.

Todo mejora y se orienta gracias a la diversión. El día en que la vida esté llena de verdaderas diversiones se habrá acabado el rencor maligno y todos los monstruos que crea el aburrimiento.

---

[9] I take it for granted that the reader has some idea of the characteristics of the *greguería*. The uninitiated can consult a lucid overview in Alan Hoyle's "El problema de la greguería." Soldevila's definition can usefully be reproduced here: "una unidad autónoma textual constituida por una frase o un grupo mínimo de frases—párrafo breve—en torno a una impresión sensorial o sensorializada, que se quiere creativa, informadora de realidad" (49). I would simply stress that the *greguería* functions primarily on the basis of metaphorical association. Its comic element usually results from incongruity.

Y que los juguetes del mundo sean juguetes nuevos. (*T* 138)[10]

These two strategies are at work—and have been conscientiously studied—in much of Ramón's writing, rejuvenating forms of expression, heightening the reader's awareness of the world around him through the articulation of a hitherto unperceived dimension of reality, festively blurring the distinction between art and everyday life. But nowhere do they come together more powerfully, in my view, than in the least studied—and least studyable—aspect of his creativity, namely in oral expression. By this I mean the different contexts in which he acted out *viva voce*—if not spontaneously, then at least with a high degree of improvisation—the underlying principles of his art. These contexts include all those fora he either appropriated or created for himself in order to communicate orally with a public: from the Café Pombo, with its meetings and banquets over which he regularly presided, to his radio broadcasts and public lectures.[11] These spaces functioned as extensions of his own extravagantly decorated office—where every available surface was covered with the disparate objects and images he assiduously collected[12]—and enabled him to move from silent, written communication with an unseen, imagined reader to direct, oral communication with a living, breathing, if not always visible au-

---

[10] Ramón often referred to the therapeutic value of the amusements and distractions he offered in his lectures. See, for example, the review of his 1923 lecture on streetlamps: "[Ramón] empezó exponiendo la necesidad de olvidar un tanto las preocupaciones fundamentales de la política y de la violencia social para encontrar otros temas placenteros que aplaquen la saña de la vida" (qtd. in *AM* 386).

[11] It goes without saying that Ramón's radio broadcasts are closely connected to his public lectures, the obvious difference being that the former rely on voice (and, intermittently, non-human sound) while the latter make use of voice *plus* visual effects. In short, the radio broadcast can be understood as the lecture minus the spectacle. Ramón's broadcasts could fruitfully be studied as a parallel phenomenon to his lectures in terms of the public projection of his artistic aims. There is much valuable information about them in J. Augusto Ventín Pereira's *Radiorramonismo*, though Ventín approaches the topic primarily from the point of view of a historian of social communications. While such an approach is entirely legitimate (and underlines, yet again, Ramón's pioneering use of a new medium of expression), it tends to underplay the literary significance of the writer's imaginative exploitation of the medium. On this subject, there is much that could be said about Ramón's voice.

[12] See, for example, the photos included in Flórez 140, 172.

dience. Ramón's office, where he often allowed himself to be photographed, was a creative refuge, and it is true that he isolated himself in it for the greater part of each day (and night), imposing on himself an unrelenting discipline of prolonged, undisturbed writing; but it is equally true that he thrived on opportunities to emerge from its rarefied atmosphere in order to convey directly to an audience the fruits of his solitary confinement. In one of his major pre-war essays—"Las palabras y lo indecible" (1936)—he explained, somewhat petulantly, that the ivory tower merely provided the conditions in which poetry could best be encountered; subsequently, the artist (Ramón himself, we may presume) readily renounced his isolation in order to step into the outside world and communicate his findings:

> En cuanto a que la poesía sea un tesoro colectivo, siempre lo ha sido. Si el artista quería publicidad era para poner en manos de todos lo que él había alumbrado del tesoro colectivo.
> Hasta lo que hallaba en su torre de marfil—donde se metía para mayor atención en el hallazgo—lo lanzaba después a los cuatro vientos, y todos, con mínimo esfuerzo, se apoderaban de lo que a él le había costado máximo vigilar. (*T* 199)

The oral performances—and I use this expression deliberately—that Ramón gave in the places I have mentioned (Pombo, the radio studio, the lecture venue) are difficult to discuss critically for the obvious reason that they were, by their very nature, ephemeral. They are known not through any direct record but rather through second-hand reports which, despite their occasional vividness, only give a partial, often purely anecdotal version of their nature and impact. These constraints have conspired to give the impression that these performances are marginal to an understanding of Ramón's work—mere liminal light accompaniment to the written texts that make up its solid fixed core. It is my contention, however, that they were or at least became central to his purpose and represent the most dynamic illustration of his art. In the pages that follow I propose to take on the difficulties inherent in this kind of oral creativity and to dwell on its most memorable expression: the public lecture. My argument, in essence, will be that Ramón made of the lecture a genre as distinctive as the *greguería* itself: radically innovative, highly personal, ultimately inimitable. This argument will be based on a discussion of relevant available material from different sources but will take as its key point of reference the sole surviving recorded example of Ramón speaking publicly.

As a preamble to this discussion we need to go back and pick up on two references made in passing in the selections already quoted. The first is to "el don elocuente del monólogo" and the second to "la nueva manera de hablar." Although these phrases lend themselves to different interpretations, they do suggest that Ramón attached a particular creative value to the spoken word, setting it alongside its written counterpart as an equally valid potential means of implementing the artistic revolution to which he aspired. But just as the written word needed to be revitalized and made to express new things in new ways, so too Ramón realized that conventional oratory needed to be subjected to radical revision.[13] He vehemently attacked the turgid solemnity of traditional public speaking, denouncing the hackneyed rhetoric of politicians, intellectuals and academics who used any available forum to harangue their listeners mechanically and listlessly:

> Desprecio y odio esa grotesca seriedad humana de los actos públicos que cree que no es estéril toda sensación académica que no aporte ni nueva cordialidad, ni nuevo conocimiento, ni nueva literatura. Por eso descompongo esos actos públicos siempre que puedo y rompo su patrón. (AM 383)[14]

Ramón clearly believed in the need for a fresh style of public speaking, more in tune with the times, able to convey something genuinely new in a genuinely original way. He set himself the goal of devising a new framework for the lecture, rooted in his own temperament, faithful to his artistic convictions:

> Contra la mentira de la conferencia yo quería oponer la conferencia que nace del alma como una creación espontánea [...]. Mis conferencias no han de servir para engañar a nadie ni para chocar,

---

[13] Ramón's denunciation of "eloquence" surely included its oral as well as its written forms. I am thinking of such statements as the following: "Nos llamarán estrupadores, violadores, infanticidas, parricidas, sádicos, quebrantahuesos, asesinos, pero hay que acabar con las elocuencias" ("Mis siete," T 89).

[14] In the same vein, he refers on another occasion to his deliberately subversive approach to traditional public speaking: "Una de las cosas que más irritan en mí es que descompongo la seriedad y tiesura de los otros—sus chaquets y sus levitas" (AM 382).

sino para mostrar el tono de una sinceridad no *trucada* por la oratoria, realizando ilusiones juveniles de las palabras y procurando que todo esté devuelto a sus ángulos y a sus aristas. (AM 382)

What needs to be looked at now are the ways in which Ramón developed his approach to the public lecture, gradually reinventing it as a new genre, transforming it into an original medium for communicating to the public his central concerns as a writer.

•

Ramón became accustomed to public speaking at the very outset of his career. In accordance with the general practice in Spain at the beginning of the twentieth century he delivered some of his earliest programatic texts—such as "El concepto de la nueva literatura" (1909)—to audiences at traditional venues like the Ateneo. But despite the radical content and tone of those talks, their delivery seems to have been fairly conventional, with the writer dutifully reading a prepared script that was subsequently made available in its entirety in printed form for general consumption.[15] Unsurprisingly, however, Ramón soon became dissatisfied with the academic formality and predictability of such occasions and began playfully subverting them. At a meeting of the Academia de la Jurisprudencia, for example, he caused something of a scandal by reading out his own letter of apology for absence (AM 383). When he was elected secretary of the literary section of the Ateneo, he provoked a similarly outraged response by reading the minutes of a previous meeting in what was judged to be irreverent fashion (AM 360). These were early signs of Ramón's provocative nonconformism straying into the realm of public speaking.

In his autobiography Ramón explicitly identifies the emergence of what he calls "mi nueva forma de conferenciar" (AM 382). It occurred on the occasion of the first exhibition in Madrid of paintings by his friend Gustavo de Maeztu.[16] "Yo hablo con unas casitas de nacimiento

---

[15] Antonio Ruiz Salvador describes the experience of reading a "memoria" at the Ateneo as the "vía ortodoxa" for any young aspiring intellectual of the time (76). Gaspar Gómez de la Serna notes, however, that for the occasion of his début in the Ateneo Ramón had planned to wear a "traje claro, corbata hidrofoba y guantes de color" but had been unable to do so since he was still in mourning for the death of his grandfather (59).

[16] Unhelpfully, few details are given and no precise date is attached to the event, though it seems to have taken place in 1923 (Gaspar Gómez de la Serna

sobre la mesa" (AM 382), he comments, signalling that his innovation lay in the use of props to accompany his talk. How exactly they were used and to what purpose is unclear, but the appearance of "visual aids" in front of the speaker—either to distract the audience or to illustrate in some way the topic under review—inaugurated what would become a standard feature of Ramón's lecturing style.

The year 1923 was, in fact, an important one for Ramón the lecturer. To relieve his unease at the heavily politicized atmosphere in the country produced by the advent of the military dictatorship of Primo de Rivera, he accepted invitations to speak in several cities.[17] Furthermore, it was the year of his extraordinary lecture in Madrid at the Circo Americano, given from a trapeze, to mark the publication of his book *El Circo*. I shall return to this event later. Subsequently, he seems to have given talks on an intermittent basis in response to a particular need or invitation or to commemorate a significant occasion of some kind. Worthy of mention in this context would be the talk he gave in 1930 "pintado de negro" (AM 389) at the Cineclub Español in Madrid when Al Jolson's *The Jazz Singer* was first screened in Spain: "Difícil es hablar frente a una sábana de proyectar películas, porque se destaca uno frente a ella como la mosca más irresistible, la mosca que se posa en la pantalla. Quería hablar del jazz y que se me creyera un poco más y no se desconfiase de mí cuando hablase de las selvas vírgenes y del Misisipí" (AM 389).

Talks such as these must have consolidated Ramón's reputation at the time as a highly original writer with a taste for entertaining showmanship. They would certainly have provided him with a welcome source of income, helping him to maintain the independence he defended so tenaciously in financial circumstances whose precariousness belied the magnitude of his fame. But it was not until the early thirties that Ramón devoted time systematically to public speaking. In those years, undoubtedly building on the foundation of earlier performances, he developed what appears to have been a fairly coherent thematic repertoire and refined his style of delivery. Three experiences combined to give this momentum to Ramón's lecturing career. First,

---

150). Presumably Ramón's lecture involved presenting Maeztu's work at the opening of the exhibition.

[17] Gaspar Gómez de la Serna notes that in October 1923 Ramón undertook "una serie muy nutrida de conferencias con sorpresivo resultado por toda España [...] Bilbao, Gijón, Granada [...], derramando la simiente de su fama ya madura" (150).

in 1931 he was invited to Buenos Aires by Bebé Sansinena de Elizalde, a friend of Ortega, to give a series of seven lectures for the association of "Amigos del Arte." He enjoyed great success and later commented in his autobiography: "[E]l público entraba con entusiasmo en mi investigación de lo absurdo y lo arbitrario. ¡Nos entendíamos!" (*AM* 549). On the basis of this success, he was invited to lecture in other Argentinian cities (Mendoza, Córdoba, Santiago del Estero, Azul, etc.) and in neighboring countries: Uruguay, Paraguay and Chile. His stay in South America ended up lasting some eight months. Second, on his return to Spain in 1932 he was contracted by his friend Arturo Soria y Espinosa to give lectures in a variety of Spanish cities under the auspices of the "Comités de Cooperación Intelectual."[18] Using the opportunity this arrangement offered to show Spain to his new Argentinian wife, Ramón lectured in, among other cities, Santiago, Vigo, Lugo, Burgos, Alicante, Seville, Segovia and Palencia. Third, he returned to Argentina in 1933, again invited by Sansinena de Elizalde, and undertook another extensive and triumphant lecture tour of the country.

Although it is impossible to compile a definitive list of the precise subjects of these lectures, the main topics can easily be identified. These can be summarized according to the following categories:

1. Characters from the past of literary, artistic or historical interest, such as Edgar Allen Poe, Napoleon, Goya, El Greco, Velázquez, José Gutiérrez Solana, Góngora, Larra, Carolina Coronado and Quevedo.

2. Places, such as Madrid, the Rastro and the Café Pombo.

3. "Phenomena" (literary, artistic or other), such as humor, bullfighting, *lo cursi*, death, magic in literature, jazz, the circus and the *greguería*.

4. Objects and living organisms, such as streetlamps, butterflies, paper birds, fish, bottles, bells, plus all the assorted objects used in the so-called "suitcase" or "trunk" lectures.

All these subjects are related in one way or another to Ramón's published work. As is well known, he wrote long biographical sketches of several of the writers and painters mentioned above, devoted entire books to the circus, Pombo, the Rastro and Madrid, and wrote substantial essays on topics like humor, death and *lo cursi*. Similarly, countless objects and animals appear in the thousands of *greguerías* he published

---

[18] On the activities of the Comités in general, see my "Culture in the Second Republic: The *Comités de Cooperación Intelectual*;" for further details concerning Ramón's association in this context with Arturo Soria y Espinosa, see my "Cinco cartas inéditas de Gómez de la Serna."

during his lifetime. This relationship is important to bear in mind since it helps to clarify the nature of Ramón's apparently improvised oral style.

Ramón described his lectures in general as "lírico-humorísticas" (Dennis, "Cinco cartas" 14). As a generic definition, the epithet is particularly revealing and links up with my earlier remarks about the essential characteristics of Ramón's artistic enterprise as a whole. On the one hand, the writer stresses how his lectures drew out the lyrical qualities of his subjects, especially the mundane objects he dwelt on with such fascination. So much of his work, after all, is bound up with what has been called "la revelación sensorial del mundo" (Soldevila 37), foregrounding—to return to a phrase already quoted—"la poesía de lo que se levanta sobre lo cotidiano." On the other hand, the allusion to the humorous dimension of his lectures frames them as amusements or entertainments, offering comic relief to his audiences with the same compassionate motives already described.

Although Ramón did not always lecture in theaters, his talks became more and more theatrical as the years went by.[19] He freely indulged his taste for histrionics in a number of different ways, consistently transforming any platform from which he spoke into a stage. First, he made abundant use of props. These allowed him to give a visual dimension to the spoken word, graphically conjuring up for his

---

[19] It would not be out of place to note, albeit in passing, Ramón's passionate interest in the theater in the early stages of his career. See, for example, the studies by Agustín Muñoz-Alonso López and Carmen Herrera Vecino and the recent edition of the writer's *Teatro muerto*. Particularly significant about this early dramatic work—at least for the purposes of this essay—is Ramón's interest in the genre of pantomime, stemming from his exposure to pantomime performances in Paris during his early stays there in 1909. His handling of the genre demonstrates an acute sensitivity towards the effects of gesture, movement and appearance, all of which would feed into his own performances as a public speaker. According to Gaspar Gómez de la Serna, at least on one occasion Ramón actually combined a pantomime—entitled *Fiesta de dolores*—with a lecture: "[La] escribió para ilustrar con su representación la conferencia que sobre la danza pronunció su autor en el Palacio de Cristal del Retiro, durante una exposición de arte decorativo" (57). There is also an obvious connection here with the silent cinema. On this point see Soldevila's remarks on the "cinematic" qualities of Ramón's prose (35-39). Agustín Sánchez Vidal argues that, from the perspective of the young Buñuel, anxious to collaborate with Ramón, the *greguería* was the verbal equivalent of the cinematic "gag" (23).

audience the subjects (and objects) he was discussing. To illustrate his lecture on butterflies he would use a large collection of artificial butterflies, especially two enormous colored ones he had cut from a chorus-girl's dress he had found in the Rastro.[20] For his fish lecture, he would place on the table a large fishbowl with a live fish swimming around inside it, interpreting its "lenguaje burbujido" and movements as he went along (AM 389).[21] When he lectured on Pombo, he would set up on stage, on an easel, the famous painting of the founding members of the group by Gutiérrez Solana (now in the Reina Sofía Museum in Madrid) and refer to it in order to illustrate the topic. He would adopt the same approach when speaking about El Greco, using a large reproduction of the famous portrait of a *Gentleman with a Hand on his Breast*, though with the twist that in this case, thanks to an elaborate hidden contraption devised by Ramón himself, the gentleman's arm could be made to move up or down according to what was being said and how long it had taken. In his 1949 lecture on "La magia en la literatura," Ramón had recourse to a "contradictor," a puppet wearing a top hat that he positioned on the table in front of him and that animatedly disputed everything he said.[22] The same lecture ended

---

[20] See Ramón's own comment in *Automoribundia*: "Saqué mis cartones de mariposas de lentejuelas, entre las que se destacaban dos enormes fulgóridas que yo había arrancado hacía años a un traje luminoso de cupletista comprado en el Rastro" (550).

[21] Ramón goes into considerable detail concerning his preparations to give the fish lecture in a curious article entitled "El falso micrófono," published in the radio journal *Ondas* in 1928. He mentions there that he also placed a false microphone on the table when he spoke, apparently to encourage the audience to believe that its responses were being broadcast and so persuade them to be benevolent. More significantly, in terms of the comments I will be making about the nature of Ramón's improvisation in his lectures, he lists some of the *greguerías* he made use of during the lecture: "La tela que tejen las arañas del mar es tela impermeable;" "Los peces tienen algo de almohadillas, tanto que se nota el pespunte con el que están cosidos;" "El lenguado es un pez al que atropelló un buque de gran carga;" "Los nenúfares son las soperas de los peces;" etc.

[22] Reported by Flórez, who notes that Ramón illustrated his lecture "colocando en una botella que saca de detrás de la mesa del estrado, su contradictor, un polichinela con sombrero de copa, con el que dialoga violentamente" (387). There are clear reminiscences here of the "Punch and Judy" tradition of children's theater. It is interesting to note that according to Agustín Muñoz-Alonso López and Jesús Rubio Jiménez in their edition of *Teatro muerto*, it was Ramón's exposure to this in his own childhood that initiated him into "la

with Ramón slipping over his own body the headless torso of a dummy constructed in his own image—even down to the detail of the color of the tie he was wearing that evening—in order to bring his talk to a stunning close.[23]

Ramón clearly used these props to great dramatic effect at times. He engineered a powerfully theatrical beginning to his lecture on streetlamps, for example, by appearing on stage carrying a lamplighter as if in readiness to light the lamp he had brought with him from home.[24] He was adept at "setting the scene," visually preparing his audience for what was to come, as can be gauged from this description of the opening scene of his lecture on Carolina Coronado:

> El escenario presenta un caballete con el retrato romántico, pintado por Federico de Medraza, de la escritora del Romanticismo [...]. En el centro, una mesa cubierta de terciopelo rojo, sobre la que lucen unos candelabros igualmente románticos con velas rojas. Ramón "está a la mesa," destacando una chistera que luego resulta ser "Castora clac." (Flórez 388)

Second, as the above description implies, Ramón had no qualms about dressing up, sometimes outlandishly, in order to act out some complementary or even central role in his lectures.[25] In fact, he seems

---

magia del teatro" (30). Ramón evidently held its liberating effects in high esteem and must have sought to reproduce them in some of his own lectures: "El teatro de los niños capta al niño, le dispone a tomar las tangencias porque su espíritu se despliega, se abre ante el espectáculo, como no lo hace en casa, en el colegio, por naturales recelos y por lo *relativo* que se hace en esos junto a los mayores" (31).

[23] It was a stunning but macabre and embittered close since the decapitation was designed to make the point that the writer sacrifices his own head in order to entertain his readers: " [Q]ueda encapuchado y hace ademán de ofrecer al público ateneístico la embriaguez de una gran copa que semeja una cabeza, y cuando la alza como para beberla 'no encuentra su boca porque el literato ofrece beber a los demás en su propio cráneo'" (Flórez 388).

[24] The audience's reaction is captured in a contemporary newspaper report reproduced in *Automoribundia*: "Cuando Ramón penetró en el salón con un encendedor de faroles de gas en la mano, a manera de báculo, se desbordó el alborozo del público, turbado y regocijado por aquella insólita entrada del conferenciante" (386).

[25] Again, there are undeniable precedents for this in Ramón's own youth. The writer's brother Julio recalled in 1963: "Le recuerdo como actor adoles-

to have taken delight in any opportunity to become himself part of the spectacle he was offering. So, when speaking about Napoleon, he would appear on stage wearing an unmistakably Napoleonic hat, would don period costume to speak about Goya, or dress in a full suit of lights in order to expound his views on bullfighting. I have already referred to the occasion in 1930 when, presenting Al Jolson in the film *The Jazz Singer*, Ramón put on blackface, ostensibly to give greater credibility to his remarks on life in the Deep South. He gave several lectures on his notorious play *Los medios seres*, appearing with one half of his body and clothes painted black and the other half white, just as the characters in the play had done when it was staged in Madrid at the end of 1929.[26]

Third, Ramón liked to heighten the visual impact of his lectures by introducing into them, at some appropriate moment, what he called "alguna experiencia expuesta" (*AM* 619). Such "experiments" ranged from a provocative gesture (revealing, for example, that the bottle on the table in front of him contained sherry instead of water) to what amounted to a magic trick. Jorge Guillén, for example, recounted how, ending his address to the "Cercle Littéraire Internationale" in Paris in 1928, Ramón surprised his audience by producing, like a white rabbit from a tophat, a string of miniature Spanish and French

---

cente haciendo uno de los papeles principales de ese drama, tan ripiosamente truculento, *El puñal del godo*, para una representación dada en nuestra casa con un público de familiares y allegados. Los jóvenes actores lucían atuendos arbitrarios y barbas y melenas de estopa" (qtd. in Herrero Vecino 1). In "El concepto de la nueva literatura" Ramón states quite boldly: "El ideal del estilo está en alcanzar la expresión de un [...] gran actor" (*T* 64). There is much theatricality in the fancy-dress banquets that he organized as a young man, particularly in Pombo. Flórez reproduces in his book a photo, taken in 1935, of Ramón, Salvador Bartolozzi and Antoniorrobles dressed up as "Los Reyes Magos de la Cabalgata del Gremio de Editores de Madrid" (106). Ramón confessed to being inspired by his own acting ability at times: "En una conferencia de escenario, al final, sintiéndome un gran actor, mimé la escena del morir, y me morí" (*AM* 620).

[26] I give details of Ramón's involvement in the production of this play in "El ir y venir de Ramón Gómez de la Serna," the introduction to my edition of his *París*, especially the section entitled "El heroico desaguisado de *Los medios seres*" (34-42).

flags.[27] In similar vein, though producing more consternation than amusement, Ramón offered a practical example of what he understood humor to be by suddenly interrupting his lecture on the topic and eating the candles in the holders in front of him on the table. He rounded off his lectures on *greguerías* in South America with a memorable festive flourish, releasing a hundred balloons into the halls he spoke in. To the string of each balloon was tied a small strip of yellow paper on which was written, in Ramón's own hand, a *greguería*, thereby providing the lucky members of the audience with a material souvenir of the genre he had been discussing.[28] But perhaps his most shocking and effective "experiencia expuesta" used to come at the beginning of his lectures on *lo cursi* when, to illustrate his contempt for the products of this style and to communicate to the audience the need to rid the world of them, he would histrionically shatter some object he had painstakingly located and purchased on the same day in a local shop. Ramón's own description of the impact this practice had is worth reproducing:

> Al principio de mis conferencias rompía con un martillo un objeto cursi en holocausto a los dioses. Quería educar de paso a los niños para que rompieran los objetos banales en vez de romper a lo mejor un importante tibor japonés. No sé si los dioses se aplaca-

---

[27] Guillén's exact words are worth reproducing: "[Ramón] tiró de un hilo, se descorrió una envoltura, y surgió un ramillete de banderitas francesas y españolas" (qtd. in *AM* 365). The gesture is manifestly that of a magician.

[28] This festive gesture of distributing mementos to the audience was repeated in other contexts. For example, Ramón gave out butterfly rattles at the end of his lecture on butterflies in Buenos Aires in 1931: "[D]i una conferencia poética que no podía repetir ya nunca pasado aquel día de credulidad y de ingenua buena fe de Buenos Aires de una singular tarde de primavera en que la calle Florida a la salida de mi conferencia tuvo alegre ruido de un clic con figura de mariposa que regalé con profusión" (*AM* 55). Interestingly, Ramón himself stresses the unrepeatability of the occasion. He did the same, though on more than one occasion, with the small bells ("cascabeles") that in a sense functioned as emblems of the joyful spirit of his public lectures: "[L]os compraba por gruesas y los tiraba al público después de mis conferencias [...]. He llegado a sembrar cascabeles por el mundo esperando que apareciese al fin el deseado árbol cascabelero [...]. Esa boca rasgada que tiene cada cascabel lleva la curvatura de la sonrisa—risa con boqueras—, y pone rumbo de fiesta donde quiera que suene" (*AM* 552).

rían con mi ofrenda votiva, pero en la sala se desmayó alguna señorita después de gritar histéricamente "¡No! ¡No!" (AM 550)

In order to pull into focus the sense of the originality of Ramón's lectures—the way they were conceived and executed—it is helpful to look briefly at a few specific examples and at a general format he used frequently. His two circus lectures of the 1920s are probably the best known and with good reason since they were without doubt his most audacious and spectacular. Despite the fact that they were, like all performances of this kind, "one-off," unique and unrepeatable, they do offer the advantage of being the best documented: Ramón himself refers to them both in his autobiography in some detail, and on each occasion notable members of the audience wrote reviews of them. As I have already mentioned, the first took place in Madrid in 1923 on the occasion of a homage paid to the writer by the Circo Americano, presumably for what might be termed "services rendered to circus culture."[29] His choice of venue to receive and to respond to this homage by way of a public address was carefully and logically made: what better place for a circus orator than the circus itself? The issue of how exactly to address the audience was quickly resolved: "Surgió el elefante en mi imaginación, como estrado magnífico para un orador; pero como ahora no tiene elefantes el Circo Americano pensé en el trapecio" (AM 352).[30] As allergic as ever to formality, Ramón chose his outfit with an appropriate sense of fun. He wore a dinner jacket but pretended it had not been finished on time by making the stitching on it clearly visible and by attaching to it a series of tailor's labels.[31] Having

---

[29] His book *El circo* had appeared in 1917; a second edition came out in 1923. Ramón prided himself on being "el primer cronista del circo."

[30] As a preparation for what I will say about the film *El orador*, we might note that Ramón took a passing swipe from his trapeze at conventional speakers, stressing the distance that separated him from them: "Así por primera vez, realizo con franqueza lo que muchos oradores hacen sin darse cuenta: columpiarse y estar en el trapecio de la coladura" (AM 352).

[31] The unfinished evening wear appears as the subject of "La prueba," one of the texts Ramón included in *Gollerías* (162-64), where he goes as far as to reproduce two of his own drawings of the outfit, commenting: " [C]on los pespuntes claros y entrecruzados, mi aire de humorista sería tan halagüeño que mi traje quedaría convertido en el traje atributivo del humorista" (164). In mock apology to his audience in 1923, he explained his appearance in the following terms: "Llevaba mi frac hilvanado y con las etiquetas del sastre pegadas. Pedí disculpa al público porque 'el sastre me había llevado tarde

climbed up a rope ladder and taken his seat on the trapeze, he explained that as a "circus orator"—"nuevo género de la oratoria" (*AM* 352)—his talk would be prudently brief. The text of his talk was written on one long roll of paper which he unfurled as he spoke. He reassured his audience by explaining the sense of this touch, evidently another defiant gesture against the traditional public speaker who usually appeared weighed down by a pile of sheets of paper: "No os asustéis. Todo lo quería traer escrito en una sola cuartilla, puesto que alarman tanto los mazos de papel con que se presentan algunos oradores" (*AM* 352). Furthermore, he pointed out that if he got into difficulty on the trapeze, he would be able to use the long roll of paper as an escape ladder: "En caso de apuro bajaré por la escala de mi larga cuartilla" (*AM* 352).

Despite the festiveness of the event, Ramón did not fail to draw attention to its underlying seriousness, referring explicitly to the sense he attached to his performance:

> El que habla desde un trapecio es como el que os habla en su lecho de muerte.
> "Soy así"—es la única disculpa que se me ocurre. Yo amo y siento esto, convencido de que la vida es una cosa grotesca, que donde se exhibe mejor es donde lo grotesco se armoniza y adquiere expresión artística, arrebatadora: en el circo. (*AM* 353)

In short, his true purpose was to provide a practical demonstration for his audience: given its nature, life needed to be lived "según la gran lección que da el circo" (*AM* 353), camouflaging its gloom with clownish entertainment.

Ramón reproduced in *Automoribundia* two eye-witness reports of his performance that appeared at the time in the Madrid press. The first, by Roberto Castrovido, published in *La Voz*, acknowledges the virtues of the lecture as Ramón himself would have perceived them: "Dar alegría, insuflar infantilismo y rejuvenecer es más de agradecer que el dinero" (qtd. in *AM* 356). The second, by the distinguished theater critic and poet, Enrique Díez-Canedo, appeared in *El Sol* and drew attention to Ramón's consummate skills as a public performer:

---

aquel frac, que yo había querido estrenar en la función que se daba en mi honor'" (*AM* 352).

> No dejaremos [...] de alabar como cumple la soltura de su presentación en la pista, la agilidad con que trepó por la escala al columpio aéreo, su perfecto *métier* al sentarse en la estrecha barra, su elegante descenso por la maroma, el arte con que saludó al público que le llamaba a la pista. (AM 357)[32]

Ramón's second circus lecture was given in Paris in 1928 on the occasion of a homage paid to him by another circus company, the Cirque d'Hiver, to commemorate the publication of the French edition of his book *El Circo*. This time he was able to execute his original plan of 1923 to deliver his address mounted on an elephant. It was possibly his finest hour, a resounding confirmation of his unmistakeable public profile. The event was witnessed and reported in the Madrid press by, among others, Ventura García Calderón, who began his remarks by broaching the problem of how exactly to define it: "¿Era una fiesta búdica, un episodio de *Las mil y una noches*, un desfile de carnestolendas o la navidad del humorismo? Era, en todo caso, la más risueña y moderna cinta" (qtd. in AM 480). García Calderón's uncertainty concerning the generic status of Ramón's performance is understandable since what he saw and described was clearly unique, entirely Ramón's own personal creation, something mid-way between a spectacle and a celebration, infused with a joyful sense of extravagant originality:

> Del lomo de su montura, como de un casillero polvoriento, [Ramón] iba sacando cuartillas para lanzarnos a la cabeza adjetivos y tropos deslumbradores. Leía en voz altisonante, con la cabeza erguida al cielo del circo, donde rebrillan los trapecios como telarañas, donde asoman la cabeza decapitada los payasos, donde están—sólo visibles para el poeta—los aros de plata y de plenilunio que destrozan las *écuyères* con un salto rubio [...].
>
> [...] Ramón iba tirando al suelo cada página leída, como si fueran cartas de amor o mensajes de Kipling. (qtd. in AM 480-81)

The report that Jean Cassou, the translator of Ramón's book, wrote for the journal *Les Nouvelles Littéraires* was entitled simply "Poésie."

---

[32] It is a tribute to Ramón's professionalism as a performer that he hid from the audience the fact that at the end of the lecture he badly burned his hands as he slid down—too fast—the rope swinging from the trapeze. He complains in his autobiography that he had to wear bandages for a month.

The word encapsulated the central impulse behind his friend's memorable performance (and behind many of his other public lectures), namely the desire to share with an audience his insights into "la poesía que se levanta sobre lo cotidiano":

> Pour lui, en effet, la poésie n'est pas une délectation secrète, mais un charme communiquable et à quoi tous les hommes d'un même temps peuvent participer, comme lui-même, dans la richesse de ses élans, participe à la joie universelle.

It is worth noting that on both these occasions Ramón read from a prepared text and that in Paris he spoke in French. Equally significant is the fact that, according to the writer's own confession, both talks included material taken directly from his book on the circus, in one case a long string of *greguerías*.[33]

The most characteristic and frequently given lecture in Ramón's repertoire was the "conferencia maleta" [suitcase lecture], subsequently expanded to become the "conferencia baúl" [trunk lecture]. In terms of public response, it was also the most successful. The writer must have considered it to be his most personal and valuable invention since on one occasion he mentioned that he had taken out a patent on it.[34] The truth is that nobody else could have devised a spectacle quite like it. Although no two suitcase lectures were identical, for the simple reason that Ramón constantly modified the material he worked with and almost certainly improvised much of what he said, the procedure he used was fairly standard—what he himself described as "prestidigitación cándida" (AM 551). He would appear on stage with a large suitcase at his side and then proceed to extract from it the various objects

---

[33] Commenting in his autobiography on the 1923 lecture, Ramón explains: "Y entonces leí una larga tirada de *greguerías* de las que después aparecieron en la segunda edición de *El circo*" (AM 355). Later in the same book, having reproduced a good portion of García Calderón's newspaper account of his 1928 lecture, he states: "Después venía mi discurso, pero sus ideas están ya en mi libro *El circo*, y no es cosa de que me repita" (481). It is a curious remark since throughout *Automoribundia* Ramón shamelessly "repeats himself," cutting and pasting from previously published work in the process of creating the collage of his own life.

[34] In "El falso micrófono," in which Ramón describes the elaborate preparations for his fish lecture, he comments: "No sólo llevaría a la conferencia la maleta con los objetos varios que la van platificando—patente de invención 927,488—y la pecera iluminadora sino un micrófono."

it contained, placing them one by one in front of him and subjecting each to a commentary. This commentary would involve an imaginative, metaphorical interpretation of the object's attributes or some kind of lyrical or comic gloss on it. The strategy was essentially the same as he used for his fish lecture or his streetlamp lecture, the only difference being that in these cases the entire lecture would be devoted to a single object.[35] How such lectures generally unfolded can be seen in this description of his reflections on the streetlamp:

> Vio el farol horrorizado que presenciaba los crímenes de la calle, el farol que da cultura a los serenos y a los cocheros, obligados a continuo velatorio, el farol de las citas y de las meditaciones [...]. Contó al farol de las revoluciones donde cabalgaban Dantón y Marat para dirigir sus alocuciones rebeldes a la muchedumbre, y al farol humano de los borrachos, que les acoge cuando todos les abandonan. (AM 386-87)

In other words, the object was seen from different angles, imagined in different contexts, brought to life by the speaker's ability to assign or extract characteristics that would not have been perceived by—or would not have occurred to—the normal onlooker. Moving from one dimension to another, Ramón accumulated nuances of meaning or "identity," humanizing, representing, revealing and recreating the object before the audience.

The objects Ramón used in his suitcase lectures could not have been more miscellaneous. They were his own possessions, gathered in an anarchic and seemingly arbitrary fashion from such places as the Rastro where he could indulge his fascination with the variety and suggestiveness of things: "Cosas carnales, entrañables, dementes, lejanas, cercanas, distintas; cosas reveladoras en su insignificancia, en su llaneza, en su mundanidad. ¡Maravillosas asociadoras de ideas!" ("Rastro," T 33). Some of these possessions were evidently quite bizarre, though many were simple everyday items that, for one reason or another, caught his attention. To the best of my knowledge, Ramón only went into detail about the objects he would typically use in a suitcase lecture on one occasion. Referring to his tour of South America in 1931 and the problems he had at various frontiers with customs officers who were understandably puzzled and suspicious of his luggage,

---

[35] Details of how his fish lecture developed are given in the text cited in the previous note.

he partially itemized the material he had been carrying around with him:

> Bolas lucientes de pasamanos de escaleras; bolas de mi brillante techo; una estrella de mar disecada; soldados de un juego de bolos; una guitarra a la que quitaba la madera de su frontis y aparecía con un corazón colgante, tripajos, el rayado de las costillas y la dorsal al fondo; peones de música; una cabeza frenológica sobre cuyos casilleros numerados ponía la peluca blanca de la experiencia; la siringa del alfilador; una cabeza de pim-pam-pum con algo de buzón de los niños; un plumero amarillo; un despertador; un candelabro de velas ante el que surgía Gerardo de Nerval; los anillos del diablo que compré en Berlín; un llamador; pisapapeles; pájaros cantores; una esponja; muñecas rusas de esas de las que se saca mucha familia, etc. etc. (AM 551)

While the disparate and undifferentiated nature of the objects may be disconcerting, they draw attention as a whole to one of the central features of Ramón's perception of reality and to the means he devised to express it. Under Ramón's gaze, reality became fragmented, atomized, broken down into its component parts.[36] Instead of embracing the world around him as a unified whole and trying to represent it as a single, harmonious, intelligible entity, he disassembled it, focusing rather on the isolated, self-contained fragment. He defined his perceptual strategy as "el punto de vista de la esponja," explaining its advantages:

> Ese pretenso ente esponjiario y agujereado que queremos ser para no soportar la monotonía y el tópico, para salvarnos a la limitación de nosotros mismos, mira en derredor como en un delirio de esponja con cien ojos, apreciando las relaciones insospechadas entre las cosas. ("Palabras [...] indecible," T 188)

It was a strategy that fed into Ramón's notion of the redemptive function of innovative art, providing a way of avoiding the constraints of repetition or predictability, and generating that expansive alertness

---

[36] My perspective on this aspect of Ramón's work is more fully developed in my introduction to *Studies on Ramón Gómez de la Serna*: "Ramón at the Centenary: The Parts of the Whole" (7-22).

which, he believed, incorporated into life the indispensable revitalizing and liberating element of revelation and surprise.

By adopting this strategy in his writing—and by extending it to his lectures—Ramón was able to break reality down into its myriad facets, compiling a kind of immense inventory of the world around him. He made no attempt to make the countless objects and phenomena he registered conform to any hierarchical order or pattern of differentiated meanings since, as he himself recognized, "el punto de vista de la esponja es la visión varia, neutralizada, sin predilecciones, multiplicada" ("Palabras [...] indecible," *T* 188).[37] This was something Borges understood about Ramón when he remarked: "[S]e encariña con [las cosas], las acaricia y las requiebra, pero la satisfacción que le dan es suelta y sin prejuicio de unidad" (125). It comes as no surprise, then, that Ramón considered himself to be "el protector de las cosas" ("Cosas," *T* 173).[38] He believed that within the disparate objects scattered throughout the world there lay some kind of key that could unlock a concealed higher truth about the universe:

> Un tarugo de madera, un gran clavo, un cenicero son elementos filosofales, claves de universo, sino que guardando la incógnita de por qué lo son. Para mí es astrolabio cualquier cosa pequeña, un enchufe desprendido, un salero cipotal [...]. De la carambola de las cosas brota una verdad superior, esa realidad transformadora del mundo que le da mayor sentido. ("Cosas," *T* 175-76)

Alert and receptive to that "higher truth," he gravitated towards those modest miscellaneous objects he saw around him, conscious of a kind of frustrated communication: "Las cosas quieren decirnos algo pero no pueden. Tienen millones de bocas, pero no pueden centrar por una sola boca una sola clase de lengua" ("Cosas," *T* 176). What Ramón did, in effect, in his capacity as "protector of things," was to take on the role of mouthpiece or spokesman for the mute contents of

---

[37] In the same connection, see his comment in "Las cosas y el 'ello'": "Las cosas siempre han sido para mí ostensorios de la fuerza cohesiva del mundo en el que es indiferente ser una cosa u otra. Igual me daba ser tintero, que jaula, que bola de cristal" (*T* 174).

[38] Ramón pursues this idea in "Los suplicios de las cosas" (*Gollerías* 195-98) where he muses about founding an "Asociación Protectora de Cosas."

the world, giving voice—his own—to the "vida incesante y sidérea" he sensed seethed unnoticed within the everyday ("Cosas," *T* 173).[39]

Such a sustained and absorbing relationship with the smallest segments of reality found its natural vehicle for expression in the micro-text of the *greguería*. As genre, the *greguería* was the aptest mold into which the writer's disconnected perceptions of the outside world could be contained and, in a sense, Ramón's books of *greguerías* are emblems of his writing as a whole: accumulations of fragments, amalgams of isolated insights and interpretations. It has often been said that in his novels Ramón simply strings together *greguerías* like so much decorative bunting—"serpentinas y farolillos venecianos," to use Max Aub's phrase (74). The same can be said of his other prose works and surely of his lectures too, especially his suitcase lectures. I have already mentioned how at least a part of one of his circus lectures was made up of a series of *greguerías* about the circus, subsequently published. The same is evidently true of his fish lecture. Similarly, the streetlamp lecture seems to have been built up on the basis of a sequence of interpretations of the streetlamp's imagined social and historical experiences. Ramón's suitcase lectures, by the very nature of the disparate material under review in them, would have comprised a discontinuous stream of lyrical/humorous comments, with mini-sequences of *greguería*-like remarks being linked together as the lecture progressed. The only determining structural principle would be the order in which the objects in question were extracted from the suitcase, a largely arbitrary one. It would seem that most, if not all, the fundamental features of Ramón's writing—fragmentation, discontinuity, spontaneity, improvisation—are also reproduced orally in the context of a public lecture. It is precisely because of this that I would argue that Ramón's voice and his pen, his written works and his lectures, are inseparable; they are simply complementary expressions of the central energies at work in his art.

---

[39] Much more could be—and probably needs to be—said about Ramón's strategies of perception. His way of seeing and revealing things did not depend solely on disassembling reality and magnifying its component parts but also involved finding the right angle of vision or access point. Consider these haunting comments on the subject: "Viendo el objeto en buena perspectiva, se ve que vive para la construcción total del universo" ("Cosas," *T* 170); "Todo estriba en saber qué ángulo es el interesante. Hay que enfocar las cosas en ángulo, no demasiado de frente o demasiado a todo lo ancho, y ¡de ninguna manera! en panorama" (*Ismos, T* 111).

•

In 1928 Ramón was filmed in Madrid by Feliciano Vitores using a rudimentary Phonofilm sound system that its American inventor Lee de Forest was trying to market in Spain at the time. Lasting some three and a half minutes, the film carries no opening credits and is known under the title that was used to refer to it in programs and reviews: *El orador* (sometimes *El orador bluff*) or *La mano*.[40] It was shown in Madrid on at least three occasions in 1930 (March, April and November), sharing the billing on the first occasion with Buñuel's *Un chien andalou* and Abel Gance's *The End of the World*, and on the second, with Giménez Caballero's *Noticiario del Cineclub Español* and, once again, the controversial Buñuel film. The fact that this film of Ramón speaking alone to the camera was made in the first place and shown in such company is worthy of comment. It bears witness to Ramón's enthusiasm for the cinema as an innovative, emphatically modern form of expression and means of communication. He clearly approached it with the same eagerness he approached live radio: ready to try it out for himself and to see how he could exploit it creatively for his own artistic ends. The decision to make the film also suggests that already by 1928 Ramón was so well known and admired as a performer and provider of original spectacles that he was judged to be a subject worthy of capturing for posterity. That *El orador* was shown alongside major experimental films of the period, films that have subsequently become milestones in the history of the cinema, indicates the privileged status it enjoyed at the time as an expression of something radically new, decidedly modern and visually compelling.

El orador is the only existing recording of Ramón that combines sound and image. Since he has recourse in it to objects or routines that he is known to have used in his lectures, it has the virtue of providing a unique insight into what Ramón must have been like "live." I offer

---

[40] I am grateful to Vicente Sánchez Biosca for having drawn my attention to this film. There has been a good deal of confusion concerning its date, the circumstances in which it was made, and the correct title for it. For example, in the "Cronología" included in *Práctica fílmica y vanguardia artística en España* (61), it appears in pride of place, dated uncertainly "191... ." It was often thought to have been shot by Giménez Caballero, though in conversation with me (and others) he denied this. According to Mariano de Paco, in his recent study "El teatro de vanguardia," the film is also known under the title *Ramón* (300). On matters of detail I have deferred to Román Gubern, who provides extensive documentation in his *Proyector de luna. La generación del 27 y el cine*.

below a transcription of what Ramón says while on camera, including in square brackets some clarifications concerning the setting and the speaker's gestures and movements.[41]

[El orador]
[*As the film begins, Ramón is already standing, facing the camera, dressed in a jacket and tie with a lighter-colored waistcoat. It is a bare, open-air, daytime setting, possibly the Retiro in Madrid. Ramón is standing in front of a waist-high stone balustrade, with an expanse of water behind him. The frame is limited to his upper body. No other person is visible at any time.*]

[Mi estética][42] no consiste más [*Ramón takes a monocle out of his waistcoat pocket and holds it up*] que en un monóculo sin cristal, monóculo sin cristal con el cual yo veo las cosas de relieve, anotando todo lo que tienen de extraordinario [*inserts monocle in his left eye*]. El monóculo sin cristal es la obsesión de mi servidumbre porque no comprende cómo se puede usar durante el trabajo. [*He replaces the monocle in his waistcoat pocket, extracts a second monocle from another pocket and places it in his eye.*]

Para los salones tengo como invención de última hora el monóculo de nuevo rico, monóculo de nuevo rico que brilla bajo la luz espléndida de las arañas y que le da a uno un tono de barón, de barón de algo.[*He takes the monocle out, puts it back in his waistcoat pocket and buttons up his jacket.*]

---

[41] I made my transcription before coming across Gubern's book, referred to in the previous note, which also includes a transcription (351-52). His coincides with mine as far as Ramón's actual words are concerned; I have adopted his method for rendering Ramón's cock-crowing. However, my punctuation is different from his on several occasions and I have divided up the transcription into shorter paragraphs, in keeping, I would argue, with Ramón's own written practice. Furthermore, this division of the paragraphs serves the case I present later in this essay concerning the close ties between written and oral discourse.

[42] Ramón's speech actually begins—in what seems to me to be mid-sentence—with the words "consiste en." Given that the purpose of his opening remarks is to explain "la base de mi estética," I have taken the liberty of reinserting here what I imagine was lost at the time the recording was made. If what Ramón began with was not "Mi estética," then it is likely that it was a very similar expression—"Mi arte" or "Mi acercamiento a la realidad."

Con estos dos elementos sencillos voy siguiendo la ruta de las cosas.

También dependen mis observaciones de cómo observo vis-à-vis la realidad de la vida. Por ejemplo, mis observaciones del corral. Yo sé hacer el canto del gallo, que es una cosa que casi todo el mundo sabe; pero estas otras cosas más sencillas del corral—por ejemplo, ese despertar en la tarde caliginosa de todo el gallinero:

—[*animated*] poa poa poa poa poa poat-poat ...

Esta cosa lenta:

—[*measured, evenly paced*] poa poa poa poa poa tati poa poa ...

Esos gritos de locura que brotan del corral caliente por agosto:

—[*piercing, drawn out*]¡puaaaaaa! ¡puaaaaa! ...

que son alboroto de todo el pueblo, que son la raya con que se señala toda la dimensión del paisaje.

Todas estas observaciones de la realidad unidas a mi monóculo sin cristal dan la base sincera de mi estética.

Pero para los discursos tengo otro elemento inapreciable, [*Ramón looks briefly away and down to a place off camera to locate the object he is about to use; he can be seen to grab it and hide it behind his back where he puts it on his hand*] elemento que lleva tras mí las multitudes, porque cuando se posee la mano convincente [*having put the glove on his right hand behind his back, he now holds it up in front of him, making the appropriate gestures from here on to accompany his remarks*], la multitud va detrás de esa mano.

Cuando se dice a la multitud "¡Por ahí!," la multitud sigue ese camino. El orador ha de tener esta mano.

Hinchazón de la elocuencia, esta mano produce también un efecto sedante en el público cuando le aconseja paz. Produce las grandes cuestaciones cuando esta mano se dirige siempre a él en son de petición.

Esta mano capta las ideas como mariposas, cogiéndolas en el ambiente y redondeando la oración, gracias a cómo las ha cazado.

Esta mano sirve para señalar cinco razones. Por ejemplo, se suele usar de ella para decir: "Por cinco razones tenéis que seguir este camino," "Cinco razones tengo para deciros esto." Todo el mundo, ante tamañas razones, baja la cabeza apabullado.

Esta mano sirve para en la tempestad del público calmarla plenamente.

Y, por fin, cuando el orador ya está próximo al final de su discurso, sirve para preparar su planear. Porque esta cosa que tiene el orador de aviador, que se remonta, parece que va seguro en sus palabras, de pronto se rompe la cabeza en una de ellas, señala la caída en barrena en esa palabra que le falla. Pero el orador que se domina espera el momento en que planear, y entonces su mano va trabajándose, va descendiendo, va señalando el párrafo final. Esto suele ser muy largo en los oradores porque buscan terreno a propósito, como también lo es en los aviadores que necesitan su terreno ad hoc.

El orador entonces ve ahí en la mesa un tintero o un vaso de agua. Tiene miedo de caer en el tintero o en el vaso de agua. Y entonces, con gran lentitud, para no caer tampoco en una pluma en punta, el orador, tomando sus medidas, concentrándose, coloca su mano sobre la mesa. [*Applause. Ramón bows to the audience, smiling, the large gloved hand across his chest, and walks off to the left out of the shot.*]

There is much that could be said about *El orador* but I will limit my comments to considerations of context, delivery, and content.

The context of the film is contrived in a number of senses. First, the recording has clearly been "staged," though not in the same way that Ramón's public lectures usually were. There is no real audience present beyond the handful of people—friends and technicians, perhaps—who witness the event and whose applause can be heard at the end. Ramón is therefore obliged to imagine an audience, to pretend that there is a crowd there to hear him. However, the artificiality of the situation is by no means a handicap for him and, drawing on his acting skills, brimming with self-confidence, looking around convincingly as if he were surrounded by people, avoiding addressing the camera directly, he maintains this illusion throughout. Second, the brevity of the recording means that any straightforward comparison between it and a public performance that Ramón might have given in normal circumstances has to be suspect.[43] The event we see on screen has been deliberately arranged simply to allow Ramón to speak—to provide an illustration, despite the constraints of time and setting, of the phenomenon of "Ramón speaking," of orally performed, live "ramonismo."[44] This ex-

---

[43] It is hard to say exactly how long Ramón's lectures lasted. He gives the impression of being able to modify the length of any talk to suit the circumstances: "Yo siempre cabalgo con un discurso de cinco minutos, otro de media hora y otro de dos horas y media" (*AM* 388).

[44] According to an editorial published in *La Gaceta Literaria* at the time, and in all probability written by Giménez Caballero, *The Jazz Singer* was shown by the Cineclub in Madrid for exactly the same reasons: "*El cantor de*

Ramón Gómez de la Serna in *El orador*.

jazz no tuvo fortuna en Madrid. Sólo en el Broadway, donde le repartieron tantos puñados de dólares como aquí pisotones. La gente no supo advertir que el Cineclub aportaba este filme de repertorio, ante todo, *para que Gómez de la Serna pudiera hablar*. Pues de no ser sobre un asunto de *jazz*, Ramón no hubiera accedido a presentarse en aquella sesión" (qtd. by Gubern 287-88; my emphasis).

plains the shape of *El orador*: it begins with the writer explaining what his work is about, how he perceives reality and how his perceptions are channelled into his writing. He then provides a few chosen examples of those perceptions, conveying them through extracts of routines he used in other oral performances. What the film offers, then, is Ramón *in nuce*: a synthesis of what a public lecture by him might have been like and of the artistic principles on which it would have implicitly been based. This underlines the fact that, far from being a casual entertainment, the lecture as genre was a fundamental expression of Ramón's world.

Earlier I drew attention to the relationship between Ramón's public lectures and the material he used elsewhere in his published work. The same kind of relationship exists between what Ramón says in *El orador* and certain ideas or routines he had previously developed. The glassless monocle, for example, was by 1928 one of the writer's trademarks since he regularly sported one at the Pombo gatherings and, one may presume, was regularly called upon to explain its significance. While it does function as a prop in the film, it also enjoys an emblematic or symbolic status, representing the unusual way in which Ramón perceived reality. It is precisely because the issue of perception is so central to his work that he makes reference to it at the beginning of his talk, defining it as the foundation of what he does. What the monocle stands for is the unmediated acuity and intensity of his gaze, a gaze which reveals hitherto unnoticed qualities in the smallest things around him. To use the words of José Díaz Fernández when he introduced Ramón at the beginning of a lecture he gave at the Gijón Ateneo in 1923, the monocle "ensancha la pupila y hace temblar a las cosas al sentirse tan escrupulosamente vigiladas" (qtd. in *AM* 386). As time went by Ramón simply made of the glassless monocle the graphic expression of his way of seeing things, stressing—as he does in *El orador*—the sincerity of his perception, his refusal to distort or falsify reality as he saw it. This was the stance he adopted in the free-flowing delirium of his novel-writing when, so he claimed, he would actually put the monocle in as he wrote: "En los momentos en que estoy más en el mundo de lo novelístico, me pongo mi monóculo sin cristal, *este monóculo que es toda mi estética desprovista de engaños*" (*AM* 544; my emphasis).[45]

---

[45] The monocle also appears elsewhere. In "Cedulario del alma" (*Gollerías* 16-19), Ramón writes: "Con mi monóculo sin cristal he observado como al microscopio, muchas almas ocultas" (16). The stress here on how magnifica-

The fact that Ramón uses in a less ambiguous way, more as a straightforward prop, a *second* monocle gives pause for thought and speculation. Could it be that, along the lines of his collections of paperweights, crystal balls and false butterflies, he also possessed several different kinds of monocles? Would they not have lent themselves perfectly to the type of mini-sequence of comments and interpretations he offered in his lectures? While I have found no written evidence to support this, his brief allusion to the nouveau riche monocle does suggest that the process of accumulating variations on a given theme is at work, albeit in truncated form, in *El orador*. Furthermore, this process is clearly applied to the crowing cock and the orator's hand, both of which are shown to perform a string of different expressive functions.

The cock-crowing routine was also a part of Ramón's oral repertoire. Román Gubern sees its origin in a brief text the writer published in 1921 on the crowing cock of the early Pathé newsreels.[46] While this may have sown the seed of an idea in Ramón's mind, he evidently developed it elsewhere and to great effect. In a review of one of his lectures on humor, for example, it appears that he had the audience rolling in the aisles with his mimicry:

> Cuando el público llegó a la mayor hilaridad fue cuando Gómez de la Serna [...] presentó un caso de humorismo imitativo, imitando al gallo con cacareo realista, el gallo perseguido, el gallo al

---

tion allows Ramón's gaze to penetrate what is hidden recalls Ortega's famous comment in *La deshumanización del arte*: "Los mejores ejemplos de cómo por extremar el realismo se le supera—no más que con atender lupa en la mano a lo minúsculo de la vida—son Proust, Ramón Gómez de la Serna y Joyce" (39). It is notable that Ramón invariably insists on the *sincerity* of his way of seeing things, defining his mission as a writer as "poner largas miradas delante de mí y recoger sin falacia y sin engañosa amenidad todo lo que vea con esas miradas a ninguna parte" (AM 345).

[46] The text in question is entitled "El corral de Pathe [sic]" and forms part of a series published under the general title "Ramonismo" in *Ultra*, 13 (10 June 1921): n.p. In it Ramón humorously imagines where the Pathé brothers live and alludes to how the cocks in their farmyard actually sound: "Lo que tienen los hermanos Pathe es un corral inmenso, el más grande corral del mundo, y en él están excluídas las gallinas. Sólo gallos infinitos, innumerables gallos que cantan como gramófonos, con aires de tenores de gramófono, gallos que las noches de luna se proyectan sobre la pantalla cinematográfica de la ley de Cierva y cacarean números. ¡BUENAS NOCHES!"

que se coge y el gallo al que, al fin, se retuerce el pescuezo." (qtd. in AM 384)

Furthermore, since cock-crowing is heard rather than seen, it could be done equally effectively during a radio broadcast. And it turns out that what he called the "psicología de los gallineros" did, in fact, figure in his radio programs.[47] Evidently, what we hear in *El orador* on this score is only a part of Ramón's "observaciones del corral."

The key prop in *El orador* is obviously the artificial hand. According to Gubern, who calls it a "prótesis grotesca," Ramón had used it before in a number of lectures (351).[48] Its exaggerated size makes it the equivalent in this context of the clown's enormous shoes or baggy trousers and as soon as it appears on the screen it becomes the visual point of reference for everything Ramón says, riveting the spectator's attention. Ramón uses it constantly, punctuating his comments with self-consciously theatrical gestures. He illustrates the order given by the orator to the crowd by pointing with one large finger into the air. When he mentions the orator's five reasons, he holds the hand up so that all five digits are clearly visible. To convey visually the analogy between the orator and the aviator,[49] he moves his hand from side to side, imitating the sweeping movements of a plane. And at the end of the talk, the hand comes purposefully down to rest on the table in front of him, tracing the movement of a plane descending to a runway. Word and gesture clearly become powerfully combined through this use of props.

---

[47] See Ventín Pereira 24. In his radio broadcasts Ramón seems to have made use of almost as many sound effects as the props he used in his lectures. In the same article quoted by Ventín Pereira, he mentions his intention to devote a broadcast to "el estudio comparado de los tic-tac." In *Automoribundia* he proudly states: "Todo lo he practicado por la Radio: ruido de llaveros de bolsillo, despertadores, copas, voz de máscara, diálogos con un mudo, diálogos con la Venus de Milo [...]" (505).

[48] Gubern gives no source for this statement. I note that the idea of the expressive hand was worked into his talk of 1930 at the Cineclub on Jolson's *The Jazz Singer*: "Tuve en aquella sesión la mano más expresiva del mundo, la mano negra que señala en los mapas, en los bosques inexplorados, en las salidas del mundo y en la salida en casos de incendio" (AM 389).

[49] This analogy was probably also a standard feature of Ramón's repertoire. In the context of his own lectures he refers to "los avionismos de la palabra hacia el cielo" (AM 549).

The bloated hand also performs a key subversive function, one that I consider central both to the film and to Ramón's whole approach to the business of public speaking. What *El orador* offers us, essentially, is "metaoratory": a speech about speech-making in which the speaker parodies through caricature the rhetoric and manipulative techniques of the traditional speech-giver—that whole style of speaking which, as we have already seen, was anathema to him. What better way to express his contempt for the posturing of the conventional public speaker than to deflate it comically through histrionic exaggeration? And what better way to posit a more attractive alternative—reconstructing in the act of demolishing—than to offer a example of his own "nueva manera de hablar," of his own "don elocuente del monólogo?"

The way in which Ramón delivers his monologue also invites comment. It is clear from what we see on camera that he is not reading from a prepared script; this is *not* a case of a writer reading from his own work. *El orador*, then, like so many of his public lectures, cannot legitimately be termed a recital. On the other hand, as I have shown, Ramón is evidently making use of pre-existing material—if not already written or performed elsewhere, then at least worked through or mentally rehearsed. It would be equally inappropriate, therefore, to describe Ramón's public speaking as pure improvisation.[50] What he does in *El orador*—and surely elsewhere, too—is to dip into a store of familiar material (ideas, objects, *greguerías*, unusual definitions or interpretations of one kind or another) and use it to make "building blocks" out of which his talk is constructed. The details of how these blocks are shaped and made to fit together would vary according to the circumstances. It is much the same performance technique that has been defined by means of "oral-formulaic theory" according to which certain fixed ingredients are memorized by the speaker-reciter but handled flexibly, being expanded, contracted or (re-)combined according to need. The element of improvisation, as in Ramón's case, lies in how the precise dimensions or emphases of each performance are orchestrated.[51]

---

[50] This is despite what Ramón himself wrote about his own style of public speaking. He described himself with some pride as "un improvisador, un nadador en las aguas peligrosas" (AM 550).

[51] See the entries for "Oral poetry" and "Oral-formulaic theory" in *The New Princeton Encyclopedia of Poetry and Poetics* (863-68). It is uncanny to see in the same reference work how performance theory (892-95) is defined (in

The above argument explains how Ramón is able to speak fluently in *El orador* though without being word-perfect. He manages his building blocks confidently because he knows them well and can fashion a coherent, if not entirely seamless, design in a matter of a few minutes. But he is still working in an oral medium and, like the orator he parodies, he too at one point stumbles on a particular word ("orador"/"aviador"), though instantly recovers his footing. Furthermore, the uncertainty in his delivery about a number of conjunctions and relative pronouns, together with a tendency to repeat certain words (the conversational "entonces," for example) and structures ("Esta mano sirve para ...") draw attention to what is, I suppose, obvious: the orality of the discourse. I make this point not to stress the problematic status of Ramón's "improvisation" but rather to underline its close links with the way he writes. For in many senses Ramón's writing bears the same marks of orality that I have outlined above.[52] By this I mean something more than the commonplace notion that Ramón wrote as he spoke or wrote *what* he spoke, though there is a degree of truth in this. The point is, rather, that as a writer Ramón explicitly cultivated and defended the virtues of improvisation: of simply sitting down with his pen in his hand and noting down whatever occurred to him. Critics have often commented on his reluctance to revise, polish or proofread his own books, attributing to that practice what have usually been seen as the defects of his prose—inconsistency, jerkiness, structural looseness, chaotic development, and so on. Ramón himself was quite clear in his own mind about the benefits of his brand of spontaneity:

> El sistema de la creación literaria es escribir sin parar y sin acordarse de personajes anteriores, seguido y sin parar, recorriendo los caminos más diversos [...].
>
> El escritor dotado de videncia, si no está distraído por nada y sigue el rumbo sin parar, tranquilo y feliz, podrá lograr novelas dignas de leerse. (AM 345)

---

terms of "a performer, a setting, an audience and a performing style") and to realize that it could be applied to the letter to Ramón's public lectures. A fundamental issue that I am not able to broach here for lack of space concerns the audience response to these lectures—a separate subject in itself.

[52] The repetition of the "Esta mano sirve para ..." structure is typical of any page of Ramón's prose where he multiplies the perspectives or *greguería*-like comments he is offering on a given topic or object.

If we make a few discreet changes to this statement, replacing "creación literaria" with "creación oral," "escribir" with "hablar," "escritor" with "orador," and so on, we get very close to defining the nature of Ramón's "spoken texts."

Since this point touches the very core of Ramón's world and the way he articulates it—in both written and oral form—it is worth pursuing briefly. Some of Ramón's best critics, like Carolyn Richmond, have in recent years encouraged a reassessment of his novels, arguing that what have conventionally been seen as their shortcomings in fact amount to a new concept of the novel whose formal characteristics (the rather vague and haphazard treatment of traditional elements of plot, character, structure, development) need to be accepted in and on the terms posited by the writer himself:

> El contenido argumental [...] de la novela ramoniana [...] es más bien una agregación, alrededor de una línea bastante arbitraria, de elementos que apelan no tanto al raciocinio del lector como a su sensibilidad, para sumergirle en un ambiente de libre fantasía: es una novela esencialmente lírica, a la que hemos de acercarnos a través de las sensaciones evocadas, sustituyendo el proceso lógico por el placer de las asociaciones intuitivas. (65)

Again, I would suggest that if we shuffled the terms of this statement in the light of what has been said about Ramón's oral discourse, adding some allusion to humor and entertainment, we would arrive at a fairly accurate description of the operating principles of his public lectures, especially—though not exclusively—his suitcase lectures. Needless to say, despite its highly condensed form, *El orador* can be said to conform to these very same notions.

•

As might be expected of any prolific professional writer, Ramón devoted a good deal of attention to the nature of words and their expressive power. Predictably, his thoughts on the subject often seem eccentric but I would argue that they are crucial in explaining why certain emphases—those I have identified in this essay, for example—recur in his own handling of words, in both written and oral form. For the young Ramón in 1911, words seemed to contain an almost tangible, fluid energy, like electricity: "La palabra es un fenómeno como el de la electricidad, rezumada por todo y viva, con una vida expandida y corriente, pintoresca y diferenciada en sus fenómenos pero identificada como fuerza viva y torrencial" ("Palabras [...] rueca," *T* 121). However, through mechanical repetition and unimaginative use— "la torpeza de la costumbre"—they had fallen into a mute and mannered torpor. They needed to be shaken up, violated, if they were to become reinvigorated: "La palabra tiene que deflorarse depravadamente, reciamente, calcinadoramente al escribirse o pronunciarse, en vez de dar su silencio y su amaneramiento siempre" ("Palabras [...] rueca," *T* 122). Ramón believed that under certain conditions—those that he himself engineered in his own work, I would argue—that energy of words could be recovered, harnessed and exploited so that language could again provide genuine revelation:

> El valor de la palabra es de improvisación y de epifanía y está en cómo se envuelve, en cómo se instruye de todo, en cómo se depura y se sedimenta y en cómo llega de invisiblemente para hacerse visible y real, con una dimensión extraña y fija. ("Palabras [...] rueca," *T* 120)

In his lectures, Ramón packaged words so that they could perform this revelatory function, making them materialize before his audience in the shape of his props and objects and become, in effect, visual spectacle: "Un orador sin más que la voz es poco," he once said. "El orador de hoy necesita otros atractivos para entretener al público. Los objetos son la alegría de la palabra; la ilustración, el gráfico, la alegría de la literatura."[53] The fact that the spectacle itself and the whole experience of the lecture were fleeting was a positive virtue for Ramón since he believed this avoided draining words of their elemental power: "Las palabras han de perderse después de pronunciadas, dejándolas ir a ese sitio abrupto, escarpado y lejano—o cercano, quién sabe—donde se metereorizan de nuevo y siguen salvajes y enteras" ("Palabras [...] rueca," *T* 120).[54]

---

[53] In F.C., "Ramón Gómez de la Serna nos habla de la radio, después de su excursión a América," *Ondas* 354 (16 April 1932) (reproduced in Ventín Pereira).

[54] There is a curious detail about Ramón's 1949 lecture on "La magia en la literatura" that links up with this idea of the desirability of ephemerality, of not leaving a permanent record. Towards the end of that lecture, according to Flórez, he put on a pair of rubber gloves "para no dejar huellas dactilares de esta conferencia" (387).

Through the public performances of the kind I have described here, Ramón undertook what he called "mi misión de hombre singular, sincero y arbitrario" (AM 355), tapping into the energy of words though without ever exhausting it. He was well aware that his success as a speaker lay in the impact that words handled in this way could have on an audience unaccustomed to such experiences. Reflecting on his South American tour of 1931-1932, he summarized the sense of what he had achieved:

> Me di cuenta de que no tenemos más misión que llevar a América la palabra amena, simpática, revelando los secretos de nuestra gesta lingüística, los avionismos de la palabra hacia el cielo.
> Después de la labor pedagógica, cultural y universitaria, el joven—y el viejo—necesitan lo que les inquiete, lo que tenga un soplo original, lo que les haga delirar un poco fuera de las retóricas anquilosadas. (AM 549)

His formula for infecting large live audiences with his own daily "delirio poético" defined his originality as a provocative, often disconcerting orator, setting him apart from all his fellow practitioners:

> Confieso que he sido el conferenciante que ha hecho dimitir más juntas directivas, pero mi creación conferencística despierta un borombonbón especial en las almas en contraste con el chirrido inaguantable como el de un cuchillo en un plato que sugieren las empalagosas y halagosas conferencias de otros. (AM 391)[55]

Ramón's commitment to originality as a public speaker and the subversive instincts at work in his lectures, all of which are contained succinctly in *El orador*, link him with other cultural terrorists of the European avant-garde at the beginning of the twentieth century. The most persuasive comparison would be with the cabaret performances of the dadaists in Zurich, performances that Ramón may well have

---

[55] The issue of the "contagiousness" of Ramón's festive oral performances is worth considering. It is clear, for example, that in Buenos Aires in 1931 and 1933 public response was overwhelmingly favorable, to such an extent that the doctors of a local hospital, entering into the spirit of his lectures, paid homage to him in an operating theater, sending an ambulance to pick the writer up at his hotel and dressing him up as a patient.

attended.[56] In them prankish humor, surprise, shock, speech and gesture were all combined to wage war on cliché and convention. Ramón would doubtless have applauded such playfully destructive exhibitionism, rooted in spontaneity, designed, in Tristan Tzara's words, to "sweep clean." On this front he shares with the dadaists the historical distinction of having anticipated the "happenings" and multi-media performance art of the 1950s and subsequent decades. The liberating randomness of those events, in which the authority of the fixed text is displaced by the more fluid live *experience* of meaning as it is being generated, owes much to their innovations.

Paradoxically, however, Ramón the lecturer and champion of novelty looks back in time as much as he looks to the present and the future. Pedro Salinas first made this point in 1936, remarking that "ningún escritor contemporáneo se parece tanto al juglar medieval como Ramón" (141). What Salinas was signalling was a different kind of comparison: a parallel between Ramón the oral entertainer who, to use Díaz Fernández's phrase, "ensancha el triste y constreñido medio literario español" (qtd. in *AM* 385), and the itinerant minstrel-jester of the thirteenth century who moved from place to place, making a living by way of public performance, bringing art, creativity and amusement into the lives of those not normally exposed to them. Salinas glosses the sense of the analogy:

> Arte y diversión se confundían; en este sentido tiene Ramón un aire primitivo, una jocundidad bulliciosa, una afición a darse en espectáculo que rompe la tiesura y rigidez que se suele atribuir al género grave de lo literario y lo asimila al hombre de buena voluntad que quiere dar un rato de placer a sus prójimos con los más variados ejercicios. (141)

In the light of what has been said in these pages, Salinas's idea could be slightly modified by saying that implicit in much of what Ramón the orator says and does is the assumption of one of the later forms of this medieval tradition, that of the travelling circus performer. I have already referred to his affiliations with the circus world and the

---

[56] According to Gaspar Gómez de la Serna, Ramón did indeed witness the birth of dada and became good friends with Picabia, Soupault and Tzara. He states that Ramón saw Tzara for the first time, alongside other founding members of the movement (Hans Arp and Huelsenbeck), at the Voltaire cabaret in Zurich (106).

memorable lectures he gave from within it. Ramón once commented that in his lectures he presented himself to his audiences "como soy, riendo y llorando" (AM 391). He felt a clear affinity for the figure of the clown who hid his mournfulness behind garish make-up, extravagant dress and the antics that became ritualized—some might say sacralized—within the protocol of the circus.[57] If he sought to conjure up its spectacle and entertainment through his lectures, it was because he believed, as he had confessed in 1928 in Paris, that the circus provided the ideal model for the world he aspired to create in his work:

> El mundo, al fin, se dará cuenta del sentido humorístico de la vida y acabará siendo un gran circo, franco, sincero, desengolado, en que los *régisseurs* lucirán las casacas ministeriales a las que habrán sacado los ojos que hoy las decoran, y la gran farsa caprichosa y disparatada del mundo habrá encontrado su sincero ritmo y su estilo verdadero. (AM 355)

Ramón's oratory constituted a clearly identifiable, consciously developed and uniquely configured avant-garde genre, but ultimately it was also something more—the enactment of his approach to the world and an affirmation of the place he sought to occupy in it. As Ramón himself said of humor: "Casi no se trata de un género literario, sino de un género de vida, o mejor dicho, de una actitud frente a la vida" ("Gravedad," T 205).[58]

---

[57] Curiously, Ramón always refused to give a lecture dressed as a clown—something that would have been entirely natural. He seems to have regarded the prospect with deep unease, as if such a lecture would have heralded his climactic exit from this world: "Hubiera intentado una conferencia final vestido de *clown*, pero no me atreví, porque hubiera sido la última. Hubiera sido la mejor, la más conmovedora [...]" (AM 551). The notion of a "sacred" dimension to Ramón's oral performances is less bizarre than it may sound. Consider this self-portrait of the live radio broadcaster: "Me siento como sacerdote de la diosa radio, esa diosa ante la que me prosterné hace años, desde el día de su advenimiento" (qtd. in Ventín Pereira 24). Pombo was, after all, known as "la sagrada cripta."

[58] Salinas saw this clearly when he drew attention to the presence in Ramón, beneath the playful exterior, of "la lucha del hombre solo e inerte, por no estar al margen, por entrar en la vida, por cobrar vida; en suma, por ser" (140).

Works Cited

Aub, Max. *Discurso de la novela española contemporánea.* México: El Colegio de México, 1945.
Borges, Jorge Luis. "Ramón Gómez de la Serna. La sagrada cripta de Pombo." *Inquisiciones.* Buenos Aires: Proa, 1925. 124-26.
Buckley, Ramón y John Crispin, eds. *Los vanguardistas españoles, 1925-1935.* Madrid: Alianza, 1973.
Cassou, Jean. "Poésie." *Les Nouvelles Littéraires.* 21 January 1928: 1.
Cernuda, Luis. "Gómez de la Serna y la generación poética de 1925." *Obras completas.* Eds. Derek Harris and Luis Maristany. Vol. II. Madrid: Siruela, 1994. 172-80.
Dennis, Nigel. "Cinco cartas inéditas de Gómez de la Serna. (El alma en pena de Ramón)." *Revista de Occidente* 80 (1988): 7-22.
———. "El ir y venir de Ramón Gómez de la Serna." Prologue. *París.* By Ramón Gómez de la Serna. Valencia: Pre-Textos, 1986. 7-69.
———. "Culture in the Second Republic: The *Comités de Cooperación Intelectual.*" *Revista Canadiense de Estudios Hispánicos* 21(1996): 87-99.
———, ed. *Studies on Ramón Gómez de la Serna.* Ottawa: Dovehouse, 1988.
Fernández Almagro, Melchor. "La generación unipersonal de Gómez de la Serna." *España* 362 (1923): 10-11.
Flórez, Rafael. *Ramón de Ramones.* Madrid: Bitácora, 1988.
Giménez Caballero, Ernesto. "Literatura española, 1918-1930." [1934]. Buckley and Crispin 48-54.
Gómez de la Serna, Gaspar. *Ramón.* Madrid: Taurus, 1963.
Gómez de la Serna, Ramón. *Automoribundia, 1888-1948.* 2 vols. Madrid: Guadarrama, 1974.
———. *Echantillons.* Trans. Valéry Larbaud. Paris: Les Cahiers Verts, 1923.
———. "El falso micrófono." *Ondas,* 10 June 1928: 5.
———. *Gollerías.* Barcelona: Bruguera, 1983.
———. *Muestrario.* Madrid: Biblioteca Nueva, 1918.
———. *El Rastro.* Valencia: Prometeo, 1915.
———. *Teatro muerto.* Ed. Agustín Muñoz-Alonso López and Jesús Rubio Jiménez. Madrid: Cátedra, 1995.
———. *Una teoría personal del arte. Antología de textos de estética y teoría de arte.* Ed. Ana Martínez-Collado. Madrid: Tecnos, 1988.
("Primera proclama de Pombo" [1915], 97-107.
"El concepto de la nueva literatura" [1909], 55-78.
Greguerías (prólogo) [1918], 124-59.
Ismos (prólogo) [1931], 105-15.
Muestrario (prólogo) [1918], 16-67
"La torre de marfil" [1943], 248-65.
"Gravedad e importancia del humorismo" [1930], 203-226.
"Las palabras y lo indecible" [1936], 184-200.
"Mis siete palabras" [1910], 84-94.

"Las cosas y el 'ello'" [1934], 173-83.
"Palabras en la rueca" [1911], 119-23.)
Gubern, Román. *Proyector de luna. La generación del 27 y el cine*. Barcelona: Anagrama, 1999.
Herrero Vecino, Carmen. *La utopía y el teatro: la obra dramática de Ramón Gómez de la Serna*. Boulder: Society of Spanish and Spanish-American Studies, 1995.
Hoyle, Alan. "El problema de la greguería." *Actas del IX Congreso de la Asociación Internacional de Hispanistas*. Ed. Sebastian Neumeister. Frankfurt am Main: Veuvert, 1989. 283-92.
Muñoz-Alonso López, Agustín. *Ramón y el teatro (La obra dramática de Ramón Gómez de la Serna)*. Universidad de Castilla-La Mancha, 1993.
The New Princeton Encyclopedia of Poetry and Poetics. Eds. Alex Preminger and T.V.F. Brogan. Princeton: Princeton UP, 1993.
Ortega y Gasset, José. *La deshumanización del arte*. Madrid: Alianza, 1983.
Paco, Mariano de. "El teatro de vanguardia." *La vanguardia en España*. Ed. Javier Pérez Bazo. Toulouse: Université de Toulouse-Le Mirail, 1998. 291-304.
Práctica fílmica y vanguardia artística en España, 1925-1981. Eds. Eugenia Bonet and Manuel Palacio. Madrid: Universidad Complutense de Madrid, 1983.
Richmond, Carolyn. "La debatida novelística de Gómez de la Serna: 'Las afueras más irrespirables del vivir.'" *Revista de Occidente* 80 (1988): 63-69.
Ruiz Salvador, Antonio. "Recuerdo y realidad: Gómez de la Serna y Ramón en el Ateneo." Dennis, ed. 71-88.
Salinas, Pedro. "Escorzo de Ramón." *Ensayos completos*. Vol. I. Madrid: Taurus, 1983. 139-43.
Sánchez Vidal, Agustín. Introducción. *Obra literaria*. By Luis Buñuel. Zaragoza: El Heraldo de Aragón, 1982. 11-79.
Soldevila, Ignacio. "El gato encerrado. (Contribución al estudio de la génesis de los procedimientos creadores en la prosa ramoniana)." *Revista de Occidente* 80 (1988): 31-62.
Ventín Pereira, J. Augusto, ed. *Radiorramonismo. Antología de textos radiofónicos de Ramón Gómez de la Serna*. Madrid: Universidad Complutense de Madrid, 1987.
Yndurain, Francisco. "Ramón en la *Revista de Occidente*." *Revista de Occidente* 80 (1988): 70-81.

Heading West with Rafael Alberti and Buster Keaton

WILLARD BOHN
Illinois State University

LIKE THEIR COLLEAGUES IN Paris, the Spanish Surrealists were strongly attracted to motion pictures which, despite the absence of sound, offered exciting new possibilities.[1] Not only was the new art form instantaneously accessible, but the invention of montage and other techniques allowed the director (and the writer) to manipulate time and space at will. While the general public flocked to the cinema seeking to be entertained, the Surrealists were intrigued by a whole range of technical innovations, which they sought to imitate in their own works. Like their counterparts in France, they were especially fond of comedies—whose madcap, slapstick humor, Virginia Higginbotham points out, was "easily distorted into the bizarre and nonsensical imagery of Surrealism" (112). Whereas the French Surrealists prized Charlie Chaplin's comedies, the Spanish Surrealists preferred films that featured Buster Keaton. Rafael Utrera reports that the Spaniards were repelled by the "excessive sentimentality" of Chaplin's films (49). What attracted them to Keaton, one surmises, was his stoic personality and manly bearing.

In 1929, Rafael Alberti composed a remarkable series of poems which was conceived as a tribute to the comics of the silent screen.[2] Seeking a title that would reflect their zany, madcap humor, which he

---

[1] Cf. Morris's *This Loving Darkness: The Cinema and Spanish Writers, 1920-1936.*

[2] Some, but not all, of the poems were eventually collected in his *Poesías completas*. For a more authoritative edition, see *Sobre los ángeles. Yo era un tonto y lo que he visto me ha hecho dos tontos.*

strove to capture in his own compositions, Alberti chose a line from a seventeenth-century play by Pedro Calderón de la Barca: "Yo era un tonto y lo que he visto me ha hecho dos tontos." Since "tonto" can also be translated as "jester" or "clown," the title aptly describes the boisterous pranks and verbal clowning that give the volume its distinctive tone. In addition, as C. B. Morris notes, it conveys the poet's increasing dissatisfaction with the status quo and his willingness to provoke, even outrage his audience (*Generation* 107). Despite Alberti's growing reputation, Anthony Geist remarks, *Yo era un tonto y lo que he visto me ha hecho dos tontos* has received relatively little critical attention. For various reasons, it remains "uno de sus libros más originales y menos estudiados" (10). Alberti sought to document each of the comics' originality, Morris explains, "by enabling them to do in his poems what they could not do in the films in which they made their names: talk" (*This Loving Darkness* 97). The challenge lay not just in translating his visual impressions into verbal equivalents but in creating a different poetic discourse for each comic.

On May 4, 1929, the members of the Cineclub in Madrid were treated to a dramatic reading of the initial three poems of his book by Alberti himself. The first composition was devoted to Charlie Chaplin, the second was concerned with Harold Lloyd, and the third was entitled "Buster Keaton busca por el bosque a su novia, que es una verdadera vaca." As Edgar O'Hara points out, the lengthy title recalls the explanatory captions that were utilized in silent films (167). We know from contemporary witnesses that Alberti dazzled his audience, accompanying his words with sound effects, gestures, and an expressive pantomime. Indeed, traces of this memorable experience can be found in the work's subtitle: "poema representable." Carlos Alberto Pérez claims that each poem constitutes its own dramatic scenario, reproducing Chaplin's nervous gestures, Harry Langdon's somnambulistic style, and Lloyd's dynamism according to its respective protagonist (211). The same principle can be detected in "Buster Keaton busca por el bosque a su novia," which possesses the same rhythm (and the same structure) as many of Keaton's movies. In the poem, as on the screen, the stone-faced comic ambles aimlessly through life with no idea where he is going.

As Pérez was the first to perceive, each of the poems is constructed around one film in particular, which it simultaneously imitates and parodies. Entitled *Go West* (1925), the movie that inspired "Buster Keaton busca por el bosque a su novia" tells the story of a drifter who rides the boxcars to Arizona, where he attempts to become a cowboy. "A hapless, unloved, pathetic creature named Friendless," as one film critic puts it, Keaton falls in love with a cow named Brown Eyes, who loves him in return (Edwards 71). Cast in the form of a monologue, Alberti's poem depicts the pitiful protagonist searching for his bovine sweetheart, who has inexplicably wandered off. As in *Go West*, we should imagine that he is dressed in full cowboy regalia including chaps, a leather vest, and a bandana tied around his neck. Except for his ridiculous porkpie hat—a Keaton trademark—the transformation is complete.

> 1, 2, 3 y 4.
> En estas cuatro huellas no caben mis zapatos.
> Si en estas cuatro huellas no caben mis zapatos,
> ¿de quién son estas cuatro huellas?
> ¿De un tiburón,
> de un elefante recién nacido o de un pato?
> ¿De una pulga o de una codorniz?
> (Pi, pi, pi.)

Not surprisingly, "Buster Keaton busca por el bosque a su novia" shares numerous stylistic traits with the other poems in the volume. In addition to its capricious imagery, O'Hara calls attention to the frequency with which Arabic numerals appear, which are usually gratuitous (172). This device was inspired not by the cinema but by contemporary advertisements, which led many poets to experiment with "poster poems" following World War I. Alberti seems to have adopted it, in conjunction with his efforts to modernize Spanish poetry, in order to give his works a brand new look. That his poetry is filled with phonic echoes reflects a larger problem in O'Hara's opinion, demonstrating "the profound difficulty the poet experiences in trying to escape from rhyme" (173). However, this interpretation ignores the possibility that the rhymes and near rhymes are deliberate. It is clear from "Buster Keaton busca por el bosque a su novia" that Alberti does not wish to abandon rhyme but rather to redefine it, to expand the number of phonic possibilities in order to gain more flexibility. He varies not only the length of his lines, therefore, but the way in which they end, incorporating assonance and approximate rhymes into his prosodic arsenal. As often as not, moreover, two lines will end with the same word, in keeping with the dominant stylistic principle: repetition. Not content to rhyme "zapatos" with "zapatos," Alberti repeats entire phrases such as "estas cuatro huellas" again and again. In the last analysis, this is basically what makes "Buster Keaton busca por el bosque a su novia" a performance poem. Together with the various sound effects, the phonic patterns produce an extraordinary effect that can only be realized by reading the poem aloud.

Whereas the protagonist of Federico García Lorca's "El paseo de Buster Keaton" (1928) is abstracted from a whole series of films, Alberti's character is drawn from a single movie. Whereas the former is a poetic dreamer, the latter is a social misfit, a perpetual outsider who is ignored or dismissed by everyone around him. "Of all the Keaton heroes," Daniel Moews remarks, the character portrayed in *Go West* is "the one absolute loner" (164). So complete is his estrangement that "he seems to live apart in the alien realm of a madman or simpleton" (169). If anything, this tendency is even more pronounced in "Buster Keaton busca por el bosque a su novia," whose hero seems to be either mentally retarded or insane. Although his initial perplexity is probably intended to be comical, it is also extremely puzzling. Pursuing the elusive Brown Eyes—whom Alberti has renamed Georgina—he encounters four footprints which are almost certainly hers but which for some reason he fails to recognize. Having laboriously counted them, he tries them on to see if perhaps they are his own footprints. What finally dissuades him is not that there are four of them or that they are obviously the wrong shape or that he has never come this way before, but the discovery that his feet are too big.

Still refusing to admit the obvious, Friendless speculates about who could have left the footprints. Of the five animals that he proposes, each of which is more ridiculous than the other, only the elephant possesses the correct number of feet. But elephants live too far away, and in any case their feet are too large. Similar objections prevent the shark—which has no feet at all—the duck, the flea, and the quail (which we hear cheeping in the underbrush) from being viable candidates. Unable to reach a conclusion, Friendless resumes his quest for his errant sweetheart.

    ¡Georginaaaaaaaa!
    ¿Dónde estás?
    ¡Que no te oigo, Georgina!
    ¿Qué pensarán de mí los bigotes de tu papa?
    (Paaa páááááááááá.)

¡Georginaaaaaaaa!
¿Estás o no estás?
Abeto, ¿dónde está?
Alisio, ¿dónde está?
Pinsapo, ¿dónde está?

For some reason, perhaps in order to make her seem more human, Alberti has rechristened the cow Georgina. While "Brown Eyes" sounds nicer in Spanish ("Ojos Castaños") than in English, it would have been a strange name for Friendless to shout and would have emphasized the difference between them. Morris suggests that Alberti borrowed the name from Chaplin's *The Gold Rush* (1925), which contains the following subtitle: "Georgia! GEORGIA!! GEORGIA!!! (*This Loving Darkness* 100). Like these exclamations, Friendless's cries increase in intensity (and length) as the poem progresses. With a little ingenuity, one could doubtless discover many other features that are duplicated in various films, especially those directed by Keaton. The reference to "un pato" recalls the family of ducks in *The Scarecrow* (1920), for example, and the duck that Keaton tries to shoot from a canoe in *Battling Butler* (1926). Similarly, the mysterious "bigotes" recall the fake mustache worn by the detective in *Sherlock Jr.* (1924) and the pencil-thin mustache affected by the foppish son in *Steamboat Bill Jr.* (1928). And yet, in contrast to many critical poets who reproduce motifs from the work(s) they are "reviewing," Alberti refers to Keaton's films only sporadically. The animals and objects invoked in the poem are taken not from a catalogue of motifs but from the poet's imagination.

Advancing amid the echoes created by his desperate cries, Friendless is struck by a very peculiar thought: "¿Qué pensarán de mí los bigotes de tu papá?" Since bulls do not have mustaches, which in any case are incapable of thinking, the question appears to make no sense. Perhaps he dreads having to confess to the cow's mustachioed owner, who is also his boss, that he has no idea where she is. Out of desperation, like countless Romantic poets before him, he calls on Nature to aid him in his quest. Receiving no response from the wind or the trees, he turns to the birds around him, from whom he learns that he is on the right track.

¿Georgina pasó por aquí?
(Pi, pi, pi, pi)
Ha pasado a la una comiendo yerbas.
Cucú,
el cuervo la iba engañando con una flor de reseda.
Cuacuá,
la lechuza, con una rata muerta.
¡Señores, perdonadme, pero me urge llorar!
(Guá, guá, guá.)

Although the birds' reply could conceivably be uttered by the birds themselves, the fact that it alternates with their original cries suggests that it is a translation, that Friendless is simply repeating what they have told him. Despite his limited intelligence and his strange appearance, he possesses at least one redeeming quality: like St. Francis (and Dr. Dolittle), he is able to converse with the birds around him. These particular birds are unusually intelligent, it would seem, for they are able to tell Friendless what time they spied Georgina eating grass. Since they presumably do not own watches, which would be difficult to wear in any case, one wonders how they knew it was one o'clock. Perhaps they heard a clock chime in the distance. As Morris remarks in his critical edition, the animals in the poem resemble those that appear in children's stories possessing the same abilities as human beings. That the crow and the owl should seek to deceive Georgina, however, introduces a sinister note into the proceedings—reinforced by the image of the dead rat. A rapid review of their traditional symbolism reveals that all three are associated with darkness and death, with demonic forces and evil impulses.[3] As far as one can tell, the two birds sought to cast some kind of spell on the cow. In contrast to the dead rat, the reseda blossom is lovely to look at and emits a wonderful perfume. On the one hand, since it possesses certain sedative properties, named for the Latin verb *resedare* meaning "to calm," the crow may have tried to drug Georgina. On the other hand, since according to the *Grand Larousse Encyclopédique* it symbolizes (loving) tenderness, he may have tried to deceive her with tender words and false promises. In either case, the world is a very dangerous place for someone as sweet and innocent as Friendless's fiancée. In the poem as in the movie, she clearly needs someone to protect her.

---

[3] Cf. J.C. Cooper's *An Illustrated Encyclopaedia of Traditional Symbols*.

At this point, something totally unexpected occurs: Friendless suddenly bursts into tears. What makes this development so shocking, Morris observes in a note to the critical edition, is that Keaton never cried in any of his films. The perpetual victim of poverty and injustice, he maintained his rigid composure through thick and thin. His atypical behavior in Alberti's text seems to have a two-fold explanation, alluding both to his role in *Go West* and to his role in the poem. In *Go West*, Moews explains, Keaton appeared "in about the heaviest white-face makeup since *Our Hospitality*, which combined with heavily rimmed eyes [made] him seem a mask of sorrow, a crying clown" (160). In the poem, he is clearly overcome by emotion when he hears that the crow and the owl have tried to dupe his bovine sweetheart. Eventually regaining control of himself, he resumes his search for the errant Georgina.

> ¡Georgina!
> Ahora que te faltaba un solo cuerno
> para doctorarte en la verdaderamente útil carrera de ciclista
> y adquirir una gorra de cartero.
> (Cri, cri, cri, cri.)
> Hasta los grillos se apiadan de mí
> y me acompaña en mi dolor la garrapata.
> Compadécete del smokin que te busca y te llora entre los aguaceros
> y del sombrero hongo que tiernamente
> te presiente de mata en mata.

Georgina is not only a wayward animal, it turns out, but a serious scholar who was on the point of receiving her doctorate when she disappeared. Perhaps the strain of writing a dissertation was too much for her or perhaps she was having trouble with her last chapter. At the same time, Alberti indulges in a bit of (surrealist) humor that undercuts her academic pretensions. The first part of the joke, one that certainly is not lost on current job seekers, is that the doctorate would only have qualified her to become a cyclist. This was preferable to becoming a professor, Alberti assures us in the second part, because she would have been a useful member of society. In point of fact, we learn subsequently, Georgina would not have used her bicycle to compete in races but rather to deliver the mail. Unfortunately, the poet concludes, her career plans were sabotaged by the fact that, like all Jersey cows, she has no horns. And yet city ordinances required that her bicycle be equipped with a (single) horn for safety reasons.

Accompanied by crickets and at least one tick, who commiserate with him, the hapless lover continues his fruitless search. Dressed in an elegant tuxedo borrowed from any one of half a dozen films, Keaton keeps expecting to find Georgina at any moment. Unfortunately, his elegant appearance is marred by the fact that he is wearing a bowler hat, which adds to the incongruity of the situation. Together with the mailman's cap, it may allude to a scene in *Steamboat Bill, Jr.*—containing "one of Keaton's best comic routines" according to one authority—in which thirteen hats are placed on his head in rapid succession (Moews 160). Worst of all, since Friendless has been caught in several downpours, his hat and clothes are soaking wet. So much water is dripping from the tuxedo, Alberti jokes, that it appears to be crying ("te llora"). Ignoring his own increasingly desperate situation, Friendless utters a long, drawn-out cry:

> ¡Georginaaaaaaaaaaaaaaaaaa!
> (Maaaaaa.)
> ¿Eres una dulce niña o eres una verdadera vaca?
> Mi corazón siempre me dijo que eras una verdadera vaca.
> Una dulce niña.
> Una verdadera vaca.
> Una niña.
> Una vaca.
> ¿Una niña o una vaca?
> O ¿una niña y una vaca?
> Yo nunca supe nada.
>   Adiós Georgina.
>   (¡Pum!)

Returning to the question format adopted at the beginning, which never produces any answers, the final section leaves readers with quite a few questions of their own. At long last, when it seems that Friendless will never find Georgina, his cries elicit a response. While he addresses her directly in the final lines, it is not clear whether she is actually present or simply somewhere in the vicinity. Now that he has found her, he is faced with a second problem that threatens to undermine his happiness. Although the answer should be fairly obvious, he is unable to decide if Georgina is a cow or a girl. If he listened to his heart, he informs us, he would choose the first solution. And yet he confesses that, for reasons that remain inexplicable, he has never been able to make up his mind. According to Pérez, Friendless is disconcerted by the ambiguity that informs the world around us, rendering efforts to discriminate between rival phenomena completely useless (213). Geist observes that his quest for Georgina parallels Alberti's search for a new poetic language, on the one hand, and for transcendental meaning on the other. The indecision that racks Friendless at the end of the poem results from the discovery that "el lenguaje mismo parece subvertir la posibilidad de significación" (Geist 10).

By accelerating the oscillation in Friendless's mind between the girl and the cow, the final scene performs his increasing confusion even as it depicts it. As Morris has pointed out, the conclusion was suggested by a corresponding scene in Go West (*This Loving Darkness* 100). "In this film the emotions of human and animal are so alike," Moews adds, "that it is no wonder poor Friendless remains confused and incapable of distinguishing between them or of deciding to which group he belongs" (164). Once Friendless reaches Arizona and begins working for a rancher, the latter's daughter alternates with Brown Eyes as his potential romantic partner. At the end, having rescued the rancher from financial ruin, he earns the latter's eternal gratitude. "My home and anything I have is yours for the asking," the rancher proclaims. "I want her," Friendless replies, pointing not to the girl, as everyone supposes at first, but to the cow placidly chewing her cud. As the film ends, all four of them drive off into the sunset together with Friendless and Brown Eyes sitting side by side in the rumble seat. Inspired by the huge success of *The Gold Rush*, Jim Kline concludes, Go West is "one of [Keaton's] most slyly satirical films" (198). Like Keaton, Alberti parodies the sentimental endings of which Chaplin was so fond by having his protagonist fall in love with a cow.

At one level, the confusion that invades the poem reflects the dilemma Friendless faces in the film: whether to choose the rancher's daughter or one of his cattle. At another level, as we have seen, the confusion stems from the fundamental indeterminacy that undermines the text at this point. As much as anything, Friendless is confronted with a problem of identity. In both cases, he finally succeeds in dominating the confusion that threatens to destroy him by taking a decisive action. Whereas he chooses the cow over the girl in Go West, he appears to reject her in the poem. No sooner has he located Georgina, for whom he has been searching high and low, than he tells her goodbye. The only way he can dispel the confusion that besets him, be it perceptual, ontological, or semiotic, is to turn his back on it. Unable to resolve this confusion and unwilling to live with it, he decides to eliminate its immediate source. Unable and unwilling to provide true poetic closure, Alberti adopts a similar solution: he ends the poem with a shot. While Pérez assumes that Friendless commits suicide, perhaps with one of the pistols that appear in *Go West*, Friendless could solve his problem just as easily by shooting Georgina. Nevertheless, both interpretations ignore the fact that the script calls for *the poet* to perform this final sound effect, as he has performed all the previous ones. One suspects that Alberti drew a pistol at this point during his reading—as he did on at least one other occasion—and suddenly fired into the air.[4] Whether actually performed or simply evoked, the unexpected action effectively brings the poem to an end.

Works Cited

Alberti, Rafael. *Poesías completas*. Buenos Aires: Losada, 1961.

———. *Sobre los ángeles. Yo era un tonto y lo que he visto me ha hecho dos tontos*. Ed. C. B. Morris. 5th ed. Madrid: Catedra, 1992.

Cooper, J. C. *An Illustrated Encyclopaedia of Traditional Symbols*. London: Thames and Hudson, 1978.

Edwards, Larry. *Buster: A Legend in Laughter*. Bradenton, Florida: McGuinn and McGuire, 1995.

Geist, Anthony L. "Mecánica, amor, poesía: discurso e ideología en *Yo era un tonto y lo que he visto me ha hecho dos tontos*." *Insula* 44.515 (1989): 10-11.

Higginbotham, Virginia. "Lorca's Apprenticeship in Surrealism." *Romanic Review* 61 (1970): 109-22.

Kline, Jim. *The Complete Films of Buster Keaton*. New York: Citadel, 1993.

Moews, Daniel. *Keaton: The Silent Features Close Up*. Berkeley: U of California P, 1977.

Morris, C. B. *A Generation of Spanish Poets, 1920-1936*. Cambridge: Cambridge UP, 1969.

———. *This Loving Darkness: The Cinema and Spanish Writers, 1920-1936*. Oxford: Oxford UP, 1980.

O'Hara, Edgar. "Exercises in the Dark: Rafael Alberti's Cinema Poems." *The Spanish Avant-Garde*. Ed. Derek Harris. Manchester: Manchester UP, 1995. 165-77.

---

[4] Morris describes the other occasion in Alberti, *Sobre los ángeles* 172n52.

Pérez, Carlos Alberto. "Rafael Alberti: sobre los tontos." *Revista Hispánica Moderna* 32 (1966): 206-16.
Utrera, Rafael. *Garcia Lorca y el cinema*. Sevilla: EDISUR, 1982.

Alma: The First Complete Motion Picture in Print

HENRY SCHWARZ

ALMA, THE FIRST NOVEL of Oswald de Andrade, was simultaneously the first novel of the literary revolution that marked Brazil's Modernist Movement in the 1920s. The controversial work, which was first published in 1922 just after the São Paulo "Semana de Arte" by the author in an edition of 3000 copies, was not generally well-received. The novel's subject, the life of a São Paulo prostitute, was considered shocking and, on the whole, its representation was taken to be immoral. Further, in telling the story of Alma, the author adopted a decidedly unconventional narrative style. While critics recognized that the disconnected staccato of brief scenes which comprised the story reflected some kind of technical innovation, inspired perhaps by silent films, many were not impressed with the vaguely "cinematic" result, and were put off by the vulgarity of both the subject and street language.

Everyone was grateful, therefore, several years later when the author's next novel, *Memórias sentimentais do João Miramar*, was published in 1924, followed by *Serafim Ponte Grande* in 1933. The wit and pace of these subsequent works largely compensated for any suspected moral flaws. Their clipped and fragmented narrative style, apparently retained in some respects from the experiment of *Alma*, also reflected some modifications which gave a comforting semblance of greater orthodoxy, and offered the general reader at least some points of reference in both subject and structure which might be construed as more familiar and more accessible. Benedito Nunes notes that from the vantage of 1945, in *Ponta de lança*, Oswald himself decided that his first worthy contribution to Brazilian prose came with *Memórias sentimentais do João Miramar,* offering the imprimatur "primeiro cadinho da nossa prosa nova" (Nunes xv).[1]

From this point forward *Alma,* despite its appearance at a pivotal moment in Brazilian letters, has received little further attention. Later critical reviews of Oswald and *Alma* are effectively summed up by biographer Maria de Lourdes Eleutério: "A obra oswaldiana é tida como desigual: o mesmo homem que escreve 'romances-invenção' da mais extrema radicalidade, como *Miramar* e *Serafim,* também é autor de 'prosa crepuscular,' como *Os condenados*" (65). Several stylistic innovations have been respectfully acknowledged, many faults noted, and the critics have moved on. But we would argue that *Alma,* beyond the historic fact of its presence at a turning point in Brazilian letters, represents a far more daring literary experiment than critics of its time, or since, have appreciated.[2] It is the author's first novel, in fact, which may be his most completely original. How then did Oswald de

---

[1] Oswald commenced (Brito xvi) to write both *Alma* and *A estrêla de absinto* sometime in the midst of his bohemian escapades between perhaps 1917 when he established his *garçonnière* on Rua Líbero Badaró and 1919 which marked the death of his radical love, the *normalista* Deisi. It was during this period that he commenced to write *Miramar* as well, whose initial chapters at least were presented in *O Pirralho* before it ceased publication in 1917 (Fonseca 29).

[2] A full review of the critical literature on *Alma* would constitute a separate paper. A number of contemporary comments have been gathered by critic Mário da Silva Brito. Brito cites Carlos Drummond de Andrade on *Alma,* "um romance atual [...] que destoa das obras até aqui aparecidas, em vista do estilo e da emoção [...] livre das imperfeições que o maculam" (xix). Monteiro Lobato, who first published the work, stressed the cinematic effect, which he identified as a "série de quadros à Griffith" (qtd. in Brito xix) which was further echoed by A. Couto de Barros: "o livro inaugura em nosso meio técnica absolutamente nova, imprevista, cinematográfica" (qtd. in Brito xx). The review by Couto de Barros appeared originally in the arts review *Klaxon* (6 [Oct. 15, 1922], 13-14), but explained nothing more specific of Oswald's technique. The elements of brief cuts and novel quality of simultaneity were also noted by Mário de Andrade, and attributed as well to "a beneficiação do cinematógrafo" (qtd. in Brito xx). Finally, Tristão de Athayde, a leading critic of the day, liked the way the new, abbreviated chapter structure and sense of simultaneity lent a certain life and immediacy, and sensed in the work, "a influência do cinema como a proclamou Epstein ou como a ensaiou também Jules Romains" (qtd. in Brito xx). None of these observers, however, seems to have noticed more than one or two film techniques or effects employed in *Alma,* or to have identified the author's full structural intention.

Andrade actually view the purpose and role of the writer of his time, and how did this creative philosophy lead to the radical structure we will identify in the novel *Alma*?

In the briefest of terms, *Alma* is the story of a comely young girl, "risonha e esbelta," from the countryside who comes to the city to live with her grandfather, old Lucas, and his little dog. She is seduced by the pimp Mauro Glade, attracts the adoration of the idealistic young telegrapher João de Carmo, has an abortion, gives birth to a child Luquinhas who names the grandpa's dog Baubau, is kept for a time by the wealthy Teles Melo, mourns the death of Luquinhas, and finally causes the suicide of the jealous João de Carmo through an accident of mistaken identity. This, in essence, is the emotional rollercoaster of *Alma*. The author unfolds Alma's adventures and misadventures, not in conventional chapters, but in a series of 238 brief "scenes" or "cuts," ranging in length from just a single sentence of one line up to the very longest passage of 69 lines. In all, the book is composed of some 100 pages of text comprised of 2,987 lines. The separation between the "cuts" is designated, simply, by a small gap in the text before and after each scene. The "cuts" are not enumerated.

Despite the rampant sentimentality that drives the novel, it is important to recognize that the author himself almost certainly never wrote a word inspired in sentimentality. Rather, as a writer Oswald was largely moved by the elation of surprise, and he was principally focused on innovations in language and structure. It was time to replace the stale forms of the old Parnassian literature, but how was it to be done? The philosophical tenets of Positivism were viewed as key to progress in the arts, and Oswald believed that a strong clash of ideas and methods was a continuing process that was critical to the advance not only of philosophy and social structures, but literature as well. Late in his life, in *A crise de filosofia messiânica*, having rejected the Marxist model of human development, he offers the following underlying model of history:

1.º termo: tese - o homem natural
2.º termo: antítese - o homem civilizado
3.º termo: síntese - o homem tecnizado (79)

Conflict, in Oswald's view, is an inherent element of man's nature; and the arts themselves are an invention which is the outcome of this essential clash: "O homem é o animal que vive entre dois grandes brinquedos—o Amor onde ganha, a Morte onde perde. Por isso, inventou as artes plásticas, a poesia, a dança, a música, o teatro, o circo e, enfim, o cinema" (126). Bringing these views to his own case, Oswald recognizes that new ideas and new solutions—the principal characteristics of change—will always arise from the collision of adversarial elements, including advancements in culture, art, and literature. This is the principle at the heart of his brash philosophy of *antropofagia*, which, although the formal "Manifesto antropófago" was composed six years later after the publication of *Alma*, was already seen by the author as the implicit philosophical engine of the "Semana de Arte" of 1922 and the works that it introduced.

All of this affirms that as Oswald began his search for a new way to compose a Brazilian novel, outside of the formulas and expectations of Parnassian tradition, he was almost certainly seeking to create a work that was anything but *prosa crepuscular*. Rather, it would be an experimental product that would come out of the strongest possible collision he could devise between elements of old and new. For old, as he began to compose *Alma*, he had as an appropriately inflammatory subject the decadent, exploitative urban society of those who were the inheritors of Brazil's old patriarchal wealth. For new, he had his choice of several completely new models of human expression, all of which were to be found in the visual domain of human experience, rather than the verbal or literary domain. Thus they fell almost entirely outside of literary experience or precedent, and although their technical elements had been examined and discussed by European writers, they had as yet received no substantial or what might be termed *defining* reinterpretation and expression in the realm of language. The possibilities of such a synthesis between the politically unmentionable (rougher edges of contemporary urban life) and the intellectually unexplored (new structural foundations for narration) were entirely plastic and the outcome was completely unforeseen. It was the perfect moment for a personality like Oswald, whose working method was always marked by a certain reckless advance into uncertainty in his search for change. Or as Eleutério observes, "Criar o imprevisto é oswaldiano" (104).

One of these new structural models was the outcome of change in the visual arts in Europe, expressed primarily in the philosophy of Cubism. Artists were no longer obliged to reproduce, on canvas, some external reality, but began to extract elements from external reality, and then reorganize and restructure them into a new reality, which existed only as the work itself. The other model which intrigued Oswald arose, strangely, from no previous art form at all, but arrived as one of the new inventions of technology: the motion picture. Better yet, from Oswald's perspective, this enchanting development of popular culture was largely an original product of the New World. The first successful film technology was developed by an American, Thomas Edison; and as early as 1915 American films began to dominate the world and produced the new medium's most important improvements.[3]

While in *Miramar* Oswald would in fact synthesize his Brazilian subject matter with Cubist-based organizing concepts, with *Alma* he began his experiments, very deliberately, by submitting his Brazilian subject to a series of crude, fast, direct methods of expression that he derived from the patient study of film. More than that, it is possible to assert that it was Oswald's specific intent to craft a new and original structural basis for the Brazilian novel, taken as completely as possible from the whole body of the structural rules and common devices of film.[4] *Alma* was to be a novel that was written like a film — the first complete motion picture in print. It is almost a certainty that no one else had thought of such a venture in those terms, much less attempted it.

That Oswald should choose the principles of cinema as his first engine for change should surprise no one. The decades of 1900-1920 in São Paulo were marked by continuing industrialization as promised by the Positivist dream of *Ordem e Progresso*. Coming to maturity at

---

[3] In the month of August 1918, according to listings in *Correio Paulistano*, São Paulo's Centro Cinema with two *salões* showed a total of 20 films and, of these, some 60 percent or 12 films are the product of what appear to be U.S.-based studios: made or distributed by Fox-Film, Pathé, Paramount, Universal and Brady, as well as Goldwin, Triangle, Bison and L-KO (presumed predecessor to RKO). The cowboy movie is already a genre, and the leading "cow-Boy" of the period is Harry Carrey in a film by Gold Seal Studio, *O guia da morte*, as explained in the *Correio Paulistano* issue of Jan. 5, 1918, "soberbo e emocionante drama da fábrica Gold Seal, tendo como principal interprete o celebre cow-Boy, o incomparável atirador e cavalheiro Harry Carry."

[4] If this is true, we can discount the suggestion that Oswald might be in any serious debt to previous European ideas. Although European Symbolists had begun to note the potential of symbolism in films, this was by no means a symbolist undertaking. In addition, the only quality that might be termed Dada in the exercise was the daring, in some ways irrational qualities of the basic idea.

this time, the young author was inevitably focused on the future, and focused as well on the United States as a model of what the future and scientific invention together might bring to the world—and it arrived as the astonishing technology of cinema. In his "Manifesto da poesia pau-brasil" of 1924, antecedent to the debut of his first volume of poetry *Pau-brasil* (1925), Oswald offers a witty description of democratization in the arts through the continuing gifts of technology. He notes the arrival of pirogravure, the photograph machine, the piano in every parlor, and manufactured statuary. The only machine not invented, he comments dryly, is one to compose poetry, and for that there was the Parnassian poet (30). Cinema offered the technology to free both prose and poetry from the old Parnassian rules of thought and structure; and American films, in particular, already dominated the new medium.[5]

How did American cinema come to drive Oswald's creative imagination? One very basic reason for the early commercial success and presence of American films, despite the best creative efforts of filmmakers in many other nations, was the advantage of a more creative and economically efficient system of film distribution. In New York, in 1903, the Miles brothers established the first film distribution company. The brothers bought the rights to reproduce and rent films within certain territories, a method which on the one hand reduced costs to the exhibitor, but on the other hand dramatically expanded exposure and revenues to the original producer. Everyone made more money, and nothing succeeds like success. So by 1907 there were, according to Richard Schickel, "over a hundred film exchanges in thirty-five key American cities" (33). By 1908 there were also more than 8,000 established film houses, called nickelodeons by virtue of their modest ticket price, operating throughout the country. And perhaps more important, the new entertainment began to reach a previously untapped audience. As Schickel observes,

> [...I]t is well to keep in mind this central fact of movie history: that it began as mass entertainment. In the beginning the middle class,

---

[5] Oswald remains convinced of the liberating power and the future of technology throughout his life. Even many years later in "A crise da filosofia messiânica," although the author is critical of the United States and its accumulation of capital, he continues to recognize in it elements of the technological age which he has long been convinced is man's future: " [...] sem dúvida, é na América que está criado o clima do mundo lúdico e o clima do mundo técnico aberto para o futuro" (127).

a rising group still unsure of itself socially, was not only condescending, but occasionally mounted reforming crusades against movies. As for the upper classes, they were well above either interest in or antagonism toward the flickers. Only the plain people, needing no language to appreciate the silents, no great span of attention, and no particular subtlety of education, loved the movies. (33)

To keep this audience, American films also focused rapidly on material that had previously gone unnoticed: the events and characters of ordinary life. While this kind of realism had appeared in the plastic arts perhaps sixty years before, early filmmakers like the Frenchman Méliès had preferred to fix their work on magical and fantastic subjects. Other filmmakers in Europe—and even Brazil—focused on bringing to film the treasures of national literature or great events of history. Louis Jacobs notes that for American filmmakers,

> Fairy-tales, fantasies, story-book romances were far removed from their immediate interests. Subject matter was derived from American life—from the exploits of the policeman and burglar, cowboy and factory worker, farmer and country girl, clerk and politician, drunkard and servant girl, storekeeper and mechanic. (qtd. in Schickel 32)

"To represent the common man in the arts," Jacobs continues, "was still a novel if not a daring venture." It was, in fact, the inevitable outcome of the unique characteristics of the American marketplace that came together almost instantly: a vast mass audience, a low ticket price, low exhibition costs, and low manufacturing costs. To this notion of "daring venture" Schikel himself adds, "In an era when the genteel still ruled in literature and the irrelevant on the stage, it was even salutary" (32). To Oswald, the prospect of democratizing literature, utilizing new forms based on an American technology that eschewed the arcane and erudite audience in favor of the common man, must have been compelling.

Once he became determined to explore the new language of film to inspire the story and structure of his novel, where would Oswald search, and how would he identify film methods which he might successfully reconstruct on the page? Oswald, a man who enjoyed and wrote knowledgeably on all of the arts, might well have seen and collected details of technique from numerous films over a period of several years; or, in 1917 he might have looked to a single film, which is still ranked as one of the most original films in cinema history, as the principal source for his study and technical inspiration. No film in the second decade of the century could have had more impact on the young author than D.W. Griffith's masterwork, *Birth of a Nation*.

Whether Oswald actually saw this landmark film or only the ensuing explosion of films that followed and integrated all of its startling new techniques is not critical. What he did see, without question, was the birth of an important new art. How was one film able to achieve such a transcendent station? Certainly the most important film of its time, *Birth of a Nation* galvanized audiences like nothing before and shocked artists, writers and intellectuals, as well as demonstrated for the first time the possibility that film, heretofore a popular but essentially plebian entertainment, might yet emerge as an important cultural medium its own right, of the same rank as theater, the plastic arts, and literature. The film was immediately noted for its scale, dramatic action, and technical innovations in camera work and editing.

Birth of a Nation was the first twelve-reel motion picture ever made, with a running time of approximately three hours. The film tells the sweeping story of the American Civil War, its battles and its harsh aftermath from the perspective of two white families, friends to each other, the Stonemans and the Camerons, one from the North and the other from the South. An extended description of the events of the plot is beyond the scope of this review except to note that beyond a political and historic perspective that was considered as inflammatory and racist at the time of production as it would be today, the film stands as an astonishing and unique technical and artistic achievement and set a standard that was widely honored by its imitators for many years. Describing the innovative character of *Birth of a Nation*, Iris Barry notes that Griffith cut the complex film himself:

> It consists of 1,375 separate shots, most of them short. Each sequence begins with an iris-in, a fade-in or a title, and ends with an iris-out or a fade out. Punctuation is provided by masking, by panning from a vignetted close-up to a full long-shot and by the use of a split screen. Rapid cutting is resorted to both for contrast, as where a brief shot of the Cameron family at prayer is suddenly interjected into the battle scenes, or for suspense, as where the gathering and ride of the Klan is cross-cut both with the attack on the

cabin and with Lynch's final scenes with Elsie. By this astonishing piece of composition, Griffith undeniably earned the title of genius which has been so lavishly conferred on him. [...] [Played with a full orchestra] in theatres at theatre prices, the film's success finally lifted the motion picture out of social contempt. (16)

A closer look at his techniques is required to appreciate the originality of Griffith's methods, and his impact upon audiences. Even Griffith, of course, had his antecedents. He is given enormous credit for the montage, yet the reality of his contribution is far more complex, as Jean Mitry explains:

> If one considers montage as an ordering of scenes or a cross-cutting of two simultaneous actions, montage existed before Griffith. Smith and Williamson in England and Edwin Porter in the United States had been using it for a long time. But montage conceived of as the bringing together of analytic elements of the same scene, in other words, as the ordering of a succession of shots taken from different vantage points with various angles and framings, was Griffith's first great innovation. In addition, the length of a scene had always depended upon the time which the action would have lasted in real life. Through cutting and editing, Griffith showed that ellipsis and foreshortening could be introduced into the continuity. Not only did this manipulation of the temporal element enhance the interest of the scenario, but it also allowed the director to imprint his images with a certain rhythm, a pace. (n.p.)

A review by Susana Schild in the *Jornal do Brasil* offers an instructive summary of the highlights of Griffith's contributions to *linguagem cinemática* in this singular film:

- first *montagem* to create suspense
- first modifications in *luz/sombra* to create *clima*
- first *ação parallel* (simultaneity)
- first close-ups to reveal/intensify emotion
- first traveling camera (first action film)
- first flash-back

There were other discoveries that emerged from Griffith's research, invention and intuitive inspiration as well. Before Griffith, scenes were played by actors as if they were standing fixed, apart from the viewer, on a nineteenth-century theater stage. With the constant change introduced by Griffith in the location of the camera within a scene—now close to the hero, now distant, from distant angles, different vantage points—the viewer of *Birth of a Nation* comes to feel he is actually between the actors and within the scene. The new relationship between images also adds a separate connotative element that permits images and scenes to take on metaphorical levels of meaning, forming in effect a new language. *Birth of a Nation*, then, offered to its audiences in one three-hour experience an explosive demonstration of new creative and artistic possibilities such as no one, including Oswald de Andrade, had ever seen.

Whether Oswald saw the film itself or only its successors, in reading *Alma* and viewing *Birth of a Nation* today it becomes evident that the book tests a full range of techniques characteristic of and in parallel to the film. The parallel that has been perhaps most noted, and which was singularly recognized and credited by Oswald's critics at the time, is the apparently simple montage or "cut" method of placing together, one after another, scenes or text which represent discontinuous temporal or spatial events. In *Alma* this method enables the reader/viewer, as we have already seen in *Birth of a Nation*, to accept an ellipsis in the flow of events and, in effect, a compression of time. It allows the film to sweep convincingly from one scene to the next, through both great battles and small parlor conversations. In *Alma* it permits the reader to read thirteen-line chapters followed by sixty-line chapters and in the next moment even two-line chapters with the same sense of "reality."

But the montage technique, in fact, serves a number of additional uses in both the film and the book, such as the juxtaposition of two activities occurring at the same time, but in different locations. In *Birth of a Nation*, the most noted instance of this simultaneous counterpoint editing is the scene featuring a group of Klan horsemen who gather, then ride off to rescue the protagonists, whose own life-or-death struggles are intercut with the Klan riding sequences. In *Alma*, the first several chapters of the book, apparently disconnected and even unrelated, create the same sense of simultaneity. The story of *Alma* begins:

O velho e o cãozinho foram andando na sombra enjoada da tarde. Tinham passseado muito. Dobraram a esquina da Rua dos Clérigos. Os vizinhos saudavam-nos. Eram ambos antigos no bairro e na cidade.

Alma havia regressado naquele instante. Retirou a blusa, mostrando ao espelho do seu quarto guindado os alvos seios manchados de apertos.

Pensava: por que será que quando uma porta me machuca, me faz sofrer; quando bato a cabeça numa janela, choro de dor; e êle pode me cortar a navalha, não dói: é delicioso!

Mas lembrou-se da Odete, que estivera com Mauro [...]. (5)

The old man and his dog suddenly disappear without explanation from the opening scene. Instead, the "cut" leaps immediately to a new location and situation ("Alma havia regressado"). Because conventional narrative does not permit this sort of disconnection, the events appear to be simultaneous. In the use of this technique, as Brito notes, Oswald himself claimed primacy for its introduction to literature: "Oswald orgulhava-se mesmo de haver introduzido, entre nós, a técnica de contraponto, de Huxley, praticando-a antes até do que o famoso escritor inglês, fato êste registrado pelo ensaísta de *Sal da Heresia*" (xxv).

Another service of montage is to suggest, through the repeat of an earlier image in a later scene, the process of memory at work. In *Birth of a Nation*, the scene cuts from young Flora Cameron for several seconds—Schild's "first flashback"—to revisit an image from an earlier scene, the death of her brother on the battlefield; we readily interpret this as her "remembering" his death, although of course she was never there to see it. In *Alma* the author might simply say "she remembered" but the same result is achieved with more effect using montage, as Oswald demonstrates in the following passages. João, separated again from Alma, is in a bar drinking with his friend:

Na inconsciência de noite longa, no barzinho eleito do Braz, João e Frederico Carlos, no confessionário dos copos, disseram mal de Dagoberto.

Era um estraga-tudo irrequieto, que pairava numa suspensa ironia, sôbre a beleza dos seus vivos sentimentos, sôbre a credulidade e a força dos seus devotados corações.

> Ela era a sua vida, tôda sua vida.
>
> A cidade noturna festejava São João. Havia fogueiras, rojões, estouros de bombas.
> Num remorso, o seu coração fagulhava como os pobres fogos da cidade, trêmulos e curtos [...]. (97-8)

With the chapter of a single line—"Ela era a sua vida, tôda sua vida"—floating between the two longer chapters, Oswald creates the illusion that we have leapt from the bar scene to the secret interior of João's mind. We are, for the moment, witnessing two concurrent events, one exterior and the other interior, the latter something in-between a recollection of past happy moments and current lament of ongoing loss. Either way, the abrupt shift of time/place, exterior/interior, even slightly ambiguous, is achieved solely by the disconnection/isolation of the montage.

Yet another service of montage is simply to compress time. *Birth of a Nation* does not require three years to present the American Civil War. On a smaller scale, the quality of cinematic speed and the resulting time ellipsis in *Alma* enable the author and reader to share the early development of baby Luquinhas—recording in brief scenes all of the important moments of baby life along the way, from sickly infancy to the point of sturdy health, walking and talking, with a many other events thrown in—in just five pages (62-66).

Another optical technique exploited strongly in *Birth of a Nation* is the "iris-shot," which, by reducing the visible image to a small, circular portion of the whole screen, leaving the balance dark, allows the director to bring special attention to one small element within a larger scene. For example, a solitary mother sitting on the top of a hill weeps as she overlooks a great battle in the distance. In *Alma* this is achieved with spatial isolation as well, as the location of the narrative is shifted, but also through the use of an isolated single- or double-line chapter to turn the reader's attention momentarily to one small anecdotal detail. In *Alma*, an effect which parallels the iris-shot is achieved when, after Alma has fled her grandfather's house, the notice of her absence is recorded in a minuscule two-line chapter and the discovery is made, not by the grandfather himself, but by his surrogate, the tiny dog: "O cachorro pequenino, eriçado de pêlos sujos, foi, num tique-taque matinal, saudar a patroazinha no quarto vazio" (14).

The technical parallels between *Birth of a Nation* and *Alma* continue in what might be termed film mannerisms. One popular mannerism of early films was the way that scenes frequently opened or concluded in fixed, sentimental tableaus. In *Birth of a Nation*, Senator Stoneman and his daughter Elsie are shown in a scene in his library, the daughter curled lovingly around her father. A title introduces the tableau, but the scene offers no action, only the two actors fixed in place. In *Alma*, scenes that feature a tranquil moment between the characters are similarly framed with a sense of the characters curled together in a fixed pose, frozen in an eternally perfect moment, as if for some unseen camera. For example, Alma and João share a moment of peace and harmony in João's humble room: "Ela enroscava-se tôda no homem forte e bom" (39). The expression of this moment would appear to be overly coy and sentimental. Reviewing silent film mannerisms, however, we can see that the text actually reflects a highly characteristic, otherwise overlooked reference to cinematic staging.

Beyond its qualities as a tableau, the same citation points us back to a more general parallel in manners between the film and book—a certain hyper-expressive quality in the actions and physical attitudes of characters in both. Without words to capture the nuance of emotions, it is easy to appreciate that early film actors resorted to the techniques of stage actors before them, who employed exaggerated gestures and over-expressed emotions to communicate with audiences across the gulf of the orchestra. With its own exaggerated poses, actions and reactions, *Alma* seems to wish to invoke in the reader some unconscious recollection of the film experience, as if the author had in mind a test: to see if the reader, like the filmgoer, would "suspend disbelief" confronted by improbable and overly-expressive emotional reactions and unnaturally strong responses.[6]

---

[6] What we are also seeing in Oswald's penchant for heroic language, such as the dactylic "homem forte e bom" which occurs with some frequency in *Alma*, is perhaps, beyond a maneristic duplication of cinematic melodrama, an echo from Oswald's relationship with the very young schoolgirl Deisi, and the teasing, mock-heroic, melodramatic parody that appears in their notes to each other in Oswald's astonishing *garçonnière* diary, which was ultimately published as *O perfeito cozinheiro das almas deste mundo*. Of Oswald's relationship with Deisi, whom he married on her deathbed, Haroldo de Campos notes, in essence, that the author saw her fierce independence as the contemporary version of one or another of Alencar's proto-mythical Indian women: a new Iracema, innocent and pure, yet whose natural sensuality and instinct for seduction, a consequence of living outside of "civilized" norms, must ultimately lead to her death (17). Thus, Oswald's sappy melodramatic

The numbing series of hyperbolic crises encountered in the plotline of *Alma*, in terms of their sheer frequency, may itself be seen as another, independent element of cinematic or at least *cine-folhetim* origin. The *cine-folhetim*, or film serial—like the "cliffhanger" *folhetim* published serially in newspapers—became an economic mainstay for the cinema of the period and came to represent perhaps thirty percent or more of cinema revenues. The exact economic importance is hard to estimate, since almost every program came to have at least one film serial episode as part of the show. This brought filmgoers back again and again, even if the other films on the bill were less than compelling. Initial promotional interest in the *cine-folhetim* was generated by running the story first as a regular *folhetim* in the newspapers. This served to maintain newsstand sales and subscription renewals, but it also drove the curiosity of readers to see the real thing: the film. A daily like *Correio Paulistano* frequently had several *folhetins* appearing at once. Theaters throughout São Paulo might ultimately have 4 to 6 episodes of the *cine-folhetim* running on different bills at the same time. One French-produced *cine-folhetim* mystery, *Judex*, appeared in 63 segments in *Correio Paulistano* from October 23, 1917, through December 31, 1917. The story opens, "Num dos bairros de mais luxo de Paris, installado num apartamento elegante, vivia um rapaz de aparência distincta" (4). By December 30 episodes 1, 4, 7, 8, 10 and 11 of *Judex* were all running in São Paulo theaters. Meanwhile, episode 6 of the U.S.-produced serial *Ravengar* was showing as well. All of this suggests the probability of another close stylistic link between Oswald's *Alma* and the cinema of the time. The sharp emotional ups and downs of the *Alma* story line, certainly, begin to look less like an accident of Oswald's over-stimulated prose than part of a deliberate soap-opera style and organization parallel to the immensely popular *cine-folhetim*. Sérgio Milliet, troubled by the same gyrations of the plot in translating *Alma* to French, actually suggested to Oswald that the term "Romance Folhetim" might serve as part of the title of *Os condenados*, as *Alma* was called in its premiere edition (Boaventura 80).

Yet another novel element characteristic of early cinema arose from film's unique power to present something of a highly improbable nature that at least *appeared* real. Filmmakers from the beginning ex-

---

mately lead to her death (17). Thus, Oswald's sappy melodramatic language is both a parody and a genuine expression of his feeling at the same time, and in no case would it appear to represent the simple and unconscious overwriting that critics seem to have assumed.

ploited the photo-realism of the medium to stage improbable events, suggest infeasible results, or invoke the most unlikely coincidences, with the expectation that audiences would readily accept and believe. Neither *Birth of a Nation* nor *Alma* presents an exception to this desire of directors to move a story along through the most farfetched developments. In *Birth of a Nation*, we are expected to believe that two of the younger brothers in the Stoneman and Cameron clans, marching along with millions of soldiers that they do not know, somehow come to the same battlefield, engage in hand-to-hand combat, and even manage to drop dead in an artful side-by-side tableau, still essentially innocent and friendly, in a poignant scene of comrades in death. Almost as statistically unlikely, at the end of the novel Alma's adoring lover, João de Carmo, happens to spot her walking along in the park in a warm and flirtatious manner with a handsome, unidentified young man. With the discovery of this latest coquettry, even considering that it is only one of many betrayals, the emotionally fragile João is finally driven to suicide. Only later, as Alma waits in vain for João to return home, do we learn another shocking and equally improbable coincidence—that the handsome young man in the park was actually Alma's cousin Jorge d'Alvelos, a young sculptor returning from Europe.[7]

Another striking and unexpected point of comparison between *Birth of a Nation* and *Alma* appears in the element of dialogue. While a shortage of conversation is to be expected in a silent film, there is also a notable absence of complex, direct dialogue in *Alma*. This appears to be a serious gesture to accept, in the author's experimental design of this first novel of his projected series, what is perhaps the most inconvenient limitation of the silent film, which is that complex interactive conversations become impossible and are generally omitted. Indeed, in *Alma*, dialogue, the essential element on which both theater and literature so heavily depend, is left on the cutting-room

---

[7] Enchanted by the circus as a child, Oswald is hopelessly addicted to these highly gymnastic but improbable story twists. He continues their use in the sequel to *Alma*, *A estrêla de absinto*, when Jorge d'Alvelos, now a suicide himself, is taken to the morgue: when grieving friends come to visit him on the slab they discover, guess what, the bullet struck just below his heart. Rushed to the hospital, he lives! In *Estrêla* Oswald also maintains his penchant for shock openings, as the book commences with a sultry affair between Jorge and his tawny young cousin who remains, as before, *risonha e esbelta*. Of course, the histories of both literature and the theater record the shameless deployment of the improbable coincidence, and Oswald's appropriation of it here might almost be applauded as Shakespearean as much as cinematic.

floor. Altogether, the author permits his characters just 143 lines of conversation in a novel of 2,987 lines, and perhaps almost half of these are only single lines of exclamation and might not actually qualify as conversation. Further, the total of 143 lines amounts to less than 5 percent of the novel, or as much language as might be found in a few of the title cards which, again, were part of the essential vocabulary of the silent film. That this sharp limitation of dialogue in *Alma* might be a reflection of the author's experimental approach to translating methods from film is indirectly suggested as well by the way the use of dialogue here contrasts with its use in the next book in the *Os condenados* trilogy, *A estrêla de absinto*. The sequel, published five years later in 1927, is a direct continuation of the story from *Alma*. Featuring the same principal characters of Alma and her cousin Jorge d'Alvelos, it moves away from some of the most extreme structural experiments of *Alma* in several interesting ways. It is as if the author, having taken his experiment to its absolute limits in the first novel, is now ready to readjust the balance in his use of techniques from film and to focus, in other words, on what works, to skip what doesn't, and to synthesize — to use that word here in a new sense — the optimum result. The most noticeable of these changes in *A estrêla de absinto* includes a sharp reduction in the high number of very brief cuts, the addition of many more chapters of substantial length, and the inclusion of more dialogue — all reversing some of the most visible characteristics just noted in both early silent films and in *Alma*.[8] This marked change in narra-

---

[8] A technical comparison of *Alma* and *A estrêla de absinto* reveals the clear evolution of the author's methodical structural experiment. Specifically *Alma* breaks down into 238 chapters of a total of 2,987 lines. Of these chapters, 78 are from 1-to-5 lines (33.2 percent of the total), and another 75 are from 6-to-10 lines (31.9 percent of the total), so that the total of short "snapshot" chapters constitutes more than 65 percent of all chapters in the book. Chapters of 40 lines or more (chapters longer than a single page), meanwhile, represent just 31.6 percent of the total content (lines) of the book. *Alma*'s sequel, in contrast, although roughly the same length (112 pages and 3,841 lines), and featuring the same central characters, was eventually published in 105 chapters, of which brief chapters of 1-10 lines constitute just 19 percent of the book. Further, comparing just extremely brief chapters of only one or two lines, *Alma* has 23, while *Estrêla* has none. Moreover, from a total of just 143 lines of dialogue throughout *Alma*, representing a minute 4.8 percent of the book, the dialogue in *A estrêla de absinto* leaps to 598 lines of conversational development, or a hefty 16.6 percent of the book, and much of it of central importance to the story.

tive method in the sequel to *Alma*, representing a move closer to traditional, accessible storytelling, highlights its predecessor's experimental and radical nature.

On the other hand, if Oswald is "making a complete film in words," as we propose, or if by some similar description of a more complete, holistic method we may say that he is attempting to translate the entire sum of film technologies to the medium of print, is there no evidence for a counterargument? There are several obvious elements of filmmaking that Oswald does seem to ignore. For example, it has been said that one characteristic of the silent film is that the camera, director and audience are all, in a sense, "exterior" observers to all that happens; but much of *Alma* is written, not from an exterior viewpoint, but ostensibly from the interior of the principal character. Rather than describing Alma's emotions and actions with anything like the camera's objective viewpoint, as the counterargument would remind us, the author reveals her thoughts and feelings almost entirely from an inside perspective. Another problem that might be raised is the question of black and white versus color. Silent films, one might assume, represent an experience essentially in black and white, while in *Alma* the author employs many vivid descriptions of color. For example, as Alma takes her loving departure from the momentarily happy João, "À porta, ela tinha estacado, sorrindo, à espera. Êle fôra beijá-la na bôca e vê-la partir, tôda lilás e oiro, no vestido curto" (67). Should we not assume that, in recreating the experience of a film on paper, the author would be careful to omit the description of vivid colors? Further, rather than literal and external, doesn't its use here imply an intention that is rather more reflective, internal and even metaphoric?

If we propose that Oswald was attempting to invent, however it might come out, a novel written like a film, it becomes important to understand how Oswald himself might have seen and approached the problem: as a process of raw transliteration or as a more subtle exercise in authentic translation? While there is no published evidence pointing us toward the author's exact methodology, perhaps the best response to this question of process—transliteration vs. translation— might be to take note that a transliteration is fundamentally narrow and dogmatic in its application and Oswald, by all accounts, was philosophically neither narrow nor dogmatic. As a writer, Oswald would almost certainly have looked at the adaptation as an additive process. Taking this approach, it might be argued that films themselves provide the basis for this methodology because silent films, in fact, did everything possible to evoke and assist sense memory. In the films of Charlie Chaplin, as Gerald Mast comments, the artist continually implies

> the operations of all the senses (quite an accomplishment in an art apparently confined to the single sense of sight). Charlie perpetually reveals how things smell ([...] sniffing the aroma of a hot dog [...], the bottoms of his shoes [...]); how they taste [...], how they sound [...], and how they feel to the touch [...]. (92)

Even the qualities of black and white could not prevent filmmakers from evoking a poetic or, for that matter, metaphoric sense of color. *Birth of a Nation*, although technically filmed within the limits of black and white, was not actually exhibited in black and white; rather, the film was tinted in a spectrum of colors—amber, blue, green, yellow, orange—to express the mood of the scene; and some of the great battles, fought and filmed at night by the light of flares, were given added emotional intensity by their fiery red color. Tight regulations, limits, and systems of rules were for the Parnassians, not for the radical sensibilities of Oswald or for his contemporary model of creative rule-breaking, the filmmaker.

It was just this liberty of the filmmaker, unfettered by the rules of written literature, that perhaps appealed to Oswald most. Although the cinematic viewpoint was enacted on the exterior in purely visual terms, the new power of montage to observe and compress events from every direction placed the audience for the first time outside themselves and into the center of the scene and story in a way that made the unreal "real." That he was entranced by this new experience and that it became a central theme in Owsald's creative explorations are without question. It was this hypnotic quality of *encantamento*, perhaps more than anything else, that drove Oswald in his attempt to reproduce the film experience on paper. Just a few years later, in 1925, he would publish an extraordinary poem in *Pau-brasil* reflecting on the cinema's seductive power:

"Linha no escuro"

É fita de risada
A criançada hurla como o vento
Mas os cotovelos se encontram
Se acotovelam e se apalpam

Mãos descem na calada de lua quadrângula
Enquanto a orquestra cavalos e letreiros galopam

Entre saias uma lixa humana se arredonda
Mas quando amanhece
   A mulher qualquer
      Desaparece   (62)

Even the title, referring to the streak of light flashing through the haze of air above the audience from the *lanterna mágica* or projector to the theater screen, offers an additional allusion to the experience of motion and velocity as a crucial element defining both art and reality, as well as to the parallel association of cinema with other transforming manifestations of new technology: telephone line, telegraph line, rail line, airline, streetcar line, power line. With the rise of the *lua quadrângula* the restless jostling and bumping of the human sandpaper is smoothed away. In Oswald's vision of the seductive process, *saias* replace the more conventional *cortinas* and as they part, the screen, now filled with horses and galloping titles washed in the music of the orchestra, enchants like a woman. But with "daybreak," as the lights go up once more, the woman, whatever woman—each time it is the same exhilarating experience—disappears again. Perhaps no one understood the powerful artifice inherent in popular cinema better than Oswald. That it might be the centerpiece of his first large literary experiment would be most natural.

    There are additional technical indicators that would make *Alma* more than simply "cinematic." Although authors seldom explain their own methods and puncture the mystery of the process, they may sometimes leave small, witty clues. In the case of *Alma*, one helpful clue would be a "mistake." Let us examine how this functions by first begging the question, how do we know if an apparent film technique appearing in print truly was inspired by cinema? Suppose the author imbedded somewhere in *Alma*, not the literary parallel of a unique cinematic feature, but of a unique cinematic *error* or *mistake*. Might such a mistake point to Oswald's intentionality and can one be identified in *Alma*? In the preparation of early films it was easy for film editors to leave some inadvertent technical error in their work. In the original release of *Birth of a Nation*, for example, there is a brief but noticeable repeat of frames at the Cameron house, preceded by the title "Back home with the good news," between scenes 417c and 417d, as Flora enters the scene and hugs her mother (Cuniberti 81). Such miscuts in editing were particularly common in the preparation of silent films, which lacked an audible tic from a jumping soundtrack when processed on rough equipment in the primitive editing rooms of the day. Filmgoers largely ignored these small errors, which were easily observable as brief repeats of perhaps 3 or 4 frames, but they might have caught the attention of a close observer like Oswald, who would have appreciated the implications of time and reality magically interrupted and transformed by the new medium. Are there any similar errors in *Alma*? In fact, there are several interesting repeats. One, which occurs early, is the (virtual) repeat of a long complete sentence, separated only by a brief two-sentence interval:

> Continha a felicidade dentro do peito musculoso de nadador; segurava-a como um pássaro vivo. [. . .]
> Êle continha a felicidade dentro do peito musculoso de nadador, segurava-a como um pássaro vivo. (8)

The impression is that the repeat is a typesetter's editing error since the sentence could work in either location, but the repetition becomes seriously redundant appearing in both. In contrast, several pages later there is a charming and certainly intentional repeat of the same sentence, in reversed order, as the opening lines of sequential paragraphs: "Passou por ela alguém. [...] Alguém passou por ela" (10). But this is clearly a deliberate effect simply designed to reflect a character walking back and forth in the background, effectively out of focus, and would not constitute an error. A third possibility, more like the first, seems to show a double placement of a virtually identical sentence that might occur in either of two locations separated by three intervening sentences—apparently another editing error: "Num remorso, o seu coração fagulhava como os pobres fogos da cidade, trêmulos e curtos" (97). In fact, both of these two authentic typesetter's editing "errors" have been maintained through several editions after the original first edition of *As memorias do exílio: Os condenados*. Such deliberate "repeats" or sentences of text repeated in a second location, would actually suggest several alternatives in their inspiration from the cinema. One might be the intentional repeat replicating the "cinematic error" we have already mentioned. But another possibility is an homage to the cinema's custom of using the same footage twice to improve continuity or stretch suspense in crowd or chase scenes. Or, as yet another cinematic inspiration, the repeats could represent an explicit experiment in "intercut," going from interior to exterior to interior again to heighten the sense of simultaneity. In any case the repeats in *Alma* are very cinematic, and even as "errors" we can be sure that they are deliberate.

This detailed review of Oswald's design system in *Alma*, linked to specific, close parallels in the methods of film, appears to solve several interesting problems left by previous studies of the work. But certainly its most delightful and unexpected result is to explain the special problem of the dog. Curiously, not one critic who has examined *Alma*, at its introduction or since, has apparently looked down and noticed the dog.[9] Based on the sheer number of times the dog of old Lucas is recorded in *Alma*—its presence, its hair condition, its attitude, its yapping, its inner turmoil—one might easily assume the old dog, rather than Alma, João do Carmo or Lucas himself, is somehow the most indispensable character of the book. In a novel of scarcely one hundred pages, the dog Baubau is mentioned, either directly or indirectly, on at least 21 separate occasions, in every possible circumstance, beginning from the first line of the book. Here are just a few of the mentions (their order of appearance is noted in brackets):

O velho e o cãozinho foram andando na sombra enjoada da tarde. (5) [1]

Seriam cinco horas da tarde; o velho e o cão passeavam ainda. (6) [3]

---

[9] The one exception is Oswald's latest biographer, Boaventura, who suggests that Baubau may be inspired by Flon-Flon, the family dog of Oswald's parents. However, the only dog that appears anywhere in the 168 photographs found in Oswald's archives at Centro de Documentação Cultural "Alexandre Eulalio" (CEDAE), Universidade Estadual de Campinas, has the large, sleek lines of a doberman, not a mutt (Coleção: Oswald de Andrade; Série: Fotografias; Pasta: 04; No. OAF 028; CEDAE).

> [Alma] Ia fugir, deixar para sempre o velho, o moleque, o cãozinho. Teve um sorriso cruel. (11) [6]
>
> A Companhia de Desenvolvimento anunciou-lhe (o velho), numa bela escrita a máquina, que não reformaria a hipoteca vencida. O cãozinho peludo quase perdera a vista. (46) [14]
>
> Era uma colherzina de D. Genoveva, oxidada pelo uso. Chamava-se a Calalá. O Baubau era o cão bôbo do avô. (63) [18]
>
> Dez horas ... onze horas... Alma quase dormia.
> Jorge d'Alvelos, seu primo escultor, chegara de Europa. [. . .] Agora, apresentá-lo-ia a João... Que demora na noite... Ela quase dormia... Na distância, um cão ladrava: bau... bau... bau..." (104) [21]

Even death cannot entirely banish this dog who, although run over and killed by a carnival truck little more than halfway through the novel, returns from the spirit world at the end to bark in the distance. What was Oswald's intent in populating *Alma* with the omnipresent character of a dog—a small, hairy, dirty dog at that?

Dogs, from the earliest days, served as an almost indispensable agent in silent films, useful to filmmakers for a great variety of reasons. In the first years, when audiences were enthralled with the way the verisimilitude of film could make the improbable seem real, dogs provided cheap subjects for what was always a diverting demonstration. But such films were sometimes more than simply amusing; they were technically brilliant.

As film historian Kenneth MacGowan relates, dogs were ideal heroes appearing in one of the earliest and most popular film genres, the chase:

> The best picture of this kind—and perhaps the most skillfully conceived and edited film before the coming of D. W. Griffith—was Cecil Hepworth's *Rescued by Rover*, 425 feet long, which he made in 1905. The plot is a bit preposterous: a child is stolen by a beggar woman, the father's collie dog listens to the story of bereavement, jumps out of the window, tracks town the child without the aid of scent, and leads the father to the room where the child is hidden. What makes the film notable—aside from the fact

that the dog was the first film character that didn't overact—is the continuity of the chase. (45)

The dog, it turns out, provided filmmakers with an important "archetypal" character. Effective storytelling within the time constraints of early silent films was always enhanced by archetypal qualities in their characters. As Iris Barry concisely describes, *Rescued by Rover* amounts to

> Careless nursemaid, gin-sodden crone, stolen baby, sagacious dog, reunited family—the figures in this little English film were as immediately recognizable as those in a fresco series on the Life of St. Joseph to a good 14th-century Christian. The familiar if improbable incident thus translated into mobile photographic images struck audiences as particularly delightful and the film enjoyed success over a period of years. (10)

Later, as techniques developed, the sagacious dog remained a film mainstay, often taking a leading role. Beginning in 1914, in the brilliant and internationally beloved films of Charlie Chaplin, dogs—with their improbable intelligence and capabilities—served Chaplin's comedy in innumerable ways. Chaplin's films appeared regularly in Brazilian cinema houses at this time, and he was affectionately advertised to audiences as both Carlito and Bigodinho.[10] To the extent that dogs, like Chaplin himself, were always operating at the bottom of the social scale, they became a useful symbol for his stories of working class ethics and solidarity, and their emotions provided an ironic parallel to their master's own feelings. In Chaplin's *The Champion*, a two-reeler (approximately 30 minutes) released on March 11, 1915, Charlie and his loyal bulldog—both hungry—encounter an abandoned frankfurter. As a kindred soul or even a surrogate for Chaplin himself, the dog ini-

---

[10] That Chaplin enjoyed two nicknames and that Bigodinho is indeed Carlito is not immediately apparent. Cinema listings in *O Diario de Minas* located in the hemeroteca of the Biblioteca Central, Belo Horizonte, reveal the connection. *Irresistivel* by Carlito was showing at the Cinema Central on October 5, 1915. A few months later *Nenhuma me resiste* by Bigodinho was reported at the Cinema Central on January 23, 1916. This, of course, is the same film. Interestingly, outside of the journals of the period the name Bigodinho seems to have been quickly discarded in universal favor of Carlito and has otherwise been lost.

tially rejects Chaplin's amusing offer of the first bite into the hotdog. As film historian Gerald D. McDonald explains the scene, "The dog, however, refuses to touch it until Charlie sprinkles some salt on it" (88). Later, when Charlie finds himself in an boxing match, "His dog watches the fight, smiles when Charlie scores, becomes fierce, then gloomy, when Charlie is knocked down" (88). Three years later, with the release of the three-reeler *A Dog's Life* on April 14, 1918, Chaplin returned to the same premise of destitute man, dog, and the comic ambiguity of identity between the two. Initially Chaplin saves the dog, Scraps; and later, when Scraps digs up a cash-filled wallet buried by crooks, the dog returns the favor. At the end, Chaplin marries the cute cabaret girl, buys the farm ... and Scraps delivers a litter of puppies.

Finally, even in *Birth of a Nation*, the more serious film which has been our principal subject for comparison and discussion, dogs provide, early in the film, a crucial metaphor presaging the conflict that is to come. As we have seen, *Birth of a Nation* astonished audiences with the brilliance of its scope and imagination. But as Gerald Mast observes, the director Griffith also played close attention to the drama of human details. One technique he used to express human feeling, almost from the first moments of the film, was with the presence of animals, and specifically dogs. Griffith, Mast tells us,

> uses animals to define his characters and their emotional states. In the film's opening sequence depicting the gentle, peaceful life of the old South (analogous to the opening sequence of Judith of Bethulia) Griffith shows Mister Cameron gently stroking two puppies. Significantly, one of the puppies is black and the other white; it is also significant that a kitten soon begins to play with the pups. The animals become visual metaphors for Griffith's idealized prewar South. [. . .] The attitudes of the characters toward animals ultimately reveal their attitudes toward people. (67)

In looking more carefully at Oswald's many mentions of the old dog Baubau in *Alma*, we can see that the small creature serves many of the same uses that early filmmakers knew it could bring to almost any story: Baubau, old and unkempt, is his master's alter ego (5) [mention no. 1]; he is Panza to the old man's Quixote (6) [3]; he is Cerebus snarling to block Alma from her path to Hell (11) [6]; he is the mirror of his master's feelings (46) [14]; he is the continuation of love across generations (63) [18]; he is the angel of fate (104) [21]. There are even dogs in *Alma*, as in *Birth of a Nation*, to serve as a metaphor for conflict and for the presence in Alma's life of both good and evil, representing a dangerous clash of choices. On the one hand, Baubau "conversava com êle aos latidos longos, expressivos, num abanar de cauda que lhe indicava corajosos caminhos" (19) [9]; on the other hand, in a single mention, the powerful, indolent beast of Alma's pimp, Mauro Glade,

> À claridade fechada, ela viu sôbre o leito exíguo, recoberto por uma colcha felpuda e multicor, um cãozinho cinzento e enorme, estirado nas duas patas tranqüilas. O animal, sem erguer a cabeça, balançou a cauda contente.(49)

With the explanation, finally, of the heretofore inexplicable Baubau the dog, we have a solution for the most glaring problem left by previous interpretations of *Alma*. Knowing from the beginning that Oswald looked closely at American cinema, we still cannot say with absolute certainty which films he saw or exactly how he approached the new art for methods he could synthesize into a new Brazilian literature. But seeing the complexity of the parallels between *Alma* and Oswald's most probable film models, we can be confident, at least, that *Alma* represents anything but *prosa crepuscular*. Rather, it shows the same remarkable gift for invention that marks *Miramar* and *Pau-brasil* that were to come just two and three years later.

We have argued that Oswald de Andrade, in undertaking to write *Alma*, was attempting to create a novel, however it might come out, written like a film. Although no one else appears to have previously thought of or attempted it, the audacity of such an endeavor—a true *romance-invenção*—would not be beyond the imagination of Oswald. The study of *Alma* presented here would appear to identify new answers to problems of interpretation that can be resolved no other way. Further study of Oswald's design process in the development of *Alma* may help us better understand the author's path to his later landmark works as well. In sum, given the numerous parallels that support the originality of Oswald's technical method in *Alma*, perhaps Oswald's earliest work merits a vigorous reassessment. Far from *prosa crepuscular*, it may well be the first complete motion picture in print.

Works Cited

Andrade, Oswald de. *Alma. Os condenados*. Rio de Janeiro: Editôra Civilização Brasileira S.A., 1970.

———. "A crise da filosofia messiânica." *Do pau-brasil à antropofagia e às utopias*. Rio de Janeiro: Editôra Civilização Brasileira S.A., 1970. 75-138.

———. *A estrêla de absinto. Os condenados*. Rio de Janeiro: Editôra Civilização Brasileira S.A., 1970.

———. "Manifesto da poesia pau-brasil." *Do pau-brasil à antropofagia e às utopias*. Rio de Janeiro: Editôra Civilização Brasileira S.A., 1970. 3-10

———. "Novas dimenções da poesia." *Estética e política*. São Paulo: Globo, 1992.

———. "Linha no escuro." *Poesias reunidas*. Rio de Janeiro: Editôra Civilização Brasileira S.A, 1971. 11-89.

———. *O perfeito cozinheiro das almas deste mundo*. São Paulo: Globo, 1992.

Barry, Iris. *The Silent Film*. New York: The Museum of Modern Art Film Library, 1949.

Boaventura, Maria Eugênia. *O salão e a selva: uma biografia ilustrada de Oswald de Andrade*. Campinas: Editora da UNICAMP, 1995.

Brito, Mário da Silva. "O aluno de romance Oswald de Andrade." Preface. *Os condenados*. By Oswald de Andrade. xv-xxxviii.

Campos, Haroldo de. Introductory essay. *O perfeito cozinheiro das almas deste mundo*. By Oswald de Andrade. *Obras completas*. São Paulo: Globo, 1992. xi-lxi.

Correio Paulistano. Oct. 23-Dec. 31, 1917; Jan. 5, 1918; Aug. 1918.

Cuniberti, John. *The Birth of a Nation, a Formal Shot-by-Shot Analysis Together With Microfiche*. Woodbridge, Connecticut: Research Publications, Inc, 1979.

Eleutério, Maria de Lourdes. *Oswald: itinerário de um homem sem profissão*. Campinas: Editora da UNICAMP, 1989.

Fonseca, Cristina. *O pensamento vivo de Oswald de Andrade*. São Paulo: Martin Claret Editores, 1987.

McDonald, Gerald D., Michael Conway and Mark Ricci. *The Films of Charlie Chaplin*. New York: Bonanza Books, Crown Publishers, 1965.

MacGowan, Kenneth. *Behind the Screen: the History and Techniques of the Motion Picture*. New York: Delacorte Press, 1965.

Mast, Gerald. *A Short History of the Movies*. New York: Macmillan Publishing Company, 1986.

Mitry, Jean. Preface. Cuniberti. n.p.

Nunes, Benedito. "Antropofagia ao alcance de todos." Preface. *Do pau-brasil à antropofagia e às utopias*. By Oswald de Andrade. Rio de Janeiro: Editôra Civilização Brasileira S.A., 1970. vi-xvii.

O Diario de Minas. Oct. 5, 1915; Jan. 23, 1916.

Schickel, Richard. *Movies*. New York: Basic Books, 1964.

Schild, Susan. "Review of D.W.Griffith." *Jornal do Brasil*. September 4, 1984.

"The New Sweaty Beauty of the Century." Avant-Garde, Sexuality, and Revolution in Mexico

RAFAEL HERNÁNDEZ-RODRÍGUEZ
Southern Connecticut State University

IN 1921, WHILE MEXICO was celebrating the centenary of the consummation of its struggle for independence, it was already clear that the country had changed dramatically since the exile of Porfirio Díaz. And perhaps one of the most interesting and radical outcomes of this change was a renaissance of patriotic feeling. The occasion was celebrated not only with elaborate civic ceremonies at the Independence Monument and the tombs of the heroes in the cathedral, but also with popular picnics, traditional rodeo-like *jaripeos*, fireworks, and *guerras floridas*—literally "flower wars," in which two sides attack each other by throwing flowers. Another activity favored by Mexicans in those days and that also was included in the celebrations was watching parades of decorated floats. One of these floats was particularly symbolic of the new times: it was shaped as a boat with an effigy of Cuauhtémoc, "the last Aztec emperor." Riding on it, in the middle of a simulated landscape of cactus and volcanic stones, was a proud young woman, María Viviana Uribe, "La India Bonita"—the "Pretty Indian Girl," who had been selected as the "most beautiful among the women of her race" in one of the first national beauty pageants.[1]

The explosion of nationalism understood as Indianism at the beginning of the century was neither rare nor peculiar to Mexico. On the contrary, similar tendencies could be observed in most American na-

---

[1] The images of the last days of the dictatorship of Porfirio Díaz described in this essay were wonderfully captured in *Memorias de un mexicano*.

tions at around the same time, including the United States and Brazil. The failure of Western culture was "confirmed" by the devastation of Europe at the end of World War I, and the reaction was immediately felt. In America such reaction took the form of a sort of "continentalism"—an identification and fascination with the new, and especially with the native.

In South America, for example, the Week of Modern Art in São Paulo in 1922 would point to a radically new path for Brazilian culture and arts. Although inspired by the European avant-garde, one of its manifestos took its cue from the cannibalistic Amazonian Indians at the time of the conquest and determined to devour European culture, assimilating what was possible to assimilate and discharging what was not. In the United States there was a revalorization of everything considered American—from crafts and the landscape to the indigenous peoples, who for the first time were not seen as a danger to the American way of life, but as an exotic addition so tame that they could even help to create an American "identity" as something other than European.

"No longer seen as a threat to white settlement of the West after the surrender at Wounded Knee in 1890, Native Americans acquired a fabled status as an embodiment of harmony and unity [. . . .] they provided a subject matter both mythic and nativist," according to Barbara Haskell (33). And if the native peoples caught the imagination of artists at the beginning of the century, it was no accident that it happened in a way that in reality reinforced the Indian's marginality since it was an attempt by mainstream culture to reach a unilateral reconciliation with the past by accepting only a sentimental one-dimensional view of indigenous life.

The Native American who suddenly became visible was not the warrior, Crazy Horse or Geronimo, but the shaman, who derived inevitably from the stereotype of Indians as people in touch with the spiritual forces of "Nature." Although it can be seen as inclusive and noble, this perception of Indians aimed to mark the division between the "pioneer" or man of action and the nature-imbedded or passive Indian. Only later, in the mid- and late-thirties, was the idea of a connection with the land and the autochthonous was extended artistically to rural white communities, particularly in the works of Thomas Hart Benton, Grant Wood, and John Steuart Curry. But even then, the identification with nature in those communities was supposed to be evidence of the indomitable American spirit rather than superstition.

"Like Benton, Curry believed that human interactions with the land and the struggle against the forces of nature were the fundamental American experiences" (Haskell 224). While Indians worshipped and conformed to Nature, white settlers dominated it.

Essentially, to be "American" meant to be modern. And that modernism was also largely identified with the urban experience. New York came to symbolize early on everything that was new and exciting. The prevailing mood in the Americas was that the weakening of Europe only would benefit them. Even the Old Continent fell under the spell of Americanism associating it with the United States, a country that became fundamental to the cultural discourse at the beginning of the century. America with its cinema, its technology, its machinery, its electricity; America with its automobiles, its architecture, its jazz bands, its bridges and skyscrapers. America represented the future. And that is how most artists of the time perceived it: "There was something celebratory and patriotic about making art out of such subjects, and artists turned to them with a newfound pride in America" (Haskell 47). The dazzle of United States capitalism was modernity itself.

In Mexico, it was obvious that the Revolution had fed and accelerated a process of identification with the indigenous that in reality was a sign of the rejection of those parts of Mexican culture that had heavily relied on the European. The armed movement that destroyed towns, dislocated populations, made possible the interaction among the classes and between the sexes brought to light a hidden but very dynamic culture that existed just beneath the official one—a culture that was at the same time rooted in the indigenous past and directly connected to the masses. Only then did it become clear that a new society was ready to emerge from the ruins of the Old Regime of Porfirio Díaz, or Porfiriato (1876-1910), and that this new society would rest greatly on its indigenous elements. This reclaiming of the indigenous was less a vindication of the Indians than a calculated decision to offer an alternative to a Eurocentric culture.

Of course, Indian cultures had persisted during the Porfiriato, but they achieved official recognition exclusively in terms of the magnificence of the remote Aztec and Maya civilizations. For all the elaborate spectacles that included parades and the unveiling of statues, this glorification of the Indian was a political manipulation—a way of overlooking the cruel marginality the descendants of those very peoples were still suffering at the beginning of the twentieth century. Perhaps the most enduring example of this political manipulation of history is the

Paseo de la Reforma. With its statues along the boulevard and others strategically placed in its traffic circles, no other public space in the capital offers a more spectacular display of national history.

What is interesting here is that among the statues, there is one dedicated to Cuauhtémoc that "vividly proclaims the government's decision that Mexico would officially identify itself with its pre-Columbian Indian past" (Tenenbaum 143). This monument to Porfirian ideals was intended not only to reinforce Mexico City's right, dating from ancient times, to rule the rest of the country, but also "to impress foreign capitalism," according to Barbara Tenenbaum. This attempt to impress foreigners was candidly captured in *Memorias de un mexicano* (compiled in 1944-50), the most important filmed document of Mexican history. The unveiling of the Independence Monument is a key scene in the film with a voice-over informing us that "Díaz liked to honor illustrious people from history, something that is reflected in his plan to dedicate statues to Queen Isabella, George Washington, and Louis Pasteur."

This gesture reveals perhaps more than anything a political desire to please the three most important nations for Mexico at the time—Spain, the United States, and France—hoping in return, one can imagine, to reinforce ties with them and gain their support for the Díaz administration. And just as the planned statues of Queen Isabella, Washington, and Pasteur were political instruments with a far more ambitious purpose than just honoring illustrious people, the statue of Cuauhtémoc was also part of a larger agenda: to reinforce so-called *criollo* nationalism.[2] Perhaps even more significant, it can be considered the beginning of what many have called the neo-indigenism as an artistic and cultural current in society. This monument, taken with all the others, was intended to declare the good news of Mexicanness as something if not entirely Indian, at least also not entirely European. Ironically, those who stumbled upon the statues were almost invariably criollos and mestizos, members of the upper and middle classes, since the poor (mostly Indian) masses did not for the most part live in Mexico City and rarely came to the Paseo de la Reforma.

Nonetheless, such a display of heroic nationalism, combined with an institutionalized indigenism during the Porfiriato, served a purpose: the unveiling of the statues with official rituals and popular fiestas signaled to all the sectors of the population that they were included in the

---

[2] *Criollo* in Mexico, since Colonial times, means a person born in the New Spain of Spanish parentage, rather than a person of mixed racial origin.

idea of one nation. The absence of the masses in this privileged space, except during ritualized (that is, controlled) ceremonies, prevented people from overexposure to that source of pride and discouraged their questioning of a social structure that had "included" them. Controlled access had the added benefit of curtailing the temptation to seize power. So when the Porfiriato finally came to an end, creating a void in the way Mexican society pictured itself, one of the biggest preoccupations that emerged with the Revolution was the redefinition of a collective identity. This should not surprise us: even at the end of the Porfiriato, the official culture was struggling between the two positions traditionally identified as the "nationalist mythologizers" and the "Francophile progressives" (Tenenbaum 147).

"The New Sweaty / Beauty of the Century"
By the mid-twenties and mainly as the result of the Revolution, Mexican society realized that it was much more diverse than anybody had acknowledged in the past regime. The "real" face or rather faces of the country were made painfully visible through the horrors of a civil war, which seemed to provide the ideal conditions to rethink national identity or in words of Guillermo Sheridan, "redefinir la *nacionalidad*" (384). New currents of cultural expression emerged and significantly most of them were popular. Everybody in the country recognized the importance of incorporating these currents in the new nation, but not everybody agreed on how exactly that should be done. The country was divided and many artistic and intellectual groups were convinced that they were the *authentic* representatives of Mexican society, turning the need to redefine nationality into a real cultural battle and Mexico City into a battlefield where different positions challenged each other sometimes in vicious confrontations and often in the name of the Revolution.

Very early the poets and artists that sympathized with the Revolution particularly *estridentistas* and *muralistas* presented themselves as the only avant-garde intellectuals, proclaiming a unifying although monolithic idea of nation. Also, they did not tolerate those who were different or disagreed with their idea of culture. In the *estridentista* manifesto this position is presented clearly when it declares that "A los que no estén con nosotros se los comerán los zopilotes" (91). Among those doomed to be eaten by vultures were the poets gathered in the pages of the magazine *Contemporáneos*, a group perceived as reactionary, anti-patriotic, and effeminate. It was to these poets that Manuel

Maples Arce, the *estridentista* leader, directed the following verses from *Urbe* in an obvious attempt to disqualify them on moral grounds:

> Los pulmones de Rusia
> soplan hacia nosotros
> el viento de la revolución social.
> Los asalta-braguetas literarios
> nada comprenderán
> de esta nueva belleza
> sudorosa del siglo. (59)

For *estridentistas*, as the poem of Maples Arce shows, avant-garde was synonymous with revolution, which was synonymous with modern, which, in turn, was synonymous with virility. This was also true for a big sector of Mexican society.

That is why revolutionary intellectuals in general, but *estridentistas* in particular, advocated the idea of radical change as much as they dismissed those who were not "men" enough to want what *they* wanted. Therefore it is not surprising to read in the manifesto mentioned above that "Ser estridentista es ser hombre. Sólo los eunucos no estarán con nosotros" (91). It is pertinent to note that sexual metaphors were so common all through the first decades of the century in the Mexican cultural debate that usually we tend to take them for granted. For example, the very famous although little studied quarrel on effeminacy and literature started with an article published by Julio Jiménez Rueda in 1924 titled, "El afeminamiento en la literatura mexicana" (*El Universal*, December 21, 1924),[3] where the author also associates revolution with virility. Jiménez Rueda's apparent intention was to show that the Mexican Revolution had not yet produced "La obra poética, narrativa o trágica que sea compendio y cifra de las agitaciones del pueblo."

He attributed such failure to the fact that what had been written until then was very soft or "feminine," while the literature that the country needed was hard and masculine. Moreover, he accused most Mexican writers and poets of being passive rather than active, which

---

[3] These articles have never been collected and the newspapers where they originally appeared are old and not always consistent or accessible, so I have decided to give the title of the publication and the date in parenthesis in the text of the essay. I believe this will assist the curious reader who wants to locate these articles.

for him was a sign of lacking sex as well as an anti-patriotic cowardice since *everybody knows*, according to him, that "[c]ualidad masculina es dar frente con valor a todas las contingencias de la vida, preferir lo fuerte, lo noble, lo altivo: las estatuas de los héroes están siempre de pie en actitud de reto, ansiosas de combate. Cualidad femenina es, en cambio, ampararse en la debilidad para herir impunemente al prójimo." In his view, sex stands for power, determination, rectitude, and love for one's own homeland, something that clearly for him men could have *naturally*, but women could not.

This article started a controversy in some of the most important Mexican papers and magazines of the time offering a completely different view from the traditional way Mexican society has been interpreted. An intellectual from the old school, Victoriano Salado Álvarez, responded to Rueda's article with an evasive note, whose title was unwittingly ironic ("No se necesitan intelectuales," *Revista de Revistas*, January 18, 1925). It was, however, a socialist and revolutionary poet, Carlos Gutiérrez Cruz, who made the debate more personal by naming specific poets including some of the *contemporáneos* and even those who had been his friends.[4] In his "Literatura con sexo y literatura sin sexo" (*La Antorcha*, January 24, 1925), Gutiérrez Cruz explains his position: "El sexo es algo que abarca todas las manifestaciones de la vida humana [pues] la simple descripción de un crepúsculo no puede ser igual, hecha por un macho que por una hembra." And yet what is evident here is that at the core of the dispute for a revolutionary culture was a struggle for power—the power that comes with erecting one's own group as the only representative of a Nation—masked in terms of gender.

In a second article, "Los poetas jóvenes sin sexo" (*El Demócrata*, February 21, 1925), González Cruz increases his personal attacks against Jaime Torres Bodet, Salvador Novo, Francisco Monterde, and Xavier Villaurrutia—these poets, in his opinion, are all asexual. Two of them, Monterde and Novo, reacted to the attacks by writing on the subject. Monterde's response ("Un poeta joven con sexo," *El Demócrata*, February 25, 1925) in particular clearly had the intention of getting his name removed from the list since he seems to agree with the equation of sex and virility: the young poet with sex he talks about in his article was, of course, himself. Among other intellectuals who intervened in the dispute, two are important to mention: José Gor-

---

[4]Xavier Villaurrutia and Gutiérrez Cruz were friends at one point and Villaurrutia even dedicated a poem about passionate love to his friend.

ostiza ("La juventud contra molino de vientos," *La Antorcha*, January 24, 1925), who seems more interested in moving the discussion to a more literary territory, and M. Glikowuskt ("El 'afeminamiento' en la literatura," *La Antorcha*, March 7, 1925), who considered "effeminacy" a characteristic present not only in Mexican, but in Western literature in general and does not deem it a problem.

The debate on effeminacy, revolution, and patriotism went on for months and involved, directly and indirectly, the most prominent intellectuals of the time. National identity was accepted as a collective priority, but it also opened the door to other concerns considered personal, if not secret. The struggle for identity felt in the public arena was mirrored in the space considered most private—sexual identity. In the verses from *Urbe* quoted above it is clear that Maples Arce was trying to discredit *contemporáneos* by questioning their sexuality as much as he was trying to incorporate Mexican *estridentismo* into a larger international and revolutionary project through the association with Russia and through a clumsy appropriation of the reactionary ideas of Italian futurism—chiefly its praise of war, patriotism, machinery, velocity, "manly" work, aggression, and disdain of women.

In fact, the avant-garde in Mexico for the most part excluded women and everything feminine was often considered fragile, unstable, and undesirable; therefore being effeminate, a woman or a homosexual—it did not matter which one—was to be *weak*. Even in those rare cases in which women held an important position in the avant-garde circles, most notably Frida Kahlo, it was evident that her acceptance had to do not only with her socialist ideas, but also with what could have been perceived as her "masculine" qualities (she was revolutionary and had to endure a harsh life in pain and illness) to the point that Diego Rivera painted her distributing arms to the workers getting ready for a social revolt dressed in manly overalls.

This seems an important aspect to consider to understand Mexican modernity because I do not believe, like most critics, that the attacks of *estridentistas* and other revolutionary artists against *contemporáneos* and all the "effeminate" poets were motivated only by homophobic prejudices,[5] a statement often mentioned, but that in my opinion explains very little, particularly because they were directed against everybody—heterosexual or homosexual—who did not write about the revolution and therefore was considered passive, soft, and

---

[5] Díaz Arciniega's opinion is that "el [centrarse en el] afeminamiento revela intereses personales y prejuicios homofóbicos" (16).

effeminate. On the contrary, I think that those attacks were the desperate cries of a dying culture stubbornly incapable of understanding the modern world in more complex terms. The traditional dualistic view of Mexican society based on the opposition of irreconcilable parts (male/female, strong/weak, national/foreigner) was losing terrain before the demands of groups that started to raise their voices, including women.

The Revolution had propitiated, after all, the rethinking of sexual roles since it had allowed and even encouraged a high degree of promiscuity; it also had allowed an increase in the expression of individuality—women would accompany men, leaving their towns in order to perform traditional domestic roles, but also in some cases to fight side by side with them and often ended up abandoned, pregnant, and dislocated. In popular music and folklore there are several stories about the role of women in the Revolution, from "soldaderas" to "valentinas," "coronelas," "adelitas," and other female figures who achieved mythological status. In a way, the Revolution abolished Porfirian morality by sexualizing the masses. Modernity was seen in Mexico in terms of gender and sexual identity very early on.[6] Better yet: modernity in that country was the struggle between a traditional patriarchal society and an emerging one that challenged the authority and the values of unification, control, determination, and integrity considered exclusively masculine and praised by that society.

Whose Sweaty Men Are They, Anyway?
Nowhere seems more evident the attempt to reduce to a monolithic and official culture the newly revealed diversity of Mexican society than ironically in Diego Rivera's revolutionary murals, particularly in those painted in the twenties and thirties in the Secretaría de Educación Pública and in the Palacio Nacional. In those murals, Rivera offers representative and populist images of the people and trades of Mexico; in the "patio de los oficios" of the Secretaría de Educación Pública we see, for example, all types of occupations and trades from refining sugar to mining to cultivating the land. And in the second floor of the same building Rivera illustrated some *corridos* and gave a

---

[6] See my essay "El poeta en la Quinta Avenida" where I explore the relationship between modernity and sexuality, particularly in the female figure as reflected in José Juan Tablada's poetry. Tablada, I propose, saw the changing female figure at the beginning of the twentieth century, associated with a modern sensibility, as a danger for a traditional society like the Mexican.

synthesis of the country's struggles for freedom in which every event of the past led to the Revolution and every future act came out of it in a way that did not leave room for different interpretations of history or other types of behavior. Along the same lines, the murals of the Palacio Nacional represent Mexican history from pre-Columbian times to the Revolution in an unquestionable version proposed by the government. However, such a restrictive view of national identity did not go unchallenged and among those openly criticizing it was Salvador Novo (1904-1974) whom I consider a barometer of what was happening in the country.

Novo is an emblematic figure of his time and its conflicts, a figure that questioned a traditional society by assuming his individuality as much as by criticizing and mocking the retrograde views of revolutionary groups. As we can observe in the poem that opens Novo's collection of "Poemas proletarios" (1931), he proposes a very funny, ironic and often precise revision of the way Mexican history and myths have been politically manipulated. What makes this poem even more important is the fact that it easily can be read as a response to the interpretation of Mexican history offered by *muralistas* and *estridentistas* and their revolutionary aspirations.

In this way, Novo bursts into the conversation about national identity, presenting a different and critical point of view. The poem's opening stanza, for example, clearly states that Mexican history is the result of the overlapping of cultures and events interacting with each other *silently*:

Del pasado remoto
sobre las grandes pirámides de Teotihuacán,
sobre los teocalis y los volcanes,
sobre los huesos y las cruces de los conquistadores áureos
crece el tiempo en silencio. (109)[7]

Time that grows in silence is a metaphor for history, certainly, but at the same time it is obviously a comment on the "strident" proposal of nation by Maples Arce and his group as well as on the visually noisy one of Rivera's murals.

Also, the poem presents a vivid and sarcastic parade of characters and heroes of Mexican history ridiculing the way they have been ele-

---

[7] Most of the quotations of Novo's poetry come from the book *Poesía*, unless otherwise indicated in parenthesis following the citation.

vated to their official pedestals. So when we move forward from the time of the Conquest to the Independence, we read:

> Nuestros héroes
> han sido vestidos como marionetas
> y machacados en las hojas de los libros
> para veneración y recuerdo de la niñez estudiosa,
> y el Padre Hidalgo,
> Morelos y la corregidora de Querétaro,
> con sus peinetas y su papada, de perfil siempre,
> y Morelos con su levita, sus botas negras y su trapo
> en la cabeza, feroz el gesto, caudillo suriano
> y la Corte de los virreyes de terciopelo, hierro y encajes
> y la figura de cera de Xóchil descalza
> entre los magueyes de cera verde. (109)

The history of Mexico, according to Novo, has been a silent, constant, collective process ridiculed both in its official version (crushed in the pages of the books) and in the murals of Rivera (dressed like marionettes).

Particularly, Novo's reference to the indigenous peoples is an irreverent statement that mocks their inclusion in the "revolutionary" rhetoric, not only the folkloric Indian girl of wax, but also a historical figure like Benito Juárez: "Y Juárez, Benemérito de las Américas, / para que vean de lo que son capaces los indios" (110). It is impossible, once more, not to read this poem as a comment on the murals of Rivera that had transformed the government buildings into "museums" for the people.

But "Del pasado remoto" goes further and pokes fun at the marriage of the indigenous and the revolutionary in what is again an open criticism of both *estridentistas* and *muralistas*:

> La literatura de la revolución,
> la poesía revolucionaria
> alrededor de tres o cuatro anécdotas de Villa
> y el florecimiento de los maussers,
> las rúbricas del lazo, la soldadera,
> las cartucheras y las mazorcas,
> la hoz y el Sol, hermano pintor proletario,
> los corridos y las canciones del campesino

y el overol azul del cielo,
la sirena estrangulada de la fábrica
y el ritmo nuevo de los martillos
de los hermanos obreros
y los parches verdes de los ejidos
de que los hermanos campesinos
han echado al espantapájaros del cura. (111)

Novo shows with these poems how those revolutionary artists with their programmatic nationalism and their official solidarity with the workers of the world miss the point of what being proletarian really means in post-revolutionary Mexico.

To make his case stronger, following "Del pasado remoto," Novo writes four poems dedicated to the working classes. In these poems, all the clichés of the proletariat, such as the beauty of sweaty arms manipulating heavy machinery or the heroic and optimistic brotherhood that the Revolution had supposedly brought to the masses are avoided. The poems talk instead of the poor devil that stops every morning by a little store on his way to work to drink alcohol and soda and again before returning home, only to start the cycle again the following morning since he earns only seventy-five cents a day.

Novo writes also about the soldiers, sub-lieutenants and privates, who at night in the barracks share their dreams and talk about their towns and get drunk with tequila and gunpowder, and smoke marijuana. Novo, the "bourgeois" poet, is writing assertively not from the perspective of the intellectual that looks at these people with contempt and finds their behavior "picturesque," but from the perspective of the man who does not romanticize them and sees their integrity as human beings in an unjust society.

Novo—it is important to clarify—is not writing out of class consciousness or because he identifies and sympathizes with a proletarian or an Indian cause; he simply refuses, like the other members of *contemporáneos*, any simplistic interpretation of history and nationalism. His poems are not didactic, since their intention is not to teach others how to write "real" proletarian or indigenous or patriotic poetry, but to expose their failure when attempting to do so. Furthermore, I think that we can read these poems as "manifestos" of the impossibility of writing such kinds of poetry. Novo's "proletarian" poems are not aesthetic declarations, but aesthetic interrogations that question the idea that poetry, to succeed, depends on its subject alone.

Voici ma douce amie
si méprisée ici car elle est sage
and numerical and temperamental.

Adiós, amigo, éxito
con Lady Gordiva.
Por mí, *Vive la France*
aunque mi amiga
no pueda ahora, materialmente,
agradecer el *compliment*. (47)

"*Forbidden silent idylls*"
After considering these aspects, the reader cannot help but wonder about this intimacy with the proletarians of Mexico in a bourgeois poet that does not claim to speak for them. Why does Novo, the intellectual and bureaucrat, feel so comfortable talking directly to these sweaty workingmen? Why does his proletarian poetry sound much more honest than that of the self-proclaimed revolutionary poets? The answer, I think, can be found in Novo's determination to live his own sexuality. If Maples Arce had said before that the "asalta-braguetas literarios" understand nothing of the new sweaty beauty of the century, "Poemas proletarios" replied that neither does Maples Arce. Novo goes further and in his best satirical poetry he makes clear that not only does he know more about those sweaty hard-working men, but also that he is responsible in part for their sweat.

This is specially evident in his erotic sonnets, which are populated by butchers, bus drivers, cops, thieves, letter carriers, soldiers, and hustlers. And such declarations have to be taken literally since they were not intended to be published, at least not while Novo was alive; further, they echo the confessions about the sexual adventures of the poet's youth that he himself registers in his memoirs:

> Una insaciable sed de carne y una audacia a la vez segura de mi belleza y mi posibilidad de comprar caricias, me arrojaban a la caza del género de muchachos que me electrizaba descubrir, tentar, exprimir: los choferes que en el México pequeño de entonces eran la joven generación lanzada a manejar las máquinas, a vivir velozmente". (*La estatua de sal* 115)

The homoerotic sonnets, also, provide particularly detailed, funny, and at times very bizarre, descriptions of sexual and sweaty encounters with those proletarians that Novo never claimed to represent. Even though the encounters described there are the result of a need to "say it" aloud perhaps only for the poet's own amusement and reaffirmation, they also have literary echoes and aspirations, so when Novo toys in a sonnet with the possibility of writing his memoirs, he imagines that people would compare him with Marcel Proust while he would write about those sweaty men:

¡Un Proust que vive en México! Y haría
por sus hojas pasar los deliciosos
y prohibidos idilios silenciosos
de un chofer, de un ladrón, de un policía. (*La estatua* 124)

Although, as we said, Novo is willing to live his sexuality to its full capacity, it is evident that in the Mexico of the twenties such practices must still be taken carefully, unless you are extremely rich and powerful.

It is this contradiction—the defiant pose and the secret practices—that could make Novo's attitude seem strange from a contemporary perspective. And yet two things must be pondered carefully. First, let us remember that Novo is writing in the twenties and thirties in the middle of a ferocious dispute for a national identity clearly identified with the masculine. In this context, the display of effeminacy is a brave protest against a macho culture, while the discretion of the actual sexual practices is a needed shield against discredit in a society that would condemn his art in the name of supposedly high moral standards. The importance of Novo resides, then, in what Monsiváis calls "La rebeldía del no ocultar" (32).

Second, we must recognize that Novo was very open about his sexuality and although he was careful not to be caught in the act, he never denied his sexual practices and even made them "public" as rumors and by association with other homosexuals. What is perhaps more striking in Novo's memoirs is the discovery that he was not the only open homosexual in Mexico at the time. In fact, through his pages we see a freedom in matters of sexuality hardly imaginable before the Revolution. The picture that emerges from the poet's memoirs is that of a society more tolerant in sexual matters—or at least more ambivalent—than we had imagined. One anecdote is particularly revealing of this. According to Novo, there was a peculiar man who, every time he ran into homosexuals he recognized and who were not as open as he was about their sexuality, would out them right there on the street calling them the most outrageous names (La Perra Collie, El Pedo Embotellado). This man also liked to stroll the streets of the city in what he would call going "[a] putear, lo cual consistía en contonearse con ellas [his male friends] por las calles, piropear atrevidamente—y a veces, con inmediata eficacia—a los hombres, en cuya cara soltaba, mirándolos, un cógeme que solía dejarles alelados" (*La estatua* 94).

Novo's ostentation of his sexual preferences, then, became a challenge to the intolerance of artists and intellectuals who understood modernity only in terms of aggressive masculinization and his mocking of the revolutionary rhetoric in "Poemas proletarios" questioned national identity. Therefore the "desacralización" and even the cannibalization of patriotic feelings through a playful integration of them into sexual practices that he recalls in his memoirs represent a symbolic ritual that comes to mark the end and the beginning of a new society. In 1921, according to him, there was a "resurrección estruendosa del nacionalismo decorativo" (*La estatua* 105) exemplified by an exhibition of Mexican art in the Hotel Regis decorated in the most stereotypical native style. This exhibition had been organized and executed by a painter that had just returned from Europe and had insisted on embellishing the space with cacti, wooden crafts, clay vases and mugs as well as with *jícaras* and ponchos that were used instead of the crystal chandeliers and Persian rugs of the Porfiriato. This seemed to have sparked Novo's imagination since, as he writes:

> Sobre ese estilo me consagré con entusiasmo, tijeras, aguja, martillo, a decorar nuestro "estudio". Un idolillo nalgón, a quien llamábamos San Polencho colgaba a la cabecera del *couch* o "piedra de los sacrificios" a presidir las escenas. Y un nacionalismo extremado me indujo a emplear una jícara pequeña como el depósito más a tono de la vaselina necesaria para los ritos. (*La estatua* 105)

The theatrical way this studio (an apartment in downtown Mexico City where he, Villaurrutia, and a couple of other friends received their conquests and entertained their acquaintances) was decorated and the ritualistic function to which that space was destined (the homosexual encounters described as "sacrifices") emphasize the marriage of nationalism and sexuality, of the public and the private, in the creation of a community that reaffirms itself and reclaims its right to belong to a larger group without losing its individuality.

In this context, the rejection of a gathering of poets considered "effeminate" by a group of intellectuals self-proclaimed revolutionary and avant-garde is clearly not derived only—or exclusively—from homophobic prejudices, but from a blind trust in the structure of a monolithic patriarchal society. The response of Novo to this rigid society was a protest, both personal and aesthetic, as much against the lack of freedom of creation as of freedom to live one's own life:

¡Qué le vamos a hacer! Ganar dinero
y que la gente nunca se entrometa
en ver si se lo cedes a tu cuero. (*La estatua* 123)

In the end, the dispute for national identity that marks the first decades of the twentieth century in Mexico turned out to be more about two specific and very different visions of modernity. Paradoxically, of these two visions the one that emphasized individuality and diversity (including sexual diversity) was more subversive than the "revolutionary" one that preached one and only one way of being Mexican. To comprehend this is essential to gain a more integral understanding of Mexican culture since it challenges the traditional belief that in that country the avant-garde was represented exclusively by a movement defined in terms of the macho, the revolutionary, and the patriotic.

Works Cited

Díaz Arciniega, Víctor. *Querella por la cultura "revolucionaria" (1925)*. México: Fondo de Cultura Económica, 1989.

Haskell, Barbara. *The American Century. Art and Culture, 1900-1950*. New York: Whitney Museum of American Art, 1999.

Hernández Rodríguez, Rafael. "El poeta en la Quinta Avenida: modernidad o el tropiezo con el cuerpo femenino." *Latin American Literary Review* 25. 49 (1997): 43-61.

"Manifiesto estridentista." *Las vanguardias literarias en Hispanoamérica. (Manifiestos, proclamas y otros escritos)*. Ed. Hugo J. Verani. México: Fondo de Cultura Económica, 1990. 90-91.

Maples Arce, Manuel. *Las semillas del tiempo. Obra poética 1919-1980*. México: Consejo Nacional para la Cultura y las Artes, 1990.

Memorias de un mexicano. Documentary filmed between 1897-1944. Fundación Carmen Toscano, IAP, compiled 1944-50.

Monsiváis, Carlos. "Introducción." Novo, *La estatua de sal.* 11-41.

Novo, Salvador. *La estatua de sal.* México: Consejo Nacional para la Cultura y las Artes, 1998.

———. *Poesía. XX poemas/Espejo/Nuevo Amor/ Poesías no coleccionadas.* México: Fondo de Cultura Económica, 1961.

Sheridan, Guillermo. "Entre la casa y la calle: la polémica de 1932 entre nacionalismo y cosmopolitismo literario." *Cultura e identidad nacional.* Comp. Roberto Blancarte. México: Consejo Nacional para la Cultura y las Artes/Fondo de Cultura Económica, 1994. 384-413.

Tenenbaum, Barbara A. "Streetwise History: The Paseo de la Reforma and the Porfirian State, 1876-1910." *Rituals of Rule, Rituals of Resistance. Public celebrations and Popular Culture in Mexico.* Eds. William Breezley, Cheryl English Martin and William French. Wilmington: SR Books, 1994. 127-150.

Transgressive Affinities (and One Difference) in Buñuel's *La edad de oro* and Lorca's *El público*

VÍCTOR FUENTES
University of California
Santa Barbara

IT IS NOT MERELY coincidental that Buñuel debuted his second film *La edad de oro* in November 1930 and Lorca dated the manuscript of his play *El público* to 22 August of the same year. These two works, pinnacles of avant-garde art—Spanish and European—and of a now-golden age which sought the fusion of art and revolution, have been gaining in critical esteem since their composition. Now, at the beginning of the twenty-first century, they stand out as essential works of twentieth-century cinema and theater, despite—or rather, due to— their previously almost underground existence. Each represented a challenge to dominant artistic, social, and sexual norms: a complete attack on bourgeois morality, taste, and order. Just a few days after its initial showing, Buñuel's film was banned, an official censorship that would last fifty years; until the 1980s, the movie could only be seen in private screenings or in clubs for cinephiles. As for *El público*, the play was never presented during the life of its author and had to wait until the mid-1980s for its successful debut on the Milan, Madrid, Paris, and London stage.[1] This recognition of *La edad de oro* and *El público* can

---

[1] In a March 1931 letter to his parents, Lorca announced that he had approached a well-known actress and theater director, Irene López Heredia, with *El público* (*Epistolario* 706). Although the latter was willing to take on anticonventional works, clearly Lorca's play was not representable in the Spain of the period.

be attributed to the rippling effect of the liberation movements of May 1968.[2]

However, at the time the two works were created, the sociopolitical revolutionary current had been overtaken by the ascendancy of reactionary forces that would culminate in fascism. The ultra-right wing protest that assaulted the auditorium where Buñuel's film was being shown, ripping the screen, destroying seats and the surrealist paintings exhibited in the vestibule, is reflected in the tumultuous response of the audience in Lorca's work, described by Student 3: "Pero después enarbolaron los cuchillos y los bastones porque la letra era más fuerte que ellos, y la doctrina cuando desata su cabellera puede atropellar sin miedo las verdades más inocentes" (174). It also anticipated the night of the "cuchillos largos" that would spread across Europe in the 1930s.

In *El público* Lorca would personally take up the attack against a complacent audience, so manifest in *Un perro andaluz* and *La edad de oro*; its title alone revealing the author's intention to create a new kind of theater. This new drama, a "mirror of the audience," would be unstageable since it represented "truths" that conventional theater and movie audiences would not, or could not face. Indeed, Buñuel's first two films received a similar reaction on the part of their viewers. It is, perhaps, the depths of these truths that led the authors to favor these works over others in their respective opuses. Lorca declared that *El público* "es lo mejor que he escrito para el teatro" (*Epistolario* 22) and Buñuel puts *La edad de oro* at the top of the list of his ten favorite films.[3]

---

[2] It is striking to note that the staging of the Lorquian drama took place during the 1980s, the decade in which the gay movement "came out of the closet." Lorca himself already had made a similar move, later celebrated in *El público*, during his 1929 stay in New York. Upon return from his trip to the United States and Cuba, Lorca wrote openly to his friend Rafael Martínez Nadal: "He escrito un drama que daría algo por leértelo en compañía de Miguel. De tema *francamente* homosexual. Creo que es mi mejor poema" (*Epistolario* 690). Later, he continues unreservedly in language that reveals a distinct "queer" sensibility: "Aquí en Granada me divierto estos días con *cosas deliciosas* también. Hay un torerillo ..."

[3] For Buñuel fans, here are the director's words and opinions of his movies: "Sólo guardo cierto cariño por una decena de ellas, lo que no es poco en relación con las que he filmado: *La edad de oro*, sobre todo; *Nazarín*; *Un Chien andalou*; *Simón del desierto*; *Los olvidados*, cuya preparación me hizo conocer la delincuencia juvenil y me sumergió en el corazón de la miseria

The multiple coincidences between Buñuel's early cinema and the work that opened Lorca's New York period point to a similar creative sensibility and will to rebellion rooted in the revolutionary ethos of the art and politics of their period and common to both the "andaluz refinado" and the "aragonés tosco," to use Buñuel's description. Despite inevitable ups and downs, from their early days at Madrid's Residencia de Estudiantes they were united by a great "politics of friendship" so valued in Foucault's later thought and from which so many notable creations of modern and contemporary Spanish literature and art derived.[4] This backdrop of friendship, with all the dialogic and creative communication at its heart, overcame the stylistic and artistic differences that Buñuel and Lorca also undeniably had. With prescient glimmers when seen in light of the creative evolution of both artists, their friendship was recorded emblematically in a fragment titled "Dialogue with Luis Buñuel" that Lorca had written in 1925. After noting the differences between them, Federico declared, "I don't have that wanderlust which haunts you, Buñuel" (qtd. in Lorca, *Unknown* 70). Yet he had opened the "Dialogue" with words that alluded prophetically to his friend's "wandering culture," a sensibility that Buñuel would increasingly develop and so enrich the director's cinematic vision. Moreover, in the same text, Lorca placed in the mouth of Augusto Centeno, a close friend of the two men, the following acute observation: "I think both of you will be able to travel in your own worlds and nobody will ever know who will bring back the fullest bag."[5]

---

mexicana; *Viridiana*; *Robinson Crusoe*; *La vida criminal de Archibaldo de la Cruz*; *La Voie Lactée, La Charme discrete de la bourgeoisie* [...]" (Buñuel 19).

[4] Didier Eribon tells us that friendship constituted a central theme of Foucault's reflexion during the last years of the philosopher's life when Foucault affirmed that in Antiquity and for subsequent centuries friendship was an important mode of social relationships. It was an intensely affectionate space within which men enjoyed certain freedoms and choices (285). This sense of friendship, so characteristic of Spaniards, as Borges has pointed out, is perhaps an important reason for which the concept of "generation" has become so prevalent in Spanish literary history (i.e. the Generations of 1898, 1914, 1927, etc.). In this way, Lorca, Dalí, and Buñuel experienced an intensely sensitive friendship, even while provoking "poetic" jealousy and rivalry between Lorca and Buñuel.

[5] Citations from "Dialogue with Luis Buñuel" are taken from the translation by John London, included in *The Unknown Federico García Lorca* (70-71). The "Dialogue" forms part of *Tres diálogos*, originally edited by Manuel Fernández Montesinos in 1985.

Although their deep friendship seems to have undergone a period of cooling between 1927 and 1929, the two men continued to coincide in different ways in their approaches to their respective genres. Both, and here we are able to detect their fundamental similarities, nurtured a profound subversion of accepted canons, uniting art and life in accordance with the surrealist directive to "transform the world and change life." Buñuel, as a member of the surrealist group, assumed this dictate consciously and seems to have lived it intuitively as well. In a similar way, Lorca, who adopted many surrealist attitudes during the late 1920s and early 1930s, heeded the movement's call for a revolutionary social art, embracing the utopic "Golden Age" so desired by the surrealists. Let us recall his words: "El día que el hambre desaparezca, va a producirse en el mundo la explosión espiritual más grande que jamás conoció la humanidad. Nunca jamás se podrán figurar los hombres la alegría que estallará el día de la Gran Revolución" (*Obras* 1759).[6]

Despite personal friction and differences of artistic taste, Lorca and Buñuel shared a common rejection of the established order and both searched for new expressions for art and life. Emblematic of the friendship that united them was an episode recollected by Buñuel that took place as the two were leaving the Madrid theater Palacio de la Prensa after a showing of *La edad de oro*:

> Al salir le dije a Federico: "Anda vente. Vámonos a comernos unas chuletas", o algo por el estilo. Federico dudó, con su corbata de moño, y dijo con acento que todavía tengo en los oídos que ya no me sirven: "Luis tu película no me ha gustado na'". Y yo le contesté que no importaba nada, que qué tenía que ver la película con las chuletas. (Aub 68)

In what follows, we shall see what *La edad de oro* has to do, not with "chuletas," but with *El público*, above and beyond the aesthetic differences that marked these two great artist-friends. *La edad de oro* provoked an entire manifesto from the surrealist group, titled "Manifi-

---

[6] With the growing social and political polarization of Second Republic Spain, Lorca's position increasingly approached the revolutionary sympathies of his friends Buñuel and poet Rafael Alberti. In 1936 he expressed a desire to visit Russia, and in May 1936 his name topped the list of the group, "Friends of Latin America," as a show of solidarity with a Brazilian political activist, jailed by dictator Getulio Vargas (*Epistolario* 822).

esto de los surrealistas a propósito de *La edad de oro*," that underlined and adopted key aspects of the film, aspects also essentially common to *El público*. These were grouped according to the following labels: "Sexual Instinct and Death Instinct," "Mythology Is What Changes," "Love and Missing," "Situation in Time," "Social Aspect-Subversive Elements." All of the foregoing are predicated on one particular component that unites them and that reveals a salient connection to love: the transgression of laws that "pretendían hacer inofensiva la obra de arte bajo la cual hay un Cristo y ante la cual, con ayuda de la hipocresía, se intenta no reconocer bajo el nombre de belleza más que una mordaza" ("Manifiesto" 59). Significantly, both in Buñuel's film and in Lorca's drama, this Christ appears physically wounded; each work virulently challenges this concept of beauty as a silencer.

The surrealist manifesto in support of *La edad de oro* underscores the association of love and sexuality, violence and death—constants that we can also apply to *El público*—and applauds an amorous passion that "se muestre iluminada por las espinas asquerosas de la sangre y que se introduzca el frenesí" (62). A similar observation could be made about *El público* in whose fifth scene a "desnudo rojo" crowned with blue thorns occupies the center of the stage. Love joined to frenzy represents the maximum propelling force in *La edad de oro* as well (Breton found in Buñuel's film one of the greatest expressions of surrealist *l'amour fou*): according to the "Manifiesto," the film makes love "prevalezca sólo fuera de los límites imaginables y domine con la profundidad del viento, del pozo de diamantes, las construcciones del espíritu y la lógica de la carne" (66). It goes on to say that Buñuel formulated a hypothesis about revolution and love, reflected in the bloody protagonist's cry—"ese alarido tan fuerte que apenas se le puede oír: AMOR...amor...Amor...AMOR..."—a cry, deafening and impassioned, that also reverberates through *El público* with the echo of the White Horse's initial refrain, "Amor. Amar. Amor" (150-52). María Clementa Millán has perceptively shown that the drama, through the intensity and near exclusivity with which the theme of love is presented, can be related to "la influencia de las teorías de Breton, que conceden una importancia capital a *l'amour fou*, como vía fundamental para la auto-realización del hombre" (61). In both the film and the drama, we find brilliant "sublime" images of this conception of love, although this "sublime" issues from subterranean depths and is linked to the excremental and to polymorphous sexuality.

With all the similarities between *La edad de oro* and *El público* there is, nevertheless, an important difference in the nature of amorous passion, the sexually liberating frenzy that each depicts. In *El público*, love, although treated as the highest value, is defined as and rooted in homoeroticism. As has been shown already, Lorca declared this work to be one with a "*frankly* homosexual theme." Even still, critics like Clementa Millán, in her over eighty-page introduction to the play, never once mentions the word "homosexual;" similarly Rafael Martínez Nadal, the very person to whom Lorca made the statement quoted above, avoided discussing the issue for decades.

In recent years, however, and due in no small measure to the staging of *El público* during a moment at which gay-oriented criticism had reached a peak, we have at our disposal various books and studies on "Lorca and the culture of homosexuality," to borrow the title of Angel Sahuquillo's investigation, which extend awareness of the theme to the rest of Lorca's work. Nevertheless, few or none of these studies separate the creative and prophetic dimensions of the texts from the proposal for a different way of life based on homosexual relationships.[7] The seed of this social and sexual revolution is overtly present in Lorca's "Oda a Walt Whitman" and finds dramatic outlet in *El público* and in his "impossible" theater, as well as in his commercially successful plays— *Yerma, Bodas de sangre, Doña Rosita la soltera*—in which the theme, as the repressed that always returns, is submerged. In Lorca's work, we find *a priori* many of the apparent keys to the vision of today's "queer" world.

As such, it is important to point out that under the auspices of the liberation of Eros, sexual as well as social, Lorca was advancing along a path before which the surrealists had halted, despite their exaltations of polymorphous perversions and the impulses of desire: the path of homosexuality. If earlier Buñuel had upbraided Lorca for pandering to bourgeois norms and taste in his early plays, even characterizing them as straight-laced, now it was Lorca who not only approached the surrealists in his work, allowing his creative imagination total freedom, but who censured them as well. Indeed, he revealed their, and especially Buñuel's position toward sexual rebellion and sexual norms as conventional and, in fact, retrograde. Xaviére Gauthier has analyzed how sexual provocation, sought by surrealists as a weapon of subversion,

---

[7] Foucault discussed the potential of these relationships in his later work; for a comprehensive synthesis of his views, see Chapter 8 of the abovementioned study by Eribon.

tripped up against the stumbling block of homosexuality, excluded from the "surrealist revolution." She underscores the totalitarian tones in which Pierre Unik and André Breton echoed the homophobia of the day. We can find similar opinions in Buñuel's statements on the topic. This despite the fact that, as Gauthier indicates, "a strong homosexual component" (239) existed among members of the surrealist group itself—a cohort of men in which homosexuality was unacknowledged, repressed, or latent. These issues manifest themselves in the relationship between Lorca and Dalí in which Buñuel's attempts to separate the painter from Lorca's "poetic sphere" played an important role.

Having made this essential distinction between the erotic visions of the two men, I would like to focus on the ways in which the subversive, transgressive force of Eros in the Buñuel film and the Lorca drama reveals aspects in common. In both, love is held up as a liberating activity, "pese a todas las escorias y los desgarramientos que nos muerden como el ácido" ("Manifiesto" 66). What the film says about Modot could also be applied to Man 1 of *El público*: "Paso, entonces, a este hombre que, de un extremo a otro del film, lo atraviesa llevando sobre sus vestimentas las marcas del polvo y de yeso, indiferente a todo lo que no es únicamente el pensamiento de amor que lo ocupa y lo conduce" (69-70). Strikingly, in the film both Modot, with his traces of dust and plaster, and his female partner could be considered protagonists of Lorca's "teatro bajo la arena": like the characters here, the protagonists of Lorca's play are determined by desire, wholly given over to the enjoyment of pleasure. "Yo no tengo más que un deseo" (156), exclaims Man 1. Significantly, Modot and the woman, Lya Lis, rolling in the sand, interrupt with their uncontrolled shouts of pleasure an entire retinue of dignitaries just as the latter are placing the cornerstone of Rome, the imperial city. Just as the wasted skeletons of the bishops and the revived city of imperial Rome frame these scenes, in Lorca's drama Roman ruins serve as the background for amorous abandon. Equally noteworthy, in both works the "mallorquines" play similar antagonistic roles. Defenders of the status quo and bourgeois (dis)order, outraged by witnessing the subversion of their values, they violently separate the lovers on the movie screen and in the dramatic scene. This abrupt end to pleasure occurs in the film when Modot and Lya Lis exalt in their embrace on the sand and in the drama when a 30-year-old man and a boy of 15 are discovered in the tomb of Romeo and Juliet, replacing the Shakespearean lovers.

In their images extolling Eros—both alone and in embrace and struggle with Thanatos—as well as in others that convey their destructive-creative vision, Buñuel and Lorca have bequeathed scenes of paramount importance to world cinema and drama of the twentieth century. Their two works discussed here make supreme use of surrealist *dépaysement*, the process that effects continuous encounters with the marvelous. The unity of the works is predicated on the surrealist concept of *identité convulsive* (to use a term coined by Max Ernst who plays the role of the raider captain in *La edad de oro*) which ruptures the discontinuity of the universe and enters both animate beings and inanimate objects into an eternally mobile relationship, subverting the order, causality, and chronology of Euclidian space. At this point I will let those familiar with these works recreate for themselves the extraordinary repository of images created by Buñuel and Lorca as they developed their themes using this associative principle.

A further achievement that *La edad de oro* and *El público* bring to the film and drama of the period is their original treatment of the subject. In the wake of Freud and coinciding with the discoveries of Lacan (who had been Buñuel's and Dalí's friend in the 1930s), the subject appears problematized, driven no longer by his "conscious" self, but by his unconscious impulses.[8] In this way, the subject not only abandons the Cartesian and Hegelian conception of the individual, but reflects, with great artistic complexity and *avant la lettre*, notions about the subject developed in the twentieth century. The origin of the subject, its mobile and "half-hidden" order, is presented formidably in the multiple transformations undergone by the couple in *La edad de oro* and the characters of *El público*, where even the costumes take on life and participate in these metamorphoses. The characters submerge themselves in the depths of their unconscious impulses,

---

[8] Julio Huélamo Kosma has studied "the influence of Freud in the theater of García Lorca" in which he tries to "prove" that "ha empleado, de modo recurrente en *El público*, de forma ocasional en *Así que pasen cinco años*, conceptos, símbolos y formulaciones teóricas vertidas por Freud en sus escritos" (75). Huélamo begins his essay with a reminder that the complete works of Freud began to be translated in Spain in the 1920s, and had great impact on the intellectual and artistic group associated with the Residencia de Estudiantes. For their part, it is well known that Buñuel and Dalí were avid readers of Freud. Perhaps the greatest objection to Huélamo's essay and his book *El teatro imposible de García Lorca. Estudio sobre "El público"* is that they attempt to give a unilateral explanation of symbols and images that are multivalent and often enigmatic.

dominated by the struggle and embrace between Eros and Thanatos, abandoning themselves to fantasy and dream.

Each work speaks, decades *avant la lettre*, to Foucault's observation that pleasure has neither passport nor identification card. In *La edad de oro* we witness how the protagonist, with total indifference, casts off his official credentials as a delegate of the International Assembly of Public Welfare in order to become a being driven exclusively by desire. And his young lover continuously renounces her social status as a marquise's daughter in order to give herself over to pleasure—lovemaking in the sand with Modot, masturbation, or sucking on the toe of a statue, a foot fetish that also appears in *El público*. In addition, when the orchestra director appears in the garden, Lya Lis abandons Modot and passionately embraces a new lover. Similar transformations of the subject and object of desire are presented in *El público*, though involving members of the same gender and alternating between bisexuality, hermaphroditism, and sadomasochism. An example of the latter takes place in scene 2, an exchange that confuses even practitioners of queer theory.

Such is the case of the rigorous critic Carlos Jerez Farrán who interprets the seductive and provocative dance between the figure of Cascabeles and Pámpanos as a "discurso homofobo." The same critic concludes, after a meticulous analysis, that the scene offers an "episodio sadomasoquista que Lorca introduce con la intención de censurar éticamente la homosexualidad afeminada" (402). Considering that Lorca's drama denounces sexual oppression and seeks all forms of liberation, I believe that it is more fruitful to view the sadomasochistic scenes from a homoerotic perspective and, taking a cue from Foucault's later thought, see them as the practice of an inventive sexuality in which a freely chosen sadomasochism plays a role. In their studies, some critics label Lorca's homoeroticism an "expresión de homofobia internalizada," to use a term that Jerez Farrán deploys in the title of his essay. I consider this a fundamental error. Even if a homophobic dimension is present in Lorca's texts, the aspect that deserves to be analyzed and celebrated is the affirmation of sexuality and the proposal of new, more creative and gratifying ways of living in the face of prescribed sexual norms and repressive sexual regimes.

Another great achievement by Buñuel and Lorca in the two works that we have been discussing is the clear and categorical way in which they destroy conventional forms of cinematic and dramatic representation—a goal to which many avant-garde artists aspired, but few attained. By the 1950s nearly all of the most groundbreaking vanguard works had been co-opted by the market and the academy. The work of Lorca himself suffered the same fate with the exception, not surprisingly, of his "teatro imposible" and his "poesía de amor oscuro." Practically unknown for much of the twentieth century, these texts have been reclaimed as liberating artistic efforts in the struggle against a regimen of imposed norms and sexual discrimination. Buñuel, whose centenary was celebrated in 2000, has been recuperated by institutions; nevertheless, his iconoclastic spirit and corrosive humor make any appropriation of his work impossible.

Recent criticism on *El público* has further developed these aspects, though rarely does it thoroughly probe the deep meaning, doubly liberating, of the destruction presented in the work. In concluding the present article, I would only add that Luis Buñuel with *La edad de oro* and Federico García Lorca in *El público* bring to life, with splendid artistic outcome, Walter Benjamin's 1930s imperative regarding the politicization of art. And in terms of aesthetics they accomplish, with an effectiveness achieved by very few writers or artists of the historic avant-garde, Benjamin's dictates on film's subversion of conventional form: "As long as the capital of cinematographic production establishes the models, as a rule no other merit can be attributed to today's film than that of the promotion of a criticism of the traditional concepts of art" (231). Buñuel's surrealist cinema and Lorca's theater-beneath-the-sand do this perfectly.[9]

Works Cited

Aub, Max. *Conversaciones con Buñuel*. Madrid: Aguilar, 1984.
Benjamin, Walter. *Illuminations*. New York: Schoken, 1969.
Buñuel, Luis. *Un perro andaluz. La edad de oro*. Mexico: Era, 1971.
———. *Buñuel en tres dimensiones*. Ed. Juan J. Vázquez. Zaragoza: Gobierno de Aragón, 1999.
Clementa Millán, María. Introducción. *El público*. By Federico García Lorca. Madrid: Cátedra, 1987. 13-112.
Eribon, Didier. *Michel Foucault et ses contemporains*. Paris: Fayard, 1994.
García Lorca, Federico. *Epistolario completo*. Eds. Andrew A. Anderson and Christopher Maurer. Madrid: Cátedra, 1997.
———. *Obras completas*. Madrid: Aguilar, 1960.

---

[9] Translated by Maria T. Pao.

———. *El público y Comedia sin título*. Eds. Rafael Martínez Nadal and Marie Laffranque. Barcelona: Seix Barral, 1978.
———. *The Unknown Federico García Lorca*. Ed. and trans. John London. London: Atlas Press, 1996.
Gauthier, Xaviére. *Surrealisme et sexualité*. Paris: Gallimard, 1971.
Huélamo Kosma, Julio. "La influencia de Freud en el teatro de García Lorca." *Boletín de la Fundación García Lorca* 6 (1989): 59-83.
———. *El teatro impossible de García Lorca*. Granada: Universidad de Granada, 1996.
Jerez Farrán, Carlos. "El sadomasoquismo homoerótico como expresión de homofobia internalizada en el cuadro 2 de *El público* de García Lorca." *Modern Philology* 93 (1996): 468-97.
"Manifiesto de los surrealistas a propósito de *La edad de oro*." *Un perro andaluz. La edad de oro*. By Buñuel. 59-72.

In Hazardous Pursuit of Chance: Mapping the Surrealists' Caribbean Sojourn (1941)*

GERARD ACHING
New York University

> The task of art is to redeem, essentially or existentially,
> the formless universe of contingency.
> —Malcolm Bradbury and James McFarlane,
> "The Name and Nature of Modernism"

> A los que en esta América tropical se imaginan el suprarrealismo como un libertinaje, les costará mucho trabajo, les será quizás imposible admitir esta afirmación: que es una difícil, penosa disciplina.
> —José Carlos Mariátegui, "La experimentación surrealista"

AROUND THE END OF 1940, in a *château* on the outskirts of Marseilles called "Air-Bel," a group of intellectuals, artists, and their families gathered to wait for the designated moment of their flight from occupied France and a hostile Vichy government. Among them were Victor Brauner, André Breton, René Char, René Daumal, Robert Delanglade, Oscar Domínguez, Marcel Duchamp, Max Ernst, Sylvain Itkine, Wifredo Lam, André Masson, Benjamin Péret, and Tristan Tzara (Breton, "Jeu" 89). Varian Fry, president of the Emergency Rescue Committee, had set up headquarters in Marseilles in order to plan

---

*I would like to thank the George A. and Elizabeth Gardner Howard Foundation for the fellowship support that has allowed me to undertake this project.

and execute the escapes.¹ While waiting for arrangements to be made, the surrealist group would meet at the *château* twice a week to indulge in games and discussions. In Antonio Núñez Jiménez's biography of Lam, the Cuban-born artist remembers that "casi nunca tenía pies ni cabeza, pero resultaba entretenido. Practicábamos el surrealismo con los impulsos automáticos del subconsciente, tratando de liberar nuestras preocupaciones y temores. Ahora, aquellos poemas están en museos y bibliotecas como piezas históricas" (155). One of the more elaborate games was the *jeu de Marseilles*, a card game in which the conventional suits (hearts, diamonds, clubs, and spades) were replaced by Love, Dream, Revolution, and Knowledge—emblematized respectively by a flame, a black star, a blood-stained wheel, and a padlock—and featured members from the surrealist pantheon such as Sade, Lautréamont, Hegel, Baudelaire, Pancho Villa, Novalis, Freud, and others. The joker was Alfred Jarry's Ubu Roi (Rosemont 84; Breton, "Jeu" 89).² In "Le Jeu de Marseilles" (March 1943), Breton claims that the surrealists in Marseilles at that time were involved in their customary disciplines such as research for the sake of research and the will to continue to interpret the world (89). Yet he also acknowledges the dire straits in which the surrealist group found itself when, for example, many of them were detained, together with the rest of Marseilles's "suspects," on board the *Sinaïa* during Marshall Pétain's official visit to the city. Hence, in recalling the *jeu de Marseilles* and the adverse conditions in which it was played, it is no surprise that Breton notes that card-game historiographers agree that the changes in rules over the centuries have always been associated with great military reversals (89)—in this case, with the retreat of an artistic, literary, and political vanguard.

---

¹ In *Surrender On Demand* (1945), Fry calls his year of living dangerously in Marseilles "an experiment in democratic solidarity" (IX). In asserting that "democrats must help democrats, regardless of nationality," he states that the sole purpose of the Emergency Committee was to rush "political and intellectual refugees out of France before the Gestapo and the Ovra and the Seguridad got them" (IX-X). The New York based organization was spearheaded by Eleanor Roosevelt and a group of American liberals. It was partly subsidized by a group of Swiss-born Jews (Núñez Jiménez 155).

² A 1942 double issue (2-3) of the surrealist journal, *VVV*, reproduces the cards in color. Most recently, the majority of the cards were placed on display in an exhibit entitled, "Los surrealistas en el exilio y el comienzo de la Escuela de Nueva York," at the Reina Sofía Museum in Madrid, December 14, 1999 to February 27, 2000.

For some of the surrealists, the day of deliverance fell on March 25, 1941, when the *Capitaine Paul Lemerle*—a creaking vessel carrying some three hundred mostly French, German, Austrian, Czech, and Spanish passengers—left Marseilles, dodged in and out along the North African coast, and eventually set out for Martinique. On board were Breton, the leader of French surrealism; Victor Serge, poet and one of Lenin's closest advisors; Lam, whose return to his native land would stimulate some of his and the Caribbean's most significant modern art; and Claude Lévi-Strauss, who subsequently became the foremost proponent of structural anthropology of his time. Even though this flight of artists and intellectuals represented the lowest ebb of the surrealists' political aspirations in Europe up to that point, it nonetheless stimulated some of the twentieth century's most influential encounters between European, Caribbean, and American artists and intellectuals.[3]

In this essay, I examine two of those chance encounters and the texts that emerged from them—namely, André Breton's *Martinique, charmeuse de serpents* (1948) and Eugenio Fernández Granell's *Isla cofre mítico* (1951)—in order to explore critical alternatives to the no-

---

[3] Despite the fact that Martinique was under Vichy control, it was a logical point of entry for the surrealists' dispersal in the Caribbean and their subsequent journeys to New York or Mexico. In the wake of their voyages of exile through the Caribbean, the European surrealists left a number of significant documents and groups. For example, André Masson, one of Paris's foremost surrealist artists, was also on board the *Capitaine Paul Lemerle* and later produced paintings such as *Antille* (1943) as well as a few lyrical pieces under the same title in Breton's *Martinique, charmeuse de serpents* (1948). Pierre Mabille, a doctor, researcher of psychoanalysis, and one of the most important writers to emerge out of surrealism, arrived afterward on a second boat to Martinique. He had visited Haiti in 1940 and after the war was appointed French Cultural Attaché there. He was instrumental, together with local writers like Jacques Roumain and Jean Price-Mars and anthropologist Louis Maximilien, in establishing the Haitian Bureau d'Ethnologie (Richardson 20; 279). By July 1941, Breton would meet his "Parisian friends" Marcel Duchamp, Max Ernst, Leonora Carrington, Yves Tanguy, Nicolas Calas, and Roberto Matta in New York. The recent exhibition at the Reina Sofía museum was organized on the premise that the origins of the New York School of Surrealists could be traced to this concentration of refugees and exiles in New York. This point is debated (see Rosemont 84-89) in terms that resemble similar discussions of the encounters between European and Caribbean Surrealists. In this study, I am interested in the events that took place in the Caribbean before some of these surrealists arrived in New York.

tion that the Latin American avant-garde movements were merely weak and peripheral versions of their European counterparts. Klaus Müler-Bergh's accurate observation that the Latin American movements "no se dan en estado químicamente puro" but express "una actitud ecléctica" should not necessarily be considered a feature that defines the Hispano-American avant-garde only (285). That the European avant-garde movements were internally conflictive, eclectic, and ephemeral is corroborated by Malcolm Bradbury's and James McFarlane's view that in order to speak about modernism roughly between 1890 and 1930, it would be essential to account for the existence of several axes of modernism, such as Paris-London-New York or Berlin-Vienna-Zürich, since they invariably produce diverse albeit overlapping modernist chronologies and maps (36). Given the degree to which the European modernists' experimentalism and desire to foment social and political changes corresponded to "a crisis of culture" and to "an unhappy view of history—so that the Modernist writer is not simply the artist set free, but the artist under specific, apparently historical strain" (26), I would like to argue that the ways in which Breton and other surrealists imagined the Americas were internal to and instrumental for their movement's regeneration.

My assertion follows in the spirit of Nelson Osorio Tejada's argument that the avant-garde movements in Latin America were not "un simple epifenómeno de la cultura europea" (228) but emerged strongly as local engagements with the profound economic, political, and artistic transformations that began taking place in the region around the time of the First World War and ended around 1930 with the consolidation of political alliances among the forces of imperialism, local bourgeoisies, and oligarchies (239). Osorio's call for a historical contextualization that would bring to light the specificities of the Latin American movements is easily appreciated. The critical scenarios that I provide in this study corroborate his argument, but they do so from the unwitting perspectives of the surrealists themselves. Because their sojourns through the Caribbean were hazardous and desperate undertakings, the surrealists on board the *Capitaine Paul-Lemerle* did not assume cultural attitudes with the degree of eurocentrism that seems to inform the claim that the Latin American avant-garde movements were for the most part epiphenomenal. Hence, even though I want to foreground the Caribbean locations and contexts in which the surrealists find themselves under "historical strain" and accompanied by an "unhappy view of history," my aim is to interrogate how they articulated their sojourns and chance encounters with intellectuals and artists in the islands and what ideological relations they established between these encounters and the survival and continuity of their movement.

Central to a mapping of the surrealists' journey through the islands are the contingencies that mediate sojourns and chance encounters. Most literary histories pay scant attention to the surrealists' Caribbean journeys of exile.[4] In this study, I would also like to think of "sojourn" as a critical and historiographical tool for examining these encounters. My definition of it dovetails with Peter Bürger's claim that "the historicity of a theory is not grounded in its being the expression of a *Zeitgeist* (the historicist view) nor in the circumstance that it incorporates earlier theories (history as prehistory of the present) but in the fact that *the unfolding of object and the elaboration of categories are connected*" (16; my emphasis). In other words, I want to position the surrealists' sojourns in the Caribbean as their contingent and speculative unfolding of certain kinds of knowledge about occidental culture. Such an approach not only corroborates Roger Shattuck's argument in the prologue to Maurice Nadeau's history of the movement that chance may be described as "blind accident working as the minimal propulsive force between one instant and the next but never bestowing meaning on happenings thus touched off" (19); it also allows me to avoid Renato Poggioli's deterministic "dialectic of movements"—successive moments of activism, antagonism, nihilism, and agonism (27)—that he ascribes to the European avant-garde.[5] Therefore, apart from alluding to the surrealists' historically verifiable journey, the "so-

---

[4] Such is the case with very detailed accounts such as Franklin Rosemont's anthology, *What is Surrealism?*, and Maurice Nadeau's *History of Surrealism*. In *Tristes tropiques*, Claude Lévi-Strauss provides some interesting insight into the journey from Marseilles to Martinique. However, by far the best collection of primary material on surrealism in the Caribbean to date is Michael Richardson's anthology (see "Works Cited").

[5] Poggioli claims that the avant-garde turned its attention to the non-western and prehistoric (55), yet he finds no room for those influences and appropriations in his "dialectic" and treats them as vestiges of a romantic spirit. However, the non-western was foundational for the surrealists. In *The History of Surrealism*, Maurice Nadeau writes that as early as the First World War's "darkest hour" in 1917, the future surrealists reflected on Apollinaire's manifesto, *L'Esprit nouveau*, in which the French poet declared that truth and the new spirit should be explored both in the ethnic domain and in the imagination (52-53).

journ" can also be seen as a conceptual precondition for their claims to happen upon and assemble "new" cultural meanings. In the next section, I examine these claims further.

Contingency and "Objective Chance"
Because of the surrealists' concerted interest in stumbling upon new meanings, it will first be necessary to describe how they approached and drew significance from the incidental. Bradbury and McFarlane could have easily been describing surrealist games when, in addressing one of European modernism's principal epistemological difficulties, they posit that "the task of art is to redeem, essentially or existentially, the formless universe of contingency" (50). Contingency generally refers to the "condition of being free from necessity with regard to existence, action, etc." (*OED*). The surrealists consistently fetishized contingent circumstances in their games and art through experimental, playful, and provocative means. Even though these practices might appear frivolous and even romantic, they nonetheless uncover a profound irony. According to Poggioli, the fact that the surrealists' techniques were researched did not prevent their experimentalism—and, for him, that of the avant-garde as a whole—from being "at once a stepping stone to something else and [...] gratuitous" (135). Nevertheless, in spite of their iconoclasm, attempts at avant-garde experimentalism retain a positivistic urge in that they provide the basis for "the technical and scientific progress of art itself" (136).

Yet the surrealists' insistence on fetishizing contingent circumstances and relations in their activities should also be seen as both rhetorical and ideological strategies. The difference, for instance, between Lam's and Breton's respective articulations of the relationship between the *jeu de Marseilles* and the "historical" is telling. Lam begins his statement by referring to the entertaining non-sense of their games at the *château*, briefly mentions technical aspects of surrealist automatism, and ends up contrasting the circumstances in which the group engaged in these activities with the latter's contemporary status as historical artifacts. His recollection suggests that the museumization of their activities was in some way accidental. Breton evinces a very different attitude toward the *jeu de Marseilles*. Omitting all but a single reference to the movement's nadir, his article gives the impression that the group's investigations had been a valiant "business as usual" in the midst of adversity. This *a posteriori* rationalization of the game is consistent with Breton's tactical skills at orchestrating and then theorizing their activities as a discipline. In his article, Breton historicizes events in Marseilles by turning what must have appeared as distressing contingencies—when escape was all but certain—into the necessity and purposefulness of their actions (89). Furthermore, his assertion that great military defeats inspired changes in card game rules—and, by implication, that the surrealists in 1941 had only lost a battle and not the war—partakes of a familiar discourse on the avant-garde as an unyielding advance. In light of Breton's practice of transforming contingencies into necessities, it is tempting to agree with Shattuck's claim that "[s]urrealism was one of the most highly disciplined and organized artistic schools that ever existed" (14). As early as 1930, José Carlos Mariátegui referred to the surrealists' experimentation as a painful and difficult quest for discipline (258).

Successively elaborated in Breton's *Nadja* (1928), *Les Vases communicants* (1932), and *L'Amour fou* (1937), the category of "objective chance" [*hasard objectif*] eventually became the surrealists' application of an ideological imperative to their fetishization of contingency. Breton described objective chance as a geometric locus of encounters, coincidences, accidents, and unexpected events and called the category "the problem of problems" since it required an understanding of the relationship between necessity and freedom (Shattuck 21; Nadeau 205). For Breton, this relationship necessarily embraced an ideological field. Bürger purports that for the surrealists objective chance and the discovery and celebration of the incidental in daily life became acts of sabotage in bourgeois societies that were organized on the basis of a means-ends rationality (65). "But what is ideological in the Surrealist interpretation of the category of chance," Bürger further states, "does not lie in the attempt to gain control of the extraordinary but in the tendency to see in chance something like an objective meaning. [...] It will never be possible to seize the meaning being searched for in chance events, because, once defined, it would become part of means-ends rationality and thus lose its value as protest" (66). Nevertheless, both the attempt to reify contingency or chance as acts of sabotage against the bourgeoisie and the need to fall short of that reification signal an ambivalence and perennial point of contention in surrealist projects as Breton and others struggled to define them.

Pierre Naville refers to the source of the discord as surrealism's "basic antinomy" (see Nadeau 128). He describes it as the opposition between a *metaphysical* attitude that was based on phenomenological speculations about the relationship between internal experiences and external objects and events and a *dialectical* one in which the mind progressed by means of its own self-consciousness (128). Even though both attitudes were intended to liberate the mind, they were, according to Naville, consistently articulated as mutually exclusive in the surrealists' internal factionalism (128).[6] Forced to take a stand on this issue at a date that coincided with the transition from the surrealists' *intuitive* to *reasoning* epochs, Breton reiterated the surrealists' alliance with the French Communist Party in an early brochure entitled "Legitimate Defence" (1926); but not without counter-attacking that the communists were politicians and as such were not achieving their revolutionary goals any better than the surrealists mostly because the party limited its concerns to material life. The surrealists' long and ambivalent competition to champion a "revolution of the mind" over social revolution was often subject to intense criticism from both within the movement and outside. In "Defence," Breton's response to the movement's opponents was to challenge them to see how the movement's intellectual engagements with phenomena such as chance, contingency, and the marvelous (249-50) went beyond the Communists' "minimum program" (243).

The surrealists' Caribbean sojourn sheds ironic light on Breton's insistence on the revolutionary character of "objective chance." Because of the already tenuous conditions of their voyages of exile, it would have been hazardous to indulge in subversive games of chance in the face of sometimes hostile colonial and foreign authorities. In the game of life and art, it seemed as though the stakes had suddenly been raised against them. Needless to say, they refrained from tinkering with

---

[6] The contention is one that lasted for several years and cannot be reduced to a Manichean polarization between phenomenological research and aesthetics and Marxist ideology and politics. Breton attempted to steer a middle course that would conserve the apparent contradiction between both "attitudes" (Nadeau 175). Early on, he had been an avid reader of Hegel, Marx, and Trotsky's *Lenin*, and there are significant aspects of the *Second Surrealist Manifesto* (1929) that were influenced by this reading. Also instrumental in Breton's insistence on a middle course was the surrealists' association with the young group of radical Marxist philosophers who founded and published the journal *Clarté* and with another group principally of university students that founded *Philosophies* (Rosemont 36-42; also see Nadeau 117-40). Finally, by taking the middle road without resolving the "antinomy," Breton succeeded in maintaining the surrealist group's autonomy in the face of demands by other surrealists, such as Louis Aragon, that the group place itself at the disposition of the French Communist Party (see Nadeau 175-82).

the arbitrary since it was life itself that had become subject to the war's profound uncertainties. Yet their sojourn is punctuated by complex encounters that require fuller explanations for the unprecedented, unplanned, and often contradictory ways in which the surrealists decentered their knowledge and critique of occidental culture.

Adrift
Breton's *Martinique, charmeuse de serpents* is divided into several parts that are not chronologically ordered.⁷ The book is composed of two lyrical sections on some of the island's natural and historical features ("Antille" by the surrealist painter, André Masson, and "Des Épingles tremblantes"); a dialogue between the painter and the artist about exoticism and the island's fauna ("Le Dialogue créole"); Breton's description of his poor treatment by island authorities ("Eaux troubles"); an essay praising the Martinican poet, Aimé Césaire ("Un Grand poète noir"); and a concluding poem ("Anciennement Rue de la Liberté"). The prologue explains why the use of different genres seemed most fitting: "A la Martinique, au printemps de 1941, notre œil se divise." [In Martinique, in the spring of 1941, our eye splits] (8). From their perspective, theirs are not "imperial eyes"—to borrow Mary Louise Pratt's coinage—but a vision that functions as if one eye were turned inward and the other outward in order to capture paradoxical circumstances: an unbearable despondency, on the one hand, and a radiant expression on the other (8). They were thus led to make use of a "langage lyrique" as well as of a "langage de simple information" because, Breton states, "[n]ous avons été follement séduits et en même temps nous avons été blessés et indignés" [we were wildly seduced and at the same time we were wounded and offended] (8). The prologue ends with the assertion that even though their mind yields to the emanation of "un lieu idéal et réel" [an ideal and real place], their purposes "gardent le tour à la fois sinueux et familier qui nous confirme moins précieusement à nos yeux comme artistes que comme personnes humaines" [stick to a simultaneously winding and familiar line that in our view less eloquently confirms us as artists than as humans beings] (8-9). They discover that what renders their human condition more

---

⁷ The book owes its title to a painting by Rousseau ("Le Douanier"), called *La Charmeuse de serpents*. It was originally published in 1948, though the section "Eaux troubles" was previously published in *Pour la Victoire* (New York, February 7 and 14, 1942). "Un Grand poète noir" was written in New York in 1943 and then published in *Tropiques* (9 [May 1944]).

eloquent than their status as artists is the irreducible experience of having been both offended and seduced.

I would like to reiterate the relevance of Breton's recognition of personal suffering in the surrealists' Caribbean sojourn for two reasons. First, the humanizing role that the susceptibility to adversity can play in histories of literary movements is a story that is seldom told because biographical vicissitudes complicate positivistic paradigms based on the notion of the avant-garde's unhindered forward march. Breton certainly helped to cultivate such paradigms, yet *Martinique, charmeuse de serpents* provides ample evidence for a critique of these models. Vicky Unruh argues that because vanguard movements sought "an active engagement between art and experience" (21), what she calls a "rehumanization of art" both represented the Latin American avant-garde's response to Ortega y Gasset's famous essay and captured the particularity of the region's relationship to the currents of modernity (25). Unruh associates "rehumanization" with the Latin American vanguards' quests for and incorporation of the autochthonous and non-universal. Second, despite its division into somewhat randomly organized sections, Breton's book gradually and coherently rectifies the split vision that the writing subject introduces in the prologue. But before examining that subliminal narrative thread, I would like to begin with Breton's and Masson's dialogue about their unplanned encounter with the Martinican landscape.

On the whole, "Le Dialogue créole" champions intuitive knowledge and the capacity to reinvent. However, because Breton and Masson are also struck by nature's perfection (22), the interlocutors distance themselves from arbitrary inventiveness: "Nous sommes très loin ici des perspectives inventées" [We are very far here from invented perspectives] (31). For Breton and Masson, there is no paradox in simultaneously advocating the capacity to reinvent and rejecting invented perspectives. Standing in the heart of the forest, they seek a middle-ground of aesthetic and intellectual responses between the supremacy of the imagination—they claim that "[t]out est à réinventer" [everything is to be reinvented] (25)—and the completely arbitrary. This humility is short-lived, however. They defend their intuitive knowledge about the forest by claiming to have known it before they arrived (19) and substantiate this claim by recalling various European artists and travel writers who experienced and recorded similar encounters with nature. In their subsequent musings that the flight of the spirit toward an imaginary flora may be the result of the poverty of

European vegetation, Breton and Masson take their argument further claiming that "les paysages surréalistes sont les moins arbitraires. Il est fatal qu'ils trouvent leur résolution dans ces pays où la nature n'a été en rien maîtrisée" [surrealist landscapes are the least arbitrary. It is inevitable that they find their resolution in these lands where nature has in no way been tamed] (20). Toward the end of the dialogue, Martinique's vegetation and surrealist practices are symbiotically represented: "Quelles échelles pour le rêve, ces lianes implacables! Ces branches, quels arcs tendus pour les flèches de nos pensées!" [What ladders for dreaming those implacable lianas are! Those branches, what arched bows for our thoughts!] (30). Nature, in the final instance, provides tangible proof of surrealist designs.[8]

Theirs in not a simple question of exoticism but a complex admission of the fact. As if to preempt a critique of their position, Breton and Masson question the word "exoticism" and its relevance to their insights arguing that they cannot limit themselves to what they see outside their window and that "[l]a terre tout entière nous appartient" [the whole world belongs to us] (21). Moreover, they dispel any simplistic comprehension of "exoticism" by raising a familiar debate about whether or not Rousseau's paintings prove that he had known the tropics. They conclude that if the painter had never left France, his appreciation for the primitive mind allowed him to discover "primitive spaces" that conformed to reality (23). Michael Richardson argues that the surrealists never forgot their American experiences and that even if they still showed signs of exoticism, there is in surrealist work in exile by the end of the war a striking confrontation with "the appearance of the exotic" (24). In this case, Breton and Masson advance Rousseau's example to declare the imagination as an aesthetic/intellectual means of apprehending the natural world and, by extension, that their readerly and intuitive familiarity with the Martinican landscape constitutes bona fide knowledge.

Lying in stark contrast to this confident resolution of certain surrealist preoccupations is Breton's description of the offensive treatment

---

[8] What is creole about "Le Dialogue créole" is neither the inclusion of native parlance nor of local interlocutors. Two speakers, ostensibly Breton and Masson, exchange impressions about the impact of the island's landscape on them. The "dialogue" refers to this congenial exchange as well as to the role that the silent landscape plays in their shared phenomenological and cultural consciousness of their own presence on the island. Their notion of "créole" is thus restricted to Martinique's local fauna and topography.

that he and the other passengers received upon their arrival. In "Eaux troubles" [Murky Waters]—a section that he deems unworthy of lyricism—Breton begins by expressing his desire to forget the miseries on board and ends with a scathing critique of French colonial practices. While Breton avoids detailing these miseries, Lam and Lévi-Strauss do not. In Núñez Jiménez's biography, Lam describes the fear into which the passengers plunged as they skirted the North African coast. To the knowledge that a British aircraft carrier had recently been sunk in the vicinity was added the discovery that their ship was being followed. "Al descubrirlo," Lam recalls, "todos empezamos a gritar como si aulláramos. El infierno es eso: aullidos" (157). In *Tristes tropiques*, Lévi-Strauss claims that the *Capitaine Paul-Lemerle* had been transporting clandestine cargo (25). Yet the hold, "with neither air nor light, and where the ship's carpenters had hastily run up bunk beds with straw mattresses" (24) was filled with passengers who "suffered not so much from hunger, fatigue, sleeplessness, overcrowding, and the disrespect in which they had lived for the past four weeks, as from the enforced filth" (26). (Lévi-Strauss was one of only seven passengers who secured the two cabins on board the ship as it transported three hundred passengers.) Their arrival in Vichy-controlled Martinique brought a new set of tribulations. The young anthropologist's impression that their departure from Marseilles "was more like the deportation of convicts" (24) is echoed in Breton's conclusion in Fort-de-France that the colonial authorities had evidently received orders to treat them as prisoners (*Martinique* 59).[9] After being systematically insulted by local officials, the passengers were confined to Lazaret, the former leper's colony at Point-Rouge, from which they were allowed to secure transport to other ports in the Caribbean and beyond.

Given this miserable deliverance from Europe "à ses ravages" [in its ravages] (57), the pivotal point in "Eaux troubles" is Breton's caustic

---

[9] According to Breton, a distinguished young intellectual on his way to New York—Lévi-Strauss, even though Breton does not mention his name— had been greeted with the statement that as a French Jew he was worse than foreign ones (*Martinique* 59-60). The anthropologist himself writes that they had fallen "into the hands of soldiers suffering from a collective form of mental derangement" (27) and that "[i]t was rather as if the Vichy authorities, in allowing us to leave for Martinique, had sent them a cargo of scapegoats, on whom these gentlemen could relieve their feelings" (28). Because Breton considers "Eaux troubles" a section that falls outside surrealist aesthetic concerns, he does not equate what Lévi-Strauss sees as the soldiers' collective derangement with his own often stated appreciation for madness.

reaction against "le prolongement machinal, routinier, désintéressé, de cette politique de démoralisation et d'écoeurement systématiques dont on a réussi à faire l'arme la plus terrible de cette guerre" [the mechanical, routine, disinterested protraction of this politics of systematic demoralization and discouragement that has successfully been made into this war's most terrible weapon] (67). As a counterblow to this demoralization, Breton's text takes a hostile, anti-colonial turn. The surrealists were not new at publicly denouncing French colonialism. For example, their initial politicization was in part a response to the French government's war with the Rif tribesmen of Morocco in 1925, and the group mounted the Anti-Colonial Exhibition when the French Colonial Exhibition opened its doors in Vincennes in 1931. Hence, blaming an abstract French colonial system for what Breton calls the Martinican authorities' paranoid precautions and bad conscience (73) was out of the question. Concluding that local colonial authorities participated in bolstering a privileged and corrupt, *béké* (Martinican white) oligarchy, Breton names specific members of this class and uncovers some of their criminal activities in detail. Having endured the ways in which the island's officials routinely criminalized the ship's passengers in the name of Vichy law and order, Breton counterattacks by exploding the island's immoral, internal contradictions. Furthermore, even though Breton calls "Eaux troubles" mere information, he published the piece, perhaps as a contribution to the war effort, in the journal *Pour la Victoire* soon after his arrival in New York and later included it in *Martinique, charmeuse de serpents*.

Breton's renewed, anti-colonial sentiment perhaps allowed him to appreciate Aimé Césaire's.[10] But the accidental meeting between both men provides not only the book's most explicit illustration of the French surrealist's notion that "objective chance" consists of complex relationships between necessity and freedom but also reveals the ways

---

[10] By contrast, Césaire became familiar with surrealism while he studied in Paris. In 1932, he and other Martinican students published the journal, *Légitime Défense*, so called after Breton's pamphlet. The articles in the journal, *Tropiques* (1941-45), provide the most extensive coverage of the intellectual dialogues between French surrealists and local Martinican artists and intellectuals. In "1943: Surrealism and Us," Suzanne Césaire describes surrealism's usefulness against censorship on Vichy-controlled Martinique. She writes that "[n]ot for a moment during the hard years of Vichy domination did the image of freedom completely fade here, and surrealism was responsible for that. We are glad to have maintained this image of freedom under the noses of those who believed they had erased it forever" (126).

in which certain necessities are strategically brought to the fore. In Fort-de-France, Breton stumbled across a copy of the first number of Césaire's journal, *Tropiques*, in a local haberdashery. In this first intellectual contact, Breton writes in "Un grand poète noir," that he could not believe his eyes: "mais ce qui était dit là, c'était ce qu'il fallait dire" [what was said there was what needed to be said] (93). Breton sensed in these pages that Césaire was "engagé tout entier dans l'aventure" [wholly committed to the adventure] (93) and, at the same time, so persuasive on the aesthetic and moral levels as to "rendre nécessaire et inévitable son intervention" [render his intervention necessary and inevitable] (93-94). At their first meeting, Breton recalls that he was struck at the sight of so pure a blackness and took Césaire's appearance to be a *"signe des temps"* [*sign of the times*] (96): "le premier souffle nouveau, revivificant, apte à redonner toute confiance est l'apport d'un Noir. Et c'est un Noir qui manie la langue française comme il n'est pas aujourd'hui un Blanc pour la manier" [the first new, life-giving breath, well-suited to bringing back all confidence is bestowed by a black man. And it's a black man who handles the French language as no white man can today] (96). Finally, Breton finds in Césaire a model of human dignity (97). Unlike the article, "Le Jeu de Marseilles," in which Breton credited the surrealists' collective research with developing a new card game, the circumstances that make Césaire's poetry "necessary and inevitable" are less prone to Breton's direct influence. What, then, positions Césaire in the right place at the right time?

Breton's assessment of Césaire's work is enthusiastic. Comparing what he read of Césaire with the situation of poetry in war-torn Europe, the surrealist writes that the poetic instrument had not even been set off-tune by the storm (95). He calls Césaire's *Cahier d'un retour au pays natal* [Notebook of a Return to the Native Land] nothing less than the greatest lyrical monument of its time (99). Yet the purported necessity and inevitability of Césaire's intervention also satisfy Breton's quest for the certitude that surrealist projects remained vital. For Breton, a new player joins the game of life and art: Césaire "avait misé sur tout ce que j'avais jamais cru juste et, incontestablement, il avait gagné. L'enjeu, tout compte tenu du génie propre de Césaire, était notre conception commune de la vie" [had gambled on everything I held to be right and, undeniably, he had won. What was at stake, taking into account Césaire's own genius, was our common conception of life] (99). His "étroite communion" [close communion] with the Martinican poet is such that not only does Breton credit

Césaire with having won at the French surrealist's game but he then finds himself unable to distinguish Césaire's will from his own. Now, this statement can also be read as an assimilative gesture on Breton's part. After all, the French surrealist claims to be in familiar territory because Césaire quotes poets well known to him (93)—such as Lautréamont, who also figured prominently in the *jeu de Marseilles*—and because, as Breton notes referring to the land that Césaire and his friends were exploring, "c'était aussi ma terre, c'était *notre* terre" [it was my land, too, it was *our* land] (94). Yet a stronger argument can be made to assert that Césaire's "necessary and inevitable" intervention liberated Breton from a "politics of systematic demoralization and discouragement" and permitted him to reinvigorate his view of poetry and of poetic theory during the war.

Césaire's intervention convinced Breton that the ideas that they held in common were not fading into darkness (94). Specifically, it was the Martinican's "capacité de refus" [capacity for refusal] (102)—in other words, his strident, obstinate rejection of colonial exploitation by what Breton calls a handful of parasites who defy even the laws upon which they depend (104)—that persuaded the surrealist to conceptualize *refusal* as constitutive of the best poetry. Breton writes that "[p]assé outre à cette première condition absolument nécessaire et non suffisante, la poésie digne de ce nom s'évalue au degré d'abstention, de *refus* qu'elle suppose" [beyond this first absolutely necessary and non-sufficient condition, poetry worthy of its name is evaluated by its degree of abstention, by the *refusal* that it supposes] (100). Breton draws the notion of refusal from Césaire's anti-colonial conceptualization of the term. The initial impact of the concept on Breton must have been substantial. Lam recalls that Breton returned from his rendez-vous with Césaire saying that his poetry "era como una patada en la cara" (Núñez Jiménez 159). Nonetheless, Breton and Césaire walked away from their encounter each reaffirmed by his own reasoning and direction. While Breton left the island convinced that the land that Césaire was exploring was also his, Césaire stated in a 1978 interview that, even though their meeting had been extraordinary, Breton had confirmed what he had discovered on his own.[11] To claim that a shared anti-colonial sentiment based on the refusal to succumb to Vichy oppression fomented this coincidence of agencies only isolates the begin-

---

[11] From J. Leiner, "Entretien avec A.C.," in *Tropiques* (I, vi); also quoted in Clayton Eshleman's and Annette Smith's introduction to Aimé Césaire's *The Collected Poetry* (17).

nings of critical and ideological positions that both men took several years to negotiate. For what remains unresolvable in the chance encounter between both men is Breton's incorporation of certain elements of anticolonialism in order to further surrealism's aesthetic goals, on the one hand, and Césaire's use of surrealist aesthetics in order to carry on his anti-colonial struggle on the other.

Casting Anchor

The Spanish painter/poet, Eugenio Fernández Granell, is a member of that substantial group of artists and intellectuals who left Spain during and after the Spanish Civil War. In 1939, his voyage of exile took him through France, where he reunited with Lam and others who had fought in Spain, and from where he departed for Chile only to be informed while on board the *De La Salle* that the South American country would not grant entrance to anymore Spanish refugees. He and the other passengers accepted an offer of asylum from Santo Domingo, which at that time had been renamed Ciudad Trujillo. But Granell only remained in the Dominican Republic until 1946 when political crises on the island and persecution by Trujillo forced him to leave for Guatemala. He stayed in Guatemala until 1950 as tensions with both the government and Stalinist communists obliged him to flee the country under dramatic circumstances (Bonet 435). He subsequently settled in Puerto Rico and eventually moved to New York in 1959.

Within the context of the Caribbean, Granell is most celebrated for his surrealist and abstract paintings.[12] But he has also been a sculptor, essayist, poet, novelist, photographer, and musician.[13] In 1941, he met and interviewed Breton in Santo Domingo as the French surrealist was passing through the islands on his way to New York. One of Breton's statements in that interview could well have resonated in Granell's conceptualization of *Isla cofre mítico*. Responding to the

---

[12] The most complete collection of Granell's extensive artistic work can be found in *Eugenio Granell: Exposición antológica, 1940-1990*, which was published by the Consejería de Cultura of the Comunidad de Madrid on the occasion of an exhibition of his work from October 1990 to January 1991. Granell has resided in Madrid since 1985.

[13] He is the author of three novels, which include *La novela del Indio Tupinamba* (1959), *El clavo* (1965), and *Lo que sucedió* (1968); a collection of short stories called *El hombre verde* (1944); and, apart from *Isla cofre mítico*, the essay, "Arte y artistas en Guatemala" (1951).

Spaniard's request for a definition of surrealism, Breton at one point intimates: "Fui llevado a hacer valer que el escritor, el artista surrealista, trabaja, no en la creación de un mito personal, sino de un mito colectivo propio en nuestra época" (Granell, "André Breton" 425). In any case, the contact with Breton then and later in 1946 served as important catalysts for Granell's commitment to surrealism. When he in turn was interviewed by Julio-José Rodríguez, Granell recalls his encounter with Breton claiming: "en realidad yo no me hice surrealista, porque el surrealismo no es cosa de elección sino de condición" (Castro Floréz 3). In 1943, together with Franklin Mieses Burgos and several other Dominican poets, Granell founded the journal *La Poesía Sorprendida* (1943-46), the principal instrument of surrealist writing, arts, and activities on the island.

Isla cofre mítico surfaces in the wake of both Breton's sojourn and his publication of *Martinique, charmeuse de serpents* in 1948. Granell's text consists of a series of lyrical reflections on Breton's book, some approaches—loosely based on surrealist techniques—to the artistic and intellectual implications of the French surrealist's journey through the Caribbean, and Granell's drawings at the start of every brief section. In his prologue, Fernando Castro Flórez calls the text a "[l]ibro en movimiento, sacudido por el oleaje, sintetizando la intensidad poética y la reflexión literaria" (3) and employs other metaphors associated with the sea in order to capture the dynamism of the surrealists' sojourn. The prologuist writes that "Santo Domingo es, más que final de viaje, incitación a la deriva" (3). He also identifies the journey as a "*Perigrinatio* medieval de la vanguardia" and concludes that the island for Granell is conceptually a "lugar esencial por serlo del encuentro" (3). Aware that Granell's book falls outside the category of literary criticism, despite its extensive commentary on Breton's, Castro Flórez argues that *Isla cofre mítico* "abre una nueva categoría de literatura, configura su propio espacio que, de modo aproximado, podría denominarse *ejercicio de admiración*: comentario múltiple de otro libro, *Martinica, encantadora de serpientes* de André Breton" (3). Granell himself describes Breton's book in similar language stating that "[d]el barco y de la isla a que arribó, de lo que quedaba en la estela del navío y de lo que se inauguraba ante su proa [...] trata este libro" (13). However, when Granell writes *in the wake of* Breton's text, he is not interested in assuming a critical attitude toward *Martinique, charmeuse de serpents* but in disseminating a euphoric one about the foundations of a new myth. He bases this myth on the island as "oasis redentor" (14), which is his assessment of Breton's and Masson's "Le Dialogue créole," and he describes surrealism as "la sola isla salvadora capaz de mantener a flote a quienes tengan fe y coraje para acercarse a ella" (20). In promoting the Caribbean as the foundational coffer of new myths (15), Granell mostly ignores the "historical strain" that set these European artists adrift in the Americas in the first place and chooses, instead, to drop anchor.[14]

It can perhaps be substantiated that Granell's conceptualization that the island serves as a source of myth and of "descanso a Europa" (25) and the Caribbean as the site of a renewed, occidental civilization corresponds in some personal way to the asylum that Santo Domingo granted to the wandering refugees on board the *De La Salle*. More easily broached, however, is the sense of arrival and foundation that he ascribes to the Caribbean when he proffers the following statement in *Isla cofre mítico*:

> Europa viajará irresistiblemente impulsada hacia las Antillas, en donde—para Pierre Mabille—se asiste al parto doloroso de una nueva civilización. En cuyo caso, la expedición del grupo surrealista que con Breton tocó primero en la Martinica para enseguida correr por otras islas—Haití, Santo Domingo, Guadalupe, Cuba, hasta la de Buenaventura—equivale a la gesta de los pioneros de la civilización profetizada. Nuevos videntes que, como los que acompañaron a Colón, creyeron, vieron y tocaron—que es todo lo contrario del proceso racionalista de tocar, ver y creer. (25)

In Granell's insistence on creating new foundational myths, he transforms what I have described as the incertitudes, adversities, and chance encounters that constitute the surrealists' sojourn into a heroic expedition that he associates with Columbus's leap of faith. The reference to Columbus is far from arbitrary. It allows Granell to associate a

---

[14] Granell's project was also the result of conversations that he had with surrealists at that time such as Pierre Mabille and Benjamin Péret. In an interview with Mabille in Santo Domingo's *La Nación* (June 26, 1941), the French doctor claimed that "las Antillas deben compararse con las colonias de la Gran Grecia. Asistimos al nacimiento doloroso de una nueva civilización en la cual el Atlántico jugará el papel del antiguo 'mar griego y latino'" (Granell, *Isla* 15). This enthusiasm is inseparable from the wide-spread awareness of the devastation that was taking place in the continent to which the "mar griego y latino" had given cultural birth.

historical "discovery" with new acts of discovery predicated on the surrealists' intellectual and aesthetic approaches to the region. Breton, Granell writes, did not see Martinique as a tourist but as a "soñador que a la vuelta del camino descubre una región de su sueño" (20).

According to Vicky Unruh, the Latin American vanguards' frequent invocation of and/or identification with Columbus raised a complex issue because "the word *discovery* harbors the paradox of seeing for the very first time something, or somebody, that was already there" (152). As I illustrated earlier, Breton self-consciously tackles problems of vision, intuitive knowledge, and exoticism in both the prologue to *Martinique, charmeuse de serpents* and in "Le Dialogue créole." He also makes it clear that, rather than a case of discovering the native, his encounter with Césaire was an instance of self-discovery in which he was able to transcend a demoralizing situation. Nevertheless, writing in the wake of Breton's journey and text, and at a remove from the dehumanizing circumstances that surrounded the *Capitaine Paul Lemerle*'s journey and arrival, Granell transforms Breton into the triumphant Columbus of a foundational myth of the islands and asserts that the three great discoveries that the French surrealist made were the islanders Aimé Césaire, Wifredo Lam, and the Haitian painter, Hector Hippolyte (*Isla cofre mítico* 30). In this respect, Granell discards the complexities of Breton's unexpected encounters during the surrealists' sojourn and thus writes against the current of other Americanist vanguard works that employ exaggerations and parody in order to play with "the interaction of discoverer and discovered, exposing the ironies of such meetings as well as their historical and cultural contingencies" (Unruh 153). In short, Granell's account of the facts responds to the crisis of occidental culture in Europe by attempting to anchor surrealist intellectual thought and artisitic creativity in Caribbean contexts and references.

Clearly, Granell's project resembles Breton's in that they both seek to overcome an "unhappy view of history." Yet the Spanish artist and writer also provides but consistently reconstrues illuminating glimpses of a less heroic account of the facts. For example, he notes that Breton felt obliged to split his discourse into lyrical and informational languages, but then Granell drops the issue (*Isla* 14). On another occasion, he reports that upon Pierre Mabille's return to Paris, the French surrealist had remarked that, while in the Caribbean, he had been impressed to learn "cómo lo primero que hicieron los conquistadores españoles en la isla de Santo Domingo fue arrancar varias hojas de un árbol y, mediante signos especiales, transformarlas en cartas de juego: 'Así nosotros—concluye Mabille—, en un momento particularmente angustioso, nos encontramos sin baraja'" (37). Rather than provoke a self-conscious reflection on their exile at that time, especially since Mabille does not associate the Spanish "conquest" with a foundational act but with the primitive institutionalization of a game of chance, Granell—in the first line of the following section of the text—calls for all the cards to be laid out on the table (39). For him, this call ushers in a surrealist game based on using the letters in Breton's name to form a series of words that "coinciden de extraña manera en el anuncio de algo bueno, universal, que el surrealismo viene precisamente anunciando con persistente ahinco desde su instante inaugural" (39). After each of the twenty words is deciphered to substantiate Breton's voyage through the region, it is revealed that "una nueva vida, a una nueva civilización, como Pierre Mabille lo anuncia, se encamina el surrealismo. Hacia ese *norte* enfilan todas las proas surrealistas, incluso la gran proa de *Martinique, charmeuse de serpents,* bordeando las costas de una isla antillana" (43).

Finally, a similar slippage in focus greets Breton's encounter with Césaire. Granell begins the reference to Césaire with a translation of Breton's stated appreciation for the notion of refusal in the Martinican poet's work. But he privileges the French surrealist's appropriation of the term and brings the reference around to his own agenda in *Isla cofre mítico*; he describes Césaire's *Cahier d'un retour au pays natal* as the "retorno mágico de la poesía a la perdurabilidad de su isla poética y natal: isla encantada" (46). What Granell promotes in his view of the Breton-Césaire encounter is not the adversities that the surrealists faced at that time but a surrealist commitment to poetry and to the poetic mythification of the Caribbean islands.

Conclusion

The surrealists' Caribbean sojourn consists of voyages of exile that converged in the region during the Second World War and appeared afterward in texts and artwork that illustrate how the surrealists' critique of modern occidental culture had shifted site from various European capitals to the Americas. Given circumstances in which the lives of artists and intellectuals in Europe were at stake, the shift is understandable. Yet this displacement was also accompanied by the surrealists' intellectual and aesthetic recognition of Caribbean and American landscapes and cultural objects as legitimate vehicles for the recreation of a "universal" art. Michael Richardson argues that

> the exile of so many surrealists in the Americas during the Second World War undoubtedly led them to question their relation to their own culture in a fresh way and underlined in their minds sensitivity to issues of otherness, displacement and inter-cultural relations. It should not be forgotten that this was a singular occurrence. The Second World War was perhaps the only time that Western intellectuals were forced to take refuge outside Europe for political reasons and were therefore confronted with the experience of exile at first hand. (22)

Rosemont goes as far as to claim that "Breton's West Indian adventure was a decisive event in his life and in the evolution of the surrealist movement" (95). Even though Breton suppresses some telling events in *Martinique, charmeuse de serpents*, it is still possible to appreciate the roles that chance, adversity, and human fallibility play in the development of intellectual and aesthetic ideas and movements. By contrast, Granell's *Isla cofre mítico* is consistently lyrical on the subject of islands and the creation of foundational myths for a Europe in crisis. At the same time, its edification of those myths also ends up facilitating the rise of another—that of the surrealists' untrammeled march forward in an expedition of discovery against all odds. It is in this light that the Caribbean for Granell acts as a "descanso a Europa."

However, what cannot be ignored are Césaire's and Granell's stated rejection of Breton's personal ability to take them into the surrealist fold even though they had had prior exposure to and had admired the movement in Europe. At an empirical level, this refusal to succumb to the French surrealist's influence is instructive because it relativizes the assertion that the Latin American avant-garde movements were simply peripheral versions of their European counterparts. It provides local evidence of subjectivities that resist the ways in which discourses about chance encounters were employed to designate and name its recruits, as in Breton's text, and mythify Europe's rest and regeneration in the Caribbean, as in Granell's. Precisely because these encounters were not structured by historical or traditional antagonisms between colonizer and colonized and center and periphery, it behooves us to move in the direction of analyzing the relations between surrealism and anticolonial struggles during the Second World War when stakes were high in the games that fused art and life.

Works Cited

Bonet, Juan Manuel. "Eugenio F. Granell: Pistas para una biografía." *Eugenio Granell: Exposición antológica, 1940-1990*. Madrid: Consejería de Cultura, Comunidad de Madrid, 1990. 431-40.

Bradbury, Malcolm and James McFarlane. "The Name and Nature of Modernism." *Modernism: A Guide to European Literature, 1890-1930*. Eds. Malcolm Bradbury and James McFarlane. London: Penguin, 1991. 19-55.

Breton, André. "Le Jeu de Marseilles." *VVV* 2-3 (March 1943): 89-90.

———. "Legitimate Defence." Nadeau 242-56.

———. *Martinique, charmeuse de serpents*. Collections 1018. Paris: Jean-Jacques Pauvert, 1972.

Bürger, Peter. *Theory of the Avant-Garde*. Trans. Michael Shaw. Minneapolis: U of Minnesota P, 1996.

Castro Flórez, Fernando. "Territorio del deseo: Encuentro con las islas de Granell." Prólogo. Granell, *Isla cofre mítico* 3-6.

Césaire, Suzanne. "1943: Surrealism and Us." *Refusal of the Shadow: Surrealism and the Caribbean* 123-26.

Eshleman, Clayton and Annette Smith. Introduction. *The Collected Poetry*. By Aimé Césaire. Berkeley and Los Angeles: U of California P, 1983. 1-31.

Fry, Varian. *Surrender on Demand*. New York: Random House, 1945.

Granell, Eugenio Fernández. "André Breton nos habla de la actual situación de los artistas franceses. El escritor surrealista juzga las posibilidades de la cultura en Francia." *La Nación* May 21, 1941. [Reprinted in *Eugenio Granell: Exposición antológica, 1940-1990* (see Bonet), 423-29.]

———. *Isla cofre mítico*. Facsimile from Príncipe edition. Puerto Rico: Editorial Caribe, 1951.

Lévi-Strauss, Claude. *Tristes tropiques*. Trans. John and Doreen Weightman. New York: Penguin Books, 1992.

Mariátegui, José Carlos. "La experimentación surrealista." *Direcciones del vanguardismo hispanoamericano: Estudios sobre poesía de vanguardia en la década del veinte*. Gloria Videla de Rivero. Pittsburgh: Instituto Internacional de Literatura Iberoamericana, 1994. 257-59.

Müler-Bergh, Klaus. "El hombre y la técnica: Contribución al conocimiento de corrientes vanguardistas hispanoamericanas." *Philologica Hispaniensia in Honorem Manuel Alvar*. Vol. 4. Madrid: Editorial Gredos, 1987. 279-302.

Nadeau, Maurice. *The History of Surrealism*. Trans. Richard Howard. Cambridge (MA): Belknap/Harvard, 1989.

Núñez Jiménez, Antonio. *Wifredo Lam*. La Habana: Editorial Letras Cubanas, 1982.

Osorio Tejada, Nelson. "Para una caracterización histórica del vanguardismo literario hispanoamericano." *Revista Iberoamericana* 114-15 (1981): 227-54.

Poggioli, Renato. *The Theory of the Avant-Garde*. Trans. Gerald Fitzgerald. Cambridge (MA): Belknap/Harvard, 1968.

Refusal of the Shadow: Surrealism and the Caribbean. Ed. Michael Richardson. London and New York: Verso, 1996.

Richardson, Michael. Introduction. *Refusal of the Shadow: Surrealism and the Caribbean* 1-33.

Rosemont, Franklin. Introduction. *What is Surrealism?: Selected Writings*. By André Breton. New York: Pathfinder, 1978. 1-139.

Shattuck, Roger. "Love and Laughter: Surrealism Reappraised." Introduction. Nadeau 11-34.

Unruh, Vicky. *Latin American Vanguards: The Art of Contentious Encounters*. Berkeley and Los Angeles: U of California P, 1994.

The View From the Wheel[1]

MARIA T. PAO
Illinois State University

TO SOME SPANIARDS AT the beginning of the twentieth century, automobiles as a mode of reliable transportation seemed more trouble than they were worth. One observer noted,

> Cuando daban dos falsas explosiones y se paraban, sin venir a cuento y sin tener por qué, había que desmontarlos poco menos que pieza a pieza, y si dábamos al fin con la causa de la avería [...], menos mal. Por ello el automóvil no auguraba un venturoso porvenir. (qtd. in Leralta 239)

These mechanical shortcomings, though, did not deter the driving enthusiast who could afford the latest rage. In Madrid alone new car registrations quintupled from an average of 480 per year between 1908 and 1919 to 2670 per year after 1920 (Leralta 256, 258). The increase in vehicles, however, did not imply initially a significant increase in speed: in 1908 the official guidelines for municipal Madrid stipulated "una máxima velocidad de un buen tronco de caballos a trote" (qtd. in Leralta 267)—just over 6 mph; in 1924 the maximum would double to a still-sedate 12 mph.

Still, breakdowns and speed limits notwithstanding, the automobile had struck a worldwide nerve. F. M. Marinetti's "Manifesto of Futurism" appeared in *Le Figaro* on February 20, 1909, declaring, "A racing car whose hood is adorned with great pipes, like serpents of explosive breath—a roaring car that seems to ride on grapeshot—is more

---

[1] This essay is a version of an article originally titled "The View From the Wheel: De Torre, Salinas, and Hinojosa" published in *Revista Hispánica Moderna* 54 (2001): 88-107.

beautiful than the *Victory of Samothrace*" (41). Dynamic machines had replaced static painting as aesthetic signposts of modernity. The traditional artist could not keep pace with "the man at the wheel, who hurls the lance of his spirit across the Earth, along the circle of its orbit."

Two months after its publication in the French daily, the manifesto's hyperbolic rhetoric burst from the pages of the Spanish journal *Prometeo*, translated by the magazine's editor Ramón Gómez de la Serna. In September of the following year, *Prometeo* printed a new version of the manifesto which Marinetti had formulated especially for Spaniards. The rendition was preceded by Gómez de la Serna's own "Proclama futurista a los españoles" consisting of a series of affirmations set off by exclamation points. One in particular confirms the modern imperative of energy linked to a broad sense of renewal: "¡Movimiento sísmico resquebrajador que da vueltas a las tierras para renovarlas y darlas lozanía!" (173).

From here, the automobile sped into the consciousness and imagination of writers and non-writers alike. The fascination with cars as emblematic of independence, modern sensibility and a certain *joie de vivre* permeated both literary and popular journals with titles like "Ford," "El automóvil de mi sobrino," "El último modelo," "Conductora de auto," and "Canción para chófer."[2] Xavier Bóveda's "Un automóvil pasa" (1919), for example, documented the "Oú, oú, oú" of the car slowly going by, its playful motor accelerating "Trrrrrrrrr / Trrrrrrrr," then its frenetic forward charge and finally the "Po-po-po-pöc" as it disappears in the distance. Later, the car assumed somewhat more complex, though still lighthearted registers. In "Navacerrada, abril" Pedro Salinas described an automobile in loving tones more appropriate for a girlfriend—"Los dos solos"—than for a mechanical behemoth of "doce caballos." Not all approached cars with the same enamored equanimity, however. But while Rafael Alberti's "Don Homero y Doña Hermelinda" faced "coches, taxis, bicicletas" and their reckless tires with bewilderment, Ernesto Giménez Caballero revealed futurist sensibilities when he extolled Castille as the powerful engine of Spain: "carburador de sus explosiones; motor de sus ruedas, sus bielas y sus dientes."[3]

---

[2] Rosa Martín Casamitjana cites these examples in her study *El humor en la poesía española de vanguardia* (290-94).

[3] All published in 1929, the Salinas poem appeared in *Seguro azar*, Alberti's in *Cal y canto*, and Giménez Caballero's essay in *Julepe de menta*. The

Nevertheless, the most provocative car and driving texts aim beyond a simple articulation of the automobile as a shorthand for modern living and technological advance. Instead, they take as their point of departure Marinetti's simultaneous dethroning of traditional painting and apotheosis of the racing car. But rather than a literal replacement (automobile = art object), the car becomes a tool for art, an implement of aesthetic renewal. Just as quality of light or distance from the viewer can change the viewed, so can the viewer-in-motion transform the observed. The automobile—faster than walking and more autonomous than train travel—provides this motion which in turn alters visual perception.

This essay will look at three Spanish vanguard texts ostensibly about driving: one poem—Guillermo de Torre's "Al volante"—and two short prose works—"Entrada en Sevilla" by Pedro Salinas and José María Hinojosa's "Los guantes del paisaje." In each case I propose to show how speed affects what we see and how we see it. Furthermore, I suggest that the modes of perception and apprehension correspond strikingly to certain avant-garde movements—futurism, cubism and surrealism.

Guillermo de Torre (1900-1971) stands out as one of the central figures of the Spanish avant-garde. Based in Madrid until his departure from Spain in 1927, he participated on numerous journals as contributor and editor, wrote literary criticism, translated Paul Verlaine and Max Jacob, and in 1925 published the influential *Literaturas europeas de vanguardia*. *Hélices*, De Torre's first book of verse, appeared in 1923. Consisting of poems composed between 1918 and 1922, and with titles like "Canto dinámico," "Locomotora," "Madrigal aéreo," and "Aviograma," it reveals clear affinity to the futurist cult of dynamism. With an obvious nod to Marinetti, De Torre writes, "Los motores suenan mejor que endecasílabos" (32).

"Al volante" (45) describes a car trip along the countryside. It begins with two quotations from the French poet Pierre Drieu la Rochelle: "Boire la vitesse pure" [To drink pure speed], "La vision circulaire entre dans l'oeil comme un fruit pelé dans la bouche" [Round vision enters the eye like a peeled fruit into the mouth]. In these citations alone, movement and optic perception become linked as each image transmits the sense of speed and vision as palpable, pleasurable things, inviting consumption or even demanding it with the active

---

1919 Bóveda and Buendía texts cited earlier both were published in the journal *Grecia*.

"entre dans." Moreover, De Torre's placement of the "vitesse pure" epigraph before the "vision circulaire" quotation suggests that velocity propels sight into the eye of the viewer and that speed, no longer merely coincidental to visual experience, helps to determine its quality.

In some respects "Al volante" does not deviate from typical futurist rhetoric in its depiction of "el cross-country cósmico," "la embriaguez dinámica," and "trayectorias insaciables." Verbs of movement predominate—"rear up," "shoot," "bore," "jump," "gallop," "advance." Strikingly, however, these action verbs correspond as much to the surrounding panorama as to the driver and his companion. That is, while the human *we* "avanzamos" and "[t]repanamos aldeas naufragadas," the highway itself rears up, the countryside gallops, and the mountains arch their backs to jump. The sudden alacrity of the once-motionless landscape has less to do with traditional personification of inanimate objects, than with the effect of speed, as "Al volante" makes clear in its first stanza:

> En el juego de velocidades
> los pedales
> barajan un kaleidoscopio
> de perspectivas tornátiles

Besides moving the driver along, the car's movement has, simultaneously and seemingly paradoxically, also set in motion the observed landscape. The play of velocity—acceleration and deceleration—reshuffles perspective so that seeing, like a turning kaleidoscope, becomes a sort of game.

In this regard, too, the notion of play bears notice. Rather than associating speed with human dominance of the earth through the shortening of distance, driving seems actually to grant agency to the landscape. Or at least, it challenges the eye to hold steady what it sees, even as mountains leap and the countryside races by as if engaged in a game of hide-and-seek. By the end of the poem, the automobile is shuddering with its effort, but not without having produced a lasting effect on sight:

Saltos entre las mallas de itinerarios
Trepidaciones
El motor padece taquiarritmia
Las ventanillas agotan el libro de paisajes
El parabrisas multiplica nuestros ojos
que cosen los panoramas evasivos
Y el viento liquefacciona los sonidos

El la embriaguez dinámica
el auto siembra
una estela
de células aladas

The car's movement has increased the eye's range of views and provided multiple kaleidoscope lenses, but only because the viewed itself—subject to the same movement—has become elusive. Even though "Las ventanillas agotan el libro de paisajes," human eyes—unlike "car eyes"—cannot deplete the album of landscapes. Despite the Argos effect, they only manage to apprehend fragments of images to stitch together collage-like. Other parts of the panorama dance away, like the "células aladas" the car sows in its wake.

The intuition in "Al volante" that motion of both observer and observed affects the way we see recalls the paintings of Italian futurists Umberto Boccioni and Carlo Carrà. For example, Boccioni's *The City Rises* (1910-1911) shows men and beasts tugging at their loads, and Carrà's *Funeral of the Anarchist Galli* (1911-1912) portrays the riotous whirl of a workers' strike. But while the objects and events depicted undoubtedly reflect movement in space and time, most important, the spectator's line of sight moves as well. As Max Kozloff notes of Carrà, "He gives us to understand that our vision is in motion, too, and strives for a generally elusive synthesis of 'pictorial' and spectator action" (148). The futurists' expanded scope of perception "makes the world more real, more present" and "turn[s] attention toward experience rather than toward the external object" (Taylor 170). As readers of De Torres's poem, our vision aligns with that of the moving driver "al volante," as the animated landscape, also in a sense "at the wheel," converts the experience of seeing into a game of catch-as-catch-can.

In Spain, from roughly 1917 to 1919, the Uruguayan painter Rafael Barradas (1890-1929), was experimenting with similar shifts in perspective based on movement. Having spent time in Italy and

France before arriving in Barcelona in 1914, he called his style, a merging of futurist energy and cubist geometry, *vibracionismo*.[4] With the name Barradas wanted to underscore the movement, the *vibration* inherent in every object. In this way, "las cosas, la materia de que están hechas, no son inertes, poseen la energía de lo existente, trascienden las cualidades físicas de su apariencia" (Carmona, "Picasso" 30). Because visual apprehension no longer sufficed to capture these objects, Barradas painted geometric fragments and colors where allusion replaced reference. In *Calle de Barcelona* (1918) [Fig. 1], for instance, a number of faceless, partial figures compete for space with overlapping wheels, grates, tires, streetlights, plant fronds and signs. The only complete image appears to be a clock marking one o'clock, whose orderly presence merely underscores the disunity of its surroundings. As the viewer's eye moves back and forth to locate coherence, each object seems to be attempting a kind of subterfuge, hiding behind or emerging from another. This dynamism has as much to do with actual physical movement, as with perception of movement due to the beholder's own change of position and with the metaphysical notion of the essential flux of all inanimate objects. In each case the optically apprehensible is reduced to the merely notational. Though *Calle de Barcelona* depicts the space of a city street in its basic details—people, signs, suggestions of vehicles—it resists any attempt on the part of the spectator to see it as a whole, as either a tree-lined boulevard or a commercial avenue or a cart-filled sidestreet.

That Barradas combined futurism with cubism to create his virtually one-man vibrationist movement supports Max Kozloff's observation that "[b]oth schools were convinced of the essential fluidity and relativity of perception" (148).[5] In Spain, cubism had made its first formal incursion in 1912 with an *Exposició de'Art Cubista* at the Dalmau Galleries in Barcelona, which included works by Jean Metzinger, Albert Gleizes, Juan Gris, Marcel Duchamp, and others. Another smaller cubist show was arranged by Gómez de la Serna in Madrid three years later. In 1916 Gleizes held an individual exhibit of cubist

---

[4] Jaime Brihuega, describing vibrationism as a kind of "dynamic cubism" (95n10), identifies references to the futurists Marinetti, Carrà and Gino Severini (87) in Barradas's work, along with those of Robert Delaunay and Francis Picabia. Barradas worked closely with the writers of the Spanish avant-garde, providing artwork for their publications, including De Torres's *Hélices*.

[5] Robert Delaunay's simultaneism might represent another collusion of these two *isms*.

Fig. 1: Rafael Barradas, *Calle de Barcelona* (1918)
(Colección de Arte Contemporáneo, Madrid)

works, again at the Dalmau Galleries, and the following year Barcelona saw a major exhibit of French art spanning from impressionism to cubism.

In the meantime, cubist theory had reached the Peninsula as well. Extracts of Apollinaire's *Les Peintres cubistes* appeared in the journal *España* in 1918, while one year later Blaise Cendrars published an article on cubism in *Grecia*. Attention intensified during the 1920s. The Polish painter and art critic living in Madrid, Marjan Paszkiewicz, wrote a series of essays for *Horizonte*, in which he described his objections to cubism. In contrast, Manuel Abril in "Itinerario del nuevo arte plástico" praised the cubist painters' use of "representación como alusión" (134), while José Moreno Villa called the movement "la mayor aventura en la historia del Arte" (136).

Fig. 2: José Ortega y Gasset at the wheel. (Photograph courtesy of the Residencia de Estudiantes, Madrid.)

Fig. 3: Pedro Salinas: "Los dos solos." (Photograph courtesy of the Residencia de Estudiantes, Madrid)

The author of "Al volante" himself did not hesitate to make his views known. In 1925 De Torre gave a lecture at Madrid's Museum of Modern Art, in which he tried to rescue cubism from the "seres obtusos y malintencionados, que tanto oscurecieron impíamente la clara armonía de tus [cubism's] conceptos" ("Aventura" 140):

¡Cubismo! ¡Cubismo! Henos aquí, frente a frente, enigmática y mutable palabra, hermético concepto, insolente escuela, dogma revolucionario; henos aquí, sirena seductora o más bien dragón amenazador de nuestra época; henos aquí, maravilla adónica, ángel o endriago, jeroglífico y rompecabezas [...] de las mentes débiles. (140)

Against "weak minds" who see only confusion, De Torre cites "la sólida trabazón" of the movement's "luminosa arquitectura teórica." Still, the idea of cubism as hieroglyphic and puzzling is perhaps less obtuse than De Torre believes. In fact, one year earlier, José Ortega y Gasset [Fig. 2] had written "Sobre el punto de vista en las artes" for *Revista de Occidente* where he specifically described cubism's depiction of objects as fantasmagoric, partial, and thus hieroglyphic.

At this point, I would like to turn to "Entrada en Sevilla." In it, Salinas (1891-1951) [Fig. 3] depicts a cubist aesthetic in which speed influences visual perception, finally compelling optic image to give way to mental image. The discussion to follow will draw from Ortega's "Sobre el punto de vista en las artes" (1924), his 1925 essay "La deshumanización del arte," as well as more recent studies of cubism. "Entrada en Sevilla"—hereafter "Sevilla"—appeared in Salinas's first collection of prose texts titled *Víspera del gozo* (1926).[6] The protagonist Claudio attempts to capture the essence of Seville; the title reflecting Claudio's desire to enter Seville not only geographically, but also metaphysically. As he rides in the car, he expects to apprehend the city as a knowable object through sight alone.[7] We will recall that the driver "at the wheel" of De Torre's poem saw leaping landscapes set in motion by the car's movement that forced his eyes to perform a kind of continuous suturing. In a similar way, Claudio's view of Seville is stymied—first by the automobile's bulk and then by its movement.

---

[6] Both Gustavo Pérez Firmat (74) and Robert C. Spires (131, 144) have suggested that *Víspera del gozo*, which Spires considers "arguably the best example of vanguardism we have in Spanish prose fiction" (74), addresses issues of aesthetics. On a more general level, Eugenio Carmona discusses the response of the Generation of 27 writers to the intersection of painting and literature as "una voluntad integradora de las artes inherente a la inmensa mayoría de los movimientos artísticos modernos" ("Pintura" 103).

[7] Audrey R. Gertz has read Claudio's wish to "possess" Seville as metaphoric of the masculine desire to control women and the male poet's need to exert authority over the text; see her article "Sensuality, Reality, and the Poetic Process in Pedro Salinas's 'Entrada en Sevilla.'"

When he and his companion Robledo leave the house, the first thing he sees "no era paisaje de ciudad, sino la poderosa forma de un automóvil en espera, que lo tapaba todo" (33-34). The hulking vehicle, practically hugging the front door due to the narrowness of the street, is blocking his view. Claudio literally *cannot see* the city because of the car. The automobile's presence, even perfectly at rest, estranges him from the object that he desires to know (through vision). Moreover, it is pressed so tightly to the side of the building that Claudio's first step does not touch Andalusian pavement, "una faja neutra de nacionalidad lejana, un estribo de automóvil." A certain alienating or distancing effect may be detected here, a forced defamiliarization suggested by the non-domestic neutrality of the auto's running board.[8] In fact, Ortega indicates that this defamiliarization or change in perspective constitutes the primary departure point for new art. It works by deliberately unhinging emotional response from our apprehension of an object since "los grados de proximidad equivalen a grados de participación sentimental en los hechos; los grados de alejamiento, por el contrario, significan grados de liberación en que objetivamos el suceso real, convirtiéndolo en puro tema de contemplación" ("Deshumanización" 362).[9] It is important to note that the adjustment of perspective that Ortega describes is not informed by actual physical distance. What he calls "*visión próxima*" and "*visión lejana*" reflect rather "dos modos distintos de mirar" (PV 187). Whereas the first establishes a hierarchy organized around a palpable "núcleo central privilegiado" (PV 188), the second produces a homogenous field in which "no se ve una cosa mejor y el resto confusamente, sino que todo se presenta sumergido en una democracia óptica" (PV 188-189). At a standstill and physically interposed between Claudio and Seville, the automobile cuts off conventional views; in motion, it will transform the city into a blur. At every moment the car qualifies what and how Claudio sees.

But he has no inking of this yet. Once in the car and moving, he expects the city to come into focus. As they start off, Robledo remarks, "Fíjate bien, ésta es Sevilla" (36). But herein lies the problem: no matter how intensely Claudio "se fija," the car's motion makes it impossi-

---

[8] Leralta notes that the most frequently purchased cars in Spain during this period consisted of foreign models—Buicks, Citröens and Fords (258).

[9] Hereafter "La deshumanización del arte" will be designated, intratextually in parenthesis, by the initial "D" and "Sobre el punto de vista en las artes" by "PV," followed by corresponding page numbers.

ble for him really to "fijar"—limit, establish, make stable—the object that he fixes on, in this case, the city of Seville:

> La calle, inmóvil, pero *poseída con la marcha del coche de una actividad vertiginosa y teatral*, empezó a desplegar formas, líneas, espacios multicolores y cambiantes, rotos, reanudados a cada instante, sin coherencia alguna, y con idéntica rapidez y destreza con que muestra un prestimano los colorinescos objetos que le van a servir en su juego, más que para que el público los vea, con el malicioso propósito de que su rauda sucesión cree una imagen confusa y apta para cualquier engaño en la mirada del espectador.[10]
> (36-37, italics added)

As in De Torre's poem, the automobile's speed triggers an otherwise static panorama into activity. The street, no longer a thoroughfare of stable facades, becomes a magician flashing shapes and lines and colors, in a now-you-see-it-now-you-don't display very much like De Torre's depiction of cubism as a "rompecabezas" to the uninitiated. The movement of the car has produced—indeed, has forced upon Claudio—Ortega's "*visión lejana.*" If in "*visión próxima*" the object focused on is clear and distinct with the background blurred, in the other, "Nada posee un perfil rigoroso, todo es fondo, confuso, casi informe" (PV 189). The corporeal palpability of objects diminishes in what Ortega calls "pura visión," so that things become "meros entes cromáticos, sin resistencia, solidez ni convexidad" (PV 190). Through this changed way of seeing, objects' very "thingness"—predicated on their tactile quality—disappears and they take on an illusory cast, "el aspecto casi irreal de apariciones ultramundanas." I would argue that Salinas's depiction of the city street suddenly charged with the car's motion dovetails with Ortega's analysis of transformed vision in modern art. Meanwhile, the metaphor of the street as a magician flipping through a rapid succession of confusing images parallels in an uncanny way an observation on cubism by Kozloff:

---

[10] The street seen from a moving car as "formas, líneas, espacios multicolores y cambiantes" mirrors a description of Picasso's cubist paintings as "an explicit statement about the nature of visual experience—of forms, of spaces, of colors and of the relation of these quantities to each other" (Vargish and Mook 83).

> In the Cubist priorities of seeing [...] movement is rarely of an event or action depicted, but a qualification of the handling. The desire to view many conceivable unfoldings of a thing superimposed in the same space [...] exhilarates all transitions. It is the finagling of a cardsharp or conjurer—fast, purposeful, and deceptive in its executions—and it is no accident that the card game [...] was to become a prominent emblem of the Cubist sleight of hand. (52)

Kozloff's characterization of the cubist conjurer as deceptive aligns with De Torre's description of cubism as enigmatic, mutable, hermetic and insolent, as well as with the portrayal of Salinas's magician-street as malicious and given to "engaño." Kozloff suggests, moreover, that the cubists' pan-perspective agenda necessarily entailed an element of cunning, the fragmented aspects deliberately arranged to puzzle an audience accustomed to viewing objects in a certain (realist) way. Indeed, what De Torre names "mutable," Kozloff calls "sleight of hand," Ortega deems "irreal," and Salinas considers "deceit" results from cubism's renewed manner of seeing. As such, the view from Claudio's automobile presents a disconcerting sight, one that perhaps evokes the discomfort spectators experienced when first viewing cubist portraits or still lifes in which the "real" person or object depicted seemed as deranged as Seville to Claudio.

Initial disconcertion or difficulty, which Thomas Vargish and Delo E. Mook describe as epistemic trauma, characterizes the reception of modern art by a public accustomed to realist conventions. It includes a feeling of strangeness, opacity, counter-intuition, and disruption of common sense (14). Claudio's inability to "fijarse en" what he sees, either conceptually and visually, is a reaction to cubism's adjustments to the way in which it represents its object. Already with impressionism, Ortega argued that "Empiezan las figuras a ser incognoscibles. En vez de pintar los objetos como se ven, *se pinta el ver mismo.* [...] El arte, con esto, se ha retirado por completo del mundo y *empieza a atender a la actividad del sujeto* (PV 201-202, italics added). In cubism the seeing subject enhances optic perception of an object by adding to the visually apprehensible the *idea* of the object. As Vargish and Mook write, "Picasso and Braque attempted to represent nature, or the object, as it exists in the mind's eye, in what we *know* about its visual reality" (64). They go on to explain that "we know what we know about objects because *we have observed them over time and in motion*" (65, italics added).[11] Cubist painters abandoned the single-point perspective in force since the Renaissance in order to include aspects of objects gleaned not only from the vantage point of one instant and a single angle, but from their accumulated memories of those objects. From Cézanne onward, remarked Ortega, "la pintura sólo pinta ideas" (PV 203); "Picasso [...] aniquila la forma cerrada del objeto y, [...] anota trozos de él, una ceja, un bigote, una nariz—sin otra misión que servir de cifra simbólica a ideas" (PV 203-204). In "Sevilla" Claudio longs to apprehend the whole head, as it were. He desires the city, "limpia y total, [...] ofrecida como en la palma de una mano hábil en la llanada del Guadalquivir" (37).[12] But the aesthetic innovations in perspective since the late 1880s have expanded this single view. As the futurists declared on the occasion of their first Paris exhibition in 1912, "We must show the invisible which stirs and lives behind intervening obstacles, what we have on our right, on the left, and behind us, and not merely the little square of life artificially compressed, as it were, by the wings of a stage" (qtd. in Kozloff 159-60). For the cubists, "the invisible which stirs and lives behind intervening obstacles" includes, as Ortega maintained, the concept of objects "distinto del que los ojos nos transmiten y que maravillosamente emerge de los senos psíquicos" (PV 203).

In Salinas's story Claudio gazes at Seville, framed by the car window, as at a cubist painting. But whereas the cubist work depicts the artist's multiple views recollected and represented on a canvas, "Sevilla" substitutes the automobile's motion for this "knowing over

---

[11] The authors specify, "[W]e know what the bottom and the stem and the bowl and the rim of our wine glass look like because we have held it in our hand on so many occasions" (64-65).

[12] Claudio's expectation of a "clean and whole" Seville immediately follows his impression of the street as "un prestimano" unfolding all manner of shapes and lines and changing colors. The entire sentence reads, "Sí, probablemente en cuanto todo aquello se aquietara, de esta confusión de colores, iba a salir, limpia y total, Sevilla, *ofrecida como en la palma de una mano hábil*, etc." (italics added). It is significant that even this apparently objective image of a motionless and complete Seville appears as the result of the magician's clever hand; that is, his trickery. Vargish and Mook have pointed out that realist painting with its one-point perspective and linearity may itself be considered a subterfuge: "Since what we know about reality, about any object, is greater than what can be perceived from a single perspective, the limitations of single-point perspective are in fact distorting. Traditional perspective is literally *trompe-l'oeil*, visual deception" (64).

time." The car's movement in fact provides a double function: it serves as diachronic "memory" or an accumulation of impressions as the vehicle speeds along, and it gives the sensation of the city itself springing into action. With both subject (viewer) and object (viewed) no longer spatially or temporally static, objective Seville—"limpia y total"—becomes transformed, to Claudio's dismay, into cubist Seville—into Seville-the-idea, Seville-the-optical-illusion: "Todo lo que aprehendían los ojos eran fragmentos, cortes y paños de muros, rosa, verde, azul" (37-38). Vision itself does not suffice—"se hundía la mirada siempre demasiado tarde"—and even when it seems to identify some coherence, something like "un punto redondo y negro que intenta dar apariencias de orden a una prosa en tumulto" (38), it turns out that "se había equivocado la vista" (39).[13] Just when Claudio fixes on one thing and attempts to make a whole, "ya empezaba de nuevo otra cosa, dejándose atrás aquélla: una pared de colores, la arista de una esquina brusca, una reja" (38). As in Barradas's *Calle de Barcelona* and De Torre's landscape of "panoramas evasivos," the city sidesteps efforts to contain it, avoids the organization and determinacy of the serious black full-stop in favor of "espacios multicolores," "colorinescos objetos," and a "confusión de colores" (37).

Claudio can no longer trust his eyes alone to supply him with an uncomplicated objective view of Seville:

> Se le desvanecía a Claudio la Sevilla convencional de los panoramas, definición lejana en el paisaje con dos líneas—caserío, Giralda—que se cortan con una belleza estrictamente geométrica. La ciudad no se definía lejos, depurada y distinta, sino que vivía cerca, complicadísima, esquiva siempre a la línea recta [...]. (40)

Here, to demonstrate that Ortega's distinction between proximate and distant vision does not rely on actual physical distances, far-off Seville provides the "núcleo central privilegiado" of Ortega's proximate vision; meanwhile, the city up-close and "esquiva" aligns with the "optical democracy" of his distant vision. Where Claudio expects sharp geometric beauty and straight lines, Seville gives him "miradores torcidos," "balcones desenfocados" (39), and "calles onduladas" (41). The automobile's unceasing forward motion produces a sensation of

---

[13] Salinas's mention of "una prosa en tumulto" makes oblique reference to the difficulty and resistance of avant-garde (and modernist) narrative, with its recasting of temporal markers (Vargish and Mook, *passim*).

strangeness-at-close-range that duplicates Ortega's conception of distant, dehierarchized vision and forces Claudio to collect as he can disparate parts of a city "muda[ndo] rumbo constantemente" and "cambia[ndo] sin tregua" (40). He cannot get a "fix" on the streets as they all seem alike and different at the same time—"Esa calle fugitiva era otra y no la suya, otra que arrancaba de allí y se confundía con ella, toda igual y deliciosamente distinta" (39)—and as every image gives way to a succeeding one: "a cada visión se sustituía inmediatamente la de al lado" (42). Even though Claudio feels disoriented, the car's velocity propels him forward, obliging him to experience Seville in the manner of a cubist painting:

> The more succinct the contradictions in a Cubist canvas, the more fugitive are the delays, backups and retakes in the way we apprehend it. Instead of measuring and framing the intervals of our attentiveness, *we become immersed in them in an unstructured succession.* In Impressionism, incidents always seem to be flowing into each other, becoming each other in one dominant flow. With Cubism, *incidents appear to be emerging out of each other, striving to differentiate themselves.*" (Kozloff 111-12, italics added)

Claudio's visual perception of the city, modified by the speed of the car, does not transmit an image of "la Sevilla convencional," but it does give him fleeting views of streets, doorways, gates, walls, corners of buildings, balconies, and flowerpots on rooftop patios. He has to supplement each fragment with another, gleaned from his memory of it during an earlier part of the car trip. Claudio must takes his point of departure from his visual apprehension of the city—an accumulation of aspects collected through space and time—and assemble a Seville from what he has seen, but also from imagined dimensions, other perspectives, loose parts, and conventional views. In this way, he replicates the mechanism of cubism paintings, described by Vargish and Mook as "highly constructed mediations between external reality and the mind of the viewer" (82):

> Y *era preciso que la imaginación juntase* tal trozo de blanqueada pared, aquel zaguán, una cancela, con la perspectiva no suya— ésta ya se había evadido—, sino de la casa vecina, y poniendo sobre todo esto balcones y terrazas ajenos y un cielo visible, pero convencional, reconstruyese idealmente *lo que por angostura de la*

calle y rapidez de la marcha no cabía, verdadero, en la visión. (42-43, italics added)

The closeness of the street, paradoxically approximating Ortega's distant vision, along with the automobile's velocity and Claudio's own powers of reconstruction, produce an image of Seville greater, not less—as Claudio fears—than what he manages to see: "In Cubism each painting is a reassemblage that forces various 'fragments,' perspectives or aspects gathered over time, into a single visual 'instant,' and 'simultaneous' mental construct represented in a single visual frame" (Vargish and Mook 89).

But it is precisely this "mental construct," the improvement of optic reality by the engagement of the observer that Claudio does not trust. He conceives of this new vision of Seville, balanced between "real" and "imagined," as too contingent and thus precarious:

Y por eso la ciudad, tan real, tenía un temblor de fantasmagoría, un inminente peligro de que al no poder tenderse juntos, arbitrariamente ensamblados en la imaginación todos aquellos fragmentos que en realidad estaban perfectamente unidos, se viniera todo abajo, en un terremoto ideal y pintarrajeado como los que se muestran con comento de romances en los cartelones de las ferias. (43)

Unaccustomed to this renewed manner of seeing in which a formerly static vantage point is abandoned for movement in time and space, demanding greater viewer participation and replacing one discrete object with its shifting planes in changing association, Claudio finds it difficult to reconcile what he "knows" is "real" with fantasy, imagination and a provisional unity more appropriate to carnival posters. His frustration stems from the what-seems-to-him-unnecessary project of wedding optic vision (clear and direct, as he perceives it) to mental conception (ineffable and tenuous): "Estaba viendo Sevilla y aún tenía que seguir imaginándola" (43). But according to Vargish and Mook, this in-betweenness that characterizes the reception of fragmented observations constitutes a primary index for modern art (and literature). As such, (partial) visual experience assumes the register of "emotionally charged negotiations, occupying that middle ground between subject and object. The fragments do not fully become fragments of external 'reality'; nor do they remain exclusively internal or psychological phenomena" (92).[14]

The middle ground, though, here precipitated by automotive speed, causes Claudio unease, as if his mind cannot absorb a single, ostensibly external reality composed both of what he sees at a one instant and what he remembers from other instants. This counterintuitive fusion was reflected earlier when Claudio considered the dizzying streets, constantly in motion, that paradoxically took him nowhere: "Imposible estarse quieto aquí en estas calles onduladas [...]. Pero imposible, luego, ir a parte alguna, servirse de aquellos viales para el logro de un designio insertándolos en calidad de medios en una empresa racional superior" (41). The automobile, rather than facilitating a journey into the "corazón recóndito y difícil" of Seville, floats through the twisting streets like a "góndola sin rumbo, a la deriva." Unexpectedly noncomplicit, the mechanically conceived machine thwarts Claudio's positivistic intentions to know the city by the "línea recta" of her thoroughfares. Instead, the curving streets frustrate his vision and with it, the method ("medios") and realization ("logro") of his lofty epistemological enterprise ("empresa racional superior").

At last, Claudio, realizing the impossibility of an objective view, accepts the significance of his individual perceptions of Seville, mediated by motion. He finally acknowledges that *to him* the city represents ("le era") "algo incierto e inaprehensible como una mujer amada, producto de datos reales, pero dispersos y nublosos, y unificadora, lúcida fantasía que los coordina en superior encanto" (43-44).[15] For cub-

---

[14] In this discussion, the authors are referring not specifically to cubist painting, but to modernist prose—Joyce's *Dubliners* (1914). However, as the title of their book *Inside Modernism: Relativity Theory, Cubism, Narrative* (1999) implies, Vargish and Mook argue that each of these cultural articulations reflected common spatio-temporal destabilizations, so that single empirical reality was problematized in favor of (variable and multiple) observation and measurement. In fact, their examination of *Dubliners* has particular resonance for "Entrada en Sevilla" since Joyce's book also deals with the plural viewpoints and perspectives of a city. While both Dublin and Seville exist as independent of human perception, they enter "human consciousness only through the unique viewpoints of individual observers" (92).

[15] Throughout "Sevilla" Claudio compares the city to a woman—to a "gitana" quick to disappear (39), a sister mistaken for "la mujer querida," a "bailarina" (40), and again "una mujer amada" (44). Gertz reads Seville's continual evasion of Claudio's gaze as emblematic of the text's refusal of the writer's authority: "Woman, city and text retain their sensuality, beauty and

ism the object viewed has been abandoned for the experience of viewing; observations or "propositions about reality—that is, self-conscious proposals of things related or associated with each other on different levels" (Kozloff 66) move to the forefront. This realization inverts Claudio's initial assumptions about the "fact" of a visually apprehensible Seville as "limpia y total," "convencional," and "racional," and his reassembly of it as "fantasmagoría." Now the "datos reales" of what he sees become scattered and fuzzy, whereas the fantasy, the virtual reality of the imagined, is lucid, clear and unifying. As in cubism, the here-and-now visual experience of the object enriched by dimensions not spatially or temporally present provides a heightened apprehension of reality. Where Claudio once longed for the fulfillment of "una empresa racional superior," by the end of the trip, he comes to appreciate the "superior encanto" of uncertainty, shifts in pattern, and curves of color.

But old habits are hard to break, and Claudio "[s]intió gana de mirar más de cerca, de bajar del auto." The realist approach of close ("más de cerca"), single-point, static ("bajar del auto") scrutiny remains instinctive to Claudio's reaction to visual experience. This impulse is his first mistake. The second is helping to gather Robledo's things after they spill from her purse when the car turns sharply. Although gallant, this action reflects Claudio's knee-jerk acquiescence to predictable order and the touchable things of Ortega's proximate vision.[16] Claudio finally has the opportunity to stop and exit the automo-

---

essential vitality by resisting definition and control" (171). (See also note 7.) Nevertheless, we can also see the disappearing female, metaphor for the disappearing city, as a cubist subversion of the traditional portrait as in Picasso's *Ma Jolie* (1911) where vague allusions to a torso and a head compete with suggestions of a guitar, a wine glass, and so on, so that "The spectator is bid to study how parts are put together and, on that basis, to intuit the vague presence of a subject" (Kozloff 47).

[16] "Un hábito milenario [...] hace que el hombre no considere como 'cosas', en estricto sentido, más que aquellos objetos cuya solidez ofrece resistencia a sus manos. El resto es más o menos fantasma. Pues bien: al pasar un objeto de la visión próxima a la lejana, se fantasmagoriza" (PV 190). In "Sevilla" Claudio initially attributes to distance an uncomplicated clearness of vision, as opposed to the complex vagueness of closeness (to the city). This, as we have seen, inverts Ortega's sense of proximate vision offering a clean image of one object, while distant vision turns everything into blurry background. The end of the text recoups Ortega's notion of close observation—Claudio's desire to "mirar más de cerca"—as too limited and limiting.

bile, for "no había perdido de vista en la memoria la calle dislocada y multicolor" (44-45), an appropriately cubist description fusing vision ("vista") and concept over time ("memoria"). But by then, "casas de colores, calles, Sevilla, todo había desaparecido, entrevisto y maravilloso, vuelto acaso a la caja de engaños del prestimano, delicia huida" (45). When Claudio attempts to revert to an old method of seeing based on an immobile vantage point and tactile proximity, the "superior encanto" of Seville slips away. The magician ends his show and rather than narrow streets turning every which way and colorful glimpses of walls, a prosaic "reality" of "una calle ancha [...] con altas casas grises" (45) appears instead.

In "Sevilla" movement mediates observation, transforming optic perception and ultimately enhancing the apprehension of external objects, in this case a city. But it also shows the resistance to changing our accustomed manner of perceiving, no matter how much a speeding car or a cubist canvas compels us. Just as Claudio at the beginning of the narrative, "We miss those qualities or techniques on which we had customarily relied for meaning, such as perspective in painting, tonality in music, temporal sequence in narrative, unvarying temporal and spatial reference frames in physics" and feel the elimination of these markers as "bereavement and outrage" (Vargish and Mook 15). But by the end, having experienced a Seville-in-motion, Claudio wants the show to go on—as cubism indeed does throughout Western representation. He has discovered a cubist reality all the more captivating for its elusiveness, as Picasso remarked, "It's not a reality you can take in your hand. It's more like a perfume—in front of you, behind you, to the sides. The scent is everywhere, but you don't quite know where it comes from" (qtd. in Kozloff 51).

Before continuing on to Hinojosa's "Los guantes del paraíso," let us look once more at Ortega's discussion of cubism in his "Punto de vista" essay. Explaining how the movement "reached the minimum of exterior objectivity," the author traces the function of the eyes—organs of visual perception—from passive and receptive to active and projective:

> Un nuevo desplazamiento del punto de vista sólo era posible si, saltando detrás de la retina [...] invertía por completo la pintura su función y, en vez de meternos dentro de lo que está fuera, *se esforazba por volcar sobre el lienzo lo que está dentro* [...]. *Los ojos, en vez de absorber las cosas, se convierten en proyectores de paisajes y*

faunas íntimas. Antes eran sumideros del mundo real: ahora, surtidores de irrealidad. (204, italics added)

This representation of internal and external reality as communicating vessels with the balance tilting toward the internal recurs strikingly in André Breton's descriptions of surrealism's effect on painting, written between 1925 and 1927,[17] and in José María Hinojosa's 1926 story "Los guantes del paisaje"—examples that, as I show below, also make use of Ortega's liquid metaphor ("volcar," "absorber," "sumideros," "surtidores") in his depiction of an internal reality pooled in the eyes and projected outward. Both Hinojosa's text and the surrealist agenda underscore mobility as a crucial element in the production of mental images. While the first enlists the velocity of an automobile to provide the continued flow of inner reality to the exterior, the second implemented the practice of psychic automatism to reproduce the uninterrupted stream of thought.

Breton's movement, as stated in his first *Manifesto of Surrealism*, aimed at "the future resolution of [...] dream and reality, which are seemingly so contradictory, into a kind of absolute reality, a *surreality*" (14). His group believed in the salutary reintegration of the subconscious mind into ordinary waking life through oneiric narration, automatic writing, and other activities designed to trigger the appearance of the marvelous in everyday living. In December 1924 Ortega's journal *Revista de Occidente* printed a review by Fernando Vela of the new movement. This particular commentator was not impressed with the reliance of "suprarrealismo" on the dream, which he considered "un estado larvado, caótico, discontinuo, intermediario" (32). Nevertheless, 1925 saw more favorable considerations of surrealism in the magazine *Alfar* by César M. Arconada and Pierre Picón, as well as a lecture by Louis Aragon at Madrid's Residencia de Estudiantes. De Torre also included a short section on "Neodadaísmo y superrealismo" in his *Literaturas europeas de vanguardia* of the same year.[18] Malaga writer

---

[17] As is well known, Breton often used the metaphor of communicating vessels—not the least in his 1932 book titled *Communicating Vessels*—to depict the mutually touching and therefore non-exclusive realms of waking reality and dream reality.

[18] In "Hacia un superrealismo musical" Arconada wrote, "[S]e está creando una pintura y una literatura contraformal, sin desdeñar los elementos reales, antes bien afirmándoles, pero sin que de ningún modo el orden lógico de lo real intervenga mandatariamente en la construcción" (333). Picón, seeing

José María Hinojosa (1904-1936) experienced surrealism firsthand in Paris between July 1925 and April 1926. He returned to Spain enamoured of the movement and wearing extravagant costumes that included brightly colored cravats, whimsical hats, and a pipe and walking stick (Neira 276). In addition, having consorted with members of the Escuela Española de París—Spanish painters working with the French avant-garde, like Francisco Bores, Benjamín Palencia and Joaquín Peinado—Hinojosa added numerous canvases to "una de las mejores colecciones del nuevo arte español" (Carmona, "Pintura" 104).

In 1928, two years after his return from France, he issued the idiosyncratically-accented *La flor de California*. Unlike previous works, the volume consisted entirely of prose narratives, some written during his Paris stay. José Moreno Villa, in his "Carta al autor" introducing the texts, stresses both the dream-like atmosphere of the narratives ("el volante misterioso de los sueños") as well as their painterly quality, adding, "He simpatizado de golpe con esa técnica porque ya la pintura gemela me tenía preparado. Y recuerdo que comprendí mejor los cuadros de Bores y de Miró cuando leí tus narraciones y que, también éstas se me iluminaron al ver aquéllos" (180). This pictorial sensibility corresponding, as I will argue, to surrealist modes of perception, is especially evident in "Los guantes del paisaje," the book's third text.

"Guantes" presents the bizarre experience of a driver creating a landscape ("paisaje") out of his eyes as he motors along. As with "Al volante" and "Entrada en Sevilla," visual perception or, in this case, visual *creation* is mediated by the movement of an automobile. The text begins with a description of the steering-wheel given a full spin and "el automóvil giró sobre sus cuatro ruedas y se puso en dirección contraria a la que llevaba" (35). This abrupt turn-around is emblematic of the irrationality and distortion of conventional perspective that characterizes surreality, a transformation triggered by access to the

---

that surrealism began primarily as a literary movement, explained that "El super-realismo afirma y prueba que las palabras viven con una vida particular y secreta, hecha de todas las sensaciones y de todos los sentimientos que evocan en cada uno de nosotros resumiendo nuestra existencia" (132). De Torre, however, found the movement "amanerado y estéril" (*Literaturas* 233). We might note as well that the term itself caused discrepancy. While Vela preferred "suprarrealismo," most opted for "superrealismo" until Ramón Gómez de la Serna used the Gallicized "surrealismo" in 1930.

mind's reality:[19] "If the depths of our mind contain within it strange forces capable of augmenting those on the surface, [...] there is every reason to seize them" (*Manifesto* 10). And seize these forces the protagonist does, as he "[s]acaba el paisaje de sus ojos con un balde y lo vertía a lo largo de la carretera" (35). Objective phenomena have changed from an evasive countryside observed in motion in "Al volante," to a city composed of viewed fragments merged with the viewer's memories and ideas of those fragments in "Sevilla," now to a landscape created purely by the driver's eyes, drawn from the depths of himself: "Se sentía un pozo de paisaje y gozaba vertiéndolo a su gusto por donde pasaba y como es natural lo iba construyendo de la manera que más le placía" (35). The driver's hands, "asidas con fuerza al volante," change color "del rojo intenso al anaranjado y amarillo" in concert with the colors of the landscape flowing from his eyes.

Not only does "Guantes" reveal an identical fluidity of internal reality as described by Ortega in "Punto de vista," but it also aligns with surrealist ideas on painting. For although surrealism originated with a group of writers, its theoreticians soon expanded its scope to include other arts such as painting and cinema. For example, in the first issue of the journal *La Révolution Surréaliste* Max Morise considered the possibility of a "peinture surréaliste." Citing the works of Chirico and the cubists and including with his essay a sketch by André Masson, Morise posited, "Ce que l'écriture surréaliste est à la littérature, une plastique surréaliste doit l'être à la peinture, à la photographie, à tout ce qui est fait pour être vu" [What surrealist writing is to literature, a surrealist plastic must be to painting, to photography, to all that is made to be seen] (26). He felt that the visual aspect of dreams, the tracings of internal reality, could be as successfully reproduced in painting as in writing—"La peinture comme l'écriture son aptes à reconter un rêve" [Like writing, painting is capable of recounting a dream]. It cannot be coincidental that Morise titled his article "Les Yeux enchantés" [Enchanted Eyes], underscoring the instrumental role of transfixed (and transfigured) eyes in capturing these dream images.

Breton himself began a series of essays on painting in *La Révolution Surréaliste* in July 1925 and published them as a separate pamphlet called *Surrealism and Painting* in 1928. Like Morise, he signalled the importance of an enhanced faculty of vision to surrealist

---

[19] Jacqueline Rattray makes this observation in her article on "José María Hinojosa and the Surrealist Visuality" (161).

perception, which discerns the physically apprehensible and more: "[T]here are [...] those things that I see differently from other people, and those things that I begin to see and that *are not visible*" (440). Breton makes the distinction between mimetic painting whose model exists in the external world and painting that follows "a *purely interior model*" (442) where the mind begins "to occupy itself with its own life."[20] Just as Hinojosa's protagonist draws the landscape from the well of his eyes and spills it where he goes, Breton writes, "I believe that men will long continue to feel the need of following to its source the magical river flowing from their eyes, bathing with the same hallucinatory light and shade both the things that are and the things that are not" (444).[21] Breton's attention to a flowing liquid sensibility corresponds to the surrealist belief in the unceasing movement of thought, as Morise specified, "[L]a succession des images, la fuite des idées sont une condition fondamentale de toute manifestation surréaliste. Le cours de la pensée ne peut être considéré sous un aspect statique" [The succession of images, the flight of ideas are a fundamental condition of every surrealist manifestation. The flow of thought cannot be considered from a static perspective] (26).

---

[20] Ortega expressed nearly the same idea in a very similar way in "Deshumanización" where he revisited the transformation in painting that he had noted in the "Punto de vista" essay: "De pintar las cosas se ha pasado a pintar las ideas: el artista se ha cegado para el mundo exterior y ha vuelto la pupila hacia los paisajes internos y subjetivos" (376).

[21] Here we may detect clearly the metaphoric similarity to Ortega describing cubist eyes as "surtidores de irrealidad" and "proyectores de paisajes y faunas íntimas." Undoubtedly, the surrealists recognized their debt to the cubism, as evident in Morise's mention of the cubist artists in "Les Yeux enchantés" and Breton's praise of Picasso in *Surrealism and Painting* where he enthuses, "In order to be able to break suddenly away from sensible things, or with more reason from the *easiness* of their customary appearance, one has to be aware of their treason to such a high degree that one cannot escape recognizing the fact of Picasso's immense responsibility" (443). Later he continues, "It has been said that there could be no such thing as surrealist painting. Painting, literature—what are they to us, O Picasso, you who have carried the spirit, no longer of contradiction, but of evasion, to its furthest point!" Finally, as an additional point of interest, Dalí, like Ortega and Breton, conceived of internal reality as fluid. In his early writings, he adopted the images of snails, sea urchins, and other crustaceans to represent the symbiotic relationship between a hard external reality and an amorphous internal one. Later, he developed his paranoiac-critical method based on private reality flowing forth to transform objective phenomena.

"Guantes" presents anti-static thought as physical movement. The complicity between the driver's liquid vision creating an external landscape and the automobile's speed is given in the following logically-hard-to-conceive terms: the driver draws fluidified landscape from his eyes using a bucket-and-pulley system in which "[l]a cuerda era la velocidad y de garrucha le servía el horizonte" (35). Speed represents the means by which the eyes complete their function, supplying the movement to keep the colors of the landscape spilling forth. Significantly, everything grinds to a halt when the driver is stopped "por mandato de un guardia de la circulación" (36). With the abrupt suspension of movement, the driver's gaze also becomes fixed and the pulley of the horizon stops going around—"el horizonte dió un quejido al verse amarrado a un punto fijo por la mirada." As we shall see, after the automobile stops nothing is the same.

Notwithstanding civil codes for speed limits and the modest velocities of cars of the period—Hinojosa had a Chrysler convertible—"Guantes" clearly blames the end of freedom and artistic expression on the authorities, the Establishment, and the powers that be. This attitude, dear to surrealist hearts, appears in the juxtaposition of two news items reported in the evening papers after the traffic stop: "EL AUTOMÓVIL M-56565656[22] HA SIDO MULTADO POR EXCESO DE VELOCIDAD.— EL PAPA EMPEÑA SU SOLIDEO PARA COMPRAR UN MATASUEGRAS" (36). Whereas one headline points to the rigidity of limits and punitive consequences imposed by authority, the other suggests extreme anti-authority and the valoration of play and silliness in the Pope's abandonment of the trappings of hierarchy.[23] In "Guantes," unfortunately, the first item has more bearing on the fate of the driver. Indeed, it appears now that his car may have overheated; the description of an "encéfalo caldeado" (36) applying both to the driver himself as to his shaky vehicle.[24]

---

[22] An interesting note: this license plate number would correspond to a car registered in Madrid—hence the "M"—some time far in the future of when Hinojosa was writing; De Torre included a poem in Hélices titled "1422-M," right before another called "Ruedas."

[23] In this regard, we may evoke Ortega's observations of modern art as "un ensayo de crear puerilidad en un mundo viejo" (D 384).

[24] It seems that writers were not unaware of the mechanical shortcomings of automobiles, in spite of their general admiration of them. Recall that in "Al volante" De Torre noted that "El motor padece taquiarritmia."

In any case, the automobile does not resume its journey. The wells of the driver's eyes become depleted and, as a result, his hands begin to pale. To remedy this situation, he attempts to replenish the liquid landscape in his eyes by external means, putting on "una serie de guantes de distintos colores"—hence the title of the text. All this time, though, the car does not move: "Durante este periodo de convalecencia no hubo un día siquiera que llegase a dar al volante un cuarto de vuelta. El automóvil no había vuelto a girar sobre sus cuatro ruedas" (37). The absence of movement impedes the liquid landscape's release from the patient's eyes that previously balanced the intravenous effect of the "guantes del paisaje" supplying color in. The blockage causes a kind of overdose, "una intoxicación de paisaje" (38), and his internal panorama starts to lose its liquidity and to solidify, so that "aquella avalancha monótona [...] amenazaba fosilizarse en su interior." The now-stalled driver, no longer a flowing landscape of changing color, converts into a well of blackness, a "mar bituminoso."

Hope of subsequent movement vanishes entirely when the driver mistakenly puts on two gloves of different color, "uno azul y otro verde, y los paisajes también distintos a su vez por cada uno de los lados de la carretera contrarrestaban mutuamente la velocidad y la circunscribían a un punto solo" (38). The tension of the tug-of-war between the two distinctly colored landscapes causes the horizon-pulley to jump from its track, negating any further possibility of motion. As a result, the flow of internal landscape from the eyes of the driver stops for good: "El último paisaje se había solidificado a manera de escarcha sobre la retina y aprisionaba *aquella vista otras veces en constante ebullición* y que ahora reflejaba en su quietud la luz destilada del amanecer" (39, italics added). Where once the eyes swam with fluid internal landscape streaming outward and changing continuously, now they are frozen and still, the "interior model" exchanged for passive imitation ("reflejaba") of exterior ones.[25] The continued liquidity and release of internal reality was contingent upon the rope, constituted by the speed of the car, that kept the buckets of landscape in motion; when the auto stopped, all transformation ceased as well.[26]

---

[25] The verb "reflejaba" strongly suggests a return to the realist conventions of imitation, as the mirror frequently served as a metaphor for the mimetic project.

[26] Rattray points to the "return to the solid state of the conventional world" (163) at the end of the narrative, as evidenced by the reestablishment of the

Automobiles in Spain and everywhere else changed the panorama of the twentieth century. They became part of the visual landscape but, more important, they offered individuals the possibility of independent movement that altered the very act of seeing. Observed phenomena now seemed to be moving in and out of sight, in concert with (and in spite of) the observer. In some cases, automotive speed even became the mechanism by which optical perception turned active, no longer inertly absorbing images, but actively spilling them forth. The three writers discussed here not only sensed these changes, but used them ingeniously to interpret the major artistic movements of their time.

Works Cited

Abril, Manuel. "Itinerario del nuevo arte plástico." 1926. Rozas, ed. 131-35.
Arconada, César M. "Hacia un superrealismo musical." "Documents of the Spanish Vanguard." Ed. Paul Ilie. *University of North Carolina Studies in the Romance Languages and Literatures* 78 (1969): 321-36.
Breton, André. "Surrealism and Painting." *Art in Theory: 1900-1990.* Eds. Charles Harrison and Paul Wood. Oxford: Blackwell, 1993. 440-46.
Brihuega, Jaime. "The Language of the Avant-Garde in Spain: A Collage on the Margin." *The Spanish Avant-Garde.* Ed. Derek Harris. Manchester: Manchester UP, 1995. 84-96.
Carmona, Eugenio. "Picasso, Miró, Dalí y los orígenes del Arte Contemporáneo en España." *Picasso, Miró, Dalí y los orígenes del Arte Contemporáneo en España.* Exhibition catalogue. Madrid: Museo Nacional Centro de Arte Reina Sofía, 1991. 11-93.
———. "Pintura y poesía en la generación del 27." *Cuadernos Hispanoamericanos* 514-515 (1993): 102-116.
Casamitjana, Rosa Martín. *El humor en la poesía española de vanguardia.* Madrid: Gredos, 1996.
De Torre, Guillermo. "La aventura estética de nuestra edad." 1962. Rozas, ed. 139-41.
———. *Hélices.* Madrid: Editorial Mundo Latino, 1923.
———. *Literaturas europeas de vanguardia.* Madrid: Caro Raggio, 1925.
García de la Concha, Víctor, ed. *El surrealismo.* Madrid: Taurus, 1982.
Gertz, Audrey R. "Sensuality, Reality, and the Poetic Process in Pedro Salinas's 'Entrada en Sevilla.'" *La Chispa '97: Selected Proceedings.* New

---

ordinary blue sky—"the world of everyday reality contained within our normal horizon of things" (164).

Orleans: The Eighteenth Louisiana Conference on Hispanic Languages and Literatures, Tulane University, 1997. 163-73.
Gómez de la Serna, Ramón. "Proclama futurista a los españoles." 1910. *El ultraísmo*. By Gloria Videla. Madrid: Gredos, 1963. 173-74.
Hinojosa, José María. "Los guantes del paraíso." *Poesías completas*. Volume II. *Litoral* 136-138 (1983): 32-39.
Kozloff, Max. *Cubism / Futurism*. New York: Charterhouse, 1973.
Leralta, Javier. *Madrid villa y coche*. Madrid: Ediciones La Librería, 1993.
"Manifesto of Surrealism." By André Breton. *Manifestoes of Surrealism*. Trans. Richard Seaver and Helen R. Lane. Ann Arbor: The U of Michgan P, 1972. 1-47.
Marinetti, F.M. *Selected Writings*. Trans. R.W. Flint and Arthur A. Coppotelli. Ed. and intro. R.W. Flint. New York: Farrar, Straus and Giroux, 1972.
Moreno Villa, José. "Carta al autor." *Obras completas*. By José María Hinojosa. Málaga: Instituto de Cultura de la Diputación Provincial de Málaga, 1974. 179-81.
———. "El arte de mi tiempo." 1925. Rozas, ed. 135-38.
Morise, Max. "Les Yeux enchantés." *La Révolution Surréaliste*. 1 (1924): 26-27.
Neira, Julio. "El surrealismo en José María Hinojosa (Esbozo)." García de la Concha, ed. 271-85.
Ortega y Gasset, José. "La deshumanización del arte." *Obras completas*. Volume III. 5th ed. Madrid: Revista de Occidente, 1962. 353-86.
———. "Sobre el punto de vista en las artes." *La deshumanización del arte y otros ensayos estéticos*. 8th ed. Madrid: Revista de Occidente, 1964.
Pérez Firmat, Gustavo. *Idle Fictions*. Durham, N.C.: Duke UP, 1982.
Picón, Pierre. "La revolución superrealista." *Alfar* 52: 131-34.
Rattray, Jacqueline. "José María Hinojosa and the Surrealist Visuality." *IV Congreso de Posgraduados en Estudios Hispánicos / 4th Hispanic Studies Postgraduate Conference*. London: Consejería de Educación y Ciencia, Embajada de España, 1996. 159-66.
Rozas, Juan Manuel, ed. *La generación del 27 desde dentro*. 2nd ed. Madrid: Istmo, 1986.
Salinas, Pedro. "Entrada en Sevilla." *Víspera del gozo*. Madrid: Revista de Occidente, 1926. 29-46.
Spires, Robert C. *Transparent Simulacra*. Columbia: U of Missouri P, 1988.
Taylor, Joshua C. "The Futurist Goal, the Futurist Achievement." *Major European Art Movements, 1900-1945: A Critical Anthology*. Eds. Patricia Kaplan and Susan Manso. New York: E.P. Dutton, 1977. 165-92.
Vargish, Thomas and Delo E. Mook. *Inside Modernism: Relativity Theory, Cubism,Narrative*. New Haven: Yale UP, 1999.
Vela, Fernando. "El suprarrealismo." 1924. García de la Concha, ed. 31-35.

An Æsthetics of Transience: Fashion in the Spanish Avant-Garde

JULI HIGHFILL
University of Michigan

*Etimológicamente, moderno se deriva de moda [...],
se es "moderno" en cuanto se adapta uno a la moda.*
—Ernesto Giménez Caballero[1]

I. Dethroning Venus: Pedro Salinas's "París, abril, modelo"

IN HIS UNFINISHED ARCHEOLOGY of modernity, the *Arcades Project*, Walter Benjamin remarked, "Fashion prescribes the ritual according to which the fetish commodity demands to be worshipped" (8). The rituals of fashion, however, differ significantly from the seasonal celebrations that mark the cycles of nature, for as Benjamin observes, "the spring rites of fashion celebrate novelty rather than seasonal recurrence; they require not remembrance, but obliviousness to even the most recent past; fashion drinks of the river of forgetfulness" (qtd. in Buck-Morss 98).[2] Pedro Salinas's poem "París, abril, modelo" (1931) offers striking parallels with Benjamin's observations about fashion in the modern age. With tongue in cheek, the poetic speaker celebrates the fashion rites of spring, proclaiming a shop-window mannequin the incarnation of a "model spring" and happily consigning all past, "out-

---

[1] From Giménez Caballero's review of Max Born's book *La teoría de la relatividad de Einstein y sus fundamentos físicos* (156).

[2] See Susan Buck-Morss's *The Dialectics of Seeing*, a reconstruction of Benjamin's *Arcades Project* (98). She paraphrases here from various fragmentary notes left by Benjamin in his Arcades files.

moded" models to oblivion.³ After years of missteps, the new, ideal spring has sprung forth self-fashioned:

> ¡Primavera, qué acierto
> por fin,
> después de tanta prueba
> frustrada en tantos años!
> ¡Cómo conozco ahora
> que las pasadas eran
> ensayos nada más
> de tiempos aprendices! (109)

Employing concise, staccato phrases, the poetic speaker goes on to cite the defects of previous springs:

> En ellas
> sobraba siempre algo:
> demasías de viento,
> cuatro grados
> más de temperatura,
> una sombrilla abierta
> pronto, besos precoces. (109)

Cognizant of these failures, the springs that followed, "locas de inexperiencia," emulated classical models, searching through the forests and ruins of Arcadia:

> corrían los jardines
> en busca de un altar.
> ¿Fustes? ¿Troncos? Ni templo
> ni bosque... (109)

---

³ The poem pertains to the collection *Fábula y signo* (1931). A year earlier it had appeared in *Revista de Occidente* 90 (1930) under the title "Maniquí." Andrew Debicki provides commentaries on this poem in: *Estudios sobre poesía española contemporánea* (73-74); "La metáfora en algunos poemas tempranos de Salinas" (113-15); "The Play of Difference in the Early Poetry of Pedro Salinas" (277); and "La visión del mundo en la poesía temprana de Pedro Salinas" (73-74). See note 14 for a comprehensive list of critical studies on Salinas's works.

They adopted the poses of bronze and marble statues; they tried on a "un traje de azul de cielo" only to throw it aside as used clothing from the recent winter (109). But through these failed attempts, the industrious springs "estaban aprendiendo" as they continued searching for more appropriate models (109):

> Se creían los colores
> de la rosa. Buscaban
> en estanques. Arrugas
> y muecas. ¿Eran ellas? (109)

In these cryptic yet suggestive lines, the spring-nymphs seem at first to misrecognize their distorted reflections in the pond. As they grimace with displeasure, their "arrugas y muecas" merge with the ripples on the surface of the water. In the face of this misrecognition,

> Tiernas infantas rápidas,
> abdicaban, huían:
> para reinar muy jóvenes. (110)

At this point there comes a sudden shift, when a self-made model spring at last emerges triumphant. Awe-struck, the speaker proclaims in a direct address:[4]

> Tú, tú eres la primera.
> Ni en rosa ni en azul
> confiada, nunca en Venus
> buscaste forma, tú,
> inventora de formas,
> modelo,
> estatua de ti misma. (110)

Unlike her predecessors, this spring has invented herself. Rather than imitating a classical model of beauty, this spring has *modeled* herself as

---

[4] Many critics have commented on Salinas's predilection for the *yo-tú* intimate dialogue. For commentaries on his dialogue with things, see Alma Zubizarreta, *Pedro Salinas: El diálogo creador*; Lorna Shaughnessy, *The Developing Poetic Philosophy of Pedro Salinas*; Christopher Maurer, "Salinas y 'las cosas'"; and Jaime Siles, "La poesía primera de Salinas y la postmodernidad."

the new ideal. Only here does the surprised reader learn that this incomparable spring resides in a shop-window:

> Entre cristales,
> maniquí, creación
> de primavera, aguardas
> que florezcan dibujos
> en las sedas. (110)

Still undressed, with a thermometer at her side, the mannequin will wait until the temperature is just right:

> —¡cuidado, precoz no!—
> te anunciará el momento
> —¡18 grados ya!—
> de huir el escaparate,
> de saltar a los tiempos,
> en la proclamación
> imperial del desnudo (110)

Here the mock-heroic speaker, in the act of predicting the imminent "imperial proclamation" of a "nude" spring, proclaims himself the one and only judge of its quality:[5]

> —sólo yo lo sabía—
> que tú llevabas dentro,
> modelo,
> primavera modelo. (110)

---

[5] Spring is a frequent motif in Salinas's early poetry. For example, see "Cuartilla," "Rapto a primavera," "Tránsito," and "Clave de febrero." David Stixrude, in *The Early Poetry of Pedro Salinas*, shows how in "Cuartilla," spring's emergence from winter—"from the indistinguishable monotony of the white surface"—becomes "a metaphor for the first word penned onto a blank page" (85). Stixrude insightfully connects this motif to Salinas's constant preoccupation with *formation*: "The initial word, the renewing spring, are ever objects of the poet's yearning, but even more fundamental are the formless worlds that precede spring [...] a world 'en blanco'" (89). Alma Zubizarreta, in *Pedro Salinas: El diálogo creador*, devotes a chapter on Salinas's treatment of spring in both his early and later poetry (308-32).

In this ironic coronation poem the speaker dethrones Venus and crowns the mannequin as the new ideal of beauty, thus privileging artifice over nature, and the commodity over the art object.[6] While the mass-produced mannequin may lack the *aura* of the traditional object of art—its status as the unique product of an artist's hand—she has the cachet of being new, modern, and "on the move."[7] She will leap from the shop window "*au naturel*" to promenade the streets and ballrooms during this year's fashion rites.[8] She will be celebrated and imitated as the standard for the new "unadorned look," only to be replaced next year by a newer standard.

Poggioli, in *The Theory of the Avant-garde*, remarks on modernism's dismissal of classical models and its idolatry of the *new*: "Classical thinking on art admits of only a single negative category, the ugly," defined against a timeless standard of *beauty* (81). Modernism, in contrast, replaces the ugly with "ex-beauty" as a negative category and in turn associates beauty with transience—with "sleepless and fevered experimentation" (82). Herein lies the avant-garde's kinship with fashion, for both pass "through the phase of novelty and strangeness, surprise and scandal, before abandoning the new forms when they become cliché, kitsch, stereotype" (82). The task of fashion, Poggioli emphasizes, "is to maintain a continual process of standardization: putting a rarity or novelty into general and universal use, then passing on to another rarity or novelty when the first has ceased to be such" (79).

Thinking along similar lines, Gianni Vattimo has observed that modernity's defining characteristic—its faith in progress—is "the equivalent of affirming the new as the fundamental value" (101). It is significant that "moda," "modelo," and "moderno" all share a common etymology.[9] "Moda" derives from the Latin *modus*, meaning

---

[6] For discussions of the employment of the Venus and Pygmalion myths in various works by Salinas, see Vialla Hartfield-Méndez, *Woman and the Infinite* and "El dilema de Pigmalión."

[7] Walter Benjamin develops the notion of *aura* in "The Work of Art in the Age of Mechanical Reproduction."

[8] Salinas replays the anecdote of "París, abril, modelo" in *La poesía de Rubén Darío* when evoking late nineteenth-century Paris: "Venus, vestida por Worth va por la *rue de la Paix* seguida de un millonario viejo verde" (37).

[9] Noel Valis discusses the kinship of *la moda* and Hispanic *modernismo* in "The Female Figure and Writing in Fin del siglo Spain": "Like fashion, the modernist aesthetic suggests a kind of permanent transitoriness, a restlessness rooted in the displacement of desire" (370).

measure, size, limit of quantity, and manner.[10] "Modelo," as well as "molde," derive from *modellus*, a diminutive of *modus*. And finally, "moderno" originates in *modo*, an adverbial form of *modus*, meaning "just now"—based by analogy on *hodiernus*, "of today." In English the etymology of "fashion" maps out a similar semantic field: it derives from the Old French term *façon*, meaning form or shape, which in turn originates in the Latin *factionem*, a making (from *facere*, to make). The etymology of both "la moda" and "fashion" thus points to a paradox immanent in their semantic domains. On the one hand a fixed standard, form, or quantity, and on the other, a way of doing or making, fashion thus admits of both fixity and mobility; it is both normative and cutting-edge, capable of defining and defying limits.[11]

It is this process whereby the standard is forever on the move that so attracted avant-garde artists, writers, and theorists to fashion. As they saw it, to "follow fashion" was not to submit to the dictates of commodity culture, but rather to assume creative agency, to insert oneself into the ever-mobile present and to join with the creative forces of history. Georg Simmel, whose thought so influenced the Spanish avant-garde, observed:

> Fashion always occupies the dividing-line between the past and the future, and consequently conveys a stronger feeling of the present, at least while it is at its height, than most other phenomena. What we call the present is usually nothing more than a combination of a fragment of the past with a fragment of the future [...]. Few phenomena of social life possess such a pointed curve of consciousness as does fashion. As soon as the social consciousness attains to the highest point designated by fashion, it marks the beginning of the end for the latter. This transitory character of

---

[10] For these etymologies I have relied on J. Corominas, *Diccionario crítico etimológico de la lengua castellana*; the *Oxford English Dictionary*; and Walter W. Skeat, *An Etymological Dictionary of the English Language*.

[11] As theoretical studies of fashion abound, I include only a few pertinent references here. For theory of fashion contemporary to this period, see José Díaz Fernández, *El nuevo romanticismo*; J.C. Flugel, *The Psychology of Clothes*; and George Simmel, "Fashion." For more recent theorizations of fashion refer to Roland Barthes, *The Fashion System*; Shari Benstock and Susanne Ferriss, *On Fashion*; Gilles Lipovetsky, *The Empire of Fashion*; Valerie Steele, *Fashion and Eroticism*; and Elizabeth Wilson, *Adorned in Dreams*.

fashion, however, does not on the whole degrade it, but adds a new element of attraction.[12] (303)

The vanguardists, in their frenzied quest for new aesthetic models and greater freedom of invention, came to regard fashion as the "model" practice: for fashion—situated in the ineffable present and aiming toward the future—challenges the hegemony of the given, resists enslavement to conventional forms, and affirms artistic freedom. Salinas's poem, "París, abril, modelo," dating from his avant-garde phase, affirms this transitory and liberatory character of fashion.[13] In an updated replay of the traditional allegory of spring, the cycle of nature is supplanted by the cycle of fashion, the springs of the past are replaced by this year's model spring (ironically personified in a non-person, the mannequin), which presumably will be surpassed in future rites of spring.

On a metapoetic level, "París, abril, modelo" can also be read as an allegory of "making" (or modeling), for it shows how, through a process of searching and experimentation, the "made-up" becomes the "made-real" in the object of art. The poem thus offers a wry commentary on a problem inherent in the act of imagining. As Elaine Scarry has observed,

> [T]he imagination is remarkable for being the only state that is wholly its object. There is in imagining no activity, no "state," no experienceable condition or felt-occurrence separate from the objects: the only evidence that one is "imagining" is that imaginary objects appear in the mind. (162)

Perfection can only be imagined by invoking in the mind's eye a particular perfect object, in this case, a model spring; and going further, the elusive assemblage of qualities that make up a perfect spring are

---

[12] I quote here from Donald Levine's translation and collection of Simmel's writings. "Fashion," written in 1904, was translated by Fernando Vela as "Filosofía de la moda" and published in the first two issues of the *Revista de Occidente* 1 (1923): 42-66; and 2 (1923): 211-30.

[13] In *From Romanticism to Surrealism*, Robert Havard discusses Salinas's "poetics of motion" (142-92), and in "The Reality of Words," he connects this prevailing theme to Bergson's thought. David Stixrude, in *The Early Poetry*, also emphasizes the importance of fleetingness and changeability in Salinas's works.

here "embodied" in a metaphor, the mannequin. As he so often did in his poetry, Salinas uses metaphor to concretize the abstract; he ironically makes a concrete model stand for an abstract model of perfection—the perfect spring—which as a temporal concept is "by nature" intangible and transitory, manifested only in its objects—budding leaves, blooming flowers, warm temperatures and fair-weather clothes.[14]

Salinas is obviously playing with the double meaning of "model," which may connote an *abstract archetype* (an ultimately intangible ideal), or a *concrete prototype* for creation or manufacture (be it animate or inanimate—i.e., artists' models, fashion models or industrial

---

[14] Scholars have engaged in a long-running debate over the problem of abstraction and concretion in Salinas's poetry. Until recent years most critics interpreted his poetry in neo-Platonic and subjectivist terms. In their view, Salinas—ever in search of essences and absolutes—negates exterior reality, considering it a mere surface to be penetrated. See for example, Leo Spitzer, "El conceptismo interior de Pedro Salinas;" Vicente Cabrera, *Tres poetas a la luz de la metáfora*; José Francisco Cirre, *El mundo lírica de Pedro Salinas*; Julian Palley, *La luz no usada de Pedro Salinas*; Concha Zardoya, "La otra realidad de Pedro Salinas;" C.B. Morris, "*Visión* and *Mirada* in the Poetry of Salinas, Guillén and Dámaso Alonso;" Ricardo Gullón, "La poesía de Pedro Salinas;" and Alba Breitenbücher, "El vocabulario del neoplatonismo en la obra poética de Pedro Salinas." Another group of critics takes a middle ground, either seeing Salinas's work as concerned with the *relation* between reality and ideality, or arguing that his stance towards reality fluctuated and remained unresolved. For such arguments, see Carlos Feal Deibe, *La poesía de Pedro Salinas* and "Lo visible y lo invisible en los primeros libros poéticos de Salinas;" David Stixrude, *The Early Poetry of Pedro Salinas*; Philip Silver, *La casa de Anteo*; Alan Bruflat, "Entre la fábula y el signo de Pedro Salinas;" Alma Zubizarreta, *Pedro Salinas: El diálogo creador*; John Crispin, *Pedro Salinas*; Andrew Debicki, "The Play of Difference in the Early Poetry;" Robert Havard, "The Reality of Words;" Lorna Shaughnessy, *The Developing Poetic Philosophy of Pedro Salinas*; Antonio Monegal, "'Voz' y 'realidad' en la crítica de un poeta;" and Jorge Guillén's prologues to Salinas's *Poesías completas* and *Poesías escogidas*. Still another group emphasizes Salinas's exaltation of reality (particularly in the early poetry), his delight in things—a "gozoso presentismo"—in the words of Olga Costa Viva, *Pedro Salinas frente a la realidad* (28). For other such views, see Christopher Maurer, "Salinas y 'las cosas,'" and Jaime Siles, "La poesía primera de Salinas y la postmodernidad." Salinas himself discussed at length the relation between poetry and reality in *Reality and the Poet in Spanish Poetry* and "Mundo real y mundo poético."

models and mannequins).[15] If read as a parodical allegory of spring, the poem adds insult to injury by naming a mannequin—mass-produced and infinitely imitable by masses of fashion-followers—as the singular emblem of perfection. And to top off the joke, this year's "perfect look" turns out to be an *undressed* mannequin, thus spoofing the pictorial tradition of the nude female figure as emblem of spring, à la Botticelli. Read parodically then, the poem might suggest how commodity culture produces models of desire, and how advertising—in this case shop-window display—creates the vocabulary and images for modern romance.

But while these elements of parody are undeniable, it would be wrong to read the poem entirely as a spoof of traditional allegory or as criticism of commodity culture; for at the same time, the poem shows Salinas's genuine fascination with modern gadgetry, an enthusiasm he shared with the European avant-garde at large.[16] In his many poems that celebrate objects of modern technology—electric lights, typewriter, telephone, radiator, cinema, or automobile—he gleefully personifies and mythologizes each object as muse, nymph, siren, or lover.[17] And while Salinas's later works, written during and after the Spanish Civil War and World War II, reveal a pessimistic attitude towards technology and commerce, his earlier works express his delight

---

[15] Andrew Debicki addresses the allegorical aspect of "París, abril, modelo" in *Estudios sobre poesía española contemporánea* (73-74) and "The Play of Difference" (277). In the latter study he also discusses the double meaning of "modelo."

[16] A number of critics have commented on Salinas's fascination with modern commerce and technology, noting in particular, his tendency to personify, animate, and mythologize objects of modernity. Olga Costa Viva, in *Pedro Salinas frente a la realidad*, goes so far as to say, "Su entusiasmo vital brota desde la más pequeña delicia hasta observar la civilización como un inmenso escaparate" (33). Also see Antonio Barbagallo, "Elementos futuristas en la poesía de Pedro Salinas;" Christopher Maurer, "Salinas y 'las cosas;'" Jaime Siles, "La poesía primera de Salinas y la postmodernidad;" Solita Salinas de Marichal, "El primer Salinas;" Lorna Shaughnessy, *The Developing Poetic Philosophy*; and Jorge Guillén's prologues to Salinas's *Poesías completas* and *Poesías escogidas*. For a summary of critical opinions on Salinas's participation in the avant-garde, see Carlos Feal, "Lo visible y lo invisible" (194 n22).

[17] See, for example, "35 bujías," "Tránsito," "Underwood girls," "El teléfono," "Radiador y fogata," "Far West," "Cinematógrafo," "Rapto a primavera," and "Navacerrada, abril"—all from *Seguro azar* (1929) and *Fábula y signo* (1930).

with new things, machines, and spectacles.[18] In a speech of 1930, "Mundo real y mundo poético," he celebrates the proliferation of new objects of beauty in the modern age:

> La cantidad de objetos bellos creados por el hombre de hoy y que encuentra a su alrededor donde quiera que ponga los ojos no tiene comparación con el repertorio de la vida material de ninguna época. La realidad circundante ha dado un avance arrollador, irresistible. Paralelamente el concepto de belleza sufre también una ampliación enorme. Una gran cantidad de cosas que siempre estuvieron excluidas de esa consideración, un hipopótamo, una bailarina negra, una fila de cacharros de aluminio, presentan hoy su instancia a ser reconocidos como bellos. Hay una verdadera rebusca, un ardorosa y frenética persecución de bellezas inéditas. Cuando un hombre sensible sale a la calle es muy difícil que vuelva a su casa sin alguna belleza más. (70-71)

Here in the same year that he first published "París, abril, modelo," Salinas shows his enthusiasm for the "enormous expansion" in the category of beauty.[19] Providing vivid, diverse examples, he cites the "hippopotamus" (an allusion to T.S. Eliot's poem by that title), a black dancer (an allusion to Josephine Baker), and kitchen utensils made of gleaming aluminum. He goes on to praise the beautiful "gestures and faces" captured by cinematographic machines, the lovely sounds and pure voices launched into "the immense plain of air with radiophonic apparatuses," and the "new aesthetic canon" arriving from the Congo. Moreover, he commends the fact that such diverse and glorious objects of beauty are now available to the masses:

---

[18] Regarding Salinas's change of attitude towards modern technology, Carlos Feal comments, "El propio poeta, que en sus primeros libros mantenía un diálogo amoroso con los objetos mecánicos, mostrará en su obra última— *Todo más claro* especialmente—el potencial alienador del universo tecnológico" (193). Also refer to Olga Costa Viva, *Pedro Salinas frente a la realidad* and Christopher Maurer, "Salinas y 'las cosas.'" David Stixrude, in *The Early Poetry*, disagrees with most critics in that he finds continuity in Salinas's stance towards the modern world from his early to his late poetry. But in order to make his case, Stixrude must read the poems that celebrate modern gadgetry as ironic—as meaning the opposite of what they say.

[19] See Anthony Geist, *La poética de la generación del 27*, for a discussion of the vanguardist reevaluation of the concept of beauty (61-62).

Y resulta además que esta enorme riqueza y multiplicidad de la vida exterior está, como nunca lo estuvo, al alcance de todos. Las dimensiones del hombre y del mundo han cambiado. Los cuadros cuya contemplación y goce se reservaban en el siglo XVI a un grupo de señores están hoy a la vista de todos. Los países más remotos se acercan y se ponen a la altura de nuestra curiosidad. (71)

Salinas continues his tribute to the modern age by asking his listeners to consider the power of this newly expanded world reality: "Piénsese en la fuerza gigantesca, el poder sin límites que tiene el mundo real en nuestros días. La realidad llegó hoy a su gran época imperial. Estamos por bien o por mal en un formidable imperialismo de la realidad" (71). Employing the vocabulary of a previous age of globalization, Salinas affirms what we today call "world-culture"—this new "formidable imperialism of reality."

In calling attention to the expansion in the category of the aesthetic, Salinas gives lie to the claims for autonomy and purity of art, baldly stating what has been evident all along. The European vanguardists, in the literary and visual arts, found their aesthetic models in the colonial world and in the commercial world—in museums, shop windows, and advertising. Considering this broad and varied appropriation of the available models of beauty, Salinas's "París, abril, modelo" can be read allegorically from still another perspective—as an allegory of vanguardist practice at large. By dethroning Venus—the age-old emblem of beauty and proclaiming a mass-produced mannequin as emblem of beauty, he dramatizes how, to a remarkable degree, vanguardist artistic practice found its models in commodity culture.

II. "Which Venus is for you?"

In proclaiming—albeit with tongue in cheek—a fashion mannequin as the new standard of beauty, Salinas could well be responding to a tongue-in-cheek question posed earlier by Corpus Barga: "¿Cuál es la Venus de usted?" (332).[20] Barga, in his essay, "Venus novísima: Ilustra-

---

[20] Corpus Barga was the pen-name of Andrés García de la Barga, a novelist and journalist who served as a correspondent in Paris from 1914 to 1920, where he befriended many of the principal actors in the European avant-garde. His published writings include: a novel, *La vida rota* (1910); collections of short narrative, *Clara Babel* (1906), *Pasión y muerte*, and *Apocalipsis* (1930);

ciones de la desnaturalización del arte" (1924), remarks upon the recent proliferation of "Venuses," now that the classical models no longer rule; and he welcomes the new freedom of choice, now that each man may select his own "patrón de la belleza" (333). After asking his readers, presumably all gentlemen, *which* Venus they prefer, he lists options for men of different positions and tastes: the Venus de Milo for "un magistrado de provincias," the more intact Venus de Médicis for "el militar ilustrado"; or the "Venus calipigia" (esteemed for her well-developed thighs and buttocks) for "un hombre de buena posición para alimentarse espiritualmente de 'beefsteak'" (332).[21]

After this mock appeal to his readers' carnal desires, Barga shifts the discussion to the abstract plane of aesthetics:

> Pero con la pregunta "¿cuál es la Venus de usted?," no se trata de plantear una cuestión personal, sino de lo que diríase, al contrario, con términos de Ortega: "deshumanizar" a Venus; y, puesto que se trata de la plástica, se dirá mejor: desnaturalizar la belleza. (332-33)

With a nod to Ortega's influential "La deshumanización del arte," Barga admits that the *dehumanization* of Venus has opened the possibility for this question, but he favors a term more apropos to the plastic arts: the *denaturalization* of beauty. No longer bound to follow the curves of the feminine body, Beauty is now free to seek new forms of embodiment. Whereas Western artistic tradition, in melding erotic and aesthetic desires, had long upheld the nude body of European woman as the allegorical emblem of Beauty, today other models, expropriated from the colonial world, have become available—from the newly appraised art of the Khmer to the "Pharaonic beauty" of ancient Egypt (333). Citing Gauguin, who had written from the South Seas— "El gran error es griego, por bello que sea,"—Barga declares: "Toda belleza, más o menos desnaturalizada, de cualquier edad, de cualquier civilización, está ya como la griega, en los escaparates" (333-34). In

---

collections of essays and articles, *París-Madrid. Un viaje en el año 19* (1920) and *Entrevistas, semblanzas y crónicas* (1992); along with his memoirs in four volumes, *Los pasos contados* (1979). Probably best known as a journalist, his literary works have attracted little critical attention.

[21] The *Enciclopedia universal ilustrada europeo-americana* (Espasa-Calpe) of 1929 included images of 32 different "Venuses" from the history of Western art.

this sweeping statement, Barga suggests that all beauty is and has always been more or less "denaturalized," that is, abstracted and stylized. Going further, in an argument which Salinas reiterates, Barga avers that today all the available models of beauty can be found behind glass, in museums as well as in shop windows—the relics of ancient Greece, the art objects looted from the colonial world, and the new fashions of 1924.

Here Barga arrives at his main point, affirming that fashion—that art of pure transience—has become the model artistic practice for the modern age:

> Mas hay una plástica de nuestra época, y no sólo en la pintura y en la escultura. Parece que nunca haya habido tanta en la "moda." La actividad de la moda es, en cierto modo, una consecuencia de la falta de patrón en la belleza. La moda es, evidentemente, un arte periódico, periodístico, característico, más que de una época, de nuestra época. Es un arte de efecto momentáneo, el arte del momento. (335)

The possibility that fashion might be tainted by affiliation with commodity fetishism is far from Barga's mind; rather, he sees fashion as the purest of art forms. By virtue of its purity and transience, fashion is akin to the "fugaz *saeta* de Sevilla," those fervent song-arrows sent to the heart of the Virgin Mary (336). In being transitory, always new, fashion remains unaffected by *ruin*: "esa obra muerta de la naturaleza, que le despinta las estatuas, le ennegrece las piedras, le dora los óleos, le armoniza, le desmaterializa la materia" (336). And unlike art of the past, "arte fariseo," fashion is not subject to "esa pobre rapsodia cometida perpetuamente en la comprensión de las obras antiguas" (336). Fashion is wedded to the present, continually in motion, and ever aiming towards the future. Notwithstanding its status as artifice, fashion paradoxically attains a "natural" authority: "Nada más natural que el traje sea la desnaturalización de Venus, que se busque a Venus bajo el arte semoviente del vestido y al patrón de la belleza, entre los patrones de moda" (336). As emblematic of human creativity—of the perpetual remaking of the world—fashion "naturally" de-naturalizes; for rather than imitating nature, it supplements the human body. As an "arte semoviente," an "arte-saeta"—the principle of change itself—fashion is self-generating and self-propelled. And most important for Barga, fashion has rendered the singular, authoritative "patrón de la belleza" outmoded, replacing it with plural models—with the proliferation of new forms (333).

III. The "Arte-saeta" of Sonia Delaunay

If Salinas's poem can be considered one answer to Barga's question—¿cuál es la Venus de usted?—Barga's essay, in turn, answers the challenge posed by Sonia Delaunay's remarkable fashion designs—part of the radical transformation in women's fashions of the nineteen-twenties."[22] Barga, then a correspondent in Paris for the *Revista de Occidente* and no doubt a visitor to Sonia's *Boutique Simultané*, devotes the remainder of his essay to Delaunay's designs, proclaiming them as exemplary of "la denaturalización de Venus" and the new plurality of forms (336).

Born in the Ukraine to working-class parents, Sonia Delaunay was adopted by a well-to-do uncle in St. Petersburg and went on to study art in Germany and in Paris. Both she and her husband, the painter Robert Delaunay—among the first abstract artists of Europe—were active in the Parisian artistic circles before the war. Apollinaire coined the term "Orphism" to describe the Delaunays' version of cubism, but the artists themselves favored the term *simultaneism* to characterize their experimentation with dynamic color contrast.[23] During the war years, the Delaunays lived in Spain and Portugal, where they contin-

---

[22] For studies of Sonia Delaunay's painting and designs, refer to Robert T. Buck, *Sonia Delaunay, a Retrospective*; Sherry Buckberrough, "Delaunay Design;" Arthur A. Cohen, *Sonia Delaunay*; Jacques Damase, *Sonia Delaunay: Fashion and Fabrics*; Monique Maunoury, "Sonia Delaunay. The Clothing of Modernity;" Elizabeth Morano, *Sonia Delaunay: Art into Fashion*; and Deborah Rosenthal, "Primary Painting: Sonia Delaunay." Ramón Gómez de la Serna includes a chapter on the Delaunay's "Simultanismo" in his book *Ismos*. Marjorie Perloff, in *The Futurist Moment*, devotes her first chapter to the collaboration of Sonia Delaunay and Blaise Cendrars on a remarkable verbal-visual text, *La Prose du Transsibérien et de la petite Jehanne de France* of 1913. And Tag Gronberg, in *Designs on Modernity*, discusses Sonia Delaunay's *Boutique Simultanée* in the *Exposition Internationale des Arts Décoratifs et Industriel's Modernes* of 1925. For biographies of Delaunay, see Axel Madsen and Stanley Baron. For a collection of writings by Robert and Sonia Delaunay, see *The New Art of Color: The Writings of Robert and Sonia Delaunay*.

[23] The Delaunays borrowed the term *simultaneism* from Chevruel's treatise on color of 1839. Across a series of letters and articles, Robert Delaunay developed his theory of simultaneism; see *The New Art of Color*.

ued painting, enamored of the Iberian light, which, in Sonia's words, "caused every color to vibrate, without the gray haze that envelopes them in France" (195-96). When the Russian Revolution erupted in October 1917, the Delaunays celebrated the event, although it brought them financial difficulty, cutting off the income Sonia had received from family properties in St. Petersburg. Forced to earn a living for the first time, they turned to the applied arts. In 1918, the Delaunays obtained a commission to design sets and costumes for a production of *Cléopâtre* by Diaghilev's *Ballets Russes*, then in residence in Barcelona. With Diaghilev's assistance in obtaining capital, Sonia opened *La Casa Sonia* in Madrid where she designed and sold women's wear and decorative items for home interiors. While earning income from sales to wealthy Spanish clientele, her designs also attracted the interests of leading figures in the arts and literature: Manuel de Falla, Ramón Gómez de la Serna, Ramón del Valle-Inclán, Guillermo de Torre, and Vicente Huidobro. In 1921, the Delaunays returned to Paris, where Sonia opened another shop, the *Boutique Simultané* and later a textile printing workshop, *L'atelier Simultané*. There she found more customers daring enough to purchase and wear her radical designs. Never part of *haute couture*, her clients were primarily women connected to the arts—among them, Gloria Swanson, and the wives of the architects Mendelsohn, Gropius, and Greuer.

Throughout the nineteen-twenties, Sonia continued creating the fashions that so astounded Corpus Barga as well as other Spanish vanguardists for whom her art exemplified "el arte nuevo." Isaac del Vando-Villar's poem, "Sonia Delaunay," evokes the bright, dynamic color combinations that characterized her painting and design:

> De las yemas de tus dedos brotaban surtidores de luces,
> rompecabezas, carnavales y kermesses.
> La serpentina verde de tu cigarrillo
> pendía de la lámpara simultaneísta.
> [...]
> En los espejos de tu cara,
> el arte nuevo nos sonríe. (319)[24]

Ramón Gómez de la Serna likewise evoked spiraling movements in his tribute to Sonia, an "Abanico de palabras" or fan-poem, in which the names of flowers, written in a serpentine cursive, emanate from the

---

[24] Originally published in *Grecia* 48 (septiembre 1920).

center (**Fig. 1**).[25] Guillermo de Torre, in a hyperbolic essay of 1924 proclaimed Delaunay's designs as emblematic of the "new art," which has now rushed into the streets and homes, transforming the everyday environment:

> El arte nuevo se ha lanzado a la calle, proclamando sus derechos a la vía libre—affiches, fachadas y escaparates gesticulantes, automóviles, vestidos de las mujeres serpentinas. El arte nuevo se ha metido en las casas—interiores guarnecidos estéticamente por biombos centinelas, cortinas cómplices, frisos y almohadones polícromos. (160)

All these responses call attention to the dynamic effect of Sonia Delaunay's designs and, in the cases of Vando-Villar and Torre, relate them to the dynamism of modern life: the gesturing shop windows, racing automobiles, the serpentine smoke of cigarettes, and the serpentine movements of women in the street. Corpus Barga, in the essay cited earlier, also emphasizes the dynamism of Delaunay's fashions; but he goes further by addressing the consequences—for aesthetics as well as for gender relations—produced by this new kinetic design.

To demonstrate how Delaunay denaturalizes the female body, he directs his readers to a photograph of the designer herself wearing a dress with a bright, irregular zigzag running from top to bottom (**Fig. 2**).[26] Barga comments: "Ahí se ve un traje que no sigue ni por alusión a la forma natural, y busca la forma de un estremecimiento" (337). Continuing, Barga compares "el progreso desnaturalizador" in several other designs, showing preference for a dress with a large Z across the bodice (**Fig. 3**), in which "el zig-zag se ha hecho arquitectónico" (337). Through this repeated motif of the zigzag—suggesting a lightning flash, an electrical circuit, or a shiver—Delaunay transmits the idea of art in motion, or "arte-saeta," the fugitive present passing by.

---

[25] See Ramón Gómez de la Serna's chapter "Simultanismo" in *Ismos*, in which he includes a sketch of the fan-poem (173) as well has his proposal for a "traje-poemático," in which he would "escribir el poema en espiral, envolviendo y ciñendo como una serpentina de palabras la figura de la interfecta" (171-73). A number of avant-garde poets wrote "dress-poems" for Sonia, among them Tzara, Aragon, and Crevel. It is not known whether Ramón's proposal came to fruition.

[26] Figures 2 – 7 accompanied Corpus Barga's "Venus novísima" essay when it appeared in *Revista de Occidente*.

But for Barga, Delaunay's innovations, while inserting themselves in that synapse of the present, do not disdain the past; for in several illustrations showing draped garments (**Figs. 4, 5, 6, 7**), "se descubren, pues, tres patrones clásicos, rituales: la veste; la estola y la casulla" (338). The art of Sonia Delaunay, Barga claims,

> es clásico porque es casto. No adultera la forma, encuentra una forma dentro de las condiciones maquinales del cuerpo [...]. La arquitectura de sus vestidos se produce como la arquitectura del automóvil.
> Sonia, en fin, viste, forra al automóvil, la caja en donde vayan sus modelos vivos y, si es menester, convenientemente embalados. (338)

By likening the architecture of Delaunay's fashions to the architecture of an automobile, Barga is remarking first of all on a rational, "classical" principle at work in modern automotive design: the skeleton (or chassis) and vital organs (engine, drive-train, etc.) condition to a large degree the shape of the car's metallic sheath. Delaunay's fashions are likewise "designed in accordance with the female form," as the artist herself confirmed.[27] But significantly, Delaunay conceives of the female form in dynamic, rather than static terms. So when Barga asserts that Delaunay's fashions "wrap the automobile" (as illustrated by **Figs. 5** and **7**), he is referring to the kinetic energy enveloped by her fabrics. He is acknowledging that Delaunay's primary concern is mobility—the body's freedom of movement beneath clothing and the aesthetic effects of fabric in motion—hence, the claim that her art finds form in "las condiciones maquinales del cuerpo" (338). In a note of wry humor, when Barga adds that Delaunay's models are "si es menester, convenientemente embalados," he uses the past participle of the verb, *embalar*, bearing the double meaning, to package and to "rev up" an engine. And indeed, Delaunay once painted an automobile with geometric designs and designed suits with matching fabric (**Fig. 8**).

Writing in 1925, Delaunay credited the age of speed as a primary influence on her designs: "Our era is above all mechanical, dynamic, and visual. The mechanical and the dynamic are the essential elements of the practical dimension of our time. The visual element is the spiritual characteristic of it" (*The New Art* 199). That she con-

---

[27] Excerpt from a letter written by Sonia to Damase in 1968 (Damase, *Sonia Delaunay* 71).

ceived her fashions as kinetic, sculpted painting is shown by the remarkable "display machine" constructed for her exhibit in the Paris *Salon d'Automne* of 1924—a machine that "caused the textiles to move continually up and down on roller tracks, dramatizing the oppositions of the contrasting colors" (Buckberrough 51). Robert Delaunay, inventor of the machine and publicist for his wife's exhibit, described its visual effect:

> As you go by the huge entrance hall to the Grand Palais if you look around among the shops that decorate it, your attention is drawn to the unusual appearance of the moving boutique decorated with Mme. Sonia Delaunay's fabrics. All that movement undeniably produces on your retina, at first, a new sort of unaccustomed appeal. (*The New Art* 139)

It is precisely this "new, unaccustomed appeal" to which Corpus Barga was responding in his essay. For in creating her designs, Sonia Delaunay seized that access to agency that fashion proffers; she responded to that unprecedented historic opening that revolutionized feminine fashion in the nineteen-teens and twenties, and in so doing, she opened new possibilities not only for aesthetics, but also for gendered roles and relations. In her lecture, "The Influence of Painting on Fashion Design," presented at the Sorbonne in 1926, Delaunay revealed her awareness of the social implications of her designs:

> Some time before the war, couture began to free itself from academicism: the corset and the high collar were dropped, all the devices of female clothing demanded by the aesthetic of fashion but contrary to the health and free movement of women were shaken off. The change in the life of woman provoked this revolution in feminine fashion. The woman was more and more active. (*The New Art* 206)

In designing clothing that further freed the female body, that created new denaturalized forms, Delaunay transferred the locus of aesthetic-erotic interest from the veiled, but imagined body beneath to the mobile surface of her fabrics. Rather than suggesting an eroticized but still body within, her clothing invented itself as kinetic three-dimensional painting that suggests—indeed, makes patently visible—the energy and movement within.[28]

As illustrated by the response of Corpus Barga, Delaunay's designs forced the question—"¿Cuál es la Venus de usted?" They compelled masculine desire, which through the ages had conjoined aesthetic and erotic desires, to question itself and to admit the proliferation of aesthetic-erotic forms, thus transforming the domain of desirability. It is to this question that Barga returns in his conclusion, followed by a series of even more provocative questions:

> ¿Cuál es la Venus de usted? ¿Quiere usted sacar del auto a Venus, desembalarla de su abrigo, desnudar a la pelota lasciva?
>
> Venus no existe, como no existe la línea geométrica. Fue una parábola de los griegos. Su gran error, no; su gran acierto: la creación de una forma.
>
> Usted tiene en los escaparates todas las formas conocidas. ¿Tiene usted forma? La cuestión queda intacta: ¿Cuál es la Venus de usted? (339)

In the first question of this series, Barga anticipates and mocks the conditioned response of his masculine readers—their desire to undress Venus, "desnudar a la pelota lasciva." But such an unveiling, as evidenced time and again in sexual fetishism, will only uncover an absence. Beauty, Barga asserts, has always been as ungraspable an abstraction as the geometric line. What is more, in the concrete case of Delaunay's denaturalized fashions, if one seeks Venus "bajo el arte semoviente del vestido," such an unveiling would reveal not passive, receptive feminine flesh, but rather, the sheer energy of a body in motion (336). This assertion sheds light on a cryptic remark by Gauguin, which Barga cites earlier in his essay: "Que la escultura quiera decir

---

[28] Blaise Cendrars called attention to this eroticization of the surface of textile in his poem dedicated to Sonia Delaunay, "Sur la robe elle a un corps" [On her dress she has a body] (1914). The poem was written in reponse to Delaunay's first simultaneous dress, which she created in 1913 and wore to the *Bal Bullier*, which is precisely the same dress she wears in figure 2. For the original poem in French, see Jacques Damase, *Robes and gouaches simultanées*. For an English translation, see Damase, *Sonia Delaunay* (8).

bultos, pero agujeros, jamás" (334). According to this anti-Platonic stance, beauty is not a prior, ideal form to be discovered and unveiled, but rather must be invented through an ongoing process of *formation*; hence, "el gran error" and paradoxically, "[el] gran acierto" of the Greeks—"la creación de una forma" (339). Such a stance implicitly allows, indeed welcomes, the proliferation of "models" of beauty—a point which Barga restates in the conclusion to his essay: "Usted tiene en los escaparates todas las formas conocidas" (339).

Then before repeating once more "la pregunta indiscreta" that resounds through the essay—"¿Cuál es la Venus de usted?"—Barga directs a more disturbing question to the masculine reader: "¿Tiene usted forma?" (339). This remarkable query suddenly undoes the masculinist posture that Barga had maintained throughout the essay, and no doubt surprises the masculine readers to whom he at first seemed to pander by offering an array of "Venuses" for the taking. By this new question—"Do you have form?"—he shows his awareness that the propagation of new forms—of beauty, of desire, of the feminine—has placed the masculine subject in crisis, forcing him, if only momentarily, to question *his* form as well. Then in the final sentence of his essay, Barga poses still another surprising question that explicitly calls attention to this alteration in gender roles and relations: "Señor Secretario de esta Revista: Si usted cree que ha llegado la hora de hacer esa pregunta indiscreta a los occidentales—y también a las occidentales—, queda abierta la información" (339). Throughout the essay, since first posing the questio—"¿Cuál es la Venus de usted?"—Barga has allowed only for respondents of the masculine persuasion: the provincial magistrate, the illustrious military officer, and the man of high status who eats beefsteak. But now in a tongue-in-cheek address to the "Señor Secretario" of the *Revista de Occidente*, Barga suddenly broadens his readership to include women. And going further, he suggests that the time has come to posit the question—"Which Venus is for you?"—to women as well as men. He thereby allows both women and men the agency to choose their "Venuses" and reinvent their "forms," as does the self-fashioned model in Salinas's poem, "París, abril, modelo."

I am reminded here of Judith Butler's writings on gender performativity in which she contends that sex is materialized through the stylized repetition of norms: "That this reiteration is necessary is a sign that materialization is never quite complete, that bodies never quite comply with the norms by which their materialization is impelled" (2). For Butler, the possibility of agency resides in the "instabilities, the possibilities for rematerialization" opened up by the very process of reiteration (2). Sonia Delaunay assumed a certain agency by seizing a historical moment that opened previously unrealizable possibilities. Her remarkable designs not only allowed women's bodies unprecedented freedom of movement, but they forced a glimmer of understanding, at least upon Corpus Barga (and by extension Salinas), that gender itself is pure movement, continually materialized through time. Moreover, her designs transferred the site of aesthetic-erotic desire from the phantasmatic, idealized nude beneath, to the mobile, multi-colored surface. And in so doing, her designs provoked an alteration in aesthetic-erotic desire, destabilizing gender roles and relations.

Roland Barthes has argued that "as pure sentience, the body cannot signify; clothing guarantees the passage from sentience to meaning" (258). In the case of women's wear, paradoxically, fashion's "meaning" had heretofore referred back to the body it shaped and contained, pointing always to the voluptuous sentience within. Delaunay's designs worked to rewrite that signifying surface, such that fashion referred to *itself* as artistic form in motion. And if Corpus Barga is correct, any stubborn attempt to unveil a "Venus" beneath that bright, mobile surface would expose only the zigzag flash of sheer kinetic energy.

Fig. 1: Rámon Gómez de la Serna's *Abinico de palabras* dedicated to Sonia Delaunay.

Fig. 2

Fig. 3

Fig. 4

Fig. 5

Fig. 6

Fig. 7

Fig. 8: Models wearing clothes designed by Sonia Delaunay, posing in front of a 5-CV Citroën, which was painted in accordance with one of her textile designs.

Works Cited

Barbagallo, Antonio. "Elementos futuristas en la poesía de Pedro Salinas." *Journal of Interdisciplinary Literary Studies* 3.2 (1991): 151-59.
Barga, Corpus. "Venus novísima: Ilustraciones de la desnaturalización del arte." *Revista de Occidente* 9 (1924): 332-39.
Baron, Stanley, and Jacques Damase. *Sonia Delaunay: The Life of an Artist.* New York: Harry N. Abrams, 1995.
Barthes, Roland. *The Fashion System.* Trans. Matthew Ward and Richard Howard. Berkeley: U of California P, 1990.
Benjamin, Walter. *The Arcades Project.* Trans. Howard Eiland and Kevin McLaughlin. Ed. Rolf Tiedemann. Cambridge, Mass.: Belknap of Harvard UP, 1999.
———. "The Work of Art in the Age of Mechanical Reproduction." *Illuminations.* Trans. Harry Zohn. Ed. Hannah Arendt. New York: Schocken, 1968. 217-51.
Benstock, Shari, and Suzanne Ferriss, eds. *On Fashion.* New Brunswick, N.J.: Rutgers UP, 1994.
Breitenbücher, Alba. "El vocabulario del neoplatonismo en la obra poética de Pedro Salinas." *Revista de Estudios Hispánicos* (Universidad de Puerto Rico) 18-19 (1990-91): 93-98.
Bruflat, Alan S. "Entre la fábula y el signo de Pedro Salinas." *Explicación de Textos Literarios* 19.2 (1990-91): 8-15.
Buck, Robert T., ed. *Sonia Delaunay, a Retrospective.* Buffalo: Albright-Knox Art Gallery, 1980.
Buckberrough, Sherry. "Delaunay Design: Aesthetics, Immigration, and the New Woman." *Art Journal* 54.1 (1995): 51-55.
Buck-Morss, Susan. *The Dialectics of Seeing: Walter Benjamin and the Arcades Project.* Cambridge: MIT Press, 1989.
Butler, Judith. *Bodies That Matter: On the Discursive Limits of "Sex."* London: Routledge, 1993.
Cabrera, Vicente. *Tres poetas a la luz de la metáfora: Salinas, Aleixandre y Guillén.* Madrid: Gredos, 1975.
Cirre, José Francisco. *El mundo lírico de Pedro Salinas.* Granada: Editorial Don Quijote, 1982.
Cohen, Arthur A. *Sonia Delaunay.* New York: Harry N. Abrams, 1975.
Corominas, J. *Diccionario crítico etimológico de la lengua castellana.* Vol. 3. Madrid: Gredos, 1954.
Costa Viva, Olga. *Pedro Salinas frente a la realidad.* Madrid: Alfaguara, 1969.
Crispin, John. *Pedro Salinas.* New York: Twayne, 1974.
Damase, Jacques. *Sonia Delaunay: Fashion and Fabrics.* Trans. Shaun Whiteside and Stanley Baron. London: Thames and Hudson, 1991.
———. *Robes and gouaches simultanées, 1925. L'Art et le corps. Rythmes-couleurs en mouvement.* Brussels: n.p., 1974.

Debicki, Andrew P. *Estudios sobre poesía española contemporánea: La generación de 1924-1925.* Madrid: Gredos, 1968.

———. "La metáfora en algunos poemas tempranos de Salinas." *Pedro Salinas.* Ed. Debicki. Madrid: Taurus, 1976. 113-17.

———. "The Play of Difference in the Early Poetry of Pedro Salinas." *MLN* 100.2 (1985): 65-80.

———. "La visión del mundo en la poesía temprana de Pedro Salinas." *Cuadernos Hispanoamericanos* 205 (1967): 64-80.

Delaunay, Robert and Sonia. *The New Art of Color: The Writings of Robert and Sonia Delaunay.* Trans. David Shapiro and Arthur A. Cohen. Ed. Arthur A. Cohen. New York: Viking, 1978.

Díaz Fernández, José. *El nuevo romanticismo: Polémica de arte, política y literatura.* Madrid: José Esteban, 1985.

Feal Deibe, Carlos. *La poesía de Pedro Salinas.* 2a ed. Madrid: Gredos, 1965.

———. "Lo visible y lo invisible en los primeros libros poéticos de Salinas." *Bulletin Hispanique* 93.1 (1991): 183-206.

Flugel, J.C. *The Psychology of Clothes.* London: Hogarth, 1930.

Geist, Anthony Leo. *La poética de la generación del 27 y las revistas literarias: de la vanguardia al compromiso (1918-1936).* Barcelona: Guadarrama, 1980.

Giménez Caballero, Ernesto. Reseña de *La teoría de la relatividad de Einstein y sus fundamentos físicos*, de Max Born. *Carteles.* Madrid: Espasa-Calpe, 1927. 155-56.

Gómez de la Serna, Ramón. *Ismos.* Madrid: Guadarrama, 1975.

Gronberg, Tag. *Designs on Modernity: Exhibiting the City in 1920s Paris.* Manchester: Manchester UP, 1998.

Guillén, Jorge. Prólogo. *Poesías completas.* De Pedro Salinas. 2a ed. Barcelona: Barral, 1975. 1-30.

———. Prólogo. *Poemas escogidos.* De Pedro Salinas. Madrid: Espasa Calpe, 1991. 75-78.

Gullón, Ricardo. "La poesía de Pedro Salinas." *Pedro Salinas.* Ed. Andrew P. Debicki. Madrid: Taurus, 1976. 85-98.

Hartfield-Méndez, Vialla. "El dilema de Pigmalión: El uso del personaje autónomo en Pedro Salinas." *Anales de la Literatura Contemporánea* 17 (1992): 395-408.

———. *Woman and the Infinite: Epiphanic Moments in Pedro Salinas's Art.* Lewisburg (PA): Bucknell UP, 1996.

Havard, Robert G. *From Romanticism to Surrealism: Seven Spanish Poets.* Cardiff: U of Wales P, 1988.

———. "The Reality of Words in the Poetry of Pedro Salinas." *Bulletin of Hispanic Studies* 51.1 (1974): 28-47.

Lipovetsky, Gilles. *The Empire of Fashion: Dressing Modern Democracy.* Trans. Catherine Porter. Princeton: Princeton UP, 1994.

Madsen, Axel. *Sonia Delaunay: Artist of the Lost Generation.* New York: McGraw-Hill, 1989.

Maunoury, Monique Schneider. "Sonia Delaunay. The Clothing of Modernity." *Art / Fashion* (Exhibition Catalogue). Ed. Germano Celant. New York: Guggenheim Museum SoHo, 1997. 55-70.

Maurer, Christopher. "Salinas y 'las cosas': Tradición y vanguardia." *Revista de Occidente* 126 (1991): 137-50.

Monegal, Antonio. "'Voz' y 'realidad' en la crítica de un poeta." *Signo y memoria: Ensayos sobre Pedro Salinas*. Eds. Enric Bou y Elena Gascón Vera. Madrid: Pliegos, 1993. 51-60.

Morano, Elizabeth, ed. *Sonia Delaunay: Art into Fashion*. New York: George Braziller, 1986.

Morris, C.B. "*Visión* and *Mirada* in the Poetry of Salinas, Guillén and Dámaso Alonso." *Bulletin of Hispanic Studies* 38.1 (1961): 103-12.

Palley, Julián. *La luz no usada: La poesía de Pedro Salinas*. México, D.F.: Ediciones de Andrea, 1966.

Perloff, Marjorie. *The Futurist Moment: Avant-Garde, Avant Guerre, and the Language of Rupture*. Chicago: U of Chicago P, 1986.

Poggioli, Renato. *The Theory of the Avant-garde*. Trans. Gerald Fitzgerald. Cambridge: Belknap of Harvard UP, 1968.

Rosenthal, Deborah. "Primary Painting: Sonia Delaunay." *The New Criterion* 8.6 (1990): 18-21.

Salinas, Pedro. "*Mundo real y mundo poético*" *y dos entrevistas olvidadas, 1930-1933*. Valencia: Pre-Textos, 1996.

———. *La poesía de Rubén Darío (ensayo sobre el tema y los temas del poeta)*. Buenos Aires: Losada, 1948.

———. *Poesías completas*. Vol. 1. Madrid: Alianza, 1997.

———. *Reality and the Poet in Spanish Poetry*. Trans. Edith Fishtine Helman. Baltimore: Johns Hopkins UP, 1966.

Salinas de Marichal, Solita. "El primer Salinas." *Boletín de la Fundación Federico García Lorca* 1.2 (1987): 22-28.

Scarry, Elaine. *The Body in Pain: The Making and Unmaking of the World*. New York: Oxford UP, 1985.

Shaughnessy, Lorna. *The Developing Poetic Philosophy of Pedro Salinas: A Study in Twentieth-Century Spanish Poetry*. Lewiston, NY: Mellen UP, 1995.

Siles, Jaime. "La poesía primera de Salinas y la postmodernidad (Notas para un catálogo de semicoincidencias)." *Revista de Occidente* 126 (1991): 151-57.

Silver, Philip. *La casa de Anteo: Ensayos de poética hispana (De Antonio Machado a Claudio Rodríguez)*. Trans. Salustiano Masó. Madrid: Taurus, 1985.

Simmel, Georg. "Fashion." *On Individuality and Social Forms. Selected Writings*. Ed. Donald N. Levine. Chicago: U of Chicago P, 1971. 294-323.

———. "Filosofía de la moda." Trans. Fernando Vela. *Revista de Occidente* 1 (1923): 43-65; 2 (1923): 211-230.

Skeat, Walter W. *An Etymological Dictionary of the English Language.* Oxford: Clarenden, 1910.
Spitzer, Leo. "El conceptismo interior de Pedro Salinas." In *Lingüística e historia literaria.* 2a ed. Madrid: Gredos, 1974. 188-246.
Steele, Valerie. *Fashion and Eroticism: Ideals of Feminine Beauty from the Victorian Era to the Jazz Age.* New York: Oxford UP, 1985.
Stixrude, David L. *The Early Poetry of Pedro Salinas.* Princeton: Department of Romance Languages. Madrid: Castalia, 1975.
Torre, Guillermo de. "El arte decorativo de Sonia Delaunay-Terk." *Alfar* 35 (1923): 160-61.
Valis, Noël M. "The Female Figure and Writing in *Fin del siglo* Spain." *Romance Quarterly* 36.3 (1989): 369-381.
Vando-Villar, Isaac de. "Sonia Delaunay." *Poesías y poética del Ultraísmo (antología).* Ed. Francisco Fuentes Florido. Barcelona: Mitre, 1989. 319.
Vattimo, Gianni. *The End of Modernity: Nihilism and Hermeneutics in Postmodern Culture.* Trans. John R. Snyder. Baltimore: Johns Hopkins UP, 1988.
Wilson, Elizabeth. *Adorned in Dreams, Fashion and Modernity.* Berkeley: U of California P, 1985.
Zardoya, Concha. "La 'otra' realidad de Pedro Salinas." *Poesía española del siglo XX.* Vol. 2. Madrid: Gredos, 1974. 106-48.
Zubizarreta, Alma. *Pedro Salinas: El diálogo creador.* Madrid, Gredos, 1969.

The Commodification of the Image of Spain's "New Woman" by Mass Culture and the Avant-Garde in José Díaz Fernández's *La Venus mecánica*

SUSAN LARSON
Fordham University

"LA SOCIEDAD ACTUAL ES MANCA, porque le falta el brazo activo de la mujer," posits José Díaz Fernández in *El nuevo romanticismo* (49). *El nuevo romanticismo* was a pivotal work in that it questioned the validity of the avant-garde novel and announced the emergence of the more social novel that would flourish in the 1930s.[1] This essay investigates the relationship between women's fashion in particular, mass culture in general, and the critique of the avant-garde of 1920s Madrid as found in the author's 1929 novel *La Venus mecánica*. The "woman question" was often linked to the "social question" in nineteenth- and twentieth-century essays about Spain's social, political, and economic concerns. Anxiety over the role of women in society and increasing overlap between the public and private spheres that occurs during times of rapid and uneven modernization is skillfully articulated but ultimately unresolved in *La Venus mecánica*. The novel is significant for the way in which it demonstrates—from both sides of

---

[1] David Herzberger finds in *El nuevo romanticismo* an important theory of narrative that lies squarely between what he calls "the metonymic pole of discourse" or the belief that language can reflect life as it really is and "the metaphorical pole of discourse" or the concept that language can reflect nothing except its own creation. He calls Díaz Fernández's theory a reconciliation that "turns upon a modified version of the reflection theory of literature, which takes into account the necessary split-referential functioning of the language of literary discourse" (85).

the exchange—how and why men and women come to relate to one another within an increasingly market-driven, image-conscious urban setting.

La Venus mecánica, Díaz Fernández's second novel, takes place in Madrid toward the end of the dictatorship of Primo de Rivera. The representation of the city as a cultural and political capital and the experience of a diverse group of individuals in this specific place make for the chaotic, disjointed feel of the novel. The author pieces together historical and fictional events in true avant-garde fashion, which permits him to comment on avant-garde art and popular culture, Spanish politics, and the behavior of the Spanish bourgeoisie in a time of crisis. As Víctor Fuentes points out, the years 1928 through 1936 were historically tumultuous, a moment in which the substitution of the Second Republic controlled by the moderate Left for the monarchy created an environment that was more open to the social, realist novel after a decade dominated by avant-garde literature (87-94).

The very first pages of the novel describe how its protagonist, Víctor, has a way of chasing after women that belittles both him and the women he objectifies. At one point he describes himself as "ese hombre de guardia a las puertas de una tienda, ese mendigo de palabras y sonrisas fugaces, ese misógino devorador de citas falsas y respuestas equívocas que desgasta su alma en todos los quicios y todas las esquinas" (11). A sharp observer, intelligent and good-looking, there are many allusions to him as a consumer of women. At one point Víctor describes them as

> más que mujeres, esquemas de mujeres como las pinturas de Picasso. Pura geometría, donde ha quedado la línea sucinta e imprescindible [...]. En realidad, aquella figura no era ya un producto natural sino artificial [...]. Era una sútil colaboración de la máquina y la industria, de la técnica y el arte. Alimentos concentrados, brisas artificiales del automóvil y el ventilador electrónico, iodos del tocador, sombras de cinema y claridades de gas [...]. Esa mujer [...] es hija de los ingenieros, de los modistas, de los perfumistas, de los operadores, de los mecánicos. (19-20)

Elizabeth Wilson's article "All the Rage" explores the relationship of fashion to art in the 1920s. "The fashions of the 1920s, for example, cannot just be interpreted (as they usually boringly are) as expressive of women's emancipation and a new sexual freedom. That was all happening before the First World War—Paul Poiret, the revolutionary French designer, abandoned the corset in 1904" (33). More significant, in Wilson's eyes, are the urban motifs in fashion that stem from movements such as modernism and futurism: "1920s fashion imitated aspects of modernism in featuring abstract designs and in rendering the body as two-dimensional and flat as possible. They were futurist in suggesting the speed and the clean lines of the machine" (34). Both women's fashion and the avant-garde of the 1920s—highly aesthetic pleasures—questioned traditional views of what was beautiful, sought to deny the existence of any hierarchy of aesthetic values, and recognized pleasure and beauty as important forces in the lives of modern urban citizens.

Recent contributions to feminist cultural theory have made the argument that the image of woman is a construction. As this argument goes, the image is a product of culture in several senses at once—as it has been industrially manufactured, as it has been pieced together according to aesthetic rules, and as it has been prefabricated by men. The image of woman, as this argument continues, is exactly what it is only because of the society which creates it, and in order to alter this image, we have to reconstruct that society.[2] Díaz Fernández here documents the "new woman" made not of flesh and blood but of geometry, film, aura, and clothing—all combined to produce an image of the modern woman as product (in the most literal sense of the word, in this case). It is against this synthetic, superficial, dehumanized quality that the female protagonist of *La Venus mecánica*, Obdulia, struggles, trying to find an escape from a world that for the most part considers this new type of woman a positive product of new technologies and social values.

The increasingly public role of women and the increased commodification of images of women by mass culture and the avant-garde became an important topic for European intellectuals in the early twentieth century. Volume One of the *Revista de Occidente*, for example, published in July of 1923 and edited by José Ortega y Gasset, prominently showcased an essay by one of the ideological forefathers of the discipline of sociology, Georg Simmel. In this essay, translated into Spanish as "Filosofía de la moda," he focuses specifically on the issues of social dependence, individual liberty, and class all in the con-

---

[2] For an overview of recent cultural studies approaches to the intersection of film, fashion and feminism see Jane Gaines's and Charlotte Herzog's *Fabrications. Costume and the Female Body* (1990).

text of a discussion of fashion. Fashion is completely arbitrary for Simmel: "con que una vez ordena lo que es útil, otra lo incomprensible, otra la estética o prácticamente inocuo, revela su perfecta indiferencia hacia las normas prácticas, racionales, de la vida" (48). Central to his theory is the assertion that fashion plays an important role in capitalist society, the idea of what is fashionable trickling down from the wealthier to the working classes, in reality unattainable but at the same time highly desirable because "la intervención del capitalismo no puede menos que acelerar vivamente este proceso y mostrarlo al desnudo, porque los objetos de moda, a fuera de cosas externas, son muy particularmente asequibles por el simple dinero" (51). In this way Simmel uses fashion, as symptomatic of modernity, to show how the modern is linked to purely symbolic capital and how this affects every last one of us on a very personal level:

> Es específico de la vida moderna un "tempo" impaciente, el cual indica no sólo el ansia de rápida mutación en los contenidos cualitativos de la vida, sino el vigor cobrado por el atractivo formal de cuanto es límite, del comienzo y del fin, del llegar y no irse. El caso es compendioso de este linaje en la moda, que, por su juego ante la tendencia a una expansión total y el aniquilamiento de su propio sentido que esta expansión acarrea, adquiere el atractivo peculiar de los límites y extremos, el atractivo de un comienzo y un fin simultáneos de la novedad y al mismo tiempo de la caducidad. Su cuestión no es "ser o no ser", sino que es ella a un tiempo ser y no ser, está siempre en la divisoria de las aguas que van al pasado y al futuro, y, merced a ello, nos proporciona durante su vigencia una sensación de actualidad más fuerte que casi todas las demás cosas. (58)

Even the "anti-moda," as Simmel calls it, the conscious need to be different from the crowd, is seen as dependent upon the commonly accepted concept of fashion. This modern obsession with the here and now and the tendency for one class to pass its sense of fashion on to another can be seen in the cultural climate of the avant-garde at the time the essay was written, a period when culture was becoming increasingly commodified and the avant-garde had to reinvent itself at a quickening rate in Spain just as in the rest of Europe. The often elitist values of "high culture" were passed down to those who were not "in the know" as being central to a meaningful representation of mankind's twentieth-century surroundings.

The growing modernization of Spanish society in the early twentieth century required significant shifts in economic, social, and demographic structures. This brought about social and cultural changes that, in turn, modified the ideological discourse on women. The representation of women as the *angel del hogar* was challenged by a new image of woman called the *nueva mujer moderna*, an "ideal" woman already in vogue in many European countries and in North America (Nash 25-50). Several publications of the time, such as Carmen de Burgos's *La mujer moderna y sus derechos* (1927), defended the idea and furthered its dissemination.

This new cultural representation was incorporated into both social values and collective imagery. In Nash's words, "the redefinition of women in terms of modernity was an effective symbolic device for adapting women to new social, political, economic and demographic concerns" (67). The shift from the old model of femininity to the innovative *nueva mujer moderna* allowed women to adjust to the process of modernity. It accommodated more restrictive gender roles toward the new needs of the labor market and society. This readjustment was, in fact, a mechanism that allowed women access to specific areas of public activity such as education, culture, social welfare and new sectors of the labor market (*La condición de la mujer en España* 135-86). It thus responded to the new socioeconomic needs of Spanish society and, in this way, became part of hegemonic discourse on women. Despite its modernizing effect, however, the model of the *nueva mujer moderna* also maintained the core of traditional gender identity by defining women as primarily and essentially mothers and childbearers, albeit in a new way.

The vast majority of women between 1900 and 1930 in Spain did not hold regular, full-time employment outside of the home. In fact, Spain's formal workforce has been even more heavily masculine than that of other Western European countries. Obviously, female employment contradicted all of the precepts of ideal womanhood and threatened to topple one of the pillars of masculine legitimacy. Geraldine Scanlon, in her meticulous study of women in Spain, *Polémica feminista en España* (1976), says that at the turn of the century

> la idea muy difundida de que el trabajo de la mujer era degradante (creencia que estaba muy arraigada entre la clase media) supo-

> nía una formidable barrera psicológica [...]. La deshonra de tener que trabajar era aún mayor si la mujer estaba casada, pues no sólo se humillaba ella, sino también su marido. (9)

As elsewhere, too, a double standard distinguished between what was acceptable for middle- and upper-class women versus women of a less economically privileged class. Gloria Nielfa Cristóbal's study "Las mujeres en el comercio madrileño del primer tercio del siglo XX" demonstrates how more and more women between 1900 and 1930 began to work in Madrid. The highest percentage of working women were widows. The second group most likely to work was aged 18-30, while the women least likely to work were those women who were married. It is important to note that Nielfa credits ambitious business owners even more than feminist groups and changing ideas about women in Spanish society with this increase in women's employment in the business sectors:

> A lo largo del primer tercio del siglo XX, se produce un crecimento del número de mujeres empleadas en establecimientos mercantiles, con salarios muy inferiores a los de la dependencia masculina. Este hecho no es exclusivo del mundo del comercio, sino una característica común del trabajo femenino de la época. Se puede decir que el deseo patronal de contar con mano de obra barata encontró el terrreno abandonado para ello en la situacion social de las mujeres. (323)

Social values do not change in a vacuum, as Nielfa's work shows. Rather, changing ideas about women were very closely tied to capital and new ways of exchanging goods and services in the urban context.

These changes in how Spanish women saw themselves and were seen by the rest of society were quite obvious in the mass media and in fashion in particular. Many theorists of the fashion industry claim that the characteristics of mass society have been unavoidably, if not problematically, imprinted upon twentieth-century clothing and influenced our attitudes to dress and identity (Breward, Craik, Gavarrón, Wilson). In many urban centers of Europe and the Americas, advances in the technology and materials used for clothing production undoubtedly provided more comfortable, cheaper, and more attractive items to a larger proportion of the population. Meanwhile, the mediums through which fashion change was communicated allowed for an equally wide dissemination of information and broader opportunities for the stimulation of a more homogeneous public imagination. The fashion magazine and the Hollywood film in particular brought fashionable models to a hugely expanded audience from the 1920s onwards, material examples of their dream-peddling often made available through the expansion of chain stores and mail order companies. At the same time, paradoxically, a reorganization of business practices of marketing and advertising prioritized particular strands of society as fashion leaders (Breward 181-199). A cult of the designer revolving around ideas of *haute couture* and high fashion coexisted with strong subcultural identities, resulting in contrasting notions of quality, style, and individuality. As Jennifer Craik comments:

> The new approach to fashion was schizophrenic. On the one hand, fashion was democratized as more people had access to the images and clothing preferred by the trendsetters. On the other hand, fashion producers were setting the styles. Other changes were also occurring in the fashion industry. The aristocracy was supplanted as the elite fashion community and role models. Socialites, artists and movie stars offered alternative sources of inspiration. These role models offered desirable images and behaviors that were no longer based on emulating one's superiors. Individualism and modernity prevailed. (74)

Without a doubt, the promise of the "new woman" was linked to utopian images of the modern metropolis in graphic design, film, and fashion trends.

Robust models of femininity preceded World War One and continued to be a blueprint for acceptable fashionability well into the 1920s. There are very differing opinions as to whether the turn-of-the-century look was more comfortable for women than that of the flapper of the 1920s. In terms of practicality and comfort, the earlier look was perhaps preferable to the chest-denying rubber corseting and sweaty man-made fibers of the later twenties.[3] However, as Lola Gavarrón

---

[3] Questions of comfort aside, the reasons behind the shift from the corset to the use of the mass-produced brassiere are the subject of "The Functions of Fashion and Clothing," Chapter Three of Malcolm Barnard's *Fashion as Communication*. He adheres to a "theory of the shifting erogenous zone" wherein a culture's sexual interest in the female anatomy continually shifts

points out in *Piel de angel. Historias de la ropa interior femenina*, due to women's collective liberation from the corset, "la mujer que se anuncia en los años veinte recuerda ya la figura humana. Ha recobrado los movimientos humanos. Es, por fin, un ser humano" (232).[4] The truth of the matter may lie somewhere in between. The vast majority of women in the 1920s and 1930s did not wear impractical flapper-inspired clothing, although their wardrobes did begin to include more close-fitting clothes that included details and designs inspired by men's fashions.

A careful look at the popular magazines of Madrid in the 1920s and 1930s brings to light a relatively sudden democratization of fashionability due to advances in clothing technology, a further expansion of the publicity and advertising machines to incorporate film, radio and mass-circulation periodicals, and a perceived broadening of employment and educational opportunities for women and the working class. At first glance, one is left with a simplified and overly glamorized image of the fashionable female of the 1920s, swathed in Chanel, sunburnt on the tennis court, reclining leisurely and answering to the name of flapper, a literal reflection of the advertising expertise of Hollywood and *Harper's Bazaar*. There were magazines published in and for the inhabitants of Madrid that were very similar to magazines like *Vogue* and *Harper's Bazaar* in the United States and *La Vie Parisienne* in France. Two dedicated solely to fashion and women's concerns were *Miss* and *Chic*.[5]

In the issues of the very successful popular magazine *Blanco y Negro*, founded in 1891 by Luca de Tena, one witnesses first-hand the evolution of the *angel del hogar* into the *nueva mujer moderna*. In the 1920s, the magazine proffered an image of women increasingly active in all aspects of urban society and constructed a new, radically differ-

---

from one part to another, now the chest, now the behind, now the legs and so on (54-55).

[4] Other than the collection of images of women in *Blanco y Negro* mentioned below, there are very few studies of fashion in Madrid at this time. One very informative exception is Gavarrón's just-cited investigation.

[5] It would be ideal to rely on more theoretical writings about fashion and culture that focus specifically on Spain. Unfortunately, there is very little of real theoretical interest to be found on fashion in Spain tht goes beyond the purely anecdotal. As the period in question is one of increased internationalization and homogenization of styles of dress, it can be assumed that fashion trends from the rest of Europe and the United States have a lot in common with those of Spain.

ent feminine stereotype. Human reactions to this increasingly urban, modern, capitalist system are played out in its pages. One sees visual references to new systems of relationships and hierarchies. There is a crisis of traditional values, incipient consumerism, the eruption of very different fashions in clothing and lifestyles, certain sexual, class and racial taboos are overcome or at least questioned, and a secular attitude introduced that counters Spain's traditionally Catholic outlook. Significantly, women are almost never portrayed in the private space of the home but in the city street or participating in athletic activities. Almost all of the illustrations of women include either the backdrop of an urban cityscape or leisure activity that takes place in the countryside or at the beach. A high percentage involve women in cars, trains, boats, and automobiles (**Figs. 1-3**). This was a purely bourgeois revolution of social values, but the complete unattainability of this lifestyle to the vast majority of *Blanco y Negro*'s readers seems not to have impeded, but rather assured the magazine's success.

Javier Pérez Rojas points out that

> [l]a mujer va a ser presentada como símbolo de esta nueva sociedad y mentalidad transformada, como prueba de la liberalización emprendida en una nueva época en la que caen mitos y conceptos vitales ancestrales [...]. Pero todos esos cambios y rupturas se desenvuelven en un marco estrictamente urbano y en unos ambientes sociales muy minoritarios que son los que en gran medida reflejan los ilustrados gráficos, los cuales los afrontan con ironía y humor en creaciones donde se viene a criticar la doble moral burguesa. La imagen de liberación femenina que gustan ofrecer los dibujos de las revistas ilustradas burguesas transcurren preferentemente en unos ámbitos elitistas, especialmente cuando se trata de aspectos relacionados de la moda. (16-17)

Some of the reasons behind the portrayal of the strong, independent, sensual woman are economic. Magazines such as *Blanco y Negro* created a new market for products in Madrid. Women's new values and role in society seemed to require modern clothes, shoes, perfumes, cosmetics, hairdos—even a new, slimmer body shape (**Figs. 4-6**). Images of this new woman predominate the movie screens and are also presented in the form of the art-deco-inspired *femme fatale* or urban vamp. In the face of this stream of images of independent women as athletes, airplane pilots, university graduates, professionals, and social and political progressives, feminists like Margarita Nelken caution that this independence is relative:

> Lo que no puede esta mujer española, a quien la Naturaleza "madura" mucho antes que a la escandinava o a la anglosajona; lo que no puede esta mujer, que tal vez es ya abogada, ingeniera, doctora en medicina, es, antes de los veinticinco años, viajar cuando lo estima conveniente sin permiso de sus padres o tutores. Lo que no puede es, hasta los veinticinco años [...] disponer libremente de su persona [...]. Y el enmendar esa ley nos parece bastante más decisivo, en cuanto a emancipación, que el acceso a las carreras liberales. (176)

The joyful, breezy exuberance of many of the proud, free women in the images of *Blanco y Negro* have a grain of truth in them. They must be tempered by a dose of reality, though, as Nelken reminds us. The dreamy portrayal of these wealthy, independent women appealed to women and men alike in no small part because they were worlds away from their own personal realities. These images appeal to men as well since the women are often sensual and scantily-clad in the newest fashions.

In the pages of *Blanco y Negro*, at least, fashionable women are at home on the big city street in the drawings of the most important graphic artists like Enrique Varela de Seijas, Loygorri, Ramón Manchón, Joaquín Valverde, Rafael de Penagos, Federico Ribas, Roberto Martínez Baldrich, Salvador Bartolozzi, and Ramón Roqueta, all of whom worked and lived in Madrid but whose work rarely depicted local scenes. Neither do the women look particularly Spanish. Their city backdrops are the generalized metropolises of work and leisure, movement and glamour. The magazine's writers and artists supplied their readers with what the latter demanded: a model of life that seemed always fresh, new, avant-garde, and exciting even if just out of reach.

Fashion in particular and the modern image business in general thrive precisely because styles change. Fashion drawing of the twenties and later fashion photography of the thirties, in Anne Hollander's words, "emphasized the dependence of desirable looks on completely ephemeral visual satisfaction, the harmony of the immediate moment only, which exists totally and changes totally, shifting to the next by no visible process" (163). Fashion is the illustrative costuming for a glamorized urban theater, but also a problematic means of expression that runs the risk of a dehumanizing anonymity. It is precisely this two-sided nature of fashion as it is associated with female liberation that Díaz Fernández outlines and criticizes in *La Venus mecánica*.

The novel has two main protagonists: Obdulia, a young woman from a middle-class class family that has fallen on hard times, and a young middle-class journalist named Víctor, who in many respects represents Díaz Fernández himself. According to Laurent Boetsch, there are three main themes (123-125). The first is the problematic role of the bourgeois intellectual (Víctor) who becomes active in the revolution of the proletariat. The second is the equally problematic position of young women (Obdulia) who are encouraged by feminist thought, the popular press, and images of women in movies and graphic design to strive to be independent and free in an urban environment that nevertheless remained dangerous and closed to them. The third is a harsh critique of avant-garde culture. These three themes are increasingly intertwined towards the end of the novel when the alienated Obdulia and Víctor reconcile their previously frustrated relationship. All three themes hinge on the same dilemma, voiced by Víctor: "Pero es que no sé si soy individualista o colectivista" (87). The end of the novel testifies to the saving power of the true, committed love relationship (though significantly still outside of marriage), the identification with society at large, and concern with the working class as opposed to what Díaz Fernández saw as the bourgeois values and avant-garde aesthetic of the time. Obdulia and Víctor, after a series of difficult personal experiences, eventually grow together and decide to take revolutionary action. In the very last phrases of the novel, Obdulia goes to the prison where Víctor has been incarcerated to tell him that their infant son has died.

> —Cuando salgas, yo te ayudaré a preparar nuestra venganza. Venganza. Venganza. Qué bien sonaba la palabra allí, bajo las bóvedas sombrías, bajo el techo ingrato y polvoriento. La boca de Obdulia parecía morderla como un fruto, el único que rueda, verde y apetecible, por el piso de todas las cárceles. (310-11)

The words spoken by Obdulia strengthen, inspire, and unite both characters. It is with a similar purpose that Díaz Fernández wrote his novels of political and social critique: in order to enlighten his readers and motivate them to act politically.[6]

Some of *La Venus mecánica* is narrated in a first- or third-person objective manner which, aside from maintaining the linear progression of the plot, describes the political situation and specific demonstrations in the streets of Madrid. However, unlike the prototypical realist novel, *La Venus mecánica* is highly subjective. Díaz Fernández uses avant-garde literary techniques in the more pensive, introspective chapters while he uses more realistic, objective language to discuss, to great effect, the general sensation and experience of life in Madrid in the 1920s. As mentioned above, Díaz Fernández's fiction lies somewhere between the traditionally demarcated realms of the social and the avant-garde novel. A look at the cover of the first edition, designed by Catalan graphic artist Joan Puyol, informs the reader of its avant-garde tendencies (**Fig. 7**). With its Cubist representation of the image of a nude woman further depersonalized by the metal grating on the bottom left, the wheel on the right, and the grim, overly-simplified figure of the male spectator on the top right, the book's cover skillfully sets the tone for the reader and encompasses the main themes of the novel in an abstract sense. Once begun, the novel's persistent, specific and detailed attack on the social construction of gender, economic inequality and political corruption in the specific context of Madrid in the 1920s locates it squarely within the category of the social novel. It is not an exaggeration to say that Díaz Fernández can be credited for drawing on the avant-garde and combining it with what the social novel as a genre had to offer in order to initiate a new literary movement.[7]

There are many artists, authors, journalists, and intellectuals who make up Madrid's cultural environment in *La Venus mecánica*. With

---

[6] It is the opinion of scholars of Díaz Fernández and the social novel of the 1920s and 1930s in Spain such as Boetsch, Gonzalo Santonja, and José Esteban that the author stopped writing fiction after the publication of *La Venus mecánica* because he doubted the power of his words to further political change in Spain. It does seem significant that after the publication of *La Venus mecánica*, Díaz Fernández only wrote political articles and biographies of revolutionaries until his untimely death in 1941.

[7] Only a handful of literary critics and historians such as Fulgencio Castañar and Laurent Boetsch have located Díaz Fernández (along with Ramón Sender, Andrés Carranque de Ríos and Joaquín Arderíus) at the intersection between these two literary currents.

few exceptions, the representation of these characters serves as a means to harshly criticize the avant-garde aesthetic of the 1920s which is portrayed as frivolous, pedantic and foolish. While on the whole the intellectuals and the art presented in the novel are divorced from the real human problems that surround them, there is an attempt by some to paternalistically elevate the cultural level of the masses. Perhaps the best example is the American Miss Mary, who "era el tipo perfecto de la mujer 'snob'. Residía en París y viajaba con frecuencia por Europa a pretexto de hacer propaganda bíblica. Conocía a los artistas de moda y se jactaba de descubrir genios desconocidos en el intricado bosque de las vanguardias" (161). Her extreme elitism is present in the Ayn Rand-like, proto-Fascist religion that she invents based on fervent individualism, which she thinks is "la fuente de la personalidad que va imponiéndose y triunfando sobre el montón informe de los pusilánimes, de los débiles, de los conformistas" (175). Miss Mary invites Víctor to the Club Femenino on the Gran Vía, where men are only allowed in the very elegant Tea Room. Miss Mary's ideology stems from a wide variety of influences, from the Futurist fascination with technology and power and the mystification of physical perfection, to the Nietzschean concept of the individual living life as if it were his or her personal work of art. In complete control of her circumstances as the widow of a powerful American industrialist, Miss Mary's existence is protected from any contact with the real world. Another character involved in this strange, elitist cultural show of strength and wealth is the nameless poet who forces Víctor to touch the poet's biceps to prove his physical strength, because "se necesita ser un buen atleta para ser gran poeta" (182). There also appears the "Communist" sculptress who sculpts "el hombre integral," whom she defines as one that "no pierde el tiempo en romanticismos ni en literatura. Para él no existe ni el amor, ni el honor, ni la familia" (258). Nevertheless, she is thrilled and considers her exhibition in Madrid a great success only when the king attends.

Popular culture is also the target of Díaz Fernández's criticism. The shallow and ultimately destructive nature of the fashion industry as related to the construction of individual identity has already been outlined above. In Chapter 42 of the novel, "Fábula del boxeador y la paloma," Díaz Fernández points out how extremely ideologically-motivated sports are, specifically mentioning soccer and, of course, boxing. The chapter briefly chronicles the fight of the Spanish boxer Eusebio and the German Schemeling. Eusabio is ultimately undone by the stress of representing his country against a rival country. "En realidad, a Eusebio no le había vencido su contrincante, sino el nacionalismo deportivo, que es, probablemente, el más intransigente de los nacionalismos" (283). *La Venus mecánica* explores how popular culture insinuates itself into daily life and what it means to those for whom it is ostensibly created. Díaz Fernández sees similarities between avant-garde and popular culture in that they are often both products of those who run the instruments of the dissemination of informational control and ideological power linked to a desire for profit. Díaz Fernández and some of the other writers and intellectuals he worked with in Madrid in the 1920s were deeply involved aesthetically with the avant-garde movements taking place between the major world wars in Europe. They also tried to create art that would politically motivate and inspire the masses by speaking directly to the experience of living in an increasingly industrialized, modern Madrid.

The young, very fashionable Obdulia is characterized throughout the novel as a woman trapped within the social and economic barriers of her time. She is portrayed not as a human being but as a "mujer-mercancía," as the "Venus mecánica" of the title. Chapter 13, titled "Capítulo para muchachas solas," briefly sketches the lives of women such as Obdulia, painting them as works in progress, as inevitable products of the modern city:

> Algún día ha de llegar en que no existan esas muchachas perdidas, indecisas, que merodean alrededor del bar económico donde han comido alguna vez. No se atreven a entrar porque en el fondo de su bolso no hay más que la polvera exprimida, la barra de carmín, sangrienta y chiquita como un dedo recién mutilado, y la factura sin pagar de la última fonda. Muchachas de zapatos gastados y sombreros deslucidos, que buscan un empleo y terminan por encontrar un amante. Un pintor actual podría retratar en ellas la desolación de una urbe: al fondo, la valla de un solar; a la izquierda, un desmonte, y más lejos, la espalda iluminada de un rascacielos. (93).

The dynamic, youthful excitement of the city street is influenced by and in turn influences the young women who have flocked to Madrid looking for work, forming new versions of themselves based on images of the feminine they see in other women, store windows, the popular press, and film.

To elaborate on this one need look no further than the title of the novel as it is an obvious reference to the modern fabrication of women described above. In this image of the title are synthesized youth, eroticism, and the mechanical—three characteristics that the avant-garde saw as desirable. When Obdulia is described in these terms, however, the reader understands them to be quite problematic. In fact, the development of Obdulia's character involves her increasing strength to fight off the burden of being the "Venus mecánica." She is forced to mature in an environment where her body is the only thing she has to offer in exchange for the money she needs to survive. The "mechanized" aspect of the woman of the title suggests a dehumanization which certainly applies to Obdulia during the first half of the novel. The image is gradually worn away as Obdulia adopts more of an awareness of how society has forced her into her situation, a personal and political resistance to this society and, most of all, an identification with the underprivileged working class. Obdulia is not an avant-garde heroine at all, as Ramón Buckley suggests (170-174); rather, when she speaks in her own voice she loses all of the mystery and flirtatious nature associated with the flapper-inspired woman she first appears to be.

The reader first meets Obdulia in the cabaret where she works as a "tanguista," dancing with men for a fee with the promise of sexual favors after hours (40-54). She rails against the situation in which she has found herself. "Es que aborrezco esta vida. No me acostumbro. Cada vez que entro allí siento un frío en las entrañas [...], pero eso era lo de menos. Lo peor era tener que devorar mis pensamientos" (56). The thoughts to which she refers are of the circumstances that have brought her to this point in her life—namely, the economic downfall of her previously-stable middle class family: her father runs off never to be heard from again, her mother tries to force Obdulia to marry a policeman she finds unbearable (in no small part because he is her mother's lover), and Obdulia runs away to find her own way in the world. There is much of the typical serialized romance novel here, with the young, beautiful, hard-working, well-intentioned heroine being abandoned to a cruel world until she cleverly manages to redeem her situation by hooking a rich man who will save her from certain doom and launch her into a safe, bourgeois existence. Díaz Fernández paints a different picture, however. The rich man in *La Venus mecánica* is not Obdulia's salvation but her cross to bear, as she gets pregnant by him. Obdulia then decides to sacrifice her comfortable existence with the wealthy mine owner for her uncertain love for Víctor. By the end of the novel she vows to change her world by engaging in revolutionary activities. Her liberation comes from an evolution from her comfortable but solitary existence to solidarity with Víctor and the revolutionary ideals they share.

Obdulia is not an individual case in *La Venus mecánica*. Díaz Fernández mentions other women in similar situations, abandoned to their own devices to survive in a world where they are forced to sell the only thing they had—themselves. The death of the dancer nicknamed María Mussolini causes in Obdulia "una indefinible pesadumbre [...] una angustia difusa e indeterminada de vivir, una sensación abstracta de riesgos, y pesares futuros, una inquietud oscura y humana" (84-85). Another woman in similar circumstances is Asunción Lanza, who is perceived as a diva by her adoring public that sees nothing more than "el tipo de mujer soberbia enferma de megalomanía" when in fact she has profoundly human feelings and needs that go unseen (and unsatisfied) by her fans. These other female characters, serving as foils for the fuller development of the fictional Obdulia, together serve as a critique of the new, modern woman described in the beginning of this essay.

The way in which Obdulia ultimately achieves her freedom is both significant and problematic. As she becomes more liberated she has a real conflict resulting from her relationship with Víctor, which she feels makes her dependent on him, and her ideas about what it means to be a liberated woman, the woman she wants to be:

> Ella [Obdulia] quería trabajar, ganarse la vida como una obrera, como una de aquellas muchachas de los talleres y las oficinas que cruzaban en grupos alegres la Puerta del Sol. Y se resistía a confesarle a Víctor su pobreza, su debilidad, porque así se vería disminuida, insignificante [...]. Si su amor tenía que apoyarse en él, recibir protección y consuelo, ¿qué era lo que daba ella, gota de azar, tímido grito de la desigualdad humana? (89-90)

The only way Obdulia can resolve this conflict is to definitively reject bourgeois society altogether. When Víctor and Obdulia declare their revolutionary intentions, the inequality between them disappears and they are strengthened by their mutual support.

Part of Obdulia's problem is that her middle-class background impedes her from being able to truly belong to the working class, to "ganarse la vida como obrera." She feels her only recourse is to prostitution, to become a plaything for the very rich, to become the "Venus mecánica." It is precisely when she makes this decision that the critique of the idealized modern woman is strongest. It has been mentioned above that the "new woman" is a superficial creation, a woman who represents herself in a shroud of mystery—her clothing, her beauty, her physical appearance creating a playful image of herself to be looked upon with admiration. Díaz Fernández describes this type of woman, but from the inside where the truth behind the elaborately-made-up façade is strikingly different. In one of the most important passages of the novel, we hear in Obdulia's words one account of how it feels to play this role:

> Yo, Venus mecánica, maniquí humano, transformista de hotel, tengo también mi traje favorito, mi elegancia de muchacha que sabe vestir para la calle, para el teatro y para el "te [sic] dansant". Conozco el color que arrastra a los hombres y el que impresiona a las mujeres. Finjo que voy a las carreras, que he de cenar fuera de casa o que salgo de compras por la mañana, después de las doce, bajo el arco de cristal de los barrenderos. Soy una actriz de actitudes, una pobre actriz de trapo, que no puede siquiera llevarse las manos al corazón para hacer más patético el verso que dicta el apuntador. (117)

Here the modern Madrid in which Obdulia lives is the stage for her performance, a demeaning one where her role is imposed upon her and leaves no room for self-expression or meaningful communication with others. It is at this point in the novel that she is just beginning to be able to articulate her sense of injustice and throw off the values of middle-class society that seek to silence her completely. Having had enough of being the object of desire and her body used as merchandise, given over for the pleasure of others again and again, she finally reclaims it for herself.

Obdulia's journey from prostitute to fashion model to kept woman instills in her over time a strong hatred of the society that has used her in these ways. She hates prostitution because she cannot submit herself to the anonymous eroticism of the trade. She winds up screaming at her first client: "Te odio.... Os odio a todos. Al mundo también... Qué desgracia" (105). As a model, the conformity and boredom of bourgeois life and tastes and the lack of meaning of the fashion industry and life in general overwhelm her. Working at a department store as a human mannequin, at one point she thinks to herself: "¿Qué derecho tienen sobre mí las mujeres que triunfan, ésas para quienes trabajo? Yo no me resigno" (133). Early in the novel Obdulia is fooled into thinking she will become a film star. She quickly realizes (but only after quitting her job) that the woman who claims she is producing a film (tellingly named Esperanza Brul) is a con artist/poseur only interested in the favors granted to her by those who hope to participate in her films. Esperanza's lust for Obdulia becomes obvious when Obdulia is made to come back repeatedly for screen tests that never amount to anything. Obdulia decides to let the married, wealthy mine owner don Sebastián support her but only because she very consciously wants to make him suffer. She sees this as the only way to fight the system that has destroyed her. Obdulia derives no real power from this relationship, however, as it ends poorly for her when she becomes pregnant.

As don Sebastián's lover, Obdulia represents luxury, "ácido corruptor de la riqueza, venganza de todos los desheredos de la tierra" (14). Paradoxically, Obdulia's experience with the wealthy man is an important part of her consciousness formation which leads to her eventual liberation. When she visits one of don Sebastián's mines, she enters "un mundo distinto, el del esfuerzo muscular, el de la esclavitud asalariada" (156). She cannot but help feel solidarity with the workers and rage against Sebastián for causing such injustice. When he is shocked by her reaction, "Obdulia no replicó. Pero su alma estaba en rebelión y sentía como nunca una furiosa rabia contra el dominio y la fuerza" (147). Nevertheless, she continues to live with her lover, she suffering in boredom and he suffering her disdain. Obdulia thinks of leaving several times but decides against it:

> Era preciso seguir al lado de don Sebastián para hacerle víctima de su odio todos los días ya que él era el implacable delincuente de todos los días [...]. Atada a aquel hombre con la ligadura del odio, que sujeta más que el amor mismo, Obdulia sería cadena de su cárcel, hierro de su tormento, venganza permanente de los obreros sin pan. (199)

In the end, though, love for herself wins out over her hatred of Sebastián. Obdulia returns to Madrid, initially avoiding contacto con Víctor. When she finds out she will have Sebastián's child, however, she is devastated because "ella no quería un hijo de la esclavitud, un hijo del odio, concebido en tinieblas. Quería un hijo del amor, sembrado en su corazón primero que en su carne, un hijo a quien habría de enseñar a aborrecer la injusticia y amar la libertad y el talento" (217). She returns to Víctor, who helps her obtain an abortion in France. Díaz Fernández implicitly defends the right of a woman to an abortion primarily because it is what allows Obdulia to take back possession of her own body. As the doctor performing the operation in Paris tells her, "Nuestro cuerpo es ya lo único que nos pertenece" (190). Indeed, almost all of the action of the novel revolves around the commodification of the body of Obdulia in an increasingly urban mass market.

Víctor and Obdulia begin a relationship and their love seems to conquer all obstacles. When they both want to have a child of their own, Obdulia feels that finally this child "puede justificar de algún modo mi paso por la tierra, mi paso trémulo que no acaba de atravesar la frontera de los deseos" (256). Obdulia sees in the birth of her child the opportunity to erase the trials and mistakes of her own life. In a plot reminiscent of Pio Baroja's *El árbol de la ciencia*, the death of the infant signals the unfairness and uncertainty of life. After this personal tragedy Obdulia has to once again face her prospects in life, this time free of any vestiges of bourgeois society such as marriage and family. At the very end of the novel it is Obdulia who proposes to her jailed lover Víctor that they act as revolutionaries to change the society in which they live: "Cuando salgas de la cárcel, te ayudaré a preparar nuestra venganza"(310). It is significant that Obdulia, a female working-class citizen of Madrid, cannot find support in any of the feminist movements going on around her, but rather through her own experience. She finds that when she tries to use her good looks and stylish dress to get ahead in Madrid's fashion or film industries, she is unable to survive. Her objectification is degrading and leads to prostitution. She is also excluded from the politically and aesthetically revolutionary sphere in which Víctor and his friends circulate. Through Obdulia's exclusion Díaz Fernández locates *La Venus mecánica* between or beyond the elite high culture of the avant-garde and the mass-produced popular culture of the time. As Boetsch points out, "ella sólo ha logrado sobrevivir en una sociedad corrupta e injusta por haberse deshumanizado. Sin embargo, se impone en ella la conciencia de que esa injusticia es más general que su propio caso, de que se trata de una injusticia social colectiva de la cual ella es parte" (121). Much like the highly unusual novel itself that straddles the traditional division between the popular and the avant-garde, Obdulia is often marginalized and misunderstood, but as an outsider she has a unique perspective on Madrilenian society.

There is an inherent problem in the portrayal of Obdulia's maturation and individualization, however. The only way out of her desperate situation is tied to the prospects and professional stability of a man, namely Víctor. This unresolvable problem is also seen throughout *El nuevo romanticismo*, the first chapter of which is titled "La moda y el femenismo" and where Díaz Fernández is concerned about the limited opportunities for women in Spanish society. But he has no real solutions to propose. On the contrary, he condemns the suffragist movement on the basis of its being run by upper-middle class women. In his essays, articles, and novels Díaz Fernández repeatedly states that women unable to compete in the workplace with men due to lack of education and opportunity should be considered an underprivileged class. He also completely dismisses feminism as a consciousness-raising movement in its 1920s form. He writes in *El nuevo romanticismo*, "nuestras damas del movimiento feminista están todavía tan retrasadas que siguen pidiendo para la mujer el voto político y el escaño parlamentario" (16). This inherent contradiction in Díaz Fernández's social theories works its way into and problematizes the evolution of Obdulia into a more mature, self-actualized woman in *La Venus mecánica*.[8]

It has been argued here that Díaz Fernández in *La Venus mecánica* seeks to critique the exploitation of women in 1920s Madrid and to chronicle the way men and women came to relate to each other in an increasingly market-driven, image-conscious urban setting. In the end, though, the consumption of highly unrealistic images of women presented by both high and low culture is contained and perpetuated through the novel itself. When Víctor meets Obdulia and falls in love with her, he begins to try to overcome his previous attitudes towards women. From the very first time they meet in the cabaret, Obdulia interests Víctor for reasons that are not purely sexual. Víctor realizes, "Obdulia sí era una muchacha interesante. Tendría unos veinte años y sus ojos eran negros y hondos," "Me dejo vencer por la imaginación. Es una mujer vulgar. Un poco bonito, pero vulgar. Y me parece que se trata de una mujer de excepción," "Estoy hecho un idiota" (48-51). When Víctor falls in love, he does not entirely stop pursu-

---

[8] Susana Cavallo takes scholars of the Spanish novel of the 1920s and 30s (Pablo Gil Casado, Gonzalo Santonja, José Esteban, Fulgenio Castañar) to task for excluding women authors and asserts that writers such as Luisa Carnés, Carmen de Burgos, Concha Espina and Elisabeth Mulder subvert patriarchal narrative practices and redefine women's role in modern Spanish society

ing other women, but his encounters with them become increasingly absurd and pathetic. He begins to think of them as belonging to the same underprivileged class as Obdulia herself. Indeed, the descriptions of these other women serve to flesh out what the reader knows about the life of Obdulia and to point to the fact that Obdulia is not alone in her lifestyle of prostitution. While sexual freedom was seen as symptomatic of true rebellion and liberty for many in the 1920s, in *La Venus mecánica* it is seen in a negative light. In search of new values for his generation, Díaz Fernández values love and fidelity over the erotic for its own sake. This conflict is central to the development of Víctor's character. It is Obdulia who, willingly or not, is thrust into the day-to-day hardship of the struggles for power going on in the streets of Madrid, not Víctor. Her role as "la Venus mecánica" and, as a woman, her subordinate position as an economically-disadvantaged person informs Víctor of the day-to-day struggle for survival of the rest of Madrid society, but he never can fully share in it.

Víctor is a young, handsome, stylish man in the habit of pursuing and ultimately charming so many women that he can no longer differentiate between them. The problem is that their individual features are so confused in his mind, the encounters so brief, that he can remember no one woman in her entirety. These women appear in the narrative to be as fragmented as many of the figures in the Cubist paintings of Picasso, which Víctor specifically mentions in the quotation cited at the beginning of this essay. The constant coming and going of unaccompanied women shopping along the Calle de Alcalá and the Gran Vía provide an insurmountable temptation to him, and he waits and watches for them regularly. He is, in effect, consuming them, choosing certain women over others for their color, shape, smell, and overall style just as the women shopping for fashion and beauty products are doing, constructing an ongoing cycle of consumption and production based solely on desire. This desire for satisfaction, whether it be sexual or for ownership of the latest, most fashionable of objects is rampant in *La Venus mecánica* and goes hand in hand with the urban experience. It is only when Víctor and Obdulia step outside of this cycle of modern urban capitalism that they are able to find a way to live more authentic and fulfilling lives.

La Venus mecánica is a crucial critique of and commentary on the human side of the age of mass production, in all of its individual and collective triumphs and trials. Torn between taking pleasure in the increasingly available mass-produced products and the pain of resulting alienation, *La Venús mecánica*, like the fictional characters it portrays, is a sobering voice of dissent in the tumultuous political, social and cultural environment of Madrid at the end of the Primo de Rivera dictatorship. Díaz Fernández thought of women as members of a disadvantaged class and went so far as to assert (to repeat the quote with which this essay began) "La sociedad actual es manca, porque le falta el brazo activo de la mujer." It is telling, though, that the first edition of the book sold many copies featuring the provocative and titillating Cubist image of the nude mechanical Venus, in an obvious reference to the evil, seductive robot Eva of Fritz Lang's highly influential 1925 film *Metropolis*. *La Venus mecánica* itself, as a cultural product circulating in the cultural marketplace of early 1930s Madrid, was able to question and critique the dehumanizing nature of modern society but in the last analysis it never completely breaks from the cycle of objectification—indeed, the cover itself participates in it by capitalizing on the marketability of the avant-garde.

Fig. 1: Rafael Barradas, *Calle de Barcelona* (1918)
(Colección de Arte Contemporáneo, Madrid)

Fig. 1: Antonio Cobos, "Sin título," 1930. *La Eva Moderna* 81.

Fig. 2: Eduardo Santonja Rosales, "Alpinismo," 1932. *La Eva Moderna* 261.

Fig. 3: Ángel Cid, "Tennis," 1935. *La Eva Moderna* 66.

Fig. 4: Enrique Climent, "Portada" 1931. *La Eva Moderna* 152.

Fig. 5: Rámon Estallella, "Portada," 1930. *La Eva Moderna* 181.

Fig. 6: Roberto Martínez Baldrich, "Sin título," *La Eva Moderna* 185.

Fig. 7: Joan Puyol, cover of the first edition of *La Venus mecánica*, 1929.

Works Cited

Barnard, Malcolm. *Fashion as Communication*. London and New York: Routledge, 1996.
Boetsch, Laurent. *José Díaz Fernández y la otra generación del 27*. Madrid: Editorial Pliegos, 1985.
Breward, Christopher. *The Culture of Fashion*. Manchester and New York: Manchester UP, 1995.
Buckley, Ramón and John Crispin. *Los vanguardistas españoles (1925 – 1935)*. Madrid: Alianza, 1973.
Castañar, Fulgencio. *El compromiso en la novela de la II República*. Madrid: Siglo XXI Editores, 1992.
Cavallo, Susana. "El femenismo y la novela social de los años treinta." *Letras Peninsulares* 6 (1993): 169-178.
Craik, Jennifer. *The Face of Fashion: Cultural Studies in Fashion*. London and New York: Routledge, 1994.
Díaz Fernández, José. *El nuevo romanticismo*. Madrid: Editorial Zeus, 1930.
———. *La Venus mecánica*. Madrid: Renacimiento, 1929.
Fuentes, Víctor. *La marcha al pueblo en las letras españolas 1917 – 1936*. Madrid: Ediciones de la Torre, 1980.
Gaines, Jane and Charlotte Herzog, eds. *Fabrications: Costume and the Female Body*. New York and London: Routledge, 1990.
Gavarrón, Lola. *Piel de angel. Historias de la ropa interior femenina*. Barcelona: Tusquets, 1982.
Herzberger, David. "Representation and Transcendence: The Double Sense of Díaz Fernández's *El nuevo romanticismo*." *Letras Peninsulares* 6 (1993): 83-108.
Hollander, Anne. *Sex and Suits*. New York: Knopf, 1994.
Nash, Mary. "Un/Contested Identities: Motherhood, Sex Reform and the Modernization of Gender Identity in Early Twentieth-Century Spain." *Constructing Spanish Womanhood: Female Identity in Modern Spain*. Ed. Victoria Lorée Enders and Pamela Beth Radcliff. Albany, NY: State U of New York P, 1999. 25-49.
Nelken, Margarita. *La condición de la mujer en España. Su estado actual. Su posible desarrollo*. Barcelona: Editorial Minerva, 1922.
Nielfa Cristóbal, Gloria. "Las mujeres en el comercio madrileño del primer tercio del siglo XX." *Mujer y sociedad en España 1700 – 1975*. Ed. Rosa María Capel Martínez et al. Madrid: Ministerio de la Cultura. Instituto de la Mujer, 1986. 299- 332.
Pérez Rojas, Javier. Introduction. *La Eva moderna: Ilustración gráfica española 1914–1935*. Madrid: Fundación MAPFRE Vida, 1997.
Santonja, Gonzalo and José Esteban. *La novela social 1928 – 39. Figuras y tendencias*. Madrid: La Idea, 1987.
Scanlon, Geraldine M. *La polémica feminista en la España contemporánea 1868-1974*. Madrid: Akal, 1986.

Simmel, Georg. "Filosofía de la moda." *Revista de Occidente* 1.1 (1923): 44-53.

Wilson, Elizabeth. "All the Rage." Gaines and Herzog 28-38.